ROBERT WILSON

AND HIS COLLABORATORS

ROBERT WILSON

AND HIS COLLABORATORS

LAURENCE SHYER

THEATRE COMMUNICATIONS GROUP

Robert Wilson and His Collaborators is published by Theatre Communications Group, Inc., 355 Lexington Ave., New York, NY 10017.

Robert Wilson and His Collaborators is supported in part by a grant from the Opera-Musical Theater Program of the National Endowment for the Arts.

TCG gratefully acknowledges public funds from the National Endowment for the Arts, the New York State Council on the Arts and the New York City Department of Cultural Affairs, in addition to the generous support of the following foundations and corporations: Alcoa Foundation; Ameritech Foundation; ARCO Foundation; AT&T Foundation; Beatrice Foundation; Center for Arts Criticism; Citicorp/Citibank; Common Wealth Fund; Consolidated Edison Company of New York; Eleanor Naylor Dana Charitable Trust; Dayton Hudson Foundation; Exxon Corporation; Ford Foundation; Japan-United States Friendship Commission; Jerome Foundation; Andrew W. Mellon Foundation; Mobil Foundation; National Broadcasting Company; New York Community Trust; New York Times Company Foundation; Pew Charitable Trusts; Philip Morris Companies; Rockefeller Foundation; Scherman Foundation; Shell Oil Company Foundation; Shubert Foundation; Lila Wallace-Reader's Digest Fund; Xerox Foundation.

Designed and typeset by The Sarabande Press.

Cover photographs by Annie Leibovitz, copyright © 1989.

Library of Congress Cataloging-in-Publication Data
Shyer, Laurence.
Robert Wilson & his collaborators / by Laurence Shyer.
Bibliography:
ISBN 0-930452-96-8 : $27.50. -- ISBN 0-930452-97-6 (pbk.) : $14.95
1. Wilson, Robert, 1941-   --Criticism and interpretation.
2. Experimental theater--United States. I. Title.
II. Title: Robert Wilson and his collaborators.
PN2287.W494S49   1989
790.2′092′4--dc19   89-4406 CIP

First Edition: December 1989.

TO MY PARENTS

CONTENTS

FOREWORD BY ROBERT BRUSTEIN

This book is the story of Robert Wilson and that international army of artists who have served him as collaborators. Here is my story.

In 1983, Bob sent me a postcard, his usual means of communication from some far-off country, to ask if the American Repertory Theatre would like to work with him on a piece. It was a thrilling and scary invitation. I had become convinced that Wilson was one of the greatest artists of our time, but his work was now of such magnitude that it could be realized only by the subsidized theatres of Europe. Bob knew I was among those scandalized by the fact that an American creative genius was in virtual artistic exile. He needed an American base. How could our comparatively puny financial resources satisfy his needs?

We met at the Harvard Club over a cup of coffee. I don't know what I was expecting—I had never met Bob Wilson—but I remember being surprised by the crew-cut appearance of this shy, elegant figure. His speech was formal; he wore a blue blazer, tie, and cowboy boots; he held his back as stiff as a dancer or a drill sergeant. Bob proposed a production of *The Golden Windows*, and when I asked him to describe the piece, he pulled out a pad and drew sketches of the sets. I was to learn that Bob's descriptive language is invariably technical. Some years later, when asked to describe his workshop of *Alcestis* for the purpose of a grant application, he replied: "I intend to have the model completed by the end of the first week, and to have a run-through at the end of the third."

Frustrated by the cancellation of *the CIVIL warS* in L.A., Bob decided to substitute its Cologne section for *The Golden Windows* at the ART. I had been warned to expect demands, temperament, eruptions, erratic behavior. What he brought us, in spite of his depression over the cancellation, was warmth, sweetness, generosity, infinite flexibility, and a genuine effort to keep the budget reasonable. "I don't know why my productions are so expensive," he giggled. He couldn't restrain his visionary powers but he was always conscious of our financial limitations, always willing to help us find new sources of support to realize his ideas.

Bob auditioned our actors for their parts by asking each one to walk from one side of the room to the other in fourteen counts, to sit in a chair in eight counts, to rise in ten counts, and finally to walk to the other side of the room in twenty counts. This rattled our classically trained company, who are accustomed to auditioning from texts, and one or two asked to be spared the privilege of working with him. They were rescued for the project through my assurances—which later proved true—that Wilson's strict rhythmic approach was a liberating limitation, that within his metronomic choreography the actor could ultimately be more creative than in the free-form frame of the most permissive director (David Warrilow puts this paradox more succinctly: "The more exact the parameter, the freer I become"). At any rate, the atmosphere in the rehearsal room was notably free of tension. Rather it was permeated with humor, good will, and friendship—a mood reinforced by the sweet natures of the collaborators Bob brought with him: Ann-Christin Rommen, Tom Kamm, Hans Peter Kuhn.

Bob had the show on its feet in a week—I've often told him he's a summer-stock director—but the real work began during technical rehearsals. Bob's focused intensity when working on sets and lights and sound creates a humming quiet not unlike that of a sanctuary or a chapel, an atmosphere intensified by his silences and reflections. All the while insisting that he doesn't know what he's doing, he manages to hallow a space and fill it with textured meaning. We believed audiences would absorb this sacral atmosphere upon entering the theatre and seeing the Union soldiers in their slow underwater ballet, moving from tent to tent. But to Bob's chagrin, we lost between two and three hundred at every preview (our theatre holds only 556). He agonized over this; he reexamined his aesthetic; he lacerated himself over his artistic deficiencies. Then he found a simple and successful solution—an intermission after the first scene.

the CIVIL warS proved to be a great success in Cambridge, with audiences and most of the critics, and Bob had found his American home. At Harvard he gave lectures and demonstrations—and even participated in seminars (waiting for Bob to frame an answer to a question from the floor can sometimes take as long as one of his scenes). Best of all, he agreed to work up an entirely new piece for us—from workshop to performance—in 1985-86.

This was *Alcestis,* a play I had suggested after learning he was planning to do Gluck's opera the following year in Europe. My hope was to convert Bob Wilson to classical texts, especially now that he had found so much image-making inspiration working with a modern playwright, Heiner Müller. Written texts had previously frightened Bob, and the Euripides play was no exception until he found a way to deconstruct the translation for his own purposes (we used the Robert Fitzgerald version when William Arrowsmith refused to let Bob tamper with his words). With a set consisting of a river flowing the length of the stage and a gigantic mountain range down which rocks slowly tumbled (in the climax a blue laser pierced a jagged hole in the side of the mountain), the piece was awesome, monumental, and we thought unmovable. But we were still able to tour it that same year to the Festival d'Automne in Paris where it proved a great triumph.

Currently, we are trying to decide on Bob's next work at the ART, squeezed between his multiple projects in 1991. He has offered to do *The Waste Land*, but T.S. Eliot's widow won't grant the rights. He has expressed interest in the plays of David Mamet! And even more surprising, he wants to do a production of *Our Town*. Too bad those rights are tied up too, because it would be a little like Nixon going to China. What's interesting is his growing attraction to texts, which we will do our best to further in our next joint venture.

One day, after Bob had completed *the CIVIL warS* in Cambridge, I came upon him waiting impatiently for Heiner Müller. Bob had promised him a ride to New York, but the elusive Müller had disappeared and was not to be found at any of his haunts. Exasperated, Bob said, "I can't find Heiner," then added with a rueful smile, "Usually I can't even find myself." But Bob Wilson finds himself in his ever-growing body of work, and in the affectionate memories of all the collaborators included in this book.

Alcestis. American Repertory Theatre, 1986.

the CIVIL warS. Act I, a. Cologne, 1984.

INTRODUCTION

Robert Wilson. Artist. Director. Performer. Phenomenon. And collaborator. Behind the visionary spectacles of Robert Wilson stand a virtual army of designers, writers, dramaturgs, actors, dancers, composers and producers, some celebrated in their own right and others barely known, all of whom are essential (easily replaceable as some of them may be individually) to the works' creation. Among their ranks one finds downtown rock stars David Byrne and Laurie Anderson, composer Philip Glass, opera singer Jessye Norman, playwright Heiner Müller, poet Allen Ginsberg, choreographer Lucinda Childs, as well as friends, housewives, the elderly, mental patients, people he has found on the street and such unique individuals as Raymond Andrews, the deaf black boy whose nonverbal communication skills and crayon drawings inspired him, and Christopher Knowles, a brain-damaged young man with whom he created a whole series of theatre pieces. Perhaps Wilson's greatest gift has always been his responsiveness to people. He has an uncanny ability to draw the best from those around him and almost effortlessly assimilates their ideas and talents into his own aesthetic. Ann Wilson, an artist who worked on a number of early productions, has said it this way: "Bob's real genius is that he can see a moment, seize it, mold it, light it, heighten it and find the right place for it." His open theatrical forms also offer collaborators—writers and musicians especially—the space in which to express themselves and pursue their own interests. Wilson once compared his organizational method to that of an architect; he creates "one large structure, like an apartment building, and within it, each artist can carve out his own home." (The degree of freedom Wilson allows his collaborators, of course, varies greatly according to their own importance and his regard for them.)

Despite a wide range of gifts, Wilson is dependent on the abilities and expertise of others, especially in technical areas, for if he possesses the eye and the vision of the complete theatre artist he lacks many of the requisite skills. Collaboration is not only an innate talent and a source of inspiration, it is a necessity. People sometimes imagine that Wilson's creations play in his head like films which have only to be transferred to the stage but, in fact, they are very much created in the theatre. Like a choreographer, he needs to see something in space before him in order to move forward; he must have people around him to flesh out his mental scenario (which may be vague in the beginning) and help clarify his vision while it is evolving. Wilson also appears to be too restless to create alone for long periods of time—he has too much energy for the silence and solitude of purely contemplative work. Finally, the associates he has gathered around him fulfill his need for friendship, as they must, since he has eliminated almost everything from his life that is not directly related to his work.

Beyond Wilson's inner circle of intimate and active associates lies a wider circle of those who have directly or indirectly shaped his vision, some of whom might be called inadvertent collaborators. Although he always claims Balanchine and Cunningham as his primary influences (each has been credited with separating movement/dance from storytelling and identifiable emotional situations), Wilson is even more indebted to the artists and theorists of his own generation, to the "happenings" movement and the Judson Dance Theater (especially such "second-generation" members as Kenneth King and Meredith Monk). Wilson arrived in New York in the early 1960s and what he saw and the people he met and worked with during these years shaped his tastes, interests and ultimately the aesthetics of his theatre. Arlene Croce once characterized Jerome Robbins as a popularizer rather than an innovator and there is a sense in which Wilson, the choreographer's one-time protégé, may be seen in the same light. Wilson has always learned through imitation and assimilation, and many of his methods and perceptions have come from far more radical artists and performers. (His absorptive powers are remarkable—Maita di Niscemi, a frequent collaborator, has gone so far as to call him "the human sponge.") Such borrowings and his failure to acknowledge influence have made for misunderstandings and bad feeling, especially when, as has happened, a number of downtown performers and artists must read how *they* have been influenced by *him*.

Since Wilson tends to create through a process of recycling and reformulation it may also happen that an idea introduced into his work by a collaborator is reused in subsequent pieces until it is more associated with him than its originator. In this sense a collaboration may continue long after a collaborator has left Wilson's circle, even his active memory.

A PAINTER IN THE THEATRE

Wilson tells us he has always been "visually concerned." He attended the theatre as a young man but was bored by its emphasis on narrative, psychology and language (he believed then as now that gestures and images can say more than words) and instead found himself drawn to dance and performance: "I liked Balanchine and Merce Cunningham because I didn't have to bother about plot or meaning. I could just look at designs and patterns—that seemed enough." Wilson often says that all of the elements in his productions are equally important but in truth the visual has always been his primary concern; it is the area over which he exercises the tightest control and finally it is the glory of his theatre. In this, Wilson is very much of his age and at one with a culture in which visuals have become the primary means of transmitting information, holding the attention and activating the imagination. His is a true theatre of images and the proof of this is that design is not placed in a subordinate position to a text or dramatic situation; the visual elements are neither decoration nor elaboration, they are the work's content. (The late Edwin Denby said that in this sense Wilson's works may be called "visionary.")

Wilson originally wanted to be a painter and he has said the reason he stopped painting was that the images in his head were so much richer than anything he could get on canvas. In time he brought his painter's eye to the theatre, creating pictures not with pigment and brushstrokes but from the things and people around him, setting them in motion in time and space. Wilson's own suggestions for approaching his work (in this instance *Einstein on the Beach*) tell much about his sensibility: "Go like you would to a museum, like you would look at a painting. Appreciate the color of the apple, the line of the dress, the glow of the light. . . . My opera is easier than *Butterfly*. You don't have to think about the story, because there isn't any. You don't have to listen to words, because the words don't mean anything. You just enjoy the scenery, the architectural arrangements in time and space, the music, the feelings they all evoke. Listen to the pictures."

TIME

What newcomers to Wilson's theatre usually find most striking (or infuriating) is the liquid slow motion in which performers travel and images unfold. If Wilson does not quite "put a stop to time" as the critic Clive Barnes once suggested, he stretches it to a degree previously unknown in Western theatre. An actor has taken as much as half an hour to perform a simple task like raising a cup to his lips. In *The Life and Times of Sigmund Freud* an hour passed as a giant papier-mâché tortoise—the logical mascot for Wilson's theatre—inched its way across the stage; in *the CIVIL warS*, a wounded soldier spent the entire evening making his solitary way across the horizon. It has been said that the length of Wilson's stage is best measured not in feet but in hours.

The artist's interest in extended time and slow motion grew at least partly out of personal experience. One of the most important influences on his life, Wilson tells us, was Miss Bird Hoffman, an elderly dance instructor he met in the 1950s, and in whose honor he would later name his foundation (the artist even called himself Byrd Hoffman for a number of years). Until the age of seventeen Wilson suffered from a severe speech impediment and it was Miss Hoffman who said, "Oh, you can speak"; she worked with him for about three months, encouraging him to relax and release the tensions in his body through movement exercises. "Part of it was just slowing down," he would later explain. "I learned to speak very, very slowly. I entered a radio speaking contest, and spoke very slowly over the air—it became funny, and then it became theatrical. . . ." This critical lesson was later applied to the work he did with the handicapped and eventually to his creations for the theatre, where in a sense audiences are made to experience again and again his personal epiphany.

During his student years in New York Wilson found that most of the theatre he attended moved so quickly he had difficulty focusing and processing all the information he was being given. (The truth of slow motion was further reinforced by an encounter with Dr. Daniel Stern, a psychiatrist at Columbia whose slow-motion film studies revealed new insights into human behavior.) Here again, prolonged duration proved a means of opening up channels of perception and communication and overcoming sensory overload. Slowing down and extending performances over greater periods of time would enable the spectator to both enter into Wilson's private world and view each image clearly; time would provide the space in which to more fully see, hear and experience. (Many downtown dancers and performance artists during his early years in New York were also experimenting with slow motion, repetition and extended time.)

Wilson would come to see his theatre as an antidote to the frenetic pace of everyday life. He believed that in watching his work, the spectator was inevitably drawn into its rhythms and reached a point where the heart rate slowed, the brain began to operate at a slower frequency and the viewer's own thoughts and interior visions mingled with the spectacle on stage. The end of the 1960s, when this work was coming into being, was an era of widespread drug experimentation and Wilson's own strung-out sense of time was very much in sync with "drug time." (Performers and audience members were frequently stoned, rendering them even more susceptible to his visions; it was sometimes said that each scene lasted as long as it took to smoke a joint.) For his part, Wilson often dismisses the notion that slow motion plays a controlling role in his productions. As he told a *New York Times* interviewer a few years ago, "People talk about slow motion in my pieces. . . . That's wrong. It's NOT in slow motion, it's in natural time. Most theatre deals with speeded-up time, but I use the kind of natural time in which it takes the sun to set, a cloud to change, a day to dawn. I give you time to reflect, to meditate about other things than those happening on the stage. I give you time and space in which to think."

COLLAGE

The term describes not only Robert Wilson's art but his process and evolution as an artist; it is the basis of everything he does in the theatre. Wilson's productions are essentially vast assemblages which he creates out of initially unrelated images, actions and activities, sounds and words. Like a collage, his theatre admits all manner of matter and inspiration—a picture he saw in that morning's newspaper, an image he dreamed the previous night, a postcard brought in by a performer, a scenic element from his last production—virtually anything that seizes his imagination. Over the years new pieces are added, new elements come into prominence, some older ones are pasted over, but the process and organizational sense remain much the same. (Wilson sometimes says that all of his productions form a single creation—each being but a piece of a greater collage.) It must be understood at the outset that Wilson's original works do not spring from some motivating idea, organizing theme or even expressive urge. Only in the course of the developmental process do the issues and concerns of each piece come to define themselves. As Sheryl Sutton suggests, the emblem of Wilson's theatre might be the onion: layer upon layer but no core.

INDEPENDENCE OF ELEMENTS

Wilson often speaks of the different components that make up his work as existing independently of each other. Text, sound, action, design—all these constitute separate layers or tracks, autonomously conceived and sufficient in themselves, like the ingredients of a hero sandwich, to which he sometimes compares his productions. Wilson also likens such discontinuity to life itself, where unrelated occurrences seem to spontaneously produce correspondences: "It's just like when you're driving a car and listening to Mozart. You look out the window and see the grass blowing and it looks like the grass is moving to the music. And maybe it is. It changes just at the moment the music changes. Or you imagine a connection."

Increasingly Wilson has come to think of such juxtaposition as a perceptual aid, with each element helping one to see or hear the other more clearly. In this, of course, Wilson has been influenced by the example of Merce Cunningham and John Cage, though he applies their principles far less rigorously. In the typical Cage-Cunningham collaboration the work of choreographer, designer and composer simply coexists, sharing the same space for the same length of time. Sometimes these elements are not even brought together until the first performance. Wilson, however, is incapable of taking such precepts the distance, for while he may espouse the principle of independence, in the end he is the master of synthesis, tonal and rhythmic fusion being his ultimate aim (even if he does not quite realize it).

"Whatever you're doing, it's all one thing," Wilson often tells his performers. Independence is a relative term at best.

FREEDOM, MEANING AND INTERPRETATION

Like so much of the art having its roots in the 1960s, Wilson's theatre aspires to a condition of total freedom, freedom not only from authority and convention but the constraints of time, language, logic and even meaning. (The surrealist writer Louis Aragon, upon seeing his work for the first time in 1971, declared it to be "an extraordinary freedom machine.") First, Wilson's creations offer a release from the kind of absorption that traditional theatre demands. Edwin Denby felt that one of the artist's greatest and most radical innovations was that his plays did not demand the full attention of the audience. The spectator was free to leave the auditorium and return, to tune in and out at will, to focus on whichever of the myriad actions on stage seized his eye or imagination. There was no story to follow and therefore none to lose track of. Each member of the audience could wander through the work as one might through an art gallery. (Many of Wilson's earlier works were actually too lengthy to experience in their entirety.) His is also an art that rejects the manipulative ploys of traditional drama, which anticipates, channels and finally controls audience response. This was immediately recognized by the director and playwright Richard Foreman, who reviewed *The Life and Times of Sigmund Freud* for the *Village Voice* in 1970. "Up until now," wrote Foreman, "leading theoreticians and practitioners of theatre have seen its procedure as a series of strategies designed to manipulate audiences in various predetermined, aimed-at ways. . . .Wilson is one of a small number of artists who seem to have applied a very different aesthetic to theatre—one current among advanced painters, musicians, dancers and filmmakers—a non-manipulative aesthetic which would see art create a 'field' situation within which the spectator can examine himself (as perceptor) in relation to the 'discoveries' the artist has made within his medium. . . . Bodies and persons emerged as the impenetrable (holy) objects they really are, rather than the usual virtuoso tools used to project some play's predetermined energies and meanings."

Such work encourages what Denby called "imaginative watching," which may take many forms. One may daydream, let Wilson's visions stimulate one's own imagination, try to puzzle it out or simply float from moment to moment with the imagery. Almost inevitably the spectator is enlisted as a collaborator, completing the experience and giving meaning to the spectacle before him. Another aspect of the work's condition of freedom is its openness and accessibility to all; no prior knowledge is required of those who would enter and no social or intellectual barriers block the way. Wilson's works admit all interpretations and all meanings but at the same time resist any single view.

The artist himself usually pleads ignorance when questioned about his intentions and the possible meaning of his creations. He is, to use Max Ernst's memorable phrase, "a blind swimmer." When pressed for explanations Wilson retreats into the silence of his own work: "The fact is, I don't really understand my own stuff. Artists very seldom understand what they are doing. My work is a mystery to me, and I feel that words only confuse people about my work. I don't wish to mystify people. It's best not to say anything at all. It's best to remain silent." In the end, no matter how one approaches Wilson's work its mystery remains. It cannot be dispelled or explained away and the spectator's efforts to subdue it within his knowledge or experience will take him only so far.

THE HUMANIST IMPULSE

Wilson is not merely a manipulator of time and space but an artist genuinely concerned with basic human issues and the fate of man. The journey is a central motif in the plays and operas of Robert Wilson and in them we travel with all of humanity through time and history, from life to death and from apocalypse to rebirth. (His works abound with images of travel and discovery: automobile excursions, ocean voyages, moving trains, spaceships.) As might be expected of a theatre made of dream visions, many of the figures one encounters are mythic in dimension: the hero, the bad mother, the wise old man, the monster and such icons of the modern age as Lincoln, Stalin, Queen Victoria and Einstein. One also senses an intense longing for the lost unity of man, nature and animals—the dream of Eden which is sometimes reclaimed at the last. A child stands in the foreground of most of Wilson's plays and in some ways his is a child's coming to terms with experience and the world. As in a fairy tale, the wonders and the terrors of our lives and dreams appear at every turn, though not in opposition but, like the bright and dark side of Wilson himself, each barely aware of the other. Beauty may be the criterion of his theatre but destruction is ever present, characteristically taking the shape of the mushroom cloud or the pointed revolver. A surprising amount of his imagery is rooted in biography, which may in time provide a means of entering more deeply into his world. The family tensions and terrors of his own experience, the figure of the disabled boy-child (his youthful self), his fascination as a nonreader with words and books, his fears of aging and loss, his obsession with death and murder—all have found a place in his creations.

In spite of his formalist tendencies and refusal to reach out to his audience, Wilson says that his ultimate aim is communication and the creation of a shared experience, and in this way too his is humanist theatre. As he explained in an interview a number of years ago, "The theatre is a forum where people come together and have an exchange. One of the extraordinary aspects of theatre is that it can bring together people of different backgrounds—different economic, religious, political backgrounds; people come together for a brief period of time and share something."

OPERA

Just as the theatre can bring people together, Wilson says it "also brings together all the arts" and "opera" is his chosen designation for such a synthesis. It was actually Robert Kanters, the drama critic of *L'Express,* who first applied the term to his work, describing the six-hour version of *Deafman Glance* presented in Paris in 1971 as "an opera, the libretto of which is silent and the music lost." Its appropriation by Wilson has proved apt for no one's work better summons up the grandeur, epic scope, lyric impulse and excess of that great antiquated art form. (Edwin Denby humorously suggested that Wilson's works could also be called operas because they lasted so long and didn't make any sense.) In recent years Wilson has told those curious about his use of the term that opera comes from the Latin root for "works" and that's what he makes, "works for the theatre," a fitting description for the indescribable—that unique fusion of drama, scenic spectacle, music, sound, silence, dance and sometimes film that is Wilson's theatre.

Doubtless Robert Wilson will continue to be a subject of controversy, simultaneously hailed as the kind of theatre genius that appears once in an era and dismissed as a charlatan, his name and exploits as always filling the arts pages of magazines and newspapers. What cannot be easily disputed at this point is his daring, the scope of his ambitions and the sheer abundance of his vision. To enter this vision is itself a liberation; it is to leave behind the cramped living rooms, kitchens and demarcated spaces of American drama for a realm beyond time inhabited by gods and demons and the great protagonists of human memory, a region where one is likely to encounter anything found within the dimension of imagination. (Stanley Kauffmann once wrote: "Nothing is too complex, too venturesome or too familiar for him to attempt." Wilson rushes in where wiser heads would hesitate, a very real part of his genius.) For good or ill, Robert Wilson remains our most individualistic and inspiring American theatre maker; he has made the theatre seem plausible once more, a place where astonishing things can still happen. As Roger Planchon has said, "Until Wilson, everyone felt the stage picture was weaker than the film image. . . . He showed us how one makes the stage image as strong as the images of film, painting and photography. He gave us courage."

Wilson continues to make journeys, moving restlessly through the world pursuing new challenges, new commissions and celebrity itself. It is tempting to see him as a figure in one of his own magic landscapes, a voyager moving past star-filled skies and changing vistas where planets collide and geese race with spaceships. Imagine him etched for a moment in his own golden light, taking in the surrounding horrors and wonders in a glance. Robert Wilson. Dreamer. Businessman. Genius. Fraud. Child of Wonder. Monster. Alone, even in the midst of his collaborators. Lost in his own spectacle and his success, the mystery-maker who is his own greatest mystery. Never pausing to consider his purpose or his goal, never stopping lest he stop altogether, he continues on his solitary, unknowing journey. And who can say where it will end?

Otto Sander in *Death Destruction and Detroit*. Berlin, 1979.

ROBERT WILSON

AND HIS COLLABORATORS

I

PERFORMANCE

AND

PERFORMERS

Sheryl Sutton in *Deafman Glance*. 1971.

SHERYL SUTTON

S heryl Sutton first stepped onto Robert Wilson's stage as a student actress in 1970. The production was *Deafman Glance* and she performed the silent murder scene that is both its prologue and the signature piece of Wilson's theatre.

A young black woman in a dark, high-collared Victorian dress stands motionless before a cracked gray wall, her back to the assembling audience. On a white rectangular platform beside her are two small children dressed in white night-clothes—a boy seated on a low stool reading a comic book and a girl asleep on the floor under a white sheet. To her left is a small table, also covered with a white sheet, on which are arranged a pitcher of milk, two glasses, a napkin, a black glove and a large knife whose blade gleams in the light. A monochrome still life: white, black, gray, a glint of silver. The audience take their seats and the house lights fade but the tall regal figure at the back remains perfectly still. It is only when silence has fallen over the theatre and more time has passed that she turns slowly, almost impercepti-bly, into profile. The face now becomes visible, its serene and beautiful features nearly expressionless, the hair close-cropped like a boy's, the body elegantly tapered and perfectly erect. She moves silently to the table, puts on the black glove and pours milk into a glass. Every action is measured and deliberate, at times unbearably slow. She takes the milk over to the little boy, who drinks. When he has finished she moves back to the table, takes the knife and carefully wipes it with the cloth, and then returns to the boy. With the same care and impassive concern, she slowly pushes the blade into his chest. He falls from the stool without any show of fear or pain and she gently cradles him to the floor, calmly sliding the knife into him one more time. She now returns to the table, pours a second glass of milk and wakes the girl. The sequence is repeated: the child drinks, the glass of milk is exchanged for the knife, the knife pushed gently into the child's side, each task performed with concentrated energy but also a curious inattention. In the original version of the *Deafman* prologue, an older boy named Raymond appears at the edge of the stage during the first murder and begins to scream repeatedly, the high-pitched, impotent utterance of a deaf-mute. The figure crosses to the boy, puts her black-gloved hand on his forehead and then moves it down over his mouth, stifling his cries. He is spared and together they slowly turn upstage toward the cracked gray wall, which rises to admit them into another world, a Wilsonian realm of moonlit forests, rising pyramids, full moons, angels, monsters and falling stars.

The *Deafman* prologue is perhaps the essence of Wilson's art, a haunting construction of silence and time. Sutton, its originator, describes the scene as "a kind of mechanism to define different phases of slow motion. It's a way to divide time. I think the scene approaches true slow motion, not just slow motion for the stage but near-photographic time, what the eye perceives as slow—it's that slow." Since there are few if any external cues during the sequence, which in its various incarnations has lasted anywhere from twenty minutes to an hour and a half, Sutton decided she needed to develop an internal method of gauging and controlling time. "It's very difficult. In general I think anyone can come close to approximating five minutes of real time. You have a kind of sense about it. But when you have to do something extremely slowly within that five minutes you lose all perception of clock time. It's not really possible to count out the time either and even that's very inaccurate because you inadvertently slow the count. The way I approached the scene was to break down the action into inner cells of contrasting speeds so I could pace myself through it." Each section has its own tempo: the black glove is drawn on slowly, the milk is poured and offered to the children a little faster (a kind of rising dramatic action), finally come the murders, which are slowest of all. "I developed an inner clock that was sensitive to each segment and my judgment was pretty accurate. What the audience is experiencing, though, is a kind of stopping of their inner clocks. They lose that whole judgment as to what is slow and fast. When something is fascinating and extremely slow, you can watch it for five minutes and think only a minute and a half have elapsed. People were sometimes amazed that it lasted as long as it did. There were also other people who became very anxious and wondered 'Why is this taking so long?' It's all so simple. Once you've figured out the sequence you know what's going to happen yet there's something fascinating about what's occurring and that is the element of murder and even more the absence of everything we associate with that act—emotion, violence, anger, blood. There's none of the usual emotional baggage. I think that's where the mind takes over, translating the slow motion and minimalist actions into a kind of mental terror." Sutton points to the scene's ambiguities and contradictions as one source of its strange power. "The character crosses so many cultural lines and periods. It's hard to say who it is. It's hard to say it's even a mother sometimes. She's a ritual figure. She might almost be a priest—the black dress, the severe lines and the little white collar. Because the staging is so ritualistic, the murders seem almost religious. There are so many paradoxes, it's so hard to define or delineate what you see. That's what makes it rich." As is often the case in Wilson's theatre, no causes are offered and no explanations given; the audience merely witnesses a calm, elegant, compelling and resolutely mysterious action.

The central concerns of the scene, murder and protracted time, are not unrelated. While it is often difficult to locate the sources of Wilson's most deeply felt images, the *Deafman* prologue seems to have had its origin in one of the film studies that Daniel Stern made in the 1960s of mothers interacting with their infants: at normal speed a mother appears to be comforting her crying baby but when the sequence is slowed down, she lunges at the child, who visibly recoils, perceiving her approach as a threat. As Wilson observed, "The body is moving faster than we think." This realization was to become the basis of the *Deafman* prologue, with slow motion again revealing what was unseen by the human eye: the maternal presence as the bearer of comfort (milk) and terror (knife). It may be that the woman in the black Victorian dress is also an incarnation of the artist's late mother, whom he has described as cool, distant, formal and "powerful in her silence." (He has said that he can remember her touching him only once; a number of Wilson's closest associates believe that this relationship determined the emotional horizons of his theatre.) It is not surprising then that the murder scene has continued to haunt and fascinate its creator. There have been variations on the basic premise (in one version the little girl rose from the dead to take her revenge on the mother), a 1981 television adaptation, and Wilson himself has performed the ritual numerous times throughout the world, usually dressed in a coat and tie but on one recent occasion in a long dress and blackface. The scene was also to provide the seed of his stage adaptation of Euripides' *Medea*, in which Sutton again appeared as the murdering mother.

That first encounter with Wilson's theatre in Iowa was to have a profound effect on Sutton's life and career. A native of New Orleans with an extensive background in dance, she had come to the university to study theatre because it seemed "closest to what I wanted to do which I couldn't define." While the conventional dramas and musicals being produced there held little interest for her, the emerging field of performance art seemed rich in possibilities though the opportunities Iowa provided in this area were limited. "I didn't know it then—not even after working on *Deafman Glance*—but the only person who could have really satisfied my direction and interest in theatre was Bob Wilson." Although Sutton continued to work intermittently toward a degree over the next three years, an increasing amount of her time was given over to Wilson and the Byrd Hoffman group, whose performances would take her to New York and then around the world. Just as she had discovered what she was seeking in his theatre, Wilson had found in Sutton his quintessential performer.

The murdering mother Sutton played in *Deafman Glance* was only one manifestation of a figure Wilson called the "Byrdwoman," who moved through his works of the early 1970s like a phantom presence. Wilson seems to have first had an inner vision of the Byrdwoman in 1968 when he was building a massive outdoor sculpture in Loveland, Ohio. She seemed to him a figure who was neither sad nor happy and somehow encompassed the incomprehensibility of life itself. At the completion ceremony for the structure and in such early pieces as *BYRD woMAN* and *Alley Cats* he took on her persona, appearing in a fur coat and floppy hat, with long braids on either side of his head. "In time," he later wrote, "she seemed to represent the past, present and future as one." By 1969, the year he staged *The Life and Times of Sigmund Freud* at the Brooklyn Academy of Music, this image had been transformed into a woman in a black Victorian dress with a single black glove on which was perched a stuffed black raven. The part was not then played by Sutton—she didn't meet Wilson until the following year—but by a young black woman he had cornered in a New York antique store. Upon assuming the role Sutton made it her own. In fact, so deeply did Wilson make this identification that for some years he refused to give up his vision of her as a figure in a high-collared Victorian dress. (The costume she wore in the *Deafman* prologue was reproduced in white muslin, beige and rose for various productions during the early seventies and became a kind of running joke, with Sutton finally saying, "I've had enough of this.")

As arresting in its own way as the murder scene was the Byrdwoman's silent domination over the first act of *Freud,* which was set along a sand-covered beach before an unseen ocean. For well over an hour, Sutton sat perfectly immobile in a white chair—a kind of tour de force unique to Wilson's theatre. "Absolute stillness. No expression. The facial muscles are so relaxed that the eyes nearly close, which gives the face a very strange mask. It's almost like you're looking but not seeing. It's the only thing like that I've ever done. When I was sitting for an hour like that my heart rate also slowed down. It's a near trance state. I remember one night when we were in Copenhagen a crazed woman came on stage and scared everyone. She stared at me for a while and then embraced me and my blood pressure suddenly shot sky high—it was like having a heart attack. It's usually quite relaxing but you have to be extremely centered and I think I would have a difficult time doing it now." Sutton also came to enjoy the time the scene provided for rumination and the play of the imagination. "Absolutely everything went through my mind. I thought it was wonderful for that. I was a really silent kind of person in those days and I could occupy myself very easily. I used to go for days without speaking so an hour was nothing to me. People used to tell me that after a while they'd forget about the fact that I wasn't moving and the whole idea of whether I was a statue or a person. They became fascinated because they could sense the thought process that was very much awake at the same time the body was so totally relaxed. Her peaceful presence is also related in some way to the setting—in fact, you can see the ocean through her. You look at her in the same way you would look at the sea. You can watch for a long time and just have your thoughts. I think we're attracted to her in the same way we're attracted to certain portraits. That's what the Byrdwoman is for me, she's a portrait, a three-dimensional painting. That's why she was always somehow the essence of Bob's work because he's really a painter. You can stare at a painting in a very impersonal way because it doesn't stare back at you. And good paintings also awaken some emotion in you. It's very unusual to have that relationship with an actor." The act ended with a Wilsonian *coup de théâtre*: after sitting perfectly immobile for more than an hour, Sutton rose slowly, almost imperceptibly, and advanced steadily toward the front of the now empty stage. Depositing a small green Egyptian figure on Dr. Freud's table, she then turned her eyes upward for the first time and looked out into the audience, holding the theatre in absolute silence as the curtain fell.

Naturalness (and the absence of visible effort) has always been the cornerstone of the performer's art in Wilson's theatre. From his earliest productions, he has attempted to help people find a way of presenting themselves on stage without self-consciousness, to put them in touch with their bodies and develop what he called individual vocabularies of movement. "In the beginning so much time was spent learning not to act. What Bob was interested in then was people being themselves." During the early days of the Byrd School, Wilson preferred to work with ordinary people in whom he perceived some special quality. His performers were drawn from every background and social strata: a lady chicken farmer from Ohio, a gray-haired man he pursued through Grand Central Station because he bore a resemblance to Sigmund Freud, the six-month-old infant of one of his friends from Pratt, the handicapped, artist friends, his 86-year-old grandmother—very often the young and the old, those at the beginning and the end of the journey; closest to nature in either direction. This concern with natural behavior, as both an aesthetic and physiological phenomenon, grew out of a number of personal experiences: his youthful encounter with the dancer teacher Bird Hoffman; his work with Jeannine Wagner, whose theatre programs for young people in Texas stressed naturalness and body awareness; an attraction to Martha Graham, whose choreography he admired for its "strength, simplicity, individuality and absence of artificiality" (Wilson sat in on some of her classes while a student at Pratt); perhaps even the liberated body language of such rock-and-roll performers as Elvis Presley and Mick Jagger. Through the dancer Kenneth King, Wilson was also introduced to the ideas of Isadora Duncan, whose famous pronouncement on the training of young dancers he often quoted during the early 1970s: "I shall not teach the children to imitate my movements, but shall teach them to make their own. . . . I shall help them to develop those movements which are natural to them." His use of nonactors reflected similar trends in the happenings of the 1960s and the performance art of the following decade as well. (Richard Foreman, whose Ontological-Hysteric Theatre came into being about the same time as the Byrd School, once declared: "I'm not interested in seeing actors' acts, but in seeing real people, awkward people.")

Though she was the one trained actress in a company where "acting" was discouraged, Sutton seemed naturally to possess the very qualities Wilson was seeking to inculcate in his workshops. Cindy Lubar, another of Wilson's early performers, marveled at how "little direction Bob ever needed to give her. Sheryl was doing exactly what he had spent months trying to get people to do. She intuitively understood it all and had what he was looking for, that grace, awareness and in-touchness with her body. She just had it." Sutton, however, takes a somewhat different view. "I think it was difficult for all of us in the beginning. It was very difficult for me because I had so much respect for my technique as an actor and I really felt confronted by not being able to use it. Bob doesn't deal in big dimensions and by that I mean huge emotion and self-expression. That eliminates a lot of what traditional acting technique is about. What people have to find is a way to be people somehow in a very aesthetically defined space while performing very minimalistic kinds of actions."

Although Wilson is celebrated for his spectacular images and stage effects, his works have always been fashioned from the simplest acts and gestures. In an introductory speech to *The Life and Times of Sigmund Freud* in 1969, he described the activities the audience would see as both "very mundane" and "pointedly human" — "like someone running and someone sitting, another making small talk, someone pouring a drink, someone dancing, people doing ritualistic exercises." For Wilson such ordinary acts provided a means of attaining and expressing the state of relaxation and naturalness to which the Byrd group aspired: each action was a vessel capable of containing a person's energy or inner personality, and a small piece of human truth. The ordinary and the extraordinary, the cosmic and minute (colliding planets and the shift of a finger) have always existed side by side in Wilson's works as though there were no ostensible difference between them. And in a sense there isn't — for in this theatre the mundane becomes infused with a magical energy, the everyday takes on the aura of mystery and the incidental is metamorphosed into the momentous. As one critic wrote, by slowing down the ordinary in our lives Wilson manages to "extract from it all the light it holds." No one has shown such a gift for releasing this light as Sheryl Sutton, whose elegance, ease and absolute concentration can transform the simplest gesture into something compelling and peculiarly beauti-ful, whether it be lifting a glass of milk, rising slowly from a chair or — as in *Einstein on the Beach* — simply crossing the stage in liquid slow motion.

The preparatory workshops for *KA MOUNTAIN* in 1972 provided two such memorable moments, both in some way emblematic of Wilson's theatre. In one scene Sutton appeared in her white Victorian dress at a high table and poured a fine, silvery stream of water from a pitcher into a bowl until it overflowed, an act that lasted so long she seemed, according to one witness, "to move from the past through the present on into the future": "It was one of Bob's images. I think he had a dream of a figure pouring water from a pitcher which never ran out, an action without end. The idea is that you start to pour long before the water comes and the volume of the pitcher is such that if you only pour a thin stream it can go on for a very long time. The perception is really that it's endless. Again, you take a minimalistic action, put it in slow motion and not only does it take on greater importance but our perception of it is exploded somehow. It's a fascinating idea. There was another scene in which I peeled an onion very slowly and again it seemed to take forever." Indeed, at one performance in Iran over two hours elapsed before the onion was peeled away to nothingness. "It's something probably everyone has done. I just peeled it very slowly, taking off one layer at a time. It's really another one of Bob's performance principles. He's always been interested in layers and that's how he builds his stage in a way—the images are one layer, the sound is another layer, the language another." Both these scenes attest not only to Sutton's concentration and control but to her curious ability to be both strongly present and absent at the same time. The body is absolutely still except for the action being performed (and an occasional tear running down her cheek from the onion), which is accomplished with the smallest expenditure of energy. As in the Zen arts she becomes the action she is performing; it is as though the water were flowing of its own power and the onion using her to peel itself.

"Oddly enough, Wilson's theatre is really classical theatre in that the stage is very separate from the audience. Unlike most experimental theatre, there's no interaction. We of the stage are doing something for you the audience and you have to watch—or you don't have to watch. That's the major difference, there's this possibility of choice and that's unique to Bob Wilson's theatre. Because the actors promote themselves in most kinds of theatre, the audience is obliged to watch." While Sutton also considers timing, temperament and inner personality to be essential attributes of the Wilson performer, she emphasizes relaxation above all else. "For me it's far more than a physiological state: it's being so comfortable that you don't feel the necessity to express yourself. This can be very difficult for people who perform. Always in the back of their mind is the feeling that they must project or exert themselves. And this is absolutely unnecessary—though, of course, there are roles in which a kind of projection is required. What I'm really talking about is the tendency to promote oneself. Bob works in Germany now with highly trained repertory actors and I think they're some of the best performers he's ever directed. They have all the skills but they don't acquire the ego and the falseness that's necessary if you want to be a movie star. They're like doctors with the egos of auto mechanics. Many of them finish their careers in the same theatre they started in. It's a life job and they're very respected. It's a whole other system and a wonderful thing happens. They have an enormous range of expressive ability, both physical and mental, and the self is very highly developed but it's not promoted. They're totally centered. I was fascinated to see their work in the Cologne *CIVIL warS*, they were really Bob Wilson actors. The actors in Rotterdam on the other hand had a lot of trouble learning this kind of centering, they didn't believe it was possible and never made any attempt to achieve it. One of the biggest problems Bob has had over the years with groups of people who've had little exposure to his way of working is an initial disbelief, because it's a sort of invisible technique, very subtle and hidden. There's always something going on that requires some knowing but it's never possible for anybody else to give you this knowing. Actors can get very hostile when someone is continually telling them, 'No, that's not it, that's not what I want.' And you can't get it by simple receding or not projecting yourself. That's not enough. You have to go into your own being and find a way of personalizing what he's given you. It not only has to make physical sense but mental sense. You have to embrace it."

Although the director controls every aspect of performance, Sutton sees the Wilson actor as a creative participant and not a puppet. "In specific terms actors don't contribute that much. But what they contribute is themselves, which is a lot — in fact it's everything. If a performer is really comfortable and relaxed enough to do the things Bob asks, he'll add to their part based on what comes out of them and what he sees in them. The role defines itself by the actor. It's kind of strange but in a way the creative part comes after the fact. You get your lines and action and all the technical information, and then you have to find a way for the whole thing to make sense. And it all has to be done with very little effort. You don't have lots of facial expression or literal gestures, how do you express who the person is? Bob never tells you what it's about. So you make it about something, working within the context of his coordinates. And you never have to explain what that is to him." Very often Sutton will invent a logical narrative for the random fragments of conversation she has been given. "You have to make some mental connection in a text where very often there isn't any. Somehow it's necessary that it makes sense to you so you can make the audience believe it."

For Sutton performing in Wilson's theatre is a means of simultaneously exploring the possibilities of the body and the self. "If Bob's actors all got really interested in what they had to do physically they would get a lot out of working with him. You begin to acquire a repertoire of movement like a ballet dancer — their vocabulary is enormous — and actors don't usually have that because they do everything in terms of real-life gesture. Those are larger groupings of muscles and they don't usually break them down into their components the way dancers do. If actors could do that they would have a kind of plastic system, a wide and minutely defined spectrum of physical expression. I think acting for Bob is very close to ballet." As in dance, the choreography enters into the body through repetition and muscle memory, yet Sutton believes that the performer must be careful not to perform on technique alone.

"There's something automatic about certain types of dance that I think is really dangerous. Some dancers have a kind of mindless way of using their bodies. It also happens in some conventional acting where everything is so internalized that no thought is necessary. There's no reason to turn off the head to enhance the body or vice versa; the two are there and you have to use them always. Certainly some things become automatic through repetition but I think what you do is work through it. You pass through a place somewhere in rehearsal where it's automatic but then in performance there has to be an edge on it that's about something else and that's what makes it exciting."

In Wilson's theatre performers do not relinquish their own personalities in order to take on those of other characters. Impersonation or identification does not exist in that sense. Just as the man riding atop a float in a Fourth of July parade is Lincoln by virtue of his beard and stovepipe hat, while otherwise remaining himself, appearance sufficiently expresses character. Thus it is possible to populate the stage with a host of Einsteins or Stalins without creating the friction or confusion that would result from the interactions of twenty actors all convinced they were the same person. "In most plays an actor is projecting himself and you know of course he's a human being but his whole humanity is covered under all this other junk. In other words you lose the person in the actor because he's projecting the character in the actor. Hamlet is a very rich and full characterization and any good actor is compelling to watch in the part. At the same time, any actor is a million times richer than the character of Hamlet, which is only a selection by the author. He couldn't possibly have the richness of any human being, even the most uninteresting human being." For Sutton performance is a very real extension of life that allows the audience a glimpse of the actor's inner personality. "Bob talks a lot about interior screen and exterior screen, these different ways of perceiving. I think what most people do is sublimate the inner screen when they have some exterior activity. So if they're playing a part, they have some text, some action and gestures and they concentrate on that. Even if they have some way to motivate these acts and words that's related to personal experience or psychology in order to make them more real, what they're doing is one-dimensional because that's *all* they're doing. I think what makes performing rich and multidimensional in Bob's theatre is that people don't have to stop being people just because they have to perform. If you listen very carefully, they tell you human things about themselves and who they are and what they're experiencing." In the past Wilson has said that his plays don't demand an audience's full attention and Sutton believes this is true for the actor as well. While concentration is imperative, performing does not consume all of one's physical and mental energies and this allows actors to pursue simultaneously their own thoughts, meditate or give play to the imagination. "Whatever Bob has given you to do isn't interesting enough to concentrate on alone. You also lose some depth—not only as a performer but as a person—if you're only counting numbers or thinking about what you have to do. The layers are infinite. In a work like *Einstein* you also have music, which attacks the mental faculties and makes it more difficult to concentrate. But it's surprising, the more things you have to perform the easier it is to function and still have this inner screen. I think it's part of the human experience to be able to perceive on multiple levels, that you're able to do a set of six actions and three gestures and at the same time think of something else and not have it be a distraction. Of course you need to be present in a very strong way but what I think Bob really needs is people who are dreaming when they are performing the actions and words he has given them."

Though many of Wilson's characters are drawn from history or mythology, there is little if any sense of the past in his theatre. Unlike the Broadway plays he saw when he first came to New York, the action does not rush headlong into the future while simultaneously moving back into the pasts of its characters; the length of the performance is the only timespan his actors inhabit. (As the critic Edwin Denby once said, "Everything takes place at the same time.") Sutton has chosen to capitalize on this phenomenon by giving full expression to the moment, endeavoring to become "an accurate barometer of the space and what's happening in it. For a long time I attempted to attune myself to the collective timing of the piece even if that wasn't where I was on a given evening. That's a mistake somehow. I think what's really important is to do what's going on tonight—whether you're 100 percent in time or 100 percent out of time. Because the whole thing's supposed to be about what's happening here and now. With the revival of *Einstein* at the Brooklyn Academy of Music, I had lapses of interest after the second or third night. I didn't want to be there somehow and I didn't care and I thought this was very dangerous. In fact, I was shocked and worried about it. But there was also something else in me that said, 'That's all right too. If you don't want to be here, that's something to play.' People are really astonished at that. But I think what's most important is to be honest and show what's going on. And people are really attracted to honesty. To be in a Wilson piece is somehow an extension of being in life, though it's also a bit special because everything has been chosen and set. When you don't respond to such things as what you had for dinner or what someone said that really bothered you, it's a denial of truth, and more than anything I think his works are about the truth that's happening at that moment."

Sutton has worked with Wilson over a longer period than any of his other collaborators; their association extends from *Deafman Glance* in 1970 to *Cosmopolitan Greetings* in 1988, with more than fifteen productions in between. No other performer has so successfully bridged the gap between the early years when Wilson created his productions around the Byrds and his present-day preference for highly trained professionals, natural behavior and self-expression having taken second place to exactitude and formal beauty. Sutton, in any case, excels in all of these. While she has also performed with Squat Theatre, made several European films and taught movement and dance in the intervening years, all her work is based on the performance techniques she acquired in Wilson's productions. Despite the closeness of this tie Sutton prefers to work with Wilson periodically, agreeing with so many others that he is simply "too engulfing, too exhausting" to work with on any other basis. Nevertheless the collaboration continues to sustain her ("I find I always get a lot of value from the work and realize another aspect of my self") and she continues to exemplify the technical perfection, simplicity and ease of the ideal Wilson performer, creating a kind of gravity field that draws the spectator to the stage with the smallest outlay of energy. Though few have been able to master the skill, Sutton offers a simple explanation for her own uncanny ability to hold an audience with so little. "What it is really is the ability to hold yourself back and give up so much space. Most people can't do that. It's like you turn your flame down low. That's very necessary to Bob's performing technique and it's also very attractive to an audience. Then they come to you." While Sutton believes any person could develop this quality and would be equally interesting on stage, she admits that this may be her special gift: "Bob used to tell a story about a Broadway actress who no matter where she was on stage or what she did the audience kept their eyes on her. You couldn't cover her up. I guess that's the ability I always had. I never really had skills like singing and dancing but I had this ability to be watched." As Wilson wrote in the program of that first production of *Deafman Glance,* marveling at the way she stood motionless for five minutes putting on a glove with only her fingers moving, "Geeze, she's a star!"

Deafman Glance. Act III. 1971.

DAVID WARRILOW

As a founding member of the experimental theatre company Mabou Mines, David Warrilow was active in the lively New York avant-garde scene of the 1970s, engaged like Wilson in exploring the nature of performance and extending the boundaries of the theatre. Though it was not until the fall of 1985 that the English-born Warrilow, one of the foremost interpreters of the works of Samuel Beckett, made his debut as a Wilson actor in *The Golden Windows,* he had been a keen observer of the artist's work ever since arriving in New York in 1969. "When I first saw the work I was truly shocked, I hadn't had an experience like that before and it was traumatic. Bob's work wasn't just interesting, it was essential and I feel that it has nourished me over the years. His imagery has a special kind of energy that does me good. When I saw *the Knee Plays* in Minneapolis last year, I realized that I really needed to have that experience at that time. It gave me encouragement and support in my own search and told me all over again that there's still someone doing something very important in the world of performing arts. I was fed by the work. Watching Sheryl Sutton move, for instance—I find that a nourishing experience. I don't know how else to say it. It uplifts me. For one thing it shows a divine kind of courage which sends me inside to get in touch with my own divine courage again. Bob and I have known each other for years, not intimately, not very well, but I would say there was an artist's intimacy without our even meeting very often. There was a recognition. I'd seen him after performances, he'd come and seen me after performances and one weeknight I went down to the Byrd Hoffman loft, had supper and danced with everybody. To my knowledge everyone within Mabou Mines was either tremendously fond of Bob as a person or totally in awe of his work, though there was also considerable envy of the scale of his work, envy that he had managed to pull it off somehow on a big stage while we were doing small pieces—wonderful work, of course, but inevitably there was a comparison. It goes on still and I would imagine that the resentment of Bob's achievements and self-realization has if anything intensified."

During the summer of 1985, when Wilson was preparing the American production of *The Golden Windows*, which had received its premiere two years earlier at the Munich Kammerspiele, Warrilow was contacted unexpectedly. For weeks Wilson had tried to persuade the German actress Elisabeth Bergner, then in her mid-eighties, to appear in the New York production and had purposely withheld casting the other roles. When she finally decided against doing the play some weeks into the scheduled rehearsal period, Wilson shifted into high gear and put together a company of American actors, none of whom had worked with him before. "There was no audition. He asked if I would go meet with him and he drew my way through the piece. That moment was really so beautiful that I felt it didn't matter if nothing more ever happened. We talked and I gave him some samples of vocalization. I think he wanted to know if I could do a text that wasn't Beckett. He wanted to have his fears allayed." Warrilow was cast in the leading male role and the hastily assembled company set to work that July in the Lepercq Space at the Brooklyn Academy of Music. "During the first days of rehearsals we watched a videotape of the Munich production and tried to get some idea of the actor aesthetic that was being dealt with. There were endless discussions. Bob's game is to ask 'What does this play mean?' The question was addressed to anybody and everyone, to whoever was in the room at the time or to the waitress in the restaurant. It was like a game and not a game. I think he wanted some answers and he knew there wasn't an answer. I wouldn't engage in the discussion or I did with bad grace. It really was when Bob was away during the summer break and I gave some thought to the piece that I realized that that question *is* what the play is about. What the play is about is 'What is the play about?' That's not unlike something he said early in rehearsals: 'I like it to be open-ended with questions that the audience answers.' I like that too. I like the fact that Bob asks the audience to take responsibility for its experience, to claim its experience. That's the way I feel about all the work I do. I won't engage in anything like explanations, because it's so presumptuous. Explanations of something so mysterious, no. The mystery should be in the heart of the person who sees it. I don't want to tamper with that." The rejection of manipulative audience strategies was, of course, one of the tenets of the experimental theatre movement of the 1970s to which they both belonged. Audiences were asked to carry a greater part of the imaginative burden or as Warrilow says, "to take the experience and run with it or drop it."

In the past few years Wilson has staged several revivals of his earlier works and he shows no compunction about drilling performers in the exact movements of their predecessors (whether it be the spread of the fingers or the precise angle of the head) in much the same way that a regisseur might teach a dancer the steps of an existing ballet. It was this process that occupied the *Golden Windows* company during the

early rehearsals. "It took several days for Julia Gillett, who assisted Bob, to communicate to the actors the choreography of movement and gesture. The idea was that we
would learn the vocabulary of the piece, and learn it very exactly, and then Bob
would work with us to refine and modify it to suit our physicalities so gestures could
really belong to people. I understand that principle. It's something I was a little
skeptical about but not any longer because I suppose I've had the experience a dancer
has when a choreography is slightly adapted to their body and style of expression.
Actors are not led to expect that that kind of thing will happen. To most actors giving
them gestures is as insulting as giving them a line reading." Often during these early
rehearsals Wilson would tell the actors that it was their task to "texture the space, to
make it alive and interesting." "You've got to find something," he once said, "that
doesn't make it look like the director told you to do it—so it doesn't look stupid." As
in ballet the performer must master a demanding and rigidly formalized physical
language, personalize it and finally transcend it altogether. As it turned out Warrilow
found Wilson's method wholly compatible with his own. "I love exact choreography.
I've always said that about my work. The more exact the parameters, the freer I
become. Because once my body knows how to do those things, all the rest gets to be
free. I get to be comfortable and free inside, and that gives me greater strength and
centeredness. And I know that matters to audiences, it makes them more comfortable." (Max Reinhardt similarly used to drill his actors for weeks in the tiniest
gesture and then at the last minute tell them, 'Be free.')

Such freedom is achieved through a near-endless process of repetition and
refinement. Timings are exact and gestures are often counted silently by the actors. At
the beginning of *The Golden Windows,* for example, Warrilow sat on a bench with his
head bowed for five minutes, a period that he was able to gauge exactly night after
night. "I cared very much that I counted accurately. I was very proud of the fact that I
was held up as the standard for counting seconds in the company. 'David gets it right
every time.' It was important for me to do it accurately and I don't consider myself to
be dumb or blank-headed because I sat there on that bench counting rather than
thinking deep philosophical thoughts. In fact, there's no room for that at all. It's not
important or even useful for the audience to know about this. What they experience is
an entirely different matter, though I suppose if I'm counting calmly then there's
going to be an evenness to my energy. There's going to be something musical about
the length and breath of it. Pretty delicate stuff, but I imagine it does matter and that
Bob could see that. Relaxation is also phenomenally important and I got there. By the
penultimate performance, I was able to begin the piece in total calm and I knew that I
could hold my hand out in front of me without the fear that it was going to start
shaking. It stayed exactly where I wanted it to be which gave me this tremendous
grounding for the rest of the performance."

As Warrilow became more comfortable with the material and his role he also found that time began to move much more rapidly, a common experience for the Wilson actor. "There were times in rehearsal when the piece seemed like it was four hours long but by the time we were playing previews, it was suddenly galloping and things were happening far faster than I'd ever experienced them before." Like relaxation and control (which is its complement), concentration is essential to the Wilson actor and listening, as Warrilow discovered, is a vital part of this: "You have to be listening like mad all the time. It's like playing an extremely demanding ensemble piece. There are very delicate sound balances, one has to listen to one's fellow actors and oneself. Because of the use of body mikes, sound is ultramagnified in your ear so you're listening to very intimate sounds and very much in camera with yourself."

Coming to terms with Wilson's text, a collage made up of random pieces of conversation and story fragments, represented a formidable challenge for Warrilow, who freely admits that it was the most difficult script he has ever had to learn. (In fact, he says his lines went completely out of his head during the summer rehearsal break and he had to learn them all over again when the company resumed work in the fall.) "I had some initial difficulty accepting the script because Bob told us that the actors in Munich simply chose what words they were going to say. That arbitrariness was a little difficult to get by but I did. I don't remember Bob ever telling anyone what a line meant to him. Why he had happened to use that found phrase, that overheard piece of conversation. There were times when one was curious and would wonder if that was something extremely painful for him, was that something that tickled him to death when he heard it? But we didn't get to know those things and no one asked those questions. So Bob would wait for you to fill it with your own life. Take it into your life and color it the way it got colored in your experience."

Warrilow discovered, as Sheryl Sutton had before him, that the underlying emotional currents or subtext supplied by the actor ultimately became "far more important than the literal text." (As early as *Queen Victoria*, Wilson was telling his actors that it was necessary to "get past the lines." He once spoke of his admiration for Kim Stanley, whom he had seen in Lee Strasberg's production of *The Three Sisters*, and the way she seemed to have "almost forgotten the words; they are back there in her mind, she has been programmed for them, but she is doing something else.") Yet Warrilow's approach to this text was essentially no different than it would have been toward a play by Samuel Beckett (and indeed the cryptic, ironic and often tormented fragments of memory and silence in Wilson's piece superficially resemble those of a late Beckett drama): not to create a psychological portrait or attempt to reveal the meaning of the work but simply to play the music of its verbal exchanges. "My opinion about the language in each is not the same but it's also immaterial. It doesn't matter. Once I'm given words to say I chose to give them to the audience as if they were incredibly important. I remember Richard Foreman saying about the language in his pieces, 'This is the way to look at it. Every word that you have to say is the key to the whole mystery.' I don't know to what degree Richard would defend his words or whether it's that idea that's more important than the words. I suspect it's the second and that it's the same with Bob. Really, though, my feeling about the language in *The Golden Windows* is that it isn't inevitable and that Bob could entirely rethink the sonic elements and have a completely different script tailor-made by someone like Heiner Müller. The imagery of *The Golden Windows* is inevitable, the language floats around that imagery in a way that is not satisfactorily grounded and inevitable."

It is left largely to the actor to give Wilson's dissociated words and phrases—and the predetermined gestures that accompany them—emotional or even psychological continuity. (While the visual presentation of *The Golden Windows* at BAM duplicated the original production, the emotional subtext was "totally different than Munich because the actors were different.") The suggestions that Wilson himself offers tend to be fragmentary and indirect. "Sometimes Bob would say it doesn't sound right, it's too heavy or it's too textured or it's too something or other. But he wouldn't say what. So you'd just try something and then try something else. There are, however, some places where Bob seems to know very well what he wants. He was very, very specific about the last words of the piece which are simply 'It all right.' It was very important to him, and the fun in doing that particular line reading was getting so close to what he wanted that he would be pleased." This brief yet powerful moment, which ended with the actor's image slowly dissolving in darkness, might almost be seen as the incarnation of the work's all-encompassing mystery, as well as the mutual desire of the two men to let the audience "claim its experience," to place the mystery squarely in the heart of the spectator. "Bob said, 'How do you think this last moment should be?' And I said, 'I feel that there should be so much *nothing* here that the audience can put anything they want on it.' And he said, 'That's exactly what I want.' So my job was to drain any expression out of my face, to turn around blank and receptive to what the audience wanted to put there. For 'It' he asked for a lightening of the voice to suggest the semblance of a question mark and a slow turn, looking in a particular way toward the light. By the time I said 'all right' there was no decision on the part of the actor as to what was really being said. It was so close to being a question that one really couldn't take it as a statement. There was no period so the end of the piece floated."

Looking back on *The Golden Windows* and his initiation into Wilsonian theatre Warrilow says, "I had no expectations about the work. I just wanted to find out if I could do a Robert Wilson piece well and what it was like. What I discovered was that the difference in experience between looking at Wilson's work and doing his work was so vast as to be almost indescribable. There is a moment in *Golden Windows* when I embrace the younger woman. I've been told that the moment appears elegant, calm, perfect looking and deeply emotional. Well, the process of doing that image is fraught with trauma—the getting up from the bench in such a way that you don't rock it too much, so the movement is clean and you don't look as if there's any effort involved. You're on a rake and you have to walk, calmly, slowly, steadily upstage; it may look cool and beautiful but it's a saga of muscular and balance difficulty. Sitting in the audience one doesn't connect with those things, so much of what the performer is going through must be subsumed. It makes one just a little nervous to realize that maybe the goal that's being postulated is perfection, which doesn't exist on this planet. There is in Bob's work almost an expectation of perfection. That creates a lot of stress and that's the last thing the audience should see."

The Golden Windows. "Midnight." Munich Kammerspiele, 1982.

THE BYRD HOFFMAN SCHOOL OF BYRDS
AND *KA MOUNTAIN:* THE SEVEN-DAY PLAY

Robert Wilson seems always to have had the ability to gather a group of followers around him, first as a child in Waco, then as a student at Pratt Institute in Brooklyn and later in SoHo, the downtown artistic community where following graduation he began to establish himself as a teacher and performance artist. The Byrd Hoffman School of Byrds, a group of disciples, friends and associates that formed the nucleus of Wilson's company and made possible his early work, dates from 1968 (at which time the artist was calling himself "Byrd Hoffman"), shortly after he acquired his loft at 147 Spring Street. They were a heterogeneous group with diverse interests and backgrounds, brought together by their commitment to Wilson's personal vision and theatre work as well as by the communal life that evolved around it. On the following pages former members of the Byrd School and a number of others who participated in its productions during the late sixties and early seventies recount their experiences (often at a distance of fifteen years or more) and detail the making of one of the group's most remarkable creations, the week-long *KA MOUN-TAIN AND GUARDenia TERRACE,* which was performed on a mountain in Iran during the summer of 1972.

FIRST ENCOUNTERS

ROBYN BRENTANO: Bob and I both worked for the recreation department at Goldwater Hospital on what is now Roosevelt Island. This was in 1967 or '68. It was a city-owned hospital which had recently been taken over by New York University Medical Center. They had put in a new staff and the woman who ran the department was very enlightened and hired a number of people who were artists or in the theatre in addition to the basic checkers-and-bingo people. Bob was about the only person on the staff that I felt any camaraderie with and we became friends within a very short time. Almost without exception the patients in that hospital were there because they were terminally ill or their families couldn't afford to keep them at home or they didn't have families. There were an awful lot of gunshot victims from Harlem and the Bronx, people who didn't have any means of support and were in wheelchairs or needed medical care, so they ended up at Goldwater. And it was a place where people didn't usually leave.

I remember Bob did a theatre piece with the patients on C-12 which was a ward of polio victims who were either in iron lungs or on respirators. A lot of them used mouthsticks to draw or write or turn the pages of a book and Bob tied strings between the various people in the unit. He darkened the room and brought in a black light so the strings glowed. I think it was a very moving experience for those people because it allowed them to be in contact with each other in a way other than yelling across the room. Many of the patients were completely paralyzed so the work he was doing was extremely minimal, often more mental than physical. He just basically got them to work with what they were hearing and what they were thinking and the very, very small movements they were able to make. One of the interesting things about Bob was that he was able to reach people who were terminal in their attitudes or in some way numbed by living within an institutional setting, in some cases for decades. He could get patients to respond by bringing them to the window to look at boats on the river or listen to steam in the pipes or watch the plants growing in the solarium. The whole point of his work was that he tried to get people to open up and be much more aware of the small things in their environment.

I think the thing that impressed me most about Bob was his intuition. He often professed not to know exactly what he was doing, and while he clearly knew what he was doing when it came to getting together these very complicated pieces and creating an administrative organization, I think in his human relations he was strongly intuitive. I remember there was a woman in one of the wards who had refused to eat for some time and it was causing the doctors and nurses a great deal of anguish. No one knew how to reach her. It turned out that her family had stopped coming to see her and she was probably punishing them by slowly committing suicide. Somehow the news got to us on the staff and Bob went and sat at her bedside for some time, it could have been an hour or two and I don't think he said anything, he just sat with her and then after he left she ate her first meal in a very long time. I was completely bowled over by that and I feel the debt I owe Bob from working with him over the years has to do with being aware of the unspoken, unconscious mental processes we all have and the kinds of nonverbal communication that take place between people. There was another woman who was legally blind and I remember Bob gave her an orange, a piece of sandpaper and some other tactile objects and right after that she did a watercolor that was just beautiful. I was very impressed that he was able to create a situation where someone who could barely see could make a beautiful painting. I think that's really what characterized his work at Goldwater, he transcended categories of experience—somehow listening to the steam in the pipes could be a visual experience and looking at the boats on the river could be an aural experience. What hooked me into Bob's work very early on was his deep humanitarian interest in people. Later certain individuals came into the group who were troubled or having difficulties and the fact that their work was valued alongside everybody else's—and in some cases even elevated and given special focus—and actually presented in the real world as theatre made a very valuable contribution to their lives. Bob could work with people who were intensely shy or had difficulty relating with others or with any one of us who maybe had difficulty being ourselves in our ordinary life. He paid equal attention to everyone and created a very supportive atmosphere where an awful lot could come out. It wasn't like he had to draw things out of people, he simply waited until they came out. I think that was another thing about him in those days, he had incredible patience and was willing to just wait and see what happened.

SCOTTY SNYDER: I was having my annual Christmas party in Summit, New Jersey and a friend of mine, Liba Bayrak, brought Bob to my house. I was charmed with him right from the beginning. I swore he had amber eyes, I never will forget that. He had just lost his job at the Y and Liba said, "Do you think you can get him a job at the Summit Art Center?" I said I would try, and that's how it all started. They hired Bob and I got together a class for him. I thought it was going to be a class in painting but Bob was interested in body movement. He would have us walking in all sorts of ways for exercises, or he'd just tell us to do anything we wanted. One time I brought in great big bags of leaves and we put them all over the floor and danced and jumped on them. We'd do little activities. His friends would come and do things. It was so different from anything we had ever done. Everyone looked forward to those weekly classes and loved working with him and the children adored him.

KIT CATION: I lived in Summit, New Jersey a long time ago and I heard about these workshops that Bob was doing. Someone told me, "Oh, they're the most wonderful things in the world." Most of the people in the group were housewives in their fifties and sixties and I was the youngest person. I was very shy at the time and the thought of doing all these strange things with people I didn't know overwhelmed me at first but I decided what the heck I'm going to do it anyway. Then I was hooked. Bob got us into physical contact. We'd get together in a big circle and hug. I was very intimidated by this initially but after a while I got to like it. It was almost like being in school and playing. He'd say, "All right, make everything in the room light." So you'd cover up anything that was dark. Then he'd say, "Okay, now make everything real dark," and we'd cover up anything that was light. All kinds of crazy things like that. He'd say, "Everyone sit very quietly and listen . . . do you hear that?" We'd just listen. And then he'd put on Bob Dylan—still when I hear Bob Dylan it goes right to my heart—and we'd *dance*! It was very exciting. There was such a warm feeling and he worked to create that feeling too: we're not just a bunch of people, we are a *group*.

CAROL MULLINS: A good friend of mine, S.K. Dunn, had been working with Bob for some time and I got involved through her. It seemed all very strange at first. I would get letters from my friend saying things like "I danced on a board wearing a long overcoat for four hours in midsummer and it was the most meaningful experience of my life." I was thinking, "Oh, no." Then I met Bob and got involved in his work and I just got swept away.

JIM NEU: I could see S.K. was *really* involved in this thing before I even understood what it was. That kind of intensity and involvement was so attractive. This was the early seventies. It was that hippie period and people were dropping out but they weren't finding anything else. I needed to find something worth doing and I loved the idea of working for Bob. I was real grateful to find something I could believe in after I couldn't believe in politics or so many other things. It really was something to be positive about.

SUE SHEEHY: I was working at Henry's Beef-n-Burger in Iowa City when I met Bob Wilson. It was a chain like McDonald's and I worked behind the counter. We were cleaning out the deep-fat fryer and John d'Arch-angelo [Wilson's costume designer] came over and said, "Would you be interested in being in this play we're doing?" Bob had sent him. He told me he liked the way I walked, it seemed natural to him. I thought they both were crazy. This was during the hippie period and Iowa is a very redneck society, anyone with long hair you just keep away from. Why did I decide to do it? Curiosity, I guess. I played a waitress in the banquet scene and I just held a tray — I was carrying a tray of grease when he saw me that day in Henry's. I liked performing and I liked the people. It was the first time in my life I was with people who accepted me for what I was, not for what I looked like or where I was from. All right, so what if you're fat — I hate that word — so what if you're single, so what this or that. You are a person and I'm going to judge you for what you are. Later I decided to take a week's vacation and come to New York and be in the play there. Bob and Mel Andringa met me at the Port Authority bus terminal dressed in ape suits, that was something. I had a round-trip ticket back to Iowa and a few weeks later I turned it in. When I first found out Bob was from New York my reaction was "Well that's one city I have no desire to see." I've been here sixteen years now. I often wonder what would have happened if Bob Wilson had never walked in that restaurant. I don't think I'd be alive. I was very bored and dissatisfied, I wanted to do something else but I had no skills. I'm not saying it was him who did it all but he helped me to see.

CINDY LUBAR: The summer before my senior year of high school I went to a Quaker camp whose director had taught at a school in New Jersey where Bob had also been a teacher and I first heard about Bob through his stories. He told me how on the first day of class Bob stayed underneath his desk. Another time he stuck a stalk of wheat in the ceiling and asked the students if they noticed anything different in the room — to allow that a child might notice something like that really interested me. I think one day he put a chair up on the roof of the building and sat there in the snow. His approach to consciousness and awareness through contact with others was something that had been on my mind for several years. I got in touch with Bob in the fall and he happened to be starting a workshop for teenagers on Saturdays. I felt even before I met him that his work was going to have special significance for me.

KIKUO SAITO: In 1968 Bob and I went to Ohio. That was quite an experience. I worked with him the whole summer putting up telephone poles for this huge sculpture he created at a church commune called

Loveland. The work was very tiring. We were up from early morning to late at night every day. After dinner Bob went to the chapel and danced by himself. He's a great dancer. Then he started inviting people to dance with him. Everybody joined in. Suddenly, it's no more one people, it's twenty people. It was amazing. I mean, it was very hard work we did there. What energy. From the beginning I thought he was very amazing.

MEL ANDRINGA: Do I remember our first meeting? I do. He had come to Iowa City to do *Deafman* and we met at a local bar. Bob was wearing sunglasses and he never took them off. He had sort of an autistic relation to people in those days, it was kind of oblique. He talked to you but it was like you were listening in on someone else's conversation.

SHERYL SUTTON: Bob has changed totally from someone who didn't want to talk—couldn't talk—to someone who's warm, friendly and gregarious. In the beginning whenever he had to make an announcement he would whisper it. He used to wear dark glasses and stare at the floor and fidget with a pencil, he'd never look at anyone. There was no verbal communication going on. If he needed to talk to someone he would take them off to a corner for twenty minutes and everyone else would just wait. Eight hours would go by without anyone saying anything. We never discussed the work, not specifically, not generally, nothing. It was a very slow, painful process to articulate what was going on. Gradually over the years Bob started to find a vocabulary to describe the experiences we were all having. By the time we did *Queen Victoria* a few years later we were really involved with words and everyone was extremely articulate about the process, though everyone had a different notion of what that process was.

JIM NEU: Bob was pretty inarticulate in those days. It was very hard to get specific feedback from him but you'd know if he liked something or not and that was enough. And if he liked it, without him being able to verbalize it that well, he had the kind of charisma that made you know it must be right.

CINDY LUBAR: My first impressions of Bob? I just remember very short hair, clean-cut, very clean lines and intense energy, an intense kind of inner focus. I was fascinated by both Bob and his work, which is often infused with qualities of his personality.

CHARLES DENNIS: Bob could totally charm you one minute and totally terrorize you the next. He could be speaking very nicely and then all of a sudden have a temper fit and scare the shit out of you. It was like a thunderstorm you never saw coming. Unbelievable electricity. I'm talking about sparks and lightning coming out of the man. He could really shoot the lava out of the volcano. You get the same thing in his dancing. So wild. Some people think they've never seen and never will see a dancer like that again.

LIFE AT THE BYRD LOFT

ANN WILSON: I had a huge loft on Canal Street where a lot of the Byrd group stayed. Bob paid the rent which was $250 a month in those days. Christ, there must have been twelve of us, all living on rice and moonbeans. Nobody had jobs. Nobody had friends outside the group. Not when you got up at five in the morning and didn't go to bed until three in the morning. We were at the Spring Street loft working eighteen hours every day. Oh, it was crazy.

SHERYL SUTTON: We'd work in the evenings and on the weekends we'd often have rehearsals that were eight to fifteen hours long. Hardly anyone was paid. The official sanction wasn't to communal living but it was very much a family and fairly incestuous. There were fifteen or twenty people who were very close and together every single day for intense periods of time.

KIT CATION: We didn't have much money so we all did the props and costumes and sets—it was a real group activity. I was interested in the group, not just theatre—the theatre was interesting too but that was just a part of it. I wasn't into the outside world that much when I was in this. It was like who needed the rest of the world? There was a very strong communal feeling. Bob was very much with the time. He has that ability.

CAROL MULLINS: Bob's work became the most important thing I could conceive of doing. I became interested in theatre, I became a different person. I really wasn't interested in much else. Just my family. And even that became a part of it—when my mother came to visit me in Holland the first thing Bob Wilson did was put her into the play.

KIT CATION: I always got temporary work during those years so I could take off at a moment's notice. If we were going somewhere I was ready, boy. I never got a permanent job because this was my job.

Stefan Brecht, The Theatre of Visions: Robert Wilson: *Byrds, generally white Protestants from upper middle class families or assimilated to a WASP manner, are apt to be undemonstrative, unemphatic, reserved people, superficially cool and off-hand, not given to shows of emotion, generally keeping their feelings, if any, to themselves, rather carefully controlled in their conduct, with unexpressive faces and voices. Though their living is day-to-day—no long-term projects—they are not at all hippies: conventional rather. Generally well-read and informed (and college graduates), they tend to be non-verbal, with few opinions, careful to avoid abstract terms, generalizations. . . . No intellectual discussions, no discussions of principles. They don't discuss the work or Wilson's art other than as to details—what's being done at the loft, what happened at such and such a performance. An orientation toward mysticism, but no strong commitments. Politics is never discussed. Tending toward a mild conservatism, they are quite apolitical. A terror of being phony, trivial or pretentious informs their conduct. One has the impression of a hygienic bisexuality, of experimental encounters, of strong inhibitions, promiscuity. . . . They are nice people; in truth withdrawn. The atmosphere is low-key as where marijuana smoking is quasi-continuous. Social intercourse is matter-of-fact or humorous. . . . Though, identifying as Byrds, Byrds loom huge in one another's lives, the bonds seem impersonal, dissolve when someone drops out. Most of them—I can think of only one exception—came to Wilson without any experience or training in theatre. Though perhaps more quiet than most, we are ordinary people, borderline psychotics.*

CHARLES DENNIS: It was the strangest bunch of people that I'd ever come across. Of all ages, eccentricities, gay and nongay. I'd never been exposed to that many different kinds of people before.

CINDY LUBAR: I attended my first workshop in 1969 and Bob was working on something called the seven-part movement, an exercise he had created to raise the energy level and increase one's facility for concentrating. It was designed so that people of different body types, ages and abilities could all do it.

ROBYN BRENTANO: It was very slow and meditative like yoga or tai chi. You start by sitting on the floor with your knees up and bringing yourself into a kind of squatting position. Then you stand up and sit down again, going back to your original position. You sit for some time and then get up and do a kind of movement that always reminded me of sowing grain. You do this three times and then you kneel down and go into a low crouching position with your head down on the floor, it's a very sweet animal-like movement. Then you get back up and turn around and walk back a few feet and you sit down and start the cycle all over again. It was a wonderful, calming thing to do.

CINDY LUBAR: Sometimes we would focus on a point on the wall and imagine all the energy in the body going to that point. There were a lot of silent activities and Bob would look very carefully at what people were doing and try to find a complementary action for them, something simple that he saw in a person that would reinforce their comfortableness with themselves. I recently worked with Bob in Lyon on two different versions of *Medea* and I was struck by the fact that so many of the things he was emphasizing during rehearsals were precisely the things he was emphasizing from the day I met him: listen, always listen, not just with your ears but with your body and your mind. If you're listening, your concentration is there. He would also tell the performers that the body is always moving—even when it's still, it's moving. I think in those early workshops we were always working toward an understanding of that fact. With *Medea* he would say no matter how many different things you're dealing with on stage it's always one thing. I think the moment I met him he was dealing with that one thing. That's what we were working toward in those early workshops. I can't say what this one thing is, it might be a different thing for everyone.

SUE SHEEHY: Sometimes Bob would say do what you want or he would pick someone out and have everyone follow their movements. He also worked on images and ideas he had in his head when he wanted to see what they looked like. I don't want to sound philosophical or pretentious but the workshops really put you in tune with your body, being conscious of your body and being conscious of other people without having any physical contact with them.

CAROL MULLINS: We did a lot of moving and dancing. I remember passing rocks and concentration exercises.

JIM NEU: At some point Bob had everybody in the room sit down and then each person would get up and move by themselves and everybody would *watch*. It really terrified me.

ROBYN BRENTANO: Those early workshops were interesting because sometimes there'd be a whole roomful of people while other times only two or three people would show up. One night I walked into the room— I think I was late—and no one else was there. Bob was sitting on a little flight of steps leading down from the windowsill and I went in and sat down and waited for him to get up but he didn't. And he didn't for a really long time. It really threw me. I got a little bit panicky because I wasn't sure quite what was going on and I didn't know Bob well enough in those days to know where he was coming from. There was something a little bit unpredictable about him. I remember at one point thinking he must be mad, nobody sits for half an hour perfectly still like that and yet his concentration and his focus were so sharp I had no choice but to wait and see what was going to happen. Finally, he began to get up very, very, very slowly—it must have taken him fifteen minutes—and it sort of released in me a vision of everything from infancy to old age, from primordial, prehuman beings to 21st-century man. It was like a recapitulation of individual and racial history flashing before me in slow motion. Movement was important to Bob right from the beginning and I think it triggers an awful lot in his mind. One of the stories he used to tell was about his experience doing action painting at Pratt. He'd put up a huge piece of paper and then run from one end to the other with a brush in his hand. He said at a certain point he became more interested in what was happening when he was running than in the object on the wall he was creating. One of the exercises that I loved doing was walking from one end of the loft to the other. Sometimes it took us half an hour just to cross the room. Our task was to focus on a point that we were going toward and then when we turned around and came back to remember where that point was while focusing on a point on the opposite wall. When you describe it that way it sounds sort of silly or inconsequential but what it did was help us focus on all of the things that we bring to an experience. I remember Bob saying it's very difficult to do something very simple.

CAROL MULLINS: Bob used the word "school" which isn't such a bad word for it. We were all dedicated to Bob and his work but everyone was getting something back from it too. We were learning and changing.

Robert Wilson in the New York Times, *December 2, 1973: I like bringing together all kinds of people and getting them to relate in new ways. They can get out of it what they can.*

Byrd Hoffman Foundation Prospectus (c. 1969): Nature of Work—to encourage, stimulate and develop self-awareness through a variety of individually structured and group generated activities . . . to locate sensitivity and personal self-discipline . . . freeing body tension and social repression; encouraging freedom of expression and being.

Robert Wilson in Dance Scope, *1975-6: I think it important that people be allowed to be themselves. In all cases the piece has been made around these people, their personalities or the things they want to do. . . . We just say "Okay, you can do that" and then we put it together. We try to have diversity, a theatre made of people.*

DANCING

SHERYL SUTTON: We were dancing nearly all the time. There was always an unspoken agreement that the way anyone danced was acceptable. Even though Andy de Groat was the leader and had an incredible capacity as a dancer, you never felt you had to look like him. Dancing had various purposes. It was a kind of physical warmup, a way of concentrating energy and focusing your attention on the rehearsal activities that followed. It was also a release and a way of expressing yourself and it provided a reservoir of material as well. Our workshops always involved a lot of dance improvisation from which specific actions and movements were taken for performances. I think I explored a lot of myself through dance and by experimenting with various ways of moving and copying what other people did with their bodies. I felt it was possible to learn everything I needed as a performer and a person from dancing.

KIT CATION: In a sense dancing was the way we communicated together. Bob would put on the music and we'd dance and dance and then he would stop the music. He'd give us all this high energy from dancing and then he'd have us sit down and channel that energy into something like moving one arm very slowly. And he'd always say now really focus on what you're doing, really concentrate. It was so powerful and exciting. I think we all felt that way, you could just feel the excitement in the air. We used to dance on a hard floor and we never warmed up. I always said working with Bob ruined my legs but it freed my psyche. It really did do incredible things for me. I used to be extremely shy and I felt that dancing just opened me up.

SCOTTY SNYDER: We danced all the time, we danced every night. Everybody danced the way they wanted to. Always to music, all kinds of music. There was an open house every Thursday and Jerome Robbins would come and dance. And we danced when we were traveling. We were asked not to dance many times. We were dancing on the platform while waiting for a train once and someone came up to us and said stop it. And when we were in Denmark we went to Tivoli and they asked us to stop.

CHARLES DENNIS: An important part of the Byrd studio and the Byrd ethic was Open House. Every Thursday night the door to the street was open and anyone could wander in and dance. There'd be a mix of professional dancers and Byrds and people who'd just walk in off the street. We'd start at eight or nine o'clock and sometimes go to three or four in the morning. People like Spalding Gray would come and Douglas Dunn and Jerome Robbins and Joan Jonas. It was very stimulating. There was always music, rock-and-roll usually, sometimes classical stuff or Terry Riley, music of the period. There was a piano up in the loft and people like Bob Telson, who at the time was working with Philip Glass, would come and jam. Sometimes people would use sounds or words while they were dancing. There were also places to go off and talk — the office and basement — and a lot of collaborations got formed.

Eric Bogosian in New York, April 11, 1988: I had a girlfriend and she lived in this cockroach-infested little apartment on Elizabeth Street. And she would take me by the hand, I remember, and she'd say, "Come on," and we'd go to this little doorway on Spring Street or Prince Street, I forget which, and it was the home of the Byrd Hoffman Foundation, which was where Robert Wilson was. You'd go to this little door that was around four feet high, and inside, people would just be dancing, free form, all night long. Somebody would be playing records, and it would be wild. And I found out that there was this hidden life to the city.

ROBYN BRENTANO: After Bob's work became known, the Open House on Thursday nights developed into a scene. Young people from outside New York found out about it and people would come over from Europe and the loft became sort of like Mecca.

SUE SHEEHY: In the beginning Open House was a lot of fun. In the end it was a drag. There would always be some big shot watching and you had to mind your *p*'s and *q*'s. Especially me. Different board members would bring people, especially people with money. It got to be like we were there to perform.

BRITISH COLUMBIA

JIM NEU: Bob purchased some land in British Columbia in 1972 or '73 and we spent a couple of months there one summer. His original plan was to create an international theatre center but we hadn't counted on the mosquitoes which made the place uninhabitable.

KIT CATION: A few years before, Bob had gone to a place in Ohio called Loveland, which was a kind of community for Catholic women, and that's what British Columbia was all about. In the old days, theatre was also about community. Bob also had this idea we were going to build a wall out there in the wilderness, it was like a project.

CAROL MULLINS: The place was very isolated. To get there we took a train across Canada, changed to a smaller train heading north and got off in a ghost town called Loos. Then, as I recall, you had to go to a deserted house, find a gun, fire a shot and somebody would hear it on the other side of the river and come and collect you in a canoe. Then, after crossing a raging river you would walk an hour through the forest. I'm not kidding.

KIT CATION: British Columbia was heaven. I'm a real outdoor person. I come from Illinois, I'm from the earth and I just loved it. We stayed in these little cabins and Charles built himself a tepee by the river and there were bears. The nearest town was sixty miles away but a neighbor on the next piece of land wanted to get rid of us so she called the police or the Mounties or whoever and told them that we were running a drug ring, which of course wasn't true at all. They came down the river in a boat and a couple people had a few joints. It wasn't a big deal but it was enough to shake everybody up. Here you are in the middle of nowhere, just you and the mosquitoes, and suddenly you're being surrounded by the police.

JIM NEU: They thought we were a bunch of drug-taking hippies. It was ironic to be so isolated and have so much trouble with your neighbors. We couldn't get over it. We had less privacy in a way than you do in New York.

MEL ANDRINGA: I never liked being isolated with the group. It was great traveling with them on tour because you had the stability of this family and also the opportunity of meeting people in new places but the thought of going to some very isolated place with the Byrds was too much for me. British Columbia was presented as being outdoors and hours from the train station and mosquito-infested and much too spiritual for my inclinations. I didn't want to do it. I had a whole circle of friends in New York who weren't connected with the Byrds and I always liked being able to step away from the company. I didn't do drugs either. Sobriety was another way of preserving my autonomy.

PREPARATIONS FOR *KA MOUNTAIN*

CHARLES DENNIS: I remember Bob coming back from Iran and saying I've found this mountain. We're going to do this piece there on the mountain. In the fall after the *Deafman* tour he went to British Columbia on retreat for a couple of months and he came back with all these drawings and plans and we started working on *Overture.*

In April of 1972 a weeklong series of performances titled *Overture for KA MOUN-TAIN AND GUARDenia TERRACE* was given at the Spring Street loft, marking the culmination of several months' work developing material for the seven-day play to be presented that September at the Shiraz Festival. Theatrical presentations were offered each day from six to nine in the morning and six to nine in the evening. Lunch was served in the basement every afternoon and exhibits on the top two floors of the loft were open to the public throughout the day. The following month Wilson and sixteen members of the company flew to France for the second developmental phase of the project, a four-week residency at Royaumont, a twelfth-century abbey located about forty-five minutes from Paris. There they were joined by participants from various countries. On Saturday nights work-in-progress was shown before friends and invited guests and at the end of their residency, the company presented twelve hours of plays and activities in different parts of the abbey.

MEL ANDRINGA: I didn't go along with the backpackers to British Columbia and I had somewhat the same attitude toward the thing at Royaumont, partly because of the intensity of the experience. But I did go at the very end of the workshop just before everyone set off for Iran. It was like the ship was leaving and I didn't want to be left behind. So S.K. and Carol Mullins and I looked around for really cheap airline tickets and found a flight that left from Canada. We did all this in a speculative manner, in other words we hocked the farm. The bus to Canada stopped in Buffalo for a day and we called back to New York to tell them we were on our way and they said, "Don't come." There had been some setback and it wasn't going to happen or maybe it wasn't going to happen on the scale they originally believed or maybe they just didn't want us. It didn't matter at that point, we already had our tickets and we weren't going to turn around. There was a short break after the Royaumont workshop and then the Byrds collected in Istanbul prior to leaving for Iran. That's when we learned that Bob had been imprisoned in Crete.

KIT CATION: He was on his way to Iran and he had to go through airport security. He had some dope in his pocket and forgot it was there. Stupid. Oh boy, was that awful.

SUE SHEEHY: We didn't know what to do. I remember one night going to the airport in Istanbul and just sitting.

JIM NEU: There was a lot of uncertainty in Istanbul whether we were going to go on. The way I remember it is that we already had the tickets and we would just go to Iran anyway and try to keep the thing alive.

MEL ANDRINGA: I flew with George Ashley [company manager] and Igor Demjen to Teheran and the rest of the group were told to wait in Istanbul. In Teheran it became clear that they weren't going to do the show without Bob. We got a very disappointing phone call in the hotel room in Teheran that the whole thing was canceled. Bob was what they had bought. Somehow things got fixed even though Bob's situation didn't change and they let us start.

KIT CATION: In Crete we got a telegram that said "Don't come to Iran" because the whole thing was going to fall through and there was no money to get us back home. We visited Bob in prison every day. We had to bring him food, I don't think they fed the prisoners, the families were expected to feed them. It was a very hard time. He wasn't allowed to write letters but he could write in his notebooks and he'd give us things to send on. I think that a French lawyer hired by his agent Ninon Karlweis eventually made some agreement with the government. In the end they let Bob out but they wouldn't give his passport back and told him not to leave the country. He said he couldn't get into a hotel without it so they gave it to him and he left. It was almost like they were letting him leave but they weren't going to admit it. It was very iffy if he was going to get through customs but he did.

SHERYL SUTTON: By the time we got to Iran we had very little time to put the work together. The family feeling was very, very strong and we were determined to do this despite the fact that Bob wasn't there for a month. The Iranian students were amazed at that kind of dedication and I think they respected it.

MEL ANDRINGA: We were working for about a month in Shiraz without Bob. We lived in the dormitories and there was a group of Iranian students from Pahlavi University working with us from the time we arrived. We would do *Deafman* in the halls just to give people a sense of the performing style and S.K. Dunn would teach the seven-part movement. We also rehearsed everything that had been done at Royaumont. S.K. and Sheryl were in charge of rehearsals and we were receiving daily letters with long detailed instructions from Bob and Andy, who was having long conferences with him each day in Crete. He would write that we're going to need to make fifty little houses and enclose a little drawing of a peaked-roofed house with a window. He would say do this, do that and we would go to the festival people and say this is what we need to build and they'd say okay, okay, but nothing would ever get done. After a couple of weeks of this it became clear that they weren't putting one cent into the show until they saw the whites of Bob's eyes. They would put us up, they would keep feeding us but that was it.

We also had to tell Bob we don't even know what mountain you're talking about. Shiraz is set on a plateau high in the mountains and Haft Tan does not stand out like the Matterhorn. There were three separate locations Wilson went to look at when he made a preliminary tour of Shiraz and he knew the name of the mountain but the people there kept moving us to other places. Everything was a problem. The festival administrators wouldn't be straight with us. First, they didn't want the show done on the mountain. Shabanou [Empress Farah, the wife of the Shah and patroness of the festival] had had a very bad experience the year before at Persepolis. She had to watch a performance through a little slot inside a bunker because of security problems and she was evidently very, very upset about it. They didn't want another situation like that. So they said snakes! snakes! you can't go on the mountain because of snakes. No one ever saw a snake. They said scorpions! scorpions! Actually we did see scorpion-type things but the general feeling was that they were trying to frighten us away. When Bob got there he had to take another tour of the other mountains to assure them they were unacceptable and insist on Haft Tan. As part of a compromise he agreed to make a special performance for the Shabanou in a very secure old palace in the city proper, which was the overture to *KA MOUNTAIN*. That's the only part she could come to. Then we moved out to the mountain.

CAROL MULLINS: I remember what was going to be our last night in Shiraz. We were being thrown out of the country because Bob was still in prison and people in the group decided to go to the Haft Tan to spend their last night on this holy mountain. We set off very late and part of the way up we started hearing lions roaring. We tried to convince ourselves that this was the wrong part of the country for lions and as it turned out it was the zoo down below but that didn't mean much at midnight going up a dark mountain in this very strange country. Then the next day we got the word. Somebody came running up the mountain to tell us Bob was on his way.

MEL ANDRINGA: Bob arrived and it was like the dam broke. We were nearly in tears of frustration over the fact that virtually nothing had happened, and Bob starts reading the riot act and things start happening. Everything began to move so fast. Evidently someone up high in the administration gave the nod because they made a complete turnaround from holding out on us to rushing to have everything made. I was amazed.

KIKUO SAITO: I didn't want to go to Iran. Bob asked me many times before he left but then he got jailed and I got a letter from him. Jerome Robbins offered to send me ticket so I just went. When I arrived Mel Andringa showed me the mountain. Nothing had been done. I didn't see anything, just mountain.

CHARLES DENNIS: It got nuts when Bob finally showed up.

JIM NEU: My God. I hate to remember. It was torture. He had just spent a month in a lousy Greek jail and was in terrible shape.

CHARLES DENNIS: There was such pressure to get everything done. It was so tense. I just remember being exhausted most of the time.

JIM NEU: People easily got mad at each other. It was scary.

CHARLES DENNIS: Bob's temper was outrageous. Everyone's temper was getting outrageous. I remember at that point thinking, "What am I doing here?"

MEL ANDRINGA: S.K. and Sheryl shaped *KA MOUNTAIN* and then Bob arrived and took over. When he came on the scene suddenly it was his show, his responsibility, his name. Collaboration became cut-and-dried and that turned some people off.

SHERYL SUTTON: Bob had been in prison and he had had a very strong personal experience. He had written stacks of notes and we had to make 179 hours of continuous performance out of them. We immediately started rehearsing, making new plays and redoing all the pieces we had ever done. We also danced every day, at six in the morning and after ten at night. One of his artists came and painted one side of the mountain and made hundreds of papier-mâché flamingoes. Amazing things. It astonished everyone. That's Bob Wilson. He has a way of inspiring people beyond a point they ever dreamed possible. People like to believe in someone who is motivated to that degree.

INNOCENTS ABROAD

SHERYL SUTTON: Many of the Iranians were either hostile or indifferent: "Here are these American hippies spending a fortune and doing this total idiocy."

JIM NEU: I don't think the Iranians helped us very much at all.

CAROL MULLINS: They said no. Any time you asked them for anything they said no.

CHARLES DENNIS: We lived in the dorms and at first they tried to segregate us by sex, even some of the couples who were married. Pretty wild. There was a big showdown over that.

KIT CATION: We refused to stay in the women's dorm, which had bars on the windows and was in terrible condition. They thought, "Well, obviously they're loose women." They didn't understand. It's such a different mentality. What I remember most about Iran is the low status of women. It was very disconcerting to be in a society that looked upon women almost as commodities. Some people loved the country. I had a feeling of this is fascinating, this is wonderful, let me go home now.

SUE SHEEHY: You really took a chance going anywhere alone if you were a woman. As far as the Iranians were concerned if you walked around without a chador you were a whore.

CAROL MULLINS: I usually tried to look like a guy when I went shopping. Hilda, who I suppose was the sexiest-looking of us, was stabbed in the ass in the market one day. They're just totally frustrated sexually. I remember walking home with Sheryl one night and having stones thrown at us because we refused to get into a car with some of them.

JIM NEU: My memory is that the Iranian students who worked with us were very undedicated. We were all trying to be gung-ho and they weren't traveling at the same pulse. There was a real problem motivating them.

CAROL MULLINS: Well, they were rich kids. I remember visiting the home of an Iranian who kept talking about how wonderful the Shah's revolution had been and all the progress they'd made and how everyone now went to school. And they had a servant in their home, a ten-year-old girl—obviously not going to school—who was a virtual slave. And they kept talking about how wonderful life was. There were definitely spies keeping track of us. There were very strange things going on.

ANN WILSON: The people in Shiraz were either wealthy, educated Iranians in the Shah's service or people in chadors who went with hotpots to get their soup. They were Khomeini's people, nobody suspected they had any power. We were all so politically naive it didn't occur to us that there may have been some troubles going on in Iran. You couldn't talk to the Byrds about politics, it didn't exist. Everyone else was out with signs and placards during those years. Not the Byrd group, we were making art.

KIKUO SAITO: We didn't know about all the political problems in Iran then. When we got to Paris someone asked me, "How could you do this? How could you work for these people?" We never knew.

JIM NEU: There was more unrest than anyone would dare talk about. We weren't really aware of it at the time though we were aware of a lot of government agents and we knew that some of our interpreters worked for the police. That was an open secret. I remember in *Overture* I was in one of the rooms that the audience walked past on the way to their seats. It was a scene showing a typical family sitting around a table and I was the father. At the end of the performance when the audience went out, they saw the same tableau only now I was standing up pointing a gun at the family. I was very nervous about this because the Shah's wife was supposed to come and I thought her security force was going to shoot first and ask questions later. Another thing I remember about *Overture* was that it was the first time I ever said no to Bob. There was a cage of monkeys in the room with us and Bob wanted to let them out to run around and I told him I wouldn't do it. I'd gone through two or three years of doing anything he wanted but this time I said no way, 'cause they had teeth like dogs and carried God-knows-what diseases. He said, "Okay, Jim, okay. We'll leave the monkeys in the cage."

KIT CATION: There were guards with guns everywhere. It was a little uncomfortable—why do they need all these guards? All these poor people lived in the area and one night someone said there was enough room and they could come in and see the play for free. The guards got real uptight about it.

JIM NEU: They were living right there and they wanted to know what the hell was going on. By that time there was a very small audience anyway so Bob said you don't have to charge them anything, just let them in. The guards didn't want that to happen but Bob really insisted on it.

SUE SHEEHY: We stayed at the university, which is right across from the palace. The queen was in town for the festival and there were armed guards every four feet. It was like a police state. I remember if you wanted to get a taxi in Shiraz you'd yell out where you were going and if they were headed in that direction they'd stop and find room for you. One night I just couldn't get a cab and there was this one guard who was watching me. Finally he saw a taxi coming and he pulled it over, made everybody get out and put me in. He must have told the driver not to stop for anyone. The driver wouldn't even take any money from me. I have never forgotten that. It really said something about the power of the police.

JIM NEU: We should have realized that something was wrong in Iran. There was a little village at the base of the mountain and I remember more than once as we got out of the taxi from the university some of these kids would throw rocks at us. We didn't know exactly why. We just figured they didn't like us messing with their garden but the fact is they didn't like Americans or what we represented or the Shah's festival.

CAROL MULLINS: We also had some big political problems a few years later in Brazil with *Stalin*, which was condemned by the military government.

ROBYN BRENTANO: There had been a big student uprising in Brazil ten years before and, although we didn't know it, we were scheduled to open on the night of the anniversary. I think they were worried that if we had all these students in the theatre for twelve hours it might cause a riot—or a revolution.

CAROL MULLINS: One of the things they complained about was that the script didn't have enough material for the length of the play so they concluded there must be a lot of bad stuff going on. What was filling up the rest of that time?

JIM NEU: We did a censors' performance which lasted twelve hours and those poor bastards were stupefied. "Hey guys, any questions?"

OVERTURE

Introductory evening to *KA MOUNTAIN*. Two performances were presented at midnight and at three in the morning before an invited audience in the garden of the Narenjestan, an ancient palace in the heart of the city. The two-hour presentation set forth some of the themes and images of the main work, which would begin on Haft Tan mountain the following night.

Judith Searle in the New York Times, *November 12, 1972: The perfor-mance I saw began about 2:30 A.M. in the beautiful building which the Iranians call the "House of Mourning." The audience entered at one end of a long rectangular courtyard and passed various open rooms like depart-ment store display windows which housed various scenes, most of which looked like tableaux vivants. On closer examination, these proved to be slowly changing scenes in which actors moved so gradually that their movements were almost imperceptible.*

Peter Cranston in Tehran Journal, *September 2, 1972: In the first one I saw a Thanksgiving dinner in progress, with a rather unhappy family sitting around a rather moldy-looking artificial turkey. Then there was a wedding, with the bride, groom and minister frozen in place, behind a small cage containing a bear. One room is unrestored and is excavated down to a cellar full of dust. There an "old man" is contemplating a lion in another cage. Two camels are sitting by a pool at the rear of the court, flanked by a gaggle of bearded men in goggles, and a lady setting her baby adrift in a basket. A stone mason is chipping away at old columns in another room. An old bazarri contemplates a lovely girl in a windblown gown, who is not moving at all. Finally there is a room full of grass, with about twenty-five real live rabbits hopping around. A Santa Claus is sitting with two live deer beside an "old lady" in black, played by the nine-year-old girl in Wilson's troupe, motionless. An enormous tower with a bell and a horrible stuffed eagle is inhabited by a number of people in white.*

Judith Searle in the New York Times, *November 12, 1972: The audience gradually clustered at one end of the courtyard, some sitting on bleachers or steps, some standing, and the major actions of the play began to unfold in various parts of the courtyard. Actors—some on platforms, some in side rooms, some on a kind of low stage at one end—began to perform very slowly actions related to the stated theme of the piece— "a family and some people changing." It is difficult to say when the play began, because actions had already begun to take place at their slow, imperceptible pace before I noticed them. One of the first things I noticed was a middle-aged woman in a large Texas hat who was speaking in flat tones about her childhood in an Iowa town; a very ordinary, undramatic description. She gets up from a table at which she is sitting and leaves, never to return. A slender Negro girl in a white Victorian dress enters, goes to the table and pours water from a pitcher into a bowl. She fills the bowl and continues to pour, even as it overflows, until the pitcher is empty. She then slowly begins to peel a red onion with a knife. She continues this for the duration of the play, about two and a half hours, never speaking, paying no attention to the other actors, who in turn pay no attention to her. A tall thin young man, who we later learn is Robert Wilson, appears on another platform near the center of the garden. He makes sounds, some of them intelligible, some not, sometimes resembling the speech-attempts of a spastic, sometimes animal sounds.*

Peter Cranston in Tehran Journal, *September 2, 1972: Well, all sorts of strange things happen then. It's kind of like life itself in that some of them are good and some are bad, some interesting and some dull.*

Judith Searle in the New York Times, *November 12, 1972: On a high platform of three levels farther back in the courtyard sit actors who almost never move but who speak poetry in English, French and Parsi. They, too, frequently make plays on words. A long "aria" is based on the sound similarities of the words "collection" and "eclectic." At intervals the woman sitting alone on the highest platform rings a bell. Below this high platform is a lower one on which are lying men wearing old age masks and long beards. Also lying on the platform is a young man wearing white trousers who at one point performs a kind of whirling-dervish dance to ethereal electronic music. In another part of the garden are a muscular strong man sitting on a kind of throne fondling a huge live snake and a 9-year-old girl dressed as an old woman whose entire action, stretched over several hours, is to walk from one side of the garden around the front platform to confront the strong man. He retreats from her, whereupon she curls up in an embryonic position in front of the throne he has vacated.*

CINDY LUBAR: Just before she arrives, fifty young Iranian children, all dressed as old men, wearing glasses with very large eyes glued on them, walk toward the front pool carrying candles. When they reach the pool they slowly bend over in unison and extinguish the candle flames in the water. Small white Christmas-tree lights sparkle in the garden's trees.

Judith Searle in the New York Times, *November 12, 1972: The lights come up strongly on the empty throne, then go down and out.*

Peter Cranston in Tehran Journal, *September 2, 1972: Overture is over. On the way out, we notice that the bride is being strangled by the groom, and that the father at the dinner table has taken out a gun. Everything else is the same. Except the audience. Some of them are very angry. Some are happy, maybe very happy. As for me, I am not feeling bad at all.*

KIT CATION: I really don't remember the performance very well. I hadn't slept in three days. At about that point I was so exhausted I stopped functioning basically. We were working day and night. I was so tired that one night I couldn't move. It got so sleep was more important to me than anything. That's my main memory of the show—exhaustion. And how delicious it was to lay down and sleep for a few hours.

John Ashbery and David Soroushian-Kermani in Saturday Review: *Meanwhile back on Ka Mountain, one of the most authentically bizarre events in the history of theatre was under way.*

THE SEVEN-DAY PLAY

Program note: KA MOUNTAIN AND GUARDenia TERRACE *will be given for one performance only beginning at 0:00 midnight, September 2 and ending at 12:00 midnight, September 8. The complete presentation is continuous, 24 hours a day for 7 days.*

Allan Kaprow: "The line between art and life should be kept as fluid, and perhaps indistinct, as possible."

John Cage: "I have attempted . . . to set forth a view of the arts which does not separate them from the rest of life, but rather confuses the difference between Art and Life, just as it diminishes the distinctions between space and time."

Antonin Artaud: "Between life and theatre there will be no distinct division, but instead a continuity."

Overture for KA MOUNTAIN. Shiraz, 1972.

Peter Cranston in Tehran Journal, *September 16, 1972: Wilson himself told me that eventually he hopes to reach the point where there is no longer any distinction between his life and his art, for he feels that the gulf between "ordinary life" and art, or between "jobs" and creativity, is the essential and tragic flaw of our times: "I want to do a single piece that will last for 200 years."*

Peter Wilson in Sixth Festival of the Arts, *September 8, 1972: No one or hardly anyone seems to have taken [Wilson] seriously when during* Overture *he shouted "NOT THEATRE!"*

K A MOUNTAIN was subtitled "a story of a family and some people changing" and the festival program stressed that these figures "were not just characters to be seen on the platforms and mountain . . . they are also us as we have worked to develop this piece." The symbiosis of life and art was but one thread in the epic work; another unifying theme was the journey of an old man who leaves his home and family and goes wandering. Making his first appearance in *Overture,* the old man appeared in various guises in the course of the seven-day performance (each actor played the old man at least once during the week), as well as in the form of an unbroken line of painted cutouts extending from the base of Haft Tan to its summit. As the figure of the old man moved higher and higher up the mountain each day, he passed through not only the rocky terrain of Haft Tan but the ages of man and the history of the world (represented by various totems, symbols and monuments along the way), metaphorically witnessing the creation, evolution and destruction of the world. A number of people close to Wilson believe that he identified the old man with the poet and critic Edwin Denby, who had portrayed a similar figure in the New York version of *Overture* that spring. The central image of the seven-day play was, of course, the mountain itself; an immense and arid slab of rock known as Haft Tan or "Seven Bodies" after the seven Sufi poets buried in the garden at its base. A member of the Byrd School has characterized the subject of *KA MOUNTAIN* as "big life," a fitting designation for this vast collage of myth and literature whose cast included performers of every age and nationality, much of the animal kingdom and nature itself.

FIRST NIGHT

John Ashbery and David Soroushian-Kermani in Saturday Review*: Driving up to the midnight opening of* KA MOUNTAIN *on September 2, we were hit, even from afar at the sight of the oil lamps twinkling on the slope, by a strong sense that something fantastic was about to happen.*

MEL ANDRINGA: At the base of the mountain there was a large walled courtyard where the seven Sufi poets were buried and behind this the

Iranians had built a level platform that went right up to the back of the garden wall with bleacher seats and a stage with metal scaffolding at the sides for the lighting equipment. There was also a rather ratty little collection of a half-dozen animals in a fenced-off area nearby—an elephant, some horses, a lion, maybe a camel. What rises up from there is not so much a mountain as it is solid rock.

Judith Searle in the New York Times, *November 12, 1972: The platform was not ready at midnight, when the play was scheduled to begin, and the crowd waiting on the slippery slope became impatient, then angry. We were let into the playing area barely in time to prevent a riot. Unfortunately, there was not room on the platform for all the people who had tickets, and many had to be turned away. We could hear them throughout the first part of the play, roaring and chanting in the darkness below.*

KIKUO SAITO: Big commotion. I was backstage and I heard shouting and screaming. I asked Bob what was going on. Bob as usual said "I don't know."

James Underwood in Tehran Journal, *September 4, 1972: And when they were still outside when the play began they started baying loudly at the moon each time Wilson's droning voice reached a pitch high enough to be carried out to them on the breeze. After waiting unsuccessfully for half an hour one group decided to put on its own rival show on the nearby piece of waste ground, where Wilson had gathered a collection of animals including a lion cub, baboons, horses, donkeys, sheep, camels, chickens and a young elephant, apparently obtained from Shiraz Zoo.*

Judith Searle in the New York Times, *November 12, 1972: Wilson, in a black suit dusted with white powder, entered from the left and made spastic noises and movements across the stage, holding a telephone conversation with the woman sitting at stage right. He explained to her that they were starting 40 minutes late and said he didn't think the audience would understand. The audience apparently didn't, and they began leaving in droves after the first five minutes. Wilson then addressed the audience and asked, "Why are you leaving?" One man, on his way out, replied, "Because you're not giving us any action." Wilson looked at his agent, Ninon Tallon Karlweis, in the front row and said, "I don't know what to do."*

Peter Cranston in Tehran Journal, *September 4, 1972: People were shouting for "action" when in fact action of the sort they meant is, I think, the furthest thing from Wilson's mind. As many people got up to leave, which was very difficult on the crowded platform, Wilson improvised some very funny material with them as the butts of his humor. "Why—where are you going?" he would ask them in a voice like a slowed-down recording; he jumped up out of a long motionless silence to accost one disgruntled leaver and scared the fellow half out of his wits.*

Judith Searle in the New York Times, *November 12, 1972: But the action continued to inch forward. The Negro girl picked up a knife from a table and slowly walked to the white girl and stabbed her. Then the white girl rose from her "dead" position to similarly stab the Negro girl. All the while, the telephone conversation continued and a voice behind a white wall covering the upstage left half of the stage began to read from* Moby Dick *about the sinister whiteness of the whale, then continued with passages from the Book of Jonah describing the Leviathan.*

Peter Cranston in Tehran Journal, *September 4, 1972: The theme of the first act was definitely whales. Readings from* Moby Dick *and the Bible on the subject of Leviathans and great fish were read from behind a screen as several performers acted out a slow-motion series of murders and rebirths. Meanwhile Wilson and a girl named Cindy carried on a rather surrealistic telephone conversation which had some very strong moments in it. This Cindy has an amazing voice, certainly not what I'd call pleasant, but certainly impressive. She and Wilson were both covered with powder, so that each violent motion either of them made raised a cloud of dust as if the remnants of memory were clouding off them like effluvium of the tomb. Cindy also took part in the mocking of the disgruntled audience.*

Judith Searle in the New York Times, *November 12, 1972: About three-quarters of the audience had disappeared by the end of the first intermission. It was 2:30 A.M., the cold wind had begun to blow down the mountainside, and those of us who remained were tired, thirsty and shivering.*

ANN WILSON (reading from her journal): "Last night, first night of seven. We lit candles up the mountain. Saito hung birds and palm branches across the path. I read from under the platform *Moby Dick* and talked about the mountain. It was wonderful down under there reading with a candle and hearing them read up on the platform. . . . We did the third act at dawn, the rooster punctuated it. I looked out of a window with a lion mask. We walked up the mountain at dawn."

MEL ANDRINGA: The first night we performed *Deafman Glance* in the full version—some six hours—and halfway through the sun came up. It was an amazing moment. The light of the sky made our own lighting totally ineffectual and changed the way you looked at everything. The space around us was suddenly so vast. I realized we were part of a greater show which was life.

CHARLES DENNIS: The show would end at dawn and the trumpets of *Aida* would come on. That was a great moment. At five o'clock when the sky was just getting light—no matter what was happening—you'd hear those blasting, beautiful trumpets and it was like rebirth. I mean, we had made it to another day. It was amazing. You were practically in a trance for the whole night and this was like bringing you back to life and the daylight.

CAROL MULLINS: When the trumpets of *Aida* went off, the old man would leave the stage and climb the mountain to the level where that day's activities would take place. The trumpets were the signal for whoever was on the stage to change into their old man's costume and go up the mountain. The audience was supposed to follow them but mostly we would be down to three people in the audience by dawn. We came to know those three people very well indeed.

SCOTTY SNYDER: We'd finish at dawn and people would be coming out to say their prayers. There'd be the sound of the prayers echoing along the mountainside and a man would appear from nowhere on the side of the mountain singing a chant. My God, it was beautiful.

KIT CATION: Once the sun came up the flies would also come out. I remember poor Sheryl sitting on stage trying not to move with the flies buzzing all around her face. She was very good.

CINDY LUBAR: After moving up the mountain, Andy de Groat would execute the pine-tree ritual in the area designated for a given day. A pine tree would be cut, wrapped, decorated with flowers, daubed with blood from the old man, burned, wrapped again and planted. This daily ceremony marked the commencement of the twelve-hour period of mountain activities.

DAY ACTIVITIES

Each morning performers and spectators moved up the mountain to the site of that day's activities. Every day had its own designated color, theme, season and element (water, earth, air, fire), as well as symbols, monuments and landscaping elements that marked the entrance to the respective levels. These included a navel (a small mound on which a different object was placed each day—on the first a miniature dinosaur and on the last a gardenia), a cube room (a white 8-foot-square enclosure whose appearance and contents similarly changed from level to level) and a seasonal garden. In some cases these motifs marked a chronological progression; the daily theme, for example, moved from birth to youth to marriage to death and the season from spring to winter. Each level also had its own architectural symbol, a two-dimensional cutout, past which the old man traveled on his weeklong ascent. These included Stonehenge (Day One), an obelisk (Day Two), the Parthenon (Day Three), a medieval castle (Day Five) and finally the New York skyline (Day Seven). The scenographic arrangement was cyclical as well as progressive, with a dinosaur stationed at the top of the mountain as well as at its base, where the imprint of dinosaur tracks could be seen along the rocky slope. Within each zone the rocks marking the path to the summit were painted the designated color of the day and the small triangular flags along the way were similarly color coded.

CAROL MULLINS: Bob divided the day activities up and gave them to various people. I remember sitting around at night passing scraps of paper with different ideas and activities on them. I was day captain for the second day. My day's theme was water, its color was blue-green. There were a lot of stuffed fish along the path and a giant whale and at the very top of the peak, Noah's ark. The old man fished up on the mountain, someone danced with yellow scarves, and two lizard people fought, broke away, hid and fought again. I carried a silver pitcher up the mountain and poured water. There was a press conference that day and we all went down to the stage at the base of the mountain, led by Sheryl who carried an egg on a book. I can also remember Andy dancing with the pine branches towards the end of the day with the sun kind of low, silhouetting him. It was beautiful, beautiful.

KIKUO SAITO: Mountain Two is ocean. I got involved in making lots of fish with papier-mâché. There were maybe a hundred fish on the mountain floor and cutout waves like in Kabuki. I said why don't we make huge whale you could walk into. It was so big an Iranian army truck had to bring it up the mountain. Then I made fish that would fly on a wire from one mountain to another. I think Bob liked that. Bob let me do anything. There was no time to talk detail or size or anything. Part of Bob's genius is that he lets people do things, you have to have that as much as any other talent otherwise nothing can happen. Another day I covered mountain with pink flamingoes. Lots. Also papier-mâché apples. We made with chicken wire, big and small apples. The biggest was human-size. Very red. That was a pretty thing, 'cause the mountain is brown. It was very hard work. Once one mountain was finished, there was the next to do. We were always just one step ahead. We left all the things there on the mountain when the week was over.

KATHRYN KEAN: We had no materials to work with, only newspaper, flour, water and three colors of paint. It was pretty bad. Saito made many things out of light bamboo and covered them with papier-mâché. I stayed in Shiraz after the festival and a week later there was hardly anything left on the mountain. The local people must have taken all the props and cutouts for fuel and building materials.

SUE SHEEHY: I'm petrified of heights and I always found a way out of climbing the mountain. When Bob arrived he said, "Either you get up that mountain or you can get on the next plane home." And I did. Climbing a mountain when I can't even stand on a chair!

JIM NEU: I remember one day my activity was to walk very slowly up the hill in a business suit carrying an attaché case. I think I was supposed to stop and open it part of the way up.

ANN WILSON: I remember some man's house was on the mountain and he would come out and shake his fist at us. He was pissed. We were in his backyard.

JIM NEU: On the sixth or seventh day one of the motifs were these beautiful little silver rockets which covered part of the mountain. I remember them well because I almost put one down on top of a snake. Oh, shit. No snakes, huh?

Judith Searle in the New York Times, *November 12, 1972: One day I climbed the mountain at 6 A.M. to see the company in their "Fifty Houses," a group of white pasteboard cutout houses near the top. Each of the "Byrds" had decorated a house and planned an activity inside it for the morning. One man, his walls decorated with paintings made by members of the company, read to us from Aesop's Fables. A woman, her house's tiny interior swathed in airy drapings of Indian silk, lay listening to Persian music on the radio. A boy stood in front of his house playing a kind of wooden flute.*

CHARLES DENNIS: What did I do in my house? I stayed out of the sun, that's what I did.

MEL ANDRINGA: I had the responsibility of stage managing everything that went on from six in the evening to six in the morning and then someone else would take over during the daylight hours. So I have very little recollection of what went on during the day. I assume that there was always some kind of activity. Sometimes it would just be someone somewhere on the mountain doing something—if you could find them. Maybe just one of the group wearing the old man's costume and walking around or hiding in the shade. There were people assigned to be there. I remember sitting by the swimming pool at the university one afternoon and thinking that at that very moment the play was going on somewhere up on the mountain.

ANN WILSON: There was a green pool in the garden with gold and white fish and we'd sit in the shadows when it got too hot. It was 150 degrees during the day. Nobody was really around until night. I remember what few hours of sleep I got were always between noon and three. It was just too hot to do anything.

CHARLES DENNIS: There wasn't too much daytime activity to be honest with you. I remember going over to the mountain after lunch. But it was always so goddamn hot. At two o'clock in the afternoon you'd fry. A few journalists or locals who were curious would come by but the real crowds were in the evening.

SHERYL SUTTON: Nobody saw the whole thing. It wasn't possible. A lot of things didn't even happen. It was too hot.

KIKUO SAITO: It's hard to grasp the whole thing. Hardly anybody saw it.

John Ashbery and David Soroushian-Kermani in Saturday Review: *Thus the play was truly an allegory of life which always seems to be taking place somewhere else—or when one is asleep—whose perceived fragments are tantalizing clues to what the whole might be but whose climax might easily go unperceived.*

KIT CATION: We'd rehearse on the stage at the foot of the mountain during the day for the performances that night and people would be passing out. It was that kind of heat. It was so hard to climb the mountain during the day but I tried it one night and it was nothing. You really couldn't function in that kind of heat and yet we were doing all this stuff. It was sort of crazy.

CAROL MULLINS: In the platform play the first night I was dressed like Sheryl Sutton in one of her Victorian dresses. She was in a dark one and I was in a light one. But Sheryl was much smaller than I was and there was no room in the dress to breathe. I'm not a frail person but with the incredible heat of the day and exhaustion—we had been working night and day—I couldn't control my breathing and panicked. I fainted dead away in the middle of the stage and the next thing I know, Sheryl, who was supposed to be sort of like my shadow, is laying down next to me, whispering, "Do you think we could get up now?" And I'm suddenly aware of the fact that I'm lying there with the queen and who knows who else watching me. Of course, I'm more worried about Bob Wilson, who never mentioned it.

SCOTTY SNYDER: It's a very vicious climate. I got typhoid fever and pneumonia and nearly everyone became dehydrated and had to go to the hospital for intravenous treatments.

SHERYL SUTTON: I was one of the few who didn't get sick. I dressed and ate like the Iranians and took on their time. I slept from one to four when it was about 130 degrees. I went up the mountain in the morning with a melon on my head, wrapped in a kind of chador. I looked crazy. Most people got dehydrated, they dressed in blue jeans and sweated a bucket and a half.

CAROL MULLINS: I was one of the few who didn't get sick and I attribute it to Coca-Cola. It kept you from getting dehydrated and it kills whatever's in the food.

Daytime activities also included a number of encounters between the company and members of the audience and press:

Ossia Trilling in The Drama Review, *June, 1973: Having been provocatively announced as a "press conference,"* Questions and Answers *offered false hopes of an intelligible dialog with Wilson but resolved itself into the same kind of extemporized, though well-tried, playacting sessions that typify most of his work. The sketch began not with Robert Wilson's voice at all, but with that of Ann Wilson reading from* Moby Dick *by Melville and the Book of Jonah from the* Bible. *Robert Wilson was seated alongside her on the bare stage with only a flickering oil-lamp burning downstage center to one side of a sturdy square-cut unpainted and unvarnished wooden throne-like armchair. As she read, Wilson uttered long, soft, piercing shrieks, as of someone in mortal terror of an unnamed danger. When she uttered the word "mountain," Wilson echoed it in a deep, lingering bass voice. A third character seated on stage held a broken mirror in her hand. In response to questions from the audience, the three characters on stage behaved irrationally. Wilson painted some hieroglyphs on Ann Wilson's wrist with a chinagraph pencil, as an indication of what reply she should give.*

Peter Cranston in Tehran Journal, *September 6, 1972: Several questions along the line of "what does it all mean?" received answers with little or no relation to what had been asked.*

Judith Searle in the New York Times, *November 12, 1972: When Robert Wilson and four of his Byrd Hoffman School of Byrds arrived for the "Debate on Robert Wilson" at this year's Festival of the Arts in Iran, they were wearing black blindfolds as though expecting to go before a firing squad. They were not far mistaken. The hostility in the room was palpable, and it came mostly from a large, international group of reporters whose creature comforts had been seriously interfered with in the course of covering the arts beat this past September in the Iranian city of Shiraz. Because of this quiet, lanky young man named Robert Wilson, they had been forced to climb a mountain in the middle of the night and sit with a dust storm blowing around them to watch a play which went on for seven days and seven nights without stopping. After all, they were not covering Vietnam! What right did Wilson have to demand they climb a mountain to see his* KA MOUNTAIN AND GUARDenia TERRACE? *Translator-moderator Nasser Assar tactfully rendered the furious questions from Arabic, Parsi and French into English, and Wilson diffidently asked the other members of his "panel" to answer. Nine-year-old Jessie Dunn Gilbert, youngest of the Wilson company, couldn't think of any reason for having the play on the mountain. Scotty Snyder said she thought the mountain was a beautiful space, more interesting than the platform below. Ann Wilson said they used the mountain "because it's there." The angry mutterings from the audience continued.*

Note in festival publication: By coming only at midnight you're missing some of the best stuff. Please come at any time, day or night, the odder the hour the better.

NIGHTS ON KA MOUNTAIN

CINDY LUBAR: At 6 P.M. each day the activities shifted from the mountain to the platform stage next to the garden. There was a three-sided room called the white room where different stories and plays were presented each night on the theme "a family and some people changing."

CHARLES DENNIS: I remember doing the old man one night on the platform. I was dressed in white and sat at a table with these rays of string coming out from my fingers and I think I also spit red strings out of my mouth. That was a pretty strange bit.

MEL ANDRINGA: One night Bob did a piece called the "Jail Play" which was sort of based on his experiences in Crete. All you could see of Bob was his hands moving through a little window at the back of the stage.

CINDY LUBAR: Two visitors crossed the stage together forty-five times to try to visit him but were told each time by the guard, "L.S.D.—DOPE—NOPE." On each of their forty-five journeys they stopped, faced the audience and in slowed-down, very deep voices said, "Whatever shall we do?"

MEL ANDRINGA: I just remember it lasted a long time and nothing happened.

CAROL MULLINS: Guess that's what being in jail is like.

JIM NEU: I stage-managed the fifth night. It was the only night performance that took place up the mountain and it was an incredible sight because a stage had been built out over the edge of the mountain and you could see the lights of Shiraz below. We constructed a circular platform with a well in the middle and people would go down into it and come back up during the play. I was under the stage cueing people and things to come on. There was a huge papier-mâché snake that Saito made which eventually circled the entire stage and the old man crawled into its mouth.

CAROL MULLINS: One of the pieces we performed was the "Twelve Bed Play," which later became a part of *The Life and Times of Joseph Stalin*. It was a real concentration exercise. Almost nothing happened. One person at a time got very slowly out of bed and walked *very* slowly around the stage carrying a lighted lantern. It was beautiful. I loved doing it. I loved the feeling of it.

Peter Cranston in Tehran Journal, *September , 1972: The episode begins with Wilson in his dusty black suit stage center, holding up a live white pigeon. "The bird is free to fly away at will" he intones, then goes and sits at a table to provide occasional abstract commentary on the dance of the twelve sleepers who weave in and out amongst their beds carrying lanterns at the slowest pace yet achieved in the course of* KA MOUNTAIN. *Wilson at his best.*

MEL ANDRINGA: Under the pressure of the moment we would put things together on stage to fill those twelve hours.

CAROL MULLINS: The quality of the plays varied a lot depending on what time of the night it was.

Scenes from *KA MOUNTAIN*.

JIM NEU: Most people came at eight and stayed until ten and that was their idea of theatre. They'd have their theatre experience and be home by ten o'clock.

KIT CATION: There were always a few people in the audience who would come back night after night. Some of them actually came to Paris that fall and worked with us because they loved it so much.

John Ashbery and David Soroushian-Kermani in Saturday Review, *November, 1972: Watching the play late at night or in the early morning, dozing, mingling one's own dreams with those taking place on the little white stage was an unforgettable experience. We felt we were witnessing the simultaneous birth and destruction of a world.*

Jacques Lonchampt in Le Monde, *September 14, 1972: It would take more than several volumes to describe these plays in which nothing happens and about which one understands almost nothing but in which, most of the time, everything excites wonder.*

Ossia Trilling in the Financial Times, *September 28, 1972: The dramatic episodes enacted on the ground-level platform at times achieve a halting musical rhythm that is no less unbearably wearisome, yet fascinates us, or some of us, for all that . . .*

Tehran Journal, September 10, 1972: Surely nobody in the whole course of human history ever spent so long watching nothing happen as we did.

Amir Taheri in Kayhan International, *September 10, 1972: A few days with Wilson and you can never face ordinary theatre again. This is what has happened to those among us who were interested enough, or "foolish" enough, to take the trouble of climbing Haft Tan mountain to see Wilson's company at work.*

CAROL MULLINS: Kit Cation and I were the only two people in the company who made some attempt to get eight hours of sleep a night. Every day began and ended with a meeting and I remember arguing early on that there had to be eight hours between the meeting at the end of the day and the one at the beginning and absolutely no one defended us in our needs. Once the show started, I just gave up. I was out of my mind. My brain was fried.

JIM NEU: "Wake me up for my next cue." You'd get somebody to remember when your play started and they'd go to the garden and wake you up.

SUE SHEEHY: You learned to sleep backstage or on the bare ground or anywhere. I can remember being asleep backstage once when I was supposed to be on.

KATHRYN KEAN: Most people went back to the university but I found it easier to sleep wherever I was. Some nights a few of us would stay in the shrine at the top of the mountain.

CHARLES DENNIS: There was this Sufi shrine a little off the path where we were working. This crazy, stoned-out Sufi mystic was there and one or two nights we would go up and smoke opium on the mountain and look down on the whole city. We degenerates had no difficulty finding where this other degenerate was.

KIKUO SAITO: I remember some of the French actors do lots of opium and next day they're throwing up on mountain all over.

SCOTTY SNYDER: The air was so clear and so clean, that's what I remember. It looked like you could reach up and almost touch the stars and the moon.

KIT CATION: I met an Iranian woman at the college whose name was Scheherazade. It was night and we were looking at the stars and she said, "You know how the poets talk about the stars in Shiraz." And I thought to myself, "No I don't know." I realized she was talking about a whole different tradition. It really struck me there's a lot I don't know. Nights in Shiraz like the poets talk about.

ANN WILSON: The fact of the piece was that it was outdoors—the trees were blowing, the night sky was moving, the wind and street sounds were coming from below and such a conjunction made the actuality very real. I think the most interesting thing about *KA MOUNTAIN* was that when we went to Paris that fall we brought the energy of having built the piece outdoors. When you build something outdoors and bring it indoors it goes whhhh! Tremendous excitement.

JIM NEU: The most incredible thing I have ever experienced in theatre was that 24-hour version of *KA MOUNTAIN* we did in Paris. After Iran, twenty-four hours was nothing.

Text from KA MOUNTAIN *program: The old man. The journey. The old man. The body. The old man. The stories. The old man, leaves. Birth. Ocean. Birth. Ocean. The beginning of movement. The beginning of sound. Branch. Bench. Horizontal Zone. Spring. Growing. Spring. Green. Green, grass and trees. Naming. Winding Path. One by one. Summer. Puberty. Heavens. Earth. Trojan horse. Globe of the World. Earth. Earth. Castle. Fall. Snakes and insects. Globe of the world. Earth. Earth. Castle. Fall. Snakes and insects. People as trees. Trees as breezes cut and transferred. Giant lizards crawl on rocks. Sound of a train. Sue Fishing. Winter. Burial. Jungle garden. Sand and clouds and rain and dew. Winter. Burial. White mountain. Green garden. The old man returns. The body. The old man.*

THE FINAL NIGHT

Judith Searle in the New York Times, *November 12, 1972: The grand finale of the* KA MOUNTAIN *event took place the night after the official closing of the festival, and only a few dozen hardy souls, mostly reporters, had stayed on for the final marathon on the mountaintop. The play began about 7:30, an hour and a half late, amid clouds of dust which not even the sprinkling of water and the scattering of straw could dispel. The wind continued throughout the performance, blowing out the candles which had been placed to mark the path up the mountain.*

KATHRYN KEAN: The last evening was very beautiful. I guess I didn't have any worries about the next day so I could just sit there and enjoy it. Bob made a little garden with cut grass and big papier-mâché snakes and in the middle there was an altar with a flying lamb. Part of the mountain was covered with white powder so the garden seemed to be growing out of the snow.

Peter Cranston in Tehran Journal, *September 18, 1972: A bridge had been erected over a terrace of grass and potted flowers, in the middle of which sat, like an altar, the winged lamb from* Overture *surrounded by flowers and candles. A cello player made simple but harmonious sounds on one side while on the other a fat lady sat quite still, fishing. Six figures in white, 18th century costumes climbed up on the bridge where they began to read or recite various things, sometimes simultaneously: a Molière play, the Iowa routine, American Indian poetry, etc. The Old Man, central figure of the play, enters slowly and kneels before the whole scene, resting on his cane. Church bells sound in the distance, along with a chorus of live voices, slowly approaching over the next hill. Overhead, thousands of stars. On the hill, a terrible wind, blowing dust and old newspapers across the scene. Ann Wilson, from the bridge, begins to talk about pilgrimages. A girl in a black robe comes and stands before the old man and begins to beckon him in a sort of fractured poetic tongue to follow her up the mountain. She backs away from the*

Scenes from *KA MOUNTAIN*.

audience, the old man follows to the "altar," where he fills a box with jewels, and proceeds beyond the terrace itself, toward the top of the mountain. A chorus of old men enters and kneels. Jessie begins to walk slowly across the front of the terrace, a little girl disguised as an old lady, with a doll tied around her by a thick rope. Something about her electrifies the audience, even terrifies them. The night, the cold stars, the confusion of childhood with old age. . . . The Old Man reaches a model of New York City and it bursts into flames. As it sparks and flares away to nothing, the shape of a pagoda is seen rising behind it. . . . Then the Old Man and the figure in black reach the statue of a white ape about seven feet high; its face bursts into flame, only its face. . . . Ann speaks of "Amazing Grace" and says several times that "the archangel loves heights." Jessie enters again, goes very slowly up to the altar and "dies," curling up in front of it like a sleeping child. As the Old Man reaches the top of the hill, so far away we can barely make him out, the Three Wise Men begin to enter leading a live camel from the left. Robert Wilson approaches them from the right, dancing the most intense movements I have seen him make that whole week, disturbing, poignant, full of both an agony and a joy. He dances to his favorite Otis Redding song, "I've Been Loving You Too Long To Stop Now," which he has been using in every play for the last five years. At last he disappears. The Wise Men move to the altar and bow before the still figure of Jessie. On the hill, a fire breaks out and silhouettes a gigantic dinosaur standing at the peak. The chorus reaches the top of the hill. The Wise Men rise and leave. The lights dim everywhere but on the burning hill. The week is over.

ANN WILSON: Few audience members made it to the top, the diehards in blankets and sleeping bags, mostly young people — I don't know how the hell they got there, somehow they found a way to get a plane ticket — drama students, Iranian students, people who flew in from Paris. The fancy people came to the opening or came by jeep the last night, stayed an hour and left. The ranks thinned by midnight. I don't remember that much. I had been awake for three months. I was stunned and stoned and cold and all I wanted to do was go home, go to bed and have this thing over with.

SHERYL SUTTON: Everybody had this great realization in Iran. It was an enormous challenge to everyone's physical and mental stamina and everyone grew a great deal because they directed plays or were responsible for artwork or had to take these scraps of information and make something out of them. Everybody acted, everyone directed, everyone got sick. After *KA MOUNTAIN* was over people in the group split up, some went to Tibet, some to India or the Middle East. When they came back, they were changed.

Members of the company reassembled that fall in Paris where they presented a six-day installation at the Musée Galliéra and the 24-hour *Overture* at the Opéra Comique. The Byrd School remained active over the next two years, presenting performances of *The Life and Times of Joseph Stalin* in Copenhagen and New York in 1973 and São Paulo, Brazil in 1974. But by then Wilson had begun to redirect his energies and address himself to new priorities and concerns. The days of the Byrd School were numbered. *The $ Value of Man*, presented at the Brooklyn Academy of Music in May of 1975, was to be its last hurrah, though the Byrd Hoffman Foundation would continue on as an administrative and producing organization.

THE BREAKUP

SUE SHEEHY: I remember after Copenhagen we went to Paris before coming back to the States and Bob looked at me and said, "I'm ready to do a small play. I don't want to do such big things anymore, I don't want to work with so many people." He had reached his limit.

SCOTTY SNYDER: It was getting to be too much of a burden to Bob. Taking care of all those people and their problems and no money.

SHERYL SUTTON: The breakup of the Byrd School, which was always pretty loose, came about because Bob decided he didn't want to work with a large group of people. He didn't want this intense and continuous activity in his loft anymore. There were a lot of people who were really dependent on that situation and they had a very hard time readjusting their lives. A couple of people threatened suicide because they weren't chosen to work on *A Letter for Queen Victoria*, which was the first time Bob actually cast one of his plays. It went even deeper than a family. Some people were so connected to Bob and his work, it seemed unthinkable that he shouldn't ask them to be part of it.

MEL ANDRINGA: For the first time, he actually wanted people to *audition*! It was unheard of. They had always assumed they would be part of whatever Bob did. When we left for Brazil the cast had already been selected for *Queen Victoria* so everyone was assessing what these changes would mean to them. I decided to leave and do my own work. I didn't feel jilted. Maybe some people did. I think a lot of the people are still fixated on that period in their lives.

KIT CATION: I think Bob got to feel overwhelmed because all these people looked to him. I remember in Paris there were some articles that said here's a bunch of people that Bob's giving therapy to or something like that. Sheryl was furious. "There's nothing wrong with us. We're performers not patients." But he had that quality very much. And then after a while he really wanted to do more theatre and less the community thing.

ROBYN BRENTANO: *Queen Victoria* was when he stopped working with the so-called unprofessionals in the group and began to focus on the more "professional" people. There was a lot of debate about that within the group. Some people were not willing to let go of the old image or let go of Bob and they felt very bitter about it. Others just recognized that he was growing and changing and needed to move on and they accepted it completely. I was doing other things outside the group so perhaps it wasn't as devastating for me yet there was a point where I felt that Bob had lost that vision that had drawn me to his work so much earlier.

KIT CATION: He just picked these few people. I was lucky. I was one of them. A lot of people really felt, "Hey, this is my family. How come I'm being left out?" And then came *Einstein on the Beach* and that kind of took care of the rest of us. I was devastated. In a sense, I had to find a new life. It was very hard. I never took any pictures during those years and it would have been so easy to carry a camera. You thought it was going to last forever. I knew it really wouldn't yet I was so immersed in the whole thing that it seemed unnecessary. Nothing else mattered.

SUE SHEEHY: I was very hurt that I wasn't in *Queen Victoria* and it took me a long while to forgive Bob for that. But I think it turned out to be a good thing, though it took me a few years to realize that. I believe he had taught me as much as he could and that it was time to go out on my own and develop what he had given me. That's really when I started doing my own work.

JIM NEU: It seems to me that there was a moment in 1975 when Bob made a decision not to represent himself as the leader of a homogenous group like the Living Theatre anymore. He wanted to be known as a director who could transplant his methods into the most professional situations in the world. And he was right and that's what he had to do and I don't blame him a bit. I mean, I didn't like not being in the next piece or losing touch with this thing but ultimately I'm glad it happened since I wouldn't have gone on to write my own stuff or work out my own problems in theatre and in the long run that was more important to me. I really loved the experience but it was extremely intense and just dominated my life. I felt I needed some time for myself.

MEL ANDRINGA: There's still a real sense of community among the people who were involved with those big productions. I think we're all good friends and there are still collaborations among some of us. Occasionally I get postcards from Bob, everyone gets postcards when he goes to Jamaica for Christmas. I'm not in very good communication with him but I don't feel that our relationship is strained or anything, it's just distant at this point.

BACKWARD GLANCES

ROBYN BRENTANO: I think Bob picked up a lot of what was in the air. I remember looking at some photographs of Robert Whitman's early work—Whitman was part of that group of visual artists who were doing theatre pieces in the mid-sixties—and there was a photograph of this chair hanging in space. And it was exactly the same chair that Bob used in *The Life and Times of Sigmund Freud* hanging at exactly the same angle and reified in the same way that Bob reified objects. I think there was a way in which Bob was consciously eclectic, he would lift ideas and objects from all over the place and put them in the theatre in his own way. For a while that was an issue for some people—"Bob ripping off this one and ripping off that one"—but the fact that he worked with these ideas and images in a unique way put an end to the argument for me. It's really not an issue as far as I'm concerned, though it was a big issue among people who were coming up at the same time as Bob and scrambling for recognition and support alongside of him.

ANN WILSON: Bob will always gravitate toward the person who is turning him on at that moment and providing the inspiration for where he's going next. Up until *Queen Victoria*, I was the principal one feeding him ideas. Right now it's Heiner Müller. Bob is like this great flying saucer that lands when he sees something and—szz, szz, szz, szz—sucks it up and goes off taking it with him. But it doesn't matter what you feed him because Bob is getting off on something he finds for himself. Nothing he does comes from anybody else. Don't kid yourself, Bob has the ideas. That's the nature of genius. At the same time I don't think you can consider Bob's work unless you think about the Judson and the happenings that he grew out of. His audience was that same Lower East

Side audience. Also very important to his development and persona was Kenneth King. They were both driven to all the battier ideas of Isadora Duncan and Scriabin. All that anti-intellectual stuff from the sixties. It isn't the mind, it's the body. The West has been screwed up by thinking. There are many strains coming into Bob's work. Kenneth adored Merce Cunningham and his ideas could have come to Bob through him. He also got Balanchine through Robbins. I have an early drawing that Bob made of the forest in *Deafman*. It's very different from his subsequent work, which became more severe, more elegantly staged and minimalist. It's closer to Rousseau and the Surrealists. I think the Bob of *Deafman* has more genius than the Bob who would like Cage and Cunningham's respect. There was something witty and wacky and wonderful about his work that has vanished.

CAROL MULLINS: Rarely did I ever know where anything came from. I think I remember Bob saying that the opening scene in *Deafman* with Alan Lloyd playing the Moonlight Sonata and the ladies in white slowly raising the red birds on their arms came from a dream he had. Who's to say? I think Bob's a genius of theatre. He instinctively understands theatre and drama. Those early plays when the stage was slowly filling and changing and suddenly the sheet of glass falls from above and the scene breaks. That's really drama.

JIM NEU: What would happen next in those plays was utterly unpredictable. Where did the Pope in *Deafman Glance* come from and why? And who cared? It was beautiful. Bob had an instinctive sense of what should follow what and what made a theatrical climax. He went beyond having to explain anything.

KIT CATION: Bob's genius when I first met him was that he *knew* every person. You felt that he could almost see into your mind and know what was right for you. There's no question that's why people were attracted to him. He would have a part that was *you* and he did that for everybody. In the New York version of *Overture* I was "girl sipping tea." I did it throughout the whole performance very slowly. It was a small part but very big. Amazingly enough, it's something you could really get into and you had to be very concentrated for it to work. I used to love doing that. That was me. So people just flocked to him. How could you resist someone who knew you so well? For me and a lot of other people he was irresistible.

ROBYN BRENTANO: A lot of people would ask "What was it like to work with Bob? Wasn't he a tyrant?" He had you doing things like raising your hand over a 57-second count and there was an aspect of it that seemed very mechanical. But what I learned was that you're never free until you're free from having to make decisions, and if you know exactly what you're doing and don't have to think about it, then—mentally at least— you're really free. I think for a lot of people the issue of freedom centers around creative choices and for me that wasn't such a big concern. I was quite happy for someone else to make the big creative decisions. For me the freedom was in being aware of the mental processes I was experiencing.

KIT CATION: A lot of people would say, "I couldn't stand it, I wouldn't want him telling me what to do," as if he were too controlling. I always felt he's the director, we're doing his plays. What's the big deal?

MEL ANDRINGA: I think Bob used collaboration in those situations where there was not enough time or the task was too big to do the work that he wanted to do. Perhaps he was able to work most easily with people like Chris and Raymond who didn't have their own sense of direction or were dependent on him in some way. I worked with Bob for about four years but I always thought of it as being his work.

CHARLES DENNIS: It was in Paris during the *Deafman* tour that I got to know Bob well. We would hang out in the dressing room and smoke grass together and talk a lot. He made a very strong impression on me. He started telling me about Isadora Duncan's theories of dance and how the dance of the future was a dance that wasn't taught and you can't teach people dance they have to find it for themselves—that was the whole aesthetic of the Byrd group anyway. And I was very impressed with that, because I was discovering my own dance at the time and it kind of gave me the philosophical background for the understanding of what I was doing. And Bob gave me a lot of encouragement, he was a real friend and mentor. I think he did this for a lot of people, encouraging talents which they almost didn't know they had.

JIM NEU: It's kind of amazing that Bob knew what talents people had and which way they should go. Charlie Dennis had never danced but Bob could see that about him and somehow he knew that I could do something with words and Carol could be a lighting designer. And he was right in all three cases. We've all continued to do these things and none of us did anything like that before.

CAROL MULLINS: I was the only person in *Queen Victoria* who was not on stage a lot and when Bob had an argument with his lighting designer he said "Okay, you do it." It's quite amazing. There was absolutely nothing in anything I'd done before that would indicate it would be anything less than a disaster. It changed my life totally. I used to be a tech writer, I wrote textbooks. You don't see me doing that now.

CHARLES DENNIS: I think Bob's most creative and interesting period was when he was working with talented nonprofessionals. He's become more professional and he's honed his skills as a director and a designer since then but I think there's a certain something missing that moved me very deeply in those early pieces. What really impressed me was his ability to draw all kinds of people into this experience and have a tremendous effect on them as well as audiences. We'd go into Copenhagen or Paris or Brazil and recruit all these local people and there'd be an incredible exchange. I think that in some ways they turned out to be more interesting on stage than professionals. You got a sense of the performer as a real individual, a unique personality. That continues to be a part of the work I'm doing today.

Jerome Robbins (1973): Bob is attracted, somewhat, to what the rest of us would consider the misfits of this world. He sees in them the exceptional. This is part of his caring. Theatre is all a little crazy anyway. After all, what could be madder than a lot of people in ballet shoes dancing on their toes? We're apt to say the new thing is the maddest, because we're not used to it, but maybe his work is saner than anything else around. One of Bob's great contributions is another way of looking at the question 'What is theatre?' What he does is make you think about the whole question. And I firmly believe that his contribution will be as great as that of any theatre man in America.

SCOTTY SNYDER: What was so special about Bob's work, I found, was the range of people. There was Hope Kondrat, she came from Russia around the turn of the century and had been through a lot of that trouble and she was wonderful. She just was herself and she was very good at that. And Mary Peer. She was an incredible character onstage or offstage. She did somersaults and made up her own scripts and she just delighted people. She swam every day and walked like a young girl when she was in her seventies. There were all ages from Hope who was almost eighty to an eight-month-old baby and this made the work very rich, I think. And the images! The pyramid in *Deafman* with the eye at the top and the cave in *Freud* with the bars coming down closing off the opening and, of course, the cat legs in *King of Spain*. And Sheryl walking across the stage in her beautiful Victorian gown. I never tired of watching that. Oh, there were some beautiful images and by beautiful, I mean beautiful, not pretty. That's what I remember most. And the silence. I loved that silence. It was so powerful. People were mesmerized by this work.

CAROL MULLINS: The stuff we did was *great*! And our contributions made for a really remarkable piece of art. How often do you have an opportunity like that? I felt as important as Picasso. I knew the work was important and I was a part of it. And to this day I feel that's true.

BIOGRAPHIES

MEL ANDRINGA was stage manager for many of Wilson's productions between 1970 and 1973. A painter and performance artist, he has taught at the University of Iowa, performed with Richard Foreman and Stuart Sherman and toured the United States and Europe with his own company, "The Drawing Legion." (New York City. April 30, 1987.)

ROBYN BRENTANO worked for Wilson in one capacity or another from 1968 to 1986. A filmmaker and arts administrator, she has danced with Kenneth King's company and performed with Andy de Groat and Robert Whitman. (New York City. July 28, 1987.)

KIT CATION worked with Robert Wilson from 1969 to 1975, appearing in such productions as *Deafman Glance, Overture, The Life and Times of Joseph Stalin, A Letter for Queen Victoria* and *The $ Value of Man*. She currently teaches nursery school in New York and says she prefers it. (New York City. June 11, 1987.)

CHARLES DENNIS is a dancer, performance artist and cofounder of Performance Space 122, a center for avant-garde performance and dance in New York's East Village, where he carries on the traditions of "Open House." He performed in Wilson's works from 1971 to 1976 and also appeared with Kenneth King and Andy de Groat's dance companies during the same period. (New York City. June 6, 1987.)

KATHRYN KEAN (K.K.) worked as an artist and artisan on such productions as *Deafman Glance, Overture* in Paris and New York and *Prologue to Queen Victoria* in Spoleto. She has collaborated on theatrical and film projects with Charles Ludlam, Red Grooms and Jim Neu. (New York City. June 26, 1987.)

CINDY LUBAR appeared in all of Wilson's major productions from 1970 to 1975 and more recently in the Dutch section of *the CIVIL warS* and *Medea/Médée* in Lyon. She has created a number of works with Christopher Knowles and performed in dance pieces by Kenneth King. (New York City. February 26, 1985.)

CAROL MULLINS first appeared with the Byrd School in 1970. She created the lighting for Wilson's *The $ Value of Man* in 1975 and *The Spaceman* the following year, and is currently resident lighting designer for the Danspace Project at St. Mark's Church in New York City. She has collaborated with such directors as Andrei Serban, Wilford Leach, Anne Bogart and S.K. Dunn. (New York City. June 14, 1987.)

JIM NEU, who began working with Wilson in 1970, appeared in such pieces as *The Life and Times of Joseph Stalin*, *A Letter for Queen Victoria* and *The $ Value of Man*, to which he also contributed texts. His own work has been been presented by experimental theatre companies in New York, Chicago, San Francisco and London. (New York City. June 6, 14, 1987.)

KIKUO SAITO worked as a craftsman and artist on such early Wilson productions as *BYRD woMAN* (1968), *The King of Spain* (1969) and the New York version of *Overture* (1972). Prior to coming to New York to study painting in 1966, he designed scenery for Butoh and modern dance companies in Japan. He collaborated with Tom O'Horgan and Tom Eyen at the original Café La Mama and worked for several months on Peter Brook's *The Conference of Birds*. He currently lives in New York and devotes himself to painting. (New York City. May 22, 1987.)

SUE SHEEHY was associated with Robert Wilson from 1970 to 1975, appearing in such productions as *Deafman Glance*, *Overture*, *The Life and Times of Joseph Stalin* and *The Spaceman*. More recently she has performed in works by David Nunemaker, Jim Neu and S.K. Dunn. (New York City. June 17, 1987.)

SCOTTY SNYDER was a housewife and part-time artist living in New Jersey with her husband, a retired Air Force commander, when she met Robert Wilson. She became one of the earliest members of the Byrd Hoffman School of Byrds and appeared in all of Wilson's major works from *King of Spain* in 1969 to *The $ Value of Man* in 1975. She has since become a familiar figure on the New York avant-garde scene, appearing in works by Richard Foreman, Stuart Sherman and JoAnne Akalaitis. (New York City. May 21, 1986.)

ANN WILSON, a painter, teacher and theatre artist, has worked in various capacities for the Living Theatre, Al Carmines and the Judson Church group. A friend of Allan Kaprow, Claes Oldenburg, Robert Rauschenberg and Robert Indiana, she was also active in the happenings movement of the 1950s and '60s. Wilson (no relation) was a member of the Byrd Hoffman School between 1970 and 1974 and has since served as a visual consultant for a number of Robert Wilson's productions. (Jersey City. May 29, 1986.)

CHRISTOPHER KNOWLES

BOB:	CHRIS:
A!	
	B!
A!	
	B!
ABABABABAB	
	ABABABAB AB B
A A AAAAABBB	
	B B BBBBBAAA
A Ladies and Gentle	
	(Long pause) Men
A Letter For Queen A	
	(Long pause) B
Victoria A	
	B
What are we doing	
	We're doing the four acts Act One Act Two Act Three and Act Four
What are we doing A	
	We're doing the play
What are we doing A	
	We're doing "A Letter For Queen Victoria" B
What are we doing	

We're doing the four acts

Where are we

We are in the theatre

Where are we A

B We are in New York

Where are we

We are at the theatre in Manhattan
                                                        in New York
                                                        in the world
                                                        in the world
                                                        in the world
                                                        in the world

(Prologue to *A Letter for Queen Victoria*)

Christopher Knowles is one collaborator who transcends the convenient categories of theatrical expression, having brought to Wilson's works his highly individualistic talents as a performer, poet, choreographer and visual artist. Born with severe brain damage (the result of his mother having contracted toxoplasmosis during pregnancy) and at one time diagnosed as autistic, Chris has transcended the condition of his birth and all expectation as well. Since 1973, when Wilson brought the fourteen-year-old child into the Byrd School and encouraged him to develop his natural creativity, their worlds have entwined and each has changed the other's life in ways both great and small.

For years when people asked me about Christopher Knowles I always used to tell how I met him in 1973 when I was doing *The Life and Times of Joseph Stalin* at the Brooklyn Academy of Music. But I didn't meet him there, I really met him when he was four years old or something like that.

Christmas time. 1963. That's when George Klauber—a very good friend of mine, my parents—brought you over. I was four. I was born May 4, 1959. I can tell you what time. Monday night at 11:10 P.M.

Chris was saying he remembers what he was doing. He was playing with blocks.

It's not possible.

Then ten years later we met again at the Brooklyn Academy of Music. I'd heard this tape of his.

George Klauber, one of my teachers at Pratt, had given it to me. I was fascinated. The musical sense of construction. The energy and rhythms. I was fascinated by what he was doing. I just liked listening to it. Later I had the tape transcribed and found that the words were all carefully patterned. Nothing was arbitrary. How did you make it Chris?

I wanted to meet him. I was doing *The Life and Times of Joseph Stalin* at BAM and Chris happened to be coming to New York the weekend of the first performance so I invited him to come. His mother brought him backstage to my dressing room just before the beginning of the performance and I asked him if he'd like to be in the opera tonight? He didn't say anything. He didn't look at

I still have them.

I got those blocks for Christmas in '63. I remember that.

"Emily Likes the TV."

I saw my sister Emily watching the TV. And then I made a tape. "Emily, Em Em Em Emily Likes the TV." I had one tape recorder. And another tape recorder. "Emily Likes the TV, Because she watches the TV, Because she likes it, Em Em Em Emily Likes the TV." Over and over again. So like you said, he was fascinated. After he listened to it, Robert Wilson telephoned George Klauber to say, "Who did that tape?" Me. Christopher Knowles. I did that tape.

me. Chris didn't look at people very much back then. I asked him several times. His mother wanted to know what he would do. I said I didn't know. His mother said, "Okay he can be in the play but not for very long." So I took Chris by the hand and we went out in front of the house curtain. And I said, "Emily likes the TV. Em Em Em Em."

Em Em Em Emily likes the TV. Because Emily watches the TV. Because Emily likes the TV. Because she likes Bugs Bunny. Because she likes The Flintstones. Because she watches it. Em Em Em Emily likes the TV.

We went on that way together. It was spontaneous. We also did another dialogue later in Act One and then his mother said it was time for Chris to go home and go to bed. His father called me the next morning and said they were very surprised, that Chris had enjoyed being in the play and that he would like to be in it again the next night. He appeared in all four performances.

The Life and Times of Joseph Stalin. Twelve hours. One hundred and twenty-five people. Do you believe that? I met a whole lot of people doing it. Oh, it was good, it was great, the twelve-hour play. I was in Act One and Act Two of the opening. There were seven acts. I was in the seventh act on the last performance. Robert Wilson asked me to be in Act Seven, so I had to get up very, very, very early.

Then, I went to the O. D. Heck School in Schenectady, New York where Chris was staying. He was making all these typings and drawings and the people there were throwing them away. They were discouraging him. I thought what he was doing was beautiful. I see Chris as an artist.

So I became an artist.

Well, I wanted Chris to leave. I thought he should come stay with me. I just thought Chris should be more independent and freer than in an institution. Since I was traveling and there were a lot of people around me I thought it would be good for his development. The doctors thought it would be a good idea too. So Chris came and lived with me at the loft. He had his own room downstairs with walls made out of canvas.

That brings back memories. Way back.

Chris would write his texts and we had workshops and sometimes Chris was leader of the workshops. Remember?

Yes, I remember. Let me tell you. I came to the Byrd loft and Bob did a workshop and that's the first time I was in a workshop and I did the leading role. I did the talking and somebody else did the talking. Then I did the leading, the leader to lead the workshop.

Chris spent several months at the Spring Street loft, working closely with Wilson and members of the group who would imitate his movements and gestures. Robyn Brentano recalls that "in the beginning Christopher's movement patterns would have been considered peculiar from an ordinary point of view but to those of us who had been exploring movement for several years they weren't at all peculiar. As I understand it most schools punished such behavior at the time and I think one of the things that really helped him open up was seeing other people do what he did. I think it suddenly gave him a mirror that he had never had. (Knowles was, of course, encouraged to do what the Byrds had always done, express himself naturally.) I believe the key to Bob's success in working with Christopher was that he threw out the label 'autistic,' he threw out all preconceptions and saw Chris as an individual." Rather than attempting to modify the youth's behavior as the doctors had done,

Wilson sought to enter into Chris's world, learning not only his patterns of movement but his secret codes and language. (He would later attempt to portray or at least reflect this personal reality and means of communication in such works as *A Letter for Queen Victoria* and *The $ Value of Man*.) From the beginning Wilson was fascinated by the peculiar logic of the boy's mind. He looked on Chris's perceptions as unique and not deficient. Perhaps Wilson, the daydreaming youth who liked to be alone and whose speech impediment set him somewhat apart from the rest of the world, could identify with Chris in a way others could not. In time the respect and curiosity that he showed were reciprocated by his young charge and each found himself teacher to the other.

It is clear that the beautiful, damaged boy awakened strong feelings in Wilson. Kit Cation recalls that "Bob was so excited when he met Chris. I remember he told us, 'I met this wonderful person who's doing the same kind of thing that I'm doing.'" Wilson found that they shared many interests and preoccupations, among them spatial order, temporal precision and repetition. (As one of the Byrds has said, "maybe Bob is a bit autistic too.") Both were visually oriented, excelling in those areas of of creative activity controlled by the right hemisphere of the brain. "Christopher and I just thought in a similar way. We were also doing some of the same things with language. I remember showing one of my notebooks to his mother once and she told me that they looked just like Chris's notebooks." Soon after the boy moved into the loft Wilson even found that some of the things Chris was writing reflected the way he himself was feeling.

Dr. Hugh Lafave, one of Chris's physicians at the Heck School, has detailed the stages in their developing relationship, showing how it progressed from essentially nonverbal beginnings. "There was some kind of a spark that sort of jumped the gap between those two from the moment they met," he has said, "but there was very little dialogue." Then, as Knowles became involved with leading the workshops he and Wilson began to communicate through movement and dance and later the exchange of drawings and graphics. Finally the two graduated to speech, making use of tape recordings which they would pass back and forth. According to Dr. Lafave, "in very slow progression, they went through the same stages that language itself probably passed through in its development." (He points out that in most human relationships the process is reversed, with individuals moving from verbal to nonverbal communication.) Wilson's success in communicating with the boy doubtless had to do with his gift for locking into people's internal rhythms (rhythmic atmospheres also being a characteristic feature of his theatre). A story Ed Knowles, Chris's father, tells about Wilson's visit to the Heck School conveys a sense of the artist's sensitivity to individuals: "There were perhaps eight or ten very badly damaged kids, neurologically damaged, both physically and mentally. . . . And there was one little guy who was about three feet long, about six years old, who had arms about as big around

Knowles and Wilson in Paris. 1977.

as your thumb. And he was just lying there whimpering and a woman was sitting there stroking his back and trying to console him. . . . Right adjacent to her was one of those electric organs—there were two, actually—so Bob went over and looked down at the kid and he touched the kid . . . with the back of his hand, the back of his fingers. And the kid stopped whimpering and with great effort, lifted his head up. And then Bob, with the kid still watching him, went over to one of these organs and just put his hand down on the keys and made a noise. And he just held it there, and the child looked at his hand, and then crawled over to the adjacent organ and put his hand down and made a noise. It was the first time this child had ever done anything voluntarily in the whole time he'd been at the school. And then he looked up at Bob, sort of making a communication, saying, 'Look, I can do that, too.' And then Bob very carefully raised his hand and moved it over so it made a different sound; and the kid realized that, and he made a different sound, too. No whimpering. Suddenly he was doing something that was meaningful. He'd learned something. The entire process took at least five minutes. It is a question of Bob understanding what that kid's rhythms were and being able to work with that kid in the same rhythms. And of course, everyone was stunned, that in five minutes time he suddenly had this kid operating, when no one else had been able to reach him."

Wilson seems always to have had a natural gift for working with children as well as a special affinity for the male child. His friendship and collaboration with Chris recalls an earlier relationship with Raymond Andrews, a black deaf-mute he had "adopted" about five years earlier. Raymond was eleven when Wilson rescued him from a policeman one day in Summit, New Jersey after the boy had thrown a stone through the window of a church. Wilson convinced the officer to release Raymond into his custody and started taking him to his workshops at the Summit Art Center, where the boy's keen visual intelligence soon became apparent. As was the case with Chris a few years later, Wilson realized that the child, who had never been to school, communicated with means other than language and set out to learn from his sounds, signs and signals. "Raymond didn't know any words but he was clearly very bright. He saw everything in terms of images and like Chris he had a tremendous visual memory." Wilson also noticed that the boy was attuned to emotional currents and sensations that usually went unnoticed by hearing people. Raymond's perceptions of the world, he says, greatly influenced his early works; the boy's crayon drawings provided an important source of imagery for *Deafman Glance*—Raymond was, of course, the deaf man of the title—and many of his movements and gestures were incorporated into the 1970 play.

Working with Raymond Andrews also set Wilson thinking about the nature of perception. He came to believe that "we all see and hear on two different levels": sensory information from the outside world is directly received on what he calls the "exterior screen" while our dreams, thoughts and indirect perceptions play on an "interior screen," the realm of imagination and intuition. He found that the blind and deaf were often more attuned to this second form of "seeing" and that their inner screens were, of necessity, more highly developed. This also seemed to be the case with Christopher, who would disappear into some inner world for hours at a time, oblivious to all that was happening around him. While Wilson was clearly uncomfortable with the word "autism," he would occasionally liken the condition to that of the artist or use the term as a metaphor for interior seeing and sensing; he once told an interviewer that Christopher was diagnosed as "autistic which means he's dreaming constantly even when he is awake." (Some years ago Wilson went so far as to say that everyone is autistic and suggested that with all the noise, pressures and sensory overload of contemporary life, shutting out is a beneficial and necessary act, even "a means of survival.") In time the artist came to consider his stretched-out, sloweddown theatre pieces as a place where the interior and exterior screens would merge for the audience as well as the performers.

While Wilson was his chief guide and mentor, the Byrds also played an important role in Chris's development, becoming in effect his second family—protecting and encouraging him and gradually initiating him into the ways of the world. Kit Cation recalls that "Chris could never look at anyone he talked to. I remember Jim Neu would tell him when you speak to someone you have to look at them. It was like teaching a child. Chris could freak people out and then they would act funny to him and he would get upset. He got a lot of help from normal people who liked him and who he could feel comfortable with." Within a few months members of the group began to notice a change in the boy's behavior as well as a growing self-confidence and an openness to the new experiences that came with venturing into the world outside. Robyn Brentano: "When Chris first came to work with us he was extremely shy and expressed a lot of anxiety about being left alone. He wouldn't even go across the street to get a sandwich for himself. One of the big breakthroughs came when he was in São Paulo. A member of the company was supposed to be responsible for Chris and one day he arrived at the theatre without him. About half an hour later Chris strolled in and it turned out he had walked from the hotel to the theatre, which was all the way across town. It was a big step for Christopher to take, to go out in a foreign city completely on his own. I think at that point everyone said, 'Chris can manage his life, Chris can be responsible for himself.'"

Chris stayed at the loft for about three or four months and then we went traveling.

We did *A Letter for Queen Victoria* for a ten-month tour.

We were traveling a lot. We went to Brazil, Italy, France, Iran. We've been all over the world together. There's a great story Chris could tell you about when he went to the self-service in Paris. Do it with all the sound effects.

I go to the self-service. Way back when I was performing in *A Letter for Queen Victoria* in late '74 in Paris, France. I could tell you the date. Wednesday. December 18, 1974. I went to this self-service for lunch and I sat down, had my lunch, got up, went to the cash register and then I didn't pay. They wanted cash.

I don't think Chris had any money. He didn't know that you had to have money to get food. He was just learning to go out to a restaurant by himself at the time so that was a big thing to do. And he liked the self-service because he didn't have to talk, he didn't have to say anything, he could just point. Chris, what time?

It was around three when it happened. I showed them my wallet. And the manager took me down to the private office. Then I sat down. He told me to sit down. He called the police and the police just arrested me.

You have to do the telephone dialogue, you're missing all the juicy parts.

Come on. Well, when the manager dialed the call to the police he went da-de-da-de-da-de-da-de-da-da. And I was arrested and four cops came. Well, I heard like clunk, clunk, clunkety, clunkety, clunk, clunk, clunkabies and they became four policeman—one, two, three, four policeman. Clunk, clunk, clunk, too many clunkabies. Then I was arrested. Just for the day. I was in a police truck to the police station. Anyway, we all had to go to the police station to answer questions. And then after all was straightened out I had to go back to the self-service and pay.

Chris had a great line, I have to tell it. He's forgotten it. We put it in *The $ Value of Man*, the play we wrote together. And the man said to the man, "The boy ain't got no dollars." (Laughter)

Neurologically damaged and autistic individuals sometimes display unusual, even inexplicable gifts, as though the brain were attempting to compensate for the injuries it has received. This was the case with Christopher, who possessed an extraordinary memory for dates, numbers and spatial arrangements. (His father has said that when Chris was first tested by psychologists, his communication skills were found to be sorely deficient while his aptitude for comprehending objects and their relationships was too high to measure.) But it was the boy's use of language and his ability to create elaborate visual structures in his head using words as building blocks that most deeply impressed and excited Wilson.

I was fascinated from the very beginning with what Chris was doing with language. He'd take words we all know and fracture them and then put them back together in a new way. He'd invent a new language and then destroy it a moment later. Words are like molecules which are always changing their configurations, breaking apart and recombining. It's very free and alive. Language is his own kingdom.

There's always a sense of organization in his tapes and writings, it's not an arbitrary arrangement of words and sounds. Everything he does makes sense but not in the way we're accustomed to. It has a logic of its own. His sense of organization and construction is fascinating. And his decisions—when he

one hundred songs
song
son
so
s

pirup birup pirup birup
pirup birup pirup birup
pirup birup pirup birup
pirup birup pirup birup
pirup birup pirup birup
pirup birup pirup birup
pirup birup pirup birup
pirup birup pirup birup
pirup birup pirup birup

decides to do something or not to do something. Chris has amazing abilities. He can remember complicated structures and repeat them word by word. At one time he was taking words and phrases and shifting every letter six places forward in the alphabet. And he's able to do it instantaneously, he doesn't need to figure it out with pen and paper the way you or I would have to. Chris constructs as he speaks. It's as though he sees the words before him in space. He uses language as much for its geometric structure as for its meaning. Sometimes he will take a word or a phrase and build a structure out of it. He'll extend it into a pyramid or some other shape and then reduce it back into a single phrase or letter. His constructions are very beautiful to look at. It's structured language. It's elegantly arranged on the page almost like music, like Mozart. His mind is perfectly clear.

Christopher Knowles
Puevfgbcure Xabjyrf

Bob Wilson
Obo Jvyfba

O
OK
AOKO
LAOKOK
LLAOKOKO
ELLAOKOKOK
WELLAOKOKOK
AWELLAOKOKOKO

Wilson often speaks of how much he has learned from Chris and the boy's influence on him seems to have been both subtle and pervasive. In addition to direct contributions to such works as *A Letter for Queen Victoria*, *The $ Value of Man* and the *Dia logs*, Chris may have significantly affected Wilson's use of language and his views on the independence of aural and visual elements (Wilson discovered that the things Chris was doing with his body in performance often had nothing to do with what he was saying), as well as his growing concern with structure, order and precise timings, and perhaps even his settings, which grew increasingly geometrical during the seventies. Robyn Brentano has explained it this way: "Chris was a regular part of Bob's everyday life for some time and I think because he was so special he probably had a profound influence on the way Bob looked at things. Chris has a particular brilliance for perceiving structure. He is able to carry a lot of information in his head and reveal a relationship between things in a way other people can't and I think that's what Bob was influenced by, this perception Chris has of language, space and graphic detail."

Between 1973 and 1980 Wilson created at least one project a year with Chris, most of them two-man shows called "dialogs" (their chosen form of exchange ever since the two first stepped onto the stage in *Stalin*) with Wilson playing interlocutor. These structured encounters, which usually combined live speech and Knowles' pre-recorded tape constructions with chance dialogue and music provided by one of the boy's radios, were seen in about five different installments between 1974 and 1980, changing from year to year as their relationship and preoccupations changed.

All the dialogs were based on things Chris wrote or structures that he would map out or that, sometimes, we would jointly put together. He would also improvise a lot. There was more or less a fixed structure but there was always the possibility of new material being introduced into it. Christopher and I just thought in a similar way, we were on the same wavelength so it was very easy to have these dialogs.

I'll tell you about *Dia log/Network*. First of all I saw the movie called *Network*, I saw it a couple of times in the movie theatre. And then I taped it the second time I saw it. The whole film. And then I typed it up. Then Bob saw the typing on a very long row. So me and Bob just decided to do a *Dia log/Network*. It had twelve sections. It lasted an hour and twenty-five minutes. I did the drawings, the backdrops. I did it with spray paint in black. There's twelve of them for twelve sections. So we did *Dia log/Network* in Florence, Italy in the late part of October. Then we did *Dia log/Network* in Munich. We did *Dia log/Network* in Paris, France. Let me tell you, we did more of *Dia log/Network* in Amsterdam, Holland in June, 1978. And then we did *Dia log/Network* in the United States in Boston, Massachusetts in July, 1978. And I counted one hundred and sixty-nine seats in the theatre. Then we did *Dia log/Network* in Minneapolis, Minnesota in the early part of August.

Chris can walk into a theatre and tell you how many seats are in it. It would probably take you or me five minutes to figure it out. Chris can do the mathematics instantly.

The last dialog we did was *Curious George* (1979-80). It was primarily his work. The *Curious George* books were something Chris had found. They fascinated him. I said "What shall we do for a play?" and he said *Curious George.* And I said, "How long should it be?" And he made a draft, a structure of pictures and he gave me that. I more or less realized the piece but I worked from his structure. We worked with his tapes and his drawings. Chris had done this great piece on Crazy Eddie and we put that in. When Chris was staying at the loft there were two radios and a television going all the time and sometimes he'd take things off the air like advertisements and song lyrics and turn them into typings. He just heard these things and started to see the words on the page. How did you make it?

Oh, I heard an advertisement of Crazy Eddie. It's been over ten years now since I heard that advertisement. From the radio. Crazy Eddie. That's on 8th Street and Fifth Avenue. There's another Crazy Eddie that's on East 57th Street. And also there's another Crazy Eddie at Third Avenue between 59th and 60th Street, right across from Bloomingdale's.

Chris had this big collection of alarm clocks and we put those in too.

I have around twenty-five alarm clocks. Red ones, green ones, yellow ones, orange ones. I have a big brown clock, I got it from the electricians at the De Roo Theater. The rest of the clocks I got from Holland. I have a big orange clock from Robert Wilson. He got it in Rome, Italy. I got lots of clocks after I turned fifteen.

Chris always liked alarm clocks. He would make drawings of them and carry them with him everywhere we went. I don't know why he liked them. Eventually they would creep onto the stage, he'd hide them backstage or off-stage or on stage somewhere. I used to spoil him. I would just buy them. He had two or three and suddenly he had thirty or forty.

Chris and I did *Curious George* in Belgium, Poland, Holland and the next year we did it at Lincoln Center.

We were going to do *Dialog/Curious George* in Germany and also in Italy for three weeks in 1980 but it didn't turn out. The reason we stopped doing it was people didn't ask Bob. So we just stopped doing it.

Wilson is as much taken with Chris's abilities as a performer as he is by his typings and artworks. "Performing is a real joy for Chris. It's not something he acts. He is totally honest on stage and he's always believable." In this sense Knowles may be the ultimate Wilson performer, the completely natural actor who doesn't know how to be otherwise. Christopher's presence also injects an element of spontaneity into Wilson's carefully drilled productions and provides a lively foil to the older artist, who tends to be much more formal and held-back. As Lucinda Childs, who appeared in a 1976 version of *Dia log*, has said, "Chris is usually the dominating force in any situation because he's unpredictable. You tend to play off whatever he does." Not surprisingly, reactions to these performances have varied greatly; some are fascinated or moved while others are profoundly embarrassed, even repelled by the youth's demeanor and the older artist's seeming domination over him (what the critic Erika Munk once called a "dreadful air of controlling Knowles"). Wilson has, of course, been stung by such criticism and the occasional accusation of exploiting a brain-damaged child. While finding no justification for his actions necessary, he once said, "If Christopher did what he did in a restaurant, he would be thrown out. The theatre is the only place where he can really express his unique way of being, because the theatre is an outlet for the exceptional."

Chris, what's your favorite work?

There's so many things that we did. Just let me think for a minute and then I'll tell you. I guess *The $ Value of Man* is one of my favorites. May of '75. At Lepercq Space here at BAM. I do like it. I love it. Me spinning. I was also using an adding machine and my cassette tape recorder and my radios. Bob did the directing. I acted and Bob acted. I wrote it. "The man says to the man, the boy ain't got no dollars." And I did the part about the stomach growls. Let me tell you. "Well, is this embarrassing or is this embarrassing? That was right in the middle of an English exam and it was so quiet you could hear your socks drop. When growl, growl. Oh, no. My stomach started growling because I skipped breakfast. I like Carnation Instant Breakfast to help stop the growls." I got it from the radio, the advertising, a very old one. I just remembered it.

What do you like doing best?

I like performing. I like doing drawings and I like doing typings. I paint sometimes.

The creation of art is in the end only one aspect of this collaboration. Although they no longer work together on a regular basis, Wilson has never ceased to take pride

Dialog/Curious George. 1980.

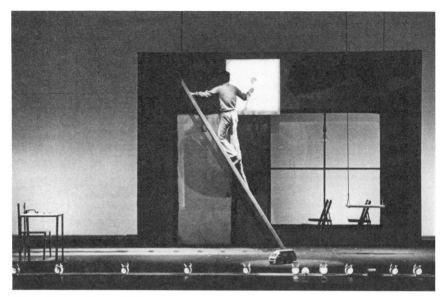

Dialog/Curious George. 1980.

in Chris's accomplishments and always makes a point of seeing him on those increasingly rare occasions when he gets to New York. (Recently he created a new piece for Knowles in Hamburg based on the medieval epic *Parzival*, resuming their collaboration after an eight-year hiatus.) Though Chris is not fully able to support himself, he has made a place for himself in the world as an individual and an artist, something his proud parents could never have envisioned that December night in 1973 when Wilson led him by the hand onto the stage of the Brooklyn Academy of Music. Chris has had one-man shows of his paintings and typings in Europe and the United States. He has presented his own theatre pieces and his poems have been published in *The New Yorker*. He's come a long way. Now nearing his thirtieth birthday (though he could pass for ten years younger), Chris lives by himself in a perfectly ordered apartment in Brooklyn and has attracted a devoted circle of friends. If he continues to dream his waking dreams, he also looks the world in the eye. As a former member of the Byrds has said, "He has a life of his own. He's his own person."

> Dia log, *1975, Final Scene: Two figures dancing on an empty, dimly lit stage, each in their own way, each expressing their own torments and joys. A door slowly opens in the back wall. Intense white light streams in and clouds of smoke envelop the stage. The two figures, man and boy, crawl one after the other toward the low portal, slowly making their way from the darkness into the blinding light beyond.*

II

WRITERS, DRAMATURGS AND TEXTS

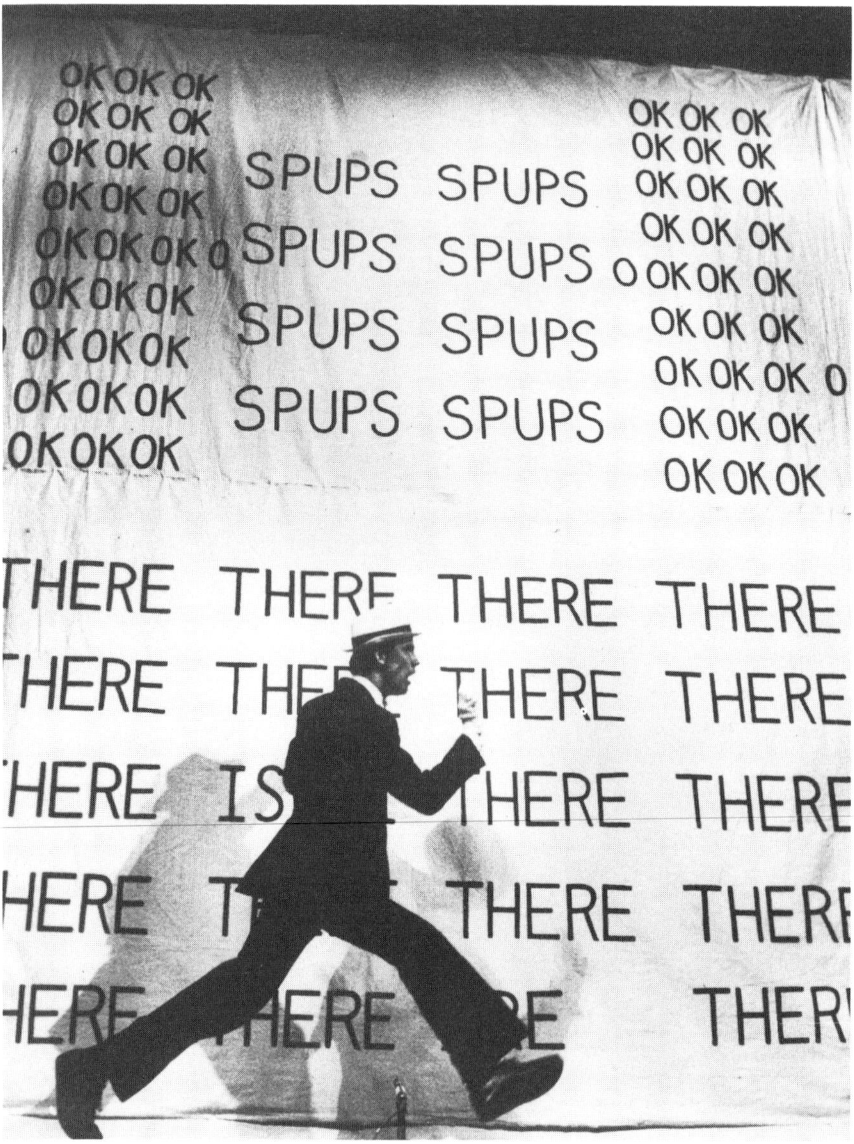

Robert Wilson in *A Letter for Queen Victoria.* 1974.

Until the New York workshop of *Overture* in 1972, the verbal silence in Wilson's theatre was broken only intermittently by the isolated monologue or odd utterance. It was not until preparations got under way for *KA MOUNTAIN* that performers were encouraged to develop their vocal resources by working with language and sound. Wilson seemed especially interested in catching the authentic voice and individual rhythms of each performer, and to that end asked many of the Byrds to devise their own monologues or, failing that, deliver texts of their own choosing. Scotty Snyder talked at length about the flatness of the landscape in her native Iowa, Cindy Lubar performed a number of stream-of-consciousness soliloquies drawn from her automatic writings, Wilson's grandmother Alma Hamilton spoke about the number of pills she took each day and told stories of her childhood. (The practice continues to this day. In *Einstein on the Beach* Samuel M. Johnson, an elderly ex-civil servant, wrote and delivered his own speeches on the delights of Paris and women's liberation; in the Dutch *CIVIL warS* a schoolboy described his daily routine; and in the ART production of the German section one actress offered a bizarre account of her rat-infested automobile.) By 1973, when *Stalin* was produced in New York, Wilson's work had absorbed a diverse body of textual materials, ranging from fragments of literature and historical writings, often in their original languages, to such simple expressions as "hm, okay" and basic introductions spoken by the company ("Hi, my name is . . ."). Even comments made during rehearsals might become part of this verbal fabric; a performer's complaint that her leg "was fucked up" found a place in *Stalin*, as did the director's response: "Keep that line!" Wilson also made use of the associational poetry he had created at the Byrd School's retreat in British Columbia while preparing *KA MOUNTAIN*—his first writings for the theatre. Much of the company's vocal explorations (as well as some of that production's visuals) sprang from the chantlike rhythms, simple rhymes, repetitions and apocalyptic imagery of these texts:

THE DINA DYE KNEE THE DINA
DYE EYE THE DINA DIE DIE
DIEING DINA SORE SORE SORE
THE DINA DYE KNEE THE DINA
DYE EYE THE DINA DIE THE
DIEING DINA SORE SORE SOWRDS!

———

RING WE ALL SING THE EARTH
IS A COLD PLANET THE SUN THE MOON
THE STARS MARS SUNDAY SUNDAY SUN CITY
CITY OF LIGHTROELECTROELELCTRACICITY, ETC.

Wilson has always been more interested in aural textures and the energy underlying language than in the meaning of words, and the texts in these early productions were often multilayered and unintelligible. As he told a reporter shortly before the New York opening of *Stalin*, "Sometimes sounds that have no real meaning mean more to us." It is a view that reflects not only Wilson's personal experience—his contact with Raymond Andrews, in particular—but the distrust of language (William Burroughs: "language is a whore") underlying the experimental theatre of his generation, a movement deeply influenced by the writings of Antonin Artaud.

Only with *A Letter for Queen Victoria* did text became a primary element in Wilson's work. For the first time language, albeit nondiscursive language, blanketed the action—an independent textual commentary running alongside the visuals. When the production reached Broadway in the spring of 1975, Wilson told John Gruen: "I became interested in language—in words, because I hadn't used many words before. I wanted to see what that experience would be. Frankly, I could never express myself in words. In school, it was even more difficult. And I always had trouble reading. I used to be very embarrassed about that." One of the drops that Wilson created for the production pictured the rough outline of a dam with a flood of words rushing through its cracked barrier wall, a fitting metaphor for the torrent of language loosed in this work. (Wilson once compared the curing of his youthful stutter and his subsequent conquest of speech to "a dam bursting.")

The script Wilson fashioned for *A Letter for Queen Victoria* (which was to become the model for such works as *Patio, Death Destruction and Detroit, Edison, The Golden Windows* and *the CIVIL warS*) was not a dramatic text at all, but a compendium of sentence fragments and found language: snatches of overheard conversation, brief personal observations, bits of dialogue taken from television and radio, hundreds of phrases that made sense in themselves but were without any recognizable connection to each other. Wilson has said that in creating the text, which one Paris critic aptly described as "a kind of huge graffiti," he became interested in tracing his own thought process. The language in the play is more a reflection of the way people think than the way they speak, moving suddenly from one thought to another unrestrained by logic or the obligations of discourse. Wilson also likes to compare his writings to a television that is continuously changing channels; he has described how his aging father would sit before a television set with the remote control in his hand, flipping restlessly from channel to channel, and how the fragments of different stories resembled his own plays. "The difference between our theatre and other theatre," Wilson once told an interviewer, "is that we don't want to belabor you with a story."Instead of a narrative his texts transmit thoughts, sensa- tions, shards of personal memory—pieces of many stories—which the audience is free to deal with as they choose. Wilson has often complained that plot and language "tend to demand too much of the audience's attention. They force us to follow what the actors are doing, which is a mental strain."

In the past Wilson has used terms like "throwaway" and "transparencies" to describe his texts, emphasizing that what he is interested in communicating lies largely beneath the surface of the language. Like the simple gestures and movements that make up his choreography, these words do not so much transmit information as act as a conduit through which the internal energy and authentic feeling of the performer can be channeled. Wilson likens his texts to musical compositions (as he does Christopher Knowles' writings), explaining that phrases are structured for sound and rhythm and sometimes manipulated like symphonic themes. "*Queen Victoria* was the beginning of this idea of using language as music," says Sheryl Sutton, "and I think it was a really ingenious way for someone who's totally nonverbal to start to deal with words, and to confront that aspect of himself. *Queen Victoria* possessed a far greater emotional range than Bob's previous works and that was breaking new ground too. There was emotion as well as language. I think those things go together."

Wilson's texts are collected and assembled without regard to the characters who will speak them or the visual imagery to which they will be joined. Typically, the play begins with snatches of conversation and observations scrawled on 3x5 cards or a yellow legal pad. Often Wilson will write in a less than fully conscious state, when he's drifting off to sleep or waking in the morning, or while listening to television or the radio, frequently incorporating phrases he hears. Such texts constitute a kind of fragmentary diary, a spontaneous account of what he is hearing, thinking or remem- bering at a given moment. Eventually this material will be typed up by an office worker (who usually receives the command "no caps, no periods, no commas") and marked "Play X," his standard designation for a new work. For Wilson the creation of a text is less a literary process than a visual one. Rather than sitting down and reading through the embryonic script, he will tack sections up on the walls of his studio, creating an architectural word mural, which can be rearranged for shape, balance and density. By standing a few steps back Wilson is able to take in the whole text at a glance. His method is not unlike that of Richard Foreman, who has said, "I don't write, I compile . . . I take fragments, pages from my notebooks, I spread them out on the floor, arrange them in a certain fashion, go from here to there, and I have a play." While Wilson might alter a word or rearrange a sentence at some point, the process of rewriting is alien to him. It is usually not until rehearsals that lines are distributed among the performers, who then invest them with emotion and significance, often independent of their literal meaning.

Critical response to Wilson's texts has always been divided; some are intrigued by the underlying principle (The Polish writer Andrzej Wirth felt such language "reproduced the absurdity and senselessness of everyday speech"; Colette Godard of *Le Monde* found in his broken verbal tapestries the "thousands of useless words accumulated in a lifetime.") while others dismiss them outright. Wilson himself has long had an ambivalent feeling toward his scripts and it is likely he senses that the formula he has employed for well over a decade has exhausted itself. Heiner Müller has said that it's "the principle rather than the actual language of his plays that's interesting," and after ten years even this principle has worn thin. The writers and dramaturgs who speak of their experiences in this section have all to some degree helped Wilson liberate himself from the limitations of his own texts and verbal capacities. Wilson is innately curious and each of these collaborators has contributed to his growing awareness of history and literature and to the opening of his work to the discursive possibilities of language and narrative.

Entr'acte to Act VI of *The Life and Times of Joseph Stalin.* 1973.

MAITA DI NISCEMI

Although Maita di Niscemi is not a name likely to produce immediate recognition even among Robert Wilson's most ardent followers, few of his collaborators have exerted such a steady influence on the visual and aural content of his works. As Wilson has come to rely less on his own personal visions and the ideas and drawings of such intimates as Raymond Andrews and Christopher Knowles, the words and images of history and literature have become an increasingly important part of his work, and it was largely through Maita di Niscemi that he first gained access to this vast realm of experience and imagery. For ten years she has functioned as his chief researcher, advisor and coauthor, encouraging and overseeing the gradual enrichment of his architecturally structured "found texts" with biographical and literary material. While Wilson has always had people around him to suggest ideas and images—in the past these included Kenneth King, Ann Wilson and Edwin Denby—no one had ever before put such a range of human incident, knowledge and iconography at his disposal.

Maita di Niscemi, a sometime novelist and poet with highly placed friends and social connections, is Robert Wilson's most devoted admirer, a one-woman cult who believes absolutely in Wilson's genius. She is only too willing to drop everything at a moment's notice and run to the library or jump on a plane should "the master" call with an urgent request. In fact, her ardor sometimes causes even Wilson's most faithful coworkers to raise their eyebrows. Di Niscemi has served Wilson (who gave her the nickname Maita) in every conceivable capacity. She has assisted in fundraising efforts, introduced him to potential sponsors and sat on the board of his foundation, translated his scripts, written program notes and press releases as well as the occasional favorable review. An Italian princess by birth, Di Niscemi is unquestionably one of the most colorful and dramatic personalities in Wilson's inner circle; proud, strong-willed, outrageously certain of her opinion and given to all kinds of sweeping judgments, wild enthusiasms and violent dislikes. While she can be somewhat cool and suspicious at first encounter, the hard exterior soon gives way to a humorous and generous personality with a ringing laugh and a well-developed sense of the absurd, an attribute which may be as useful as total devotion when dealing with Robert Wilson. She also brings to their collaboration a broad knowledge of languages, history and literature (she has degrees from Barnard College and the Sorbonne), a lightning-quick mind and a phenomenal recall for dates, names and details.

"I first met Bob Wilson in February of 1976. My cousin Gioacchino Lanza Tomasi, the head of the Rome Opera, had told me that there was only one genius working in America and it was a lunatic from Texas—so I was on the lookout for him. As it happened I was invited to go to the New York City Ballet one evening with Jean and Gordon Douglas, who were patrons of Balanchine, and Bob was to join us. There was a terrible snowstorm and I remember standing in the entranceway of the State Theater thinking he wasn't going to come when all of a sudden this great noodle came walking up to us. And that was the genius. One of the ballets that evening was Jerome Robbins' 'Dances at a Gathering.' Peter Martins played the dancer in brown and at the end of the piece he kneels and touches the ground. Bob turned to me and said, 'Some day I'm going to make a great work around that single gesture.' And I thought to myself, 'Well, the man's nuts.' We had supper after the performance and talked for a long time while the snowstorm continued outside. I didn't see him again till May when Bob invited Jean and Gordon to the first run-through of *Einstein on the Beach* and asked them to bring me along. And I loved it, I was *mad* for it. He had the most extraordinary group of people I'd ever seen, so diverse and interesting—it looked as if he had stopped a bus. Later when *Einstein* came to the Met I worked as one of his ladies getting people to buy benefit tickets. It was 1976 and hundred-dollar tickets were terribly expensive so I sold the fifty-dollar tickets. I sold over a hundred, mainly to artists but also to some snobbish friends who got bored and left—I told them, 'Okay, leave if you want to but give your ticket stubs to the people who are waiting outside in hopes of getting in.'"

The following spring di Niscemi began attending rehearsals of Wilson's next work *Patio*, sitting across from Wilson's friend and mentor Edwin Denby. Although she came to know Wilson better during this period, the possibility of contributing in some manner to his work did not present itself until nearly a year later: "There was a dinner party at Paula Cooper's in late January of 1978 and at one point during the evening Bob pulled out a photograph of Rudolf Hess taken on his eighty-second birthday two years before. It's the saddest photograph I've ever seen—it's a man staring at nothing. In fact, I had seen it in the *New York Times* shortly after reading Albert Speer's memoirs in 1976 and had cut it out and put it away. It's possible that Bob had gotten the photograph out of the newspaper just as I did. He is the kind of person who looks and sees. Bob asked me, 'Do you know who this is?' and I said 'I know absolutely who it is.'" He asked if she would be interested in providing him with information about the man in the photograph and di Niscemi immediately agreed. The following month, as Wilson was about to embark on the European tour of *Patio*, the first of the many letters she would write him in the coming years arrived: "Dear Bob—It's show-and-tell time in the case of Rudolf Hess. . . ." And so, nearly two years after that wintry evening when Wilson appeared to her out of the swirling snow, their collaboration began.

That first communication, printed in neat and gently rolling letters with a black felt-tipped pen, presented a detailed picture of the life of Hitler's Deputy Führer, from his youthful embrace of "geo-politics" (the theory justifying the need for German expansionism) and rise to power in the National Socialist Party to his abortive flight to Scotland to obtain peace in 1941 and his years of confinement in Spandau prison. Di Niscemi enclosed xeroxed articles from the *Encyclopedia Britannica*, a psychological portrait drawn from medical reports, a discussion of the motives for the ill-fated peace mission, excerpts from Albert Speer's memoirs and numerous photographs of Hess and his contemporaries. Information was characteristically presented in a simple, straightforward manner and interwoven with visual materials: "I always go very much for the visual because it's what Bob likes and what catches his eye, and otherwise he might not read it." In the months that followed di Niscemi continued to feed Wilson's ever-deepening fascination with the strange figure in the photograph, whose life and shadowy existence would ultimately provide the focus of his next major work, *Death Destruction and Detroit*.

In contrast to the mythic protagonists of Wilson's previous works, Rudolf Hess was a minor figure—a kind of living footnote to history. Yet in many ways he was a logical Wilson hero, a man whose very existence touched on the artist's most deeply felt themes and obsessions. First, of course, there was the compelling image of Hess himself: the old man with the sunken face and empty stare, standing alone in a prison courtyard—in di Niscemi's words "a man outside of time." Then there was the mystery and isolation of his shadowy life; his years of solitude and silence, his growing blindness and incapacity, his madness and sanity (Wilson would later say that Hess's rambling, incoherent defense near the end of the Nuremberg trials reminded him of the language in his own plays), and the potent image of the empty fortress in Berlin where, surrounded by armed guards, history's only survivor ruled over the past. Like the black youth in *Deafman Glance* and the small boy in *Stations* (which also dates from 1978), who gaze in isolation upon an inner world of fantasy, Wilson's Hess is a dreamer and traveler, a prisoner of the self who stares through his barred window onto a landscape of his own imagining.

The form *Death Destruction and Detroit* would ultimately take is contained in this idea: Hess sits in his bare cell in Spandau prison while his mind, unconstrained by iron bars, stone walls or human law, journeys through time and space. We move with him from a Louis Quinze salon to the interior of a Greyhound bus to a London street during the Blitz and then on to a red crater somewhere in outer space. In the course of the play's sixteen scenes (Hess was coincidentally member #16 in the Nazi Party) we travel without warning between present, past and future, observing car races in the desert, a cactus-studded landscape with cowboys and Indians, thunderstorms, a New York rooftop, a vista of palm trees by the sea and a black hole. The old man in Spandau is the force that holds all these disparate visions together, the totality of which constitutes a secret life of Rudolf Hess. (This is di Niscemi's view of the work; when asked if Wilson would agree with such an interpretation she immediately replies, "I know he would.") Though the spirit of Hess presides over *D D & D*, his name is never spoken, nor is his presence ever identified. He is, befitting his place in history, "a shadow protagonist." In fact, most of the critics and spectators who saw the work in Berlin in 1979 were unaware of its subject (though Hess lay imprisoned in the same city) until one of the Schaubühne actors, Otto Sander, revealed the play's allusive content in an interview after the premiere. Hess does not dominate *D D & D* in the manner of the great historical figures of Wilson's earlier works, rather he haunts its imagery with a phantom presence that is at once nowhere and everywhere. As a German critic later wrote, the work was not about Hess but "about the fascination Hess released" in its creator.

Curiously enough, the designs for *D D & D* predated Wilson's interest in Rudolf Hess by several months. This is possible because his scenic pictures are conceived as free and open spaces, capable of absorbing any number of themes and activities. While Hess clearly became the organizing principle of the work, he was not its starting point, for themes and meanings in Wilson's works do not invariably spring from a controlling concept or motivating idea but instead tend to emerge gradually as images and details accumulate. So it happened that the sixteen scenes Wilson created for *D D & D*, all of which were sketched out on paper in the summer of 1977 before he had chosen his protagonist (some were simply taken from old picture postcards he had been given), became enveloped by Hess's sadness and isolation, and suffused with fragments of his life drawn from di Niscemi's research: "I was very pleased. I kept writing all these cuckoo letters and I had no idea they were going into the work."

Her first letter alone provided Wilson with a number of ideas and images. A striking photo of Hess as a young man in his World War I uniform and another in his flying helmet and goggles were copied for costumes. A portrait of Karl Haushofer, the chief formulator of "geo-politics," in his academic robes inspired an assembly of identical figures in the London street scene who viewed the descent to earth of a parachutist (whose appearance was greeted with "Come, let's have a cup of tea with my mum," the same words spoken by the Scottish ploughman who witnessed Hess's crash landing in 1941). In another of her letters, di Niscemi described the events following the birth of Hess's son, when the Deputy Führer broke into a Dionysian dance and ordered all the Gauleiters to send him bags of earth from the four corners of the nation so the infant could symbolically start life on German soil (according to various versions of the story, Goebbels sent a brick or a sack of manure). In Scene 10, Otto Sander fondly performed the ritual of spreading earth under the child's cradle in a small, brilliantly lit room beneath an enormous light bulb, and then began a slow, delicate tap step that soon grew into a frenzied dance of atavistic exultation, never failing to bring down the house. Wilson also learned of how a duck flew into Spandau one year and gave birth to seven ducklings, which Hess delighted in feeding. When they grew too large for the courtyard of the prison, they were marched through the main gate to a nearby pond. The image must have captivated Wilson for a small parade of fowl later made an unexpected appearance in the second act. Typically, Wilson tended to seize on minor incidents and small human details that sparked his imagination or related to his private mythology: "It's all linked to Hess and it's all linked to Bob. He wouldn't take it if it weren't linked to himself."

With di Niscemi's assistance, Wilson assembled a collection of photographs documenting his protagonist's journey from youth to old age. One of these photos, a scene of Hess and his fellow prisoners raking leaves in the garden before a vast stone wall, was the inspiration for the prologue in which three figures similarly dressed in long winter coats and prison caps appeared one by one before a painted gray wall, slowly tapping their way across the stage with canes—the rakes of the photograph—like blind men, a poignant image of the protagonist's regimented and darkening world. This wall also served as the background for the epilogue, so that Hess's fantasies of freedom and limitless travel, which formed the main body of the play, were contained by the reality of the stone barrier that would keep him forever a prisoner.

Wilson also drew a considerable amount of textual material from *Prisoner # 7: Rudolf Hess*, a book written by the American warden of Spandau, Eugene K. Bird, which di Niscemi had urged on him. (The number seven would later appear on the tailcoat of an old man who danced in a world of his own for nearly an hour at the beginning of the second act.) From this firsthand account of Hess's confinement came fragments of the prisoner's words—reflections, observations, exchanges with his jailer—which were torn from their original context and dispersed through Wilson's text. As di Niscemi has observed, "Much more of the work refers to reality than people think." Wilson's visual books are usually made up of a series of corresponding images (the eight scenes that form the first half of *D D & D* mirror those in the second half), and sometimes the content or architectural shape of his texts reflects this arrangement. Wilson, for example, concentrated the bulk of Hess's thoughts in two corresponding sequences, Scene 7 ("A Large Rock by the Sea") and Scene 15 ("A Grove of Palm Trees by the Sea"). These included admissions ("I was putting on an act about my memory"), observations ("You should never sleep on too soft a mattress"—Wilson himself was suffering from a bad back), complaints ("The blood does not flow properly into the legs") and even Hess's parting words to Albert Speer as he stood watching coal being unloaded in the prison courtyard shortly before the other's release, "So much coal and from tomorrow only for me." These brief phrases floated by on the sea of Wilson's associative texts like shattered bits of Hess's consciousness and memory. On a few occasions Wilson chose to match text to image, so that Hess's advice to his son, "Never be so foolish as to go up in a plane without a parachute," was heard as the aviator descended from the sky in the London street scene, and the old man's comments on moon craters, space travel and airports of the future were intoned during a scene set around a crater in outer space.

Di Niscemi also brought Wilson a number of texts that, while not biographical, related in some way to Hess's life and the developing themes of the work. One of these was a children's fable by Else H. Minarik called "Mother Bear's Robin," which a six-year-old friend had recently shown her. In the story Mother Bear finds a baby robin which had fallen out of its nest. She takes the little creature home and raises it as her own, but as time passes and the robin grows up, it longs to escape its loving captivity and fly out into the world. The story, which was later woven through Scenes 2 and 10 (also mirrored sequences), had many points of contact with Hess, who was deeply attached to the birds that flew in and out of Spandau—the only outsiders to enter his world—and fed them every day in the prison garden. Like the robin, Hess was a flyer who looked out at the world from his window and yearned for the freedom of the skies. In a 1949 letter to his wife, he wrote, "How strange a thing is freedom. Never again will I shut a bird up in a cage. And now I understand so well why the Chinese and Japanese, when they wish to show gratitude for good fortune, go to the market, buy cage-birds and let them loose. I will do this, too, one day. . . ." Toward the end of the story Mother Bear exclaims, "I love you, little robin, but I want you to be happy. Fly away, if you wish. You are free"—words that di Niscemi found tremendously moving in the context of Rudolf Hess, the man who would never be free. Wilson reinforced this textual motif with numerous references to birds and a single visual manifestation: as Hess retreated from the audience for the final time in Scene 15, a small bird descended on a wire and alighted on his shoulder. Audiences watched the solitary figure pass into the distance, a stuffed bird for his only companion, and heard the words "listen / do you hear the birds" followed by Hess's complaint about crows taken from *Prisoner # 7*: "they are robbers / they will take food from any bird that is small and defenseless / I will not give them anything."

Another text that di Niscemi brought to Wilson's attention was a statistical footnote in Albert Speer's *Inside the Third Reich* on the production of ball bearings. "A factory in Schweinfort had been bombed and Speer got the plant back to full operation and produced more ball bearings than ever before. The war went on for two-and-a-half years because that factory was rebuilt." Wilson liked the fragment and wove it into two scenes, the first of which was set on a Greyhound bus and the second in the desert, where lozenge-shaped cars raced across the empty landscape. Although the only direct reference to the city named in the work's title is the recurring phrase "you're from Detroit" (Scene 6), the once great automobile-manufacturing capital is felt as an oblique presence in these two scenes, and the quotation from Speer's memoirs links the German war machine and the assembly-line production of American industry, where dreams of power and destruction are also generated. Wilson reinforced the connection between his protagonist and the automotive metropolis by outfitting the drivers of the racing cars in flying helmets and goggles similar to those worn by Hess on his famous flight.

D D & D is subtitled "a love story in 16 scenes" and love in its many guises pervades the imagery and language of the work. Wilson's own texts are saturated with protestations of love, recriminations, expressions of amatory regret, romantic clichés (many of which relate to the passion of two sixteen-year-olds, Brian and Susan, who appear from time to time) and references to marriage, friendship, parting and rejection. Most of the scenes are also duologues suggesting romantic or familial relationships. As *D D & D* evolved, these themes (which had been independently conceived) were absorbed into the life of Hess—his passion as a young man, his love for his infant son, the devotion of his aging wife, the need for human contact denied him in his solitude.

Di Niscemi wrote two original speeches which were interpolated into the existing text of *D D & D* and credited in the program. Like so much of her writing, these pieces were based on research and consciously tapped into areas of Wilson's concerns. One of her contributions was a dream speech for Frau Hess, an odd evocation of the simple woman's confusion and misfortune drawn from biographical material as well as one of di Niscemi's own dreams. "Sometimes I cook in my dreams," the speech begins, "not just simple food for children. But complicated dishes. I awoke once in the middle of the night and wrote down the recipe I was working on. It was for King's Cake. All the ingredients were correct. Butter, eggs, sugar, flour, lemon juice, rind and peel, almonds, rum, raisins, cornstarch, baking soda, almond extract and salt. There was nothing wrong with the proportions either, except the salt. Instead of a spoonful, I put in a kilo of salt. Imagine making a King's Cake with a kilo of salt." The speech, which drew gales of laughter from the audience ("'Ein kilo Saltz'—they thought it was the funniest thing they ever heard but it was actually very sad"), was spoken by an elderly woman who had been found in a Berlin rest home. Since she was unable to memorize her lines, Wilson arranged for her to pick up a telephone which played the speech back to her.

Di Niscemi's other contribution was conceived as a showpiece for Rudolf Nureyev, who was at one point interested in playing Hess. "Bob came to me and said, 'I need a

Scenes from *D D & D.* Berlin, 1979.

Prologue, "The Garden Wall."

"A Large Rock by the Sea."

"A Car Race in a White Desert."

"A Thunderstorm."

big speech for Nureyev, he has to have something dramatic.' I thought of the Nazis who were lumbering around getting their feet deeper and deeper in the glue and it seemed to me that Hess was really like a dinosaur, living on as the last of an extinct breed. Since I knew that Bob liked dinosaurs I said I'll write you a speech about dinosaurs. My six-year-old friend had a dinosaur book and I took some material from that and from the lectures of Professor Ritchie which I heard as a student at Barnard. The speech ended, 'If we were to consider the history of the world from the big bang to the present as being one year long, the dinosaurs appeared on this planet on Christmas Eve to be wiped out on December 28th. And man, who had invented agriculture at 11:59 P.M. on December 31st, only began to admit the possible preexistence of dinosaurs one hundredth of a second before midnight on New Year's Eve.' It's a classic way of getting people to see time in a different warp." It was likely to appeal to Wilson for that very reason. (When asked if he also thought of the dinosaur as a metaphor for Hess, she replies "I don't know. Bob doesn't tell you what he's thinking.")

Wilson's staging of the speech, which formed a postlude to the first act, typifies his approach to text. Although a large green Tyrannosaurus rex and a red, armor-plated triceratops cross the stage several times in *DD & D*, they do not appear here. Text and presentation remain entirely independent. As Hess, Otto Sander stood before a dark, abstract desert landscape, relating the history of the dinosaur in a flat, monotonous voice while conducting an imaginary orchestra. Wilson shows us an attentive, scholarly Kapellmeister, tracing elegant patterns in the air with his baton, and at the same time Hess the dreamer—a man blissfully shaping music no one else hears, in control once more of time and the universe. As the recitation ends the small, precise hand signals give way to grand and sweeping gestures. He raises his baton for the crescendo but suddenly freezes. The lights change and he is transformed once more into the bent old man standing before the wall of Spandau, which has descended behind him. The midnight alluded to at the end of his speech has struck and the spell is broken. As he slowly brings down his baton, it becomes the cane we first saw him holding in the prologue. The chimes of Westminster fill the theatre as if to once more assert the omnipotence of time, which has brought down both Hess and the dinosaurs. Finally the lights dim and we see only the hand grasping the stick in the darkness.

Although Wilson had incorporated literary and historical texts into past productions—Edwin Denby read excerpts from Nijinsky's autobiography in *Overture*, Stefan Brecht recited from the writings of Alfred Jarry and George Ashley from Karl Marx in *Stalin*—*DD & D* marked the first time such interpolated writings all related (though at times tenuously) to a central subject or were so deeply woven into his own text. The work also pointed the way toward increasingly literary texts and greater interrelationship between visual and aural content, which di Niscemi, as researcher and writer, would do much to encourage. Although she did not sit in on daily

Scenes from *Edison.* 1979.

rehearsals as she would with later productions, di Niscemi flew to Berlin to observe the final preparations of *D D & D* a few days before the premiere. "I went as a volunteer worker and as a member of the cheering squad. Bob called and asked me to bring him cock feathers for one of the costumes. He said, 'They won't give me any more money.' The theatre had already spent $400,000 on costumes and there were only twenty people in the cast. They had bad memories of Richard Wagner and Ludwig of Bavaria. I went out and spent a hundred and forty dollars on feathers. *D D & D* was seven hours long when I arrived in Berlin and Bob was very courageous and decided to cut an hour and a half just before the opening. He bought the house out the day previews were to begin and ran a rehearsal for himself. The first night was a great, great success. There was over fifteen minutes of applause at the final curtain. The performance ended at 12:20 and the last subway left at 11:30 so the audience, many of them students, had to decide if they were going to stay and try to find a ride or a taxi or leave. I saw three performances and you could always feel that terrible moment of decision coming, but no more than 25 percent of the audience ever left."

A few months after the premiere of *D D & D*, Wilson set to work on *Edison*, an American panorama celebrating the inventor of the electric light bulb and some of the nation's other heroes. Wilson's interest in Edison, another in a long line of dreamer-protagonists, was again rooted in his personal concerns. "Edison was very visual. He drew and the technical drawings he created are extraordinarily beautiful. He and Henry Ford used to communicate through drawings because Ford was very shy and Edison was very deaf. Bob was very, very interested in that. *Edison* also grew out of the huge light bulb in *D D & D*. Bob was mad about those old light bulbs. In fact, if you go down to his loft you'll see bulbs that look very much like those." Once again di Niscemi supplied Wilson with biographical information (sometimes directed toward his own interests, such as Edison's contempt for language), historical references, quotations and visual materials (one item, an editorial cartoon, inspired the work's poignant epilogue, in which the hooded figure of death arrives at the bedside of the dying inventor bearing a glowing light bulb in its outstretched hand). The texts she submitted were similarly dislocated bits of biography and history, a collage of Americana ranging from Lafayette's declaration on the rights of man (one day di Niscemi received a hastily scrawled note from Wilson asking, "What do you know about Layfatte?"—now one of her treasured mementos) to the words of Emma Lazarus and snatches of dialogue drawn from the life of the play's protagonist:

1 (Edison): improve my dynamo there's $50,000 in it for you if you can do it

2 (Nicolai Tesla): it's done where's my money (Act II, pt. 7)

4 (Henry Ford): how pleasant my boyhood's hero has become my later manhood's friend (Act II, pt. 13)

Wilson then inserted these and other fragments ("Everything that makes sense came from me") into his existing text, a process di Niscemi likens to trimming a Christmas tree.

In its interplay of historical imagery and related textual materials, *Edison* might be considered a transitional work leading to Wilson's most ambitious undertaking, *the CIVIL warS*, whose characters, images and texts would be drawn from all of world history and literature. Di Niscemi played a significant role in the inception of this mammoth work, which was to occupy Wilson for nearly five years. "It started when I read Susan Sontag's book *On Photography*. Bob had just finished *D D & D* and asked me, 'What shall I do now?' I knew he was interested in the Civil War [a Confederate soldier had appeared in *A Letter for Queen Victoria*], which was the first war documented in photographs, so I said, 'Why don't you do something about the photographer.' I thought of the Time-Life book on the Civil War, which contains many of Matthew Brady's photos, and showed it to him. You can never tell what Bob will pick up on. He was mesmerized by a picture showing one of Barnum's midgets sitting in the hand of the world's largest woman and that image was later integrated into the piece." Toward the end of December, 1979, the first entry for *the CIVIL warS* appeared in Wilson's journal under the heading "New Play X": an excerpt from *Mr. Lincoln's Camera Man*, a biography of Matthew Brady, followed by fourteen hastily sketched scenes. Although he initially planned to use Brady as a central character and organizing force (as he had Einstein and Edison), the rapidly evolving work soon outgrew any single personality or theme. As Wilson would later recall, "The idea of the piece just began to grow in my mind—from Japan to the industrial revolution, from there to Jules Verne and the voyages under the sea and to the moon, and then to the whole history of the world."

After Robert Fitzpatrick of the Olympic Organizing Committee approached him early the following year about presenting one of his works at the arts festival planned for the 1984 Games in Los Angeles, Wilson began to envision a spectacle of unprecedented scope and size which would be put together in a number of different countries (eventually Holland, Germany, Japan, Italy, France and the United States). As the epic work started to take shape in Wilson's head, di Niscemi immersed herself in the history of the American Civil War, from which much of its imagery would be drawn. "I read as many as twenty books on Lincoln. I read my way through the Civil War day by day. Bob has a wall where he puts up material he's working on. I used to walk into his apartment and put up all kinds of things—cartoons, slogans, admonitions, suggestions. You have to show them to Bob first—obviously you don't slap something on someone's wall without showing it to them—and he'll say either 'yes, that's interesting' or 'no, I don't find that interesting.' The wall is made up of long strips of paper which can be rolled up like a scroll when he travels somewhere. When Bob was in Paris, I walked into his room and put up a phrase from Carl Sandburg's biography of Lincoln, 'a tree is best measured when it's down.' I put it up in big black letters to catch his attention." The old folk saying, which Sandburg quoted in a chapter dealing with the public response to Lincoln's assassination, would become the subtitle of *the CIVIL warS* (much to di Niscemi's eventual regret) and the tree an allusion to its most important recurring image.

Once again requests and research materials passed back and forth through the mails. In a typical letter posted from Munich in the spring of 1982, Wilson asked for information on Madame Curie, Mrs. Lincoln, the death of Robert E. Lee and the play performed at Ford's Theatre the night Lincoln was assassinated; ideas for characters that could be played by Hildegard Behrens and Jessye Norman; and "any kind of unspectacular events of the time, stories about ordinary people as well as portraits and pictures of various people of all classes and backgrounds." During the lengthy gestation period, di Niscemi also provided preliminary scenarios for several scenes, supplied sponsoring theatres with background materials, and assembled research on general subjects Wilson wanted to introduce into the work—his request for information on families, for example, brought forth detailed reports on everyone from the Borgias to the Ewings of TV's "Dallas." In August of 1981, she traveled to Munich (once again as a volunteer) to work with a small group of performers, technicians and assistants that Wilson brought together to help him shape the project. "We were there for ten days and we mapped out the whole work. I was the historian. I brought books and explained the context of what we were doing. I did whatever was necessary. One day Bob said, 'Get up and play Grant,' so I had a marvelous scene with Hildegard Behrens, who was General Lee." Di Niscemi was also present at the four-week workshop held in the small West German city of Freiburg the following summer. "We had such a good time putting the piece together. 'Why don't we add this.' 'Let's put in some windmills, let's have ten Lincolns.' It was like making mudpies." Two of her own texts were incorporated into the opera at that time, a death scene for Robert E. Lee (III, c) and a dialogue between the general and his horse, Traveller (II, a). The latter, one of di Niscemi's personal favorites, typifies the way in which she creates associative wordscapes out of historical and literary fragments:

LEE   as long as there is a horse that can
               carry his rider and one arm that can
               wield a sword I prefer annihilation to
               submission

TRAVELLER   AND one AND two
            AND one AND two
            AND one AND two . . .

LEE   we must strike them a blow
             we must strike them a blow
             we must never let them pass us again

TRAVELLER   one two bugles
             three four cannon
             one two blood
             three four dust . . .

LEE   But what a cruel thing is war
             to separate
             and destroy
             families and friends
             and to devastate the fair face
             of this beautiful world

TRAVELLER   and one
             and one
             and one
             and one
             will it never stop raining?

LEE   I will strike that man a blow in the morning

TRAVELLER   will we never reach home
             will it never stop raining
             will we never reach home

"All of this comes from Robert E. Lee. Every phrase is from his correspondence. 'We must strike them a blow' — that was just before Gettysburg, he was talking about Grant. 'But what a cruel thing is war' — Lee really wrote that. But he was in love with war and he was a bloody, savage general. Bob and I used to have terrible fights because I'm a big Lincoln man and he's a big Lee man." The exchange between Lee and Traveller suggests some of the reasons di Niscemi and Wilson are able to work comfortably together. The text is first of all a collage like the CIVIL warS itself, made up of dislocated fragments of history and associational verbal images. It shares with Wilson's own writings (perhaps intentionally so) a preoccupation with simple numerical sequences, repetition and architecturally structured phrases. Most importantly, di Niscemi's dialogue for horse and rider is an open text; it imposes on the director neither meaning nor mood nor manner of presentation. Traveller's commentary might be either poignant or humorous; it is left to Wilson and his actors to determine its context and effect. The text is simply an arresting object that Wilson can use (di Niscemi acknowledges that in the end "everything becomes his").

While a broad outline of the text of *the CIVIL warS* had been developed at Freiburg, the dialogue for each section was to be created during later workshops in collaboration with a team of dramaturgs and researchers, who would contribute additional historical material from the various sponsoring countries. Ultimately di Niscemi played a larger role in this process than Wilson ever intended, a fact attributable to both circumstance and her special ability to gauge his needs and act quickly on them. When Wilson's collaboration with his Dutch dramaturg foundered in the spring of 1983, di Niscemi was immediately dispatched to Rotterdam to help organize the text. "Everything was wrong. No one was getting anywhere. They had nothing. At a certain point, it is better to have something you can work with than nothing." After "calming Bob down," di Niscemi began assembling texts and writing speeches to order. "Some of the best work I've done for Bob has been in rehearsals, because that's when he really gets going. I sit behind him, usually to the left, and I try to see things as he sees them. Often he'll turn around and say 'I need fifteen minutes of intense passion' or 'I need two-and-a-half minutes of this character.' I have a stopwatch and I'll go to the back of the house and write."

Di Niscemi acknowledges that quickness of response is crucial in her work with Wilson. "You have to be able to respond to him immediately. That's why you have to study in advance and have everything in your mind. 'Should it be this? Should it be that? Yes. No. Yes. No.' Response is very important. There are times I've written him letters that go unanswered for five months but when *he* wants an answer it has be *now.*" When Wilson decided that the chorus surrounding Hercules in the final scene of *the CIVIL warS* should be named for figures from his past, di Niscemi was expected to supply a list of suitable mythological characters at that moment, which she did. On their way to Freiburg some years earlier, he told her that if the work was going to be presented at the Olympics he would need "something about peace" and she immediately suggested the Duke of Burgundy's great speech on that subject from Shakespeare's *Henry V,* which was incorporated into the opening scene. This kind of facility and speed is essential, for if the collaborator hesitates or ponders a moment too long Wilson will have moved on to something else. In addition to her prodigious gift of recall and far-flung general knowledge, di Niscemi is a mighty talker, capable of shifting gears and changing directions in accordance with Wilson's reactions and filling any empty space in the conversation. "When you come up with something that really interests Bob, he suddenly becomes very quiet like a good little mouse, looks at you very seriously and says, 'Hmm, let's see if we can work this out.' Then you realize you've got it. But you can go on for hours before this happens."

Di Niscemi has also come to accept the swift rejection of some of her most cherished ideas and writings as a basic part of the process. "I would say that about 60 percent of what I give Bob is accepted. The rest is rejected and so it disappears. I did what I thought was a very good poem for Mrs. Lincoln but he disliked it and so it disappeared. I wanted to bring in Mrs. Chesnut, the lady from South Carolina who wrote a marvelous diary which Margaret Mitchell pilfered in *Gone with the Wind*, but Bob wasn't interested. I toss out a lot of characters to Bob. Some of them cling and some of them don't. It's not a problem. I trust Bob and I have a lot of imagination. I can always think of something else." Speaking of their collaboration, she proudly proclaims, "I'm not an intellectual and Bob's not an intellectual. That's why we work well together." And there's more than a measure of truth in her assertion, for like Wilson she is drawn to the colors, shapes and anecdotal details of history and literature rather than to issues, ideas or consequences.

Di Niscemi's libretto for Act V of *the CIVIL warS* might be seen as the culmination of her efforts to infuse Wilson's work with the colors and voices of history and to bring greater unity to its visual and aural content. Her pivotal role in the creation of the Italian section, which was set to music by Philip Glass and received its premiere at the Rome Opera in the spring of 1984, resulted from Wilson's preoccupation with other matters, the compelling need for a singable text and, as always, her own initiative. "Bob was busy in Japan and I realized that we couldn't arrive in Rome for the workshop that summer with nothing in hand so I hunted up Philip Glass and we created the first real scenario. Bob had told me he wanted Hercules for the final scene because Hercules was the founder of the Olympics. When I was a student at Barnard in the 1950s, there was a very great Latin scholar at Columbia named Moses Hadas whose classes I used to audit and one of the things we read was Seneca's *Hercules Furens*. T. S. Eliot has a lovely poem "Marina" which is prefaced with a tag from the play. I decided to look it up because I know Latin and Latin is a marvelous language to sing. I read the play again and thought, 'For the Italians this would be good, because they don't really know Latin—they have no real memory for it.'" Together with Seneca's last play *Hercules Oetaeus,* the text of *Hercules Furens* would become the primary source for the Rome opera.

The final act of *the CIVIL warS* begins with a prologue set on an empty plain, perhaps a battlefield, before a sky filled with stars. A snow owl is perched on a bare branch extending from the wings, while below her an "Earth Mother" sits on a tree stump cradling an infant. From the opposite side of the stage a 15-foot-tall Abraham Lincoln slowly begins to make its way across the landscape.

Such was the scene Wilson envisioned at the time of the Freiburg workshop. It was left to di Niscemi to give Wilson's evocative images a context and further animate the scene through the associative power of language. In the texts of Seneca she found a wealth of relevant themes and analogous situations that could be directly incorporated into the libretto. The first lines of the choral ode in Act I of *Hercules Furens* became the opening song of the Earth Mother (3), who observes the waning of the night and the approaching dawn just as the assembly of Theban elders had centuries before:

3   Iam rara micant sidera prono   Now stars shine few and faint
    languida mundo; nox victa vagos   above a sleeping world;
    contrabit ignis luce renata . . .   vanquished night draws in her
                                           wandering fires as the new day is
                                         born . . .

Her song is soon followed by the mournful plaint of the Snow Owl (2), whose threnody begins with the phrase di Niscemi recalled from Eliot's poem:

2   Quis hic locus, quae regio, quae   What place is this? What region
       mundi plaga?   of the world?
    Quas trahimus auras? Quod   Where am I? What soil lies
       solum fesso subest . . .   beneath me?

These words, originally spoken by Hercules after waking from his delirium and finding the bodies of the children he had murdered moments before, are now intoned after the slaughter of countless wars and the madness of centuries. (Hercules himself is seen passing silently across the stage at the beginning of the scene.) When the looming figure of Lincoln (1) speaks, it is again with the words of Seneca's hero, whose prayer for humanity and desire to wrestle with the evils of the world seem equally suited to the great American leader. The powerful apostrophe forms one of the opera's most important textual motifs, recurring in both Italian and Latin:

1   Non vi siano più veleni,   Let poisons cease to be,
    nessun'erba si gonfi di succo   let no destructive herb
    nocivo. Non regnino più tiranni   swell with harmful juice.
    feroci e crudeli. Se la terra sta   May savage and cruel tyrants
    per produrre ancora qualche   rule no more.
    nefandezza, si affretti, e se   If earth must still produce
    prepara qualche mostro, esso sia   any evil, let her make haste,
    mio.   and if she is preparing any
                                        monster,
                                      let it be mine.

Di Niscemi also wove key words and phrases into the prologue that reflected Wilson's own themes and images, so much so that her text—with its numerous references to death, stars, ships, children and peace—might be considered a thematic summation of *the CIVIL warS* itself. Even the Earth Mother and Snow Owl's cries of "Morte" (Death) heard near the beginning of the scene seem to yield at last to the promise of accord ("pace pace / O figli miei"; "peace peace / oh my children") in keeping with the opera's basic message. What di Niscemi fashioned from Wilson's visual scenario is a kind of Norn prologue: three figures gather before the dawn to review the history of the world and cast its fate (even the scene's placement before the final installment of the epic suggests Wagner's *Ring*). But while her libretto enriches and gives urgency to Wilson's imagery, it is finally only a commentary on his work, not an inseparable part of it. In fact, the visual scenario of this prologue also constituted the epilogue of the fourth act, where it was performed with an entirely different script drawn from the writings of Heiner Müller, the Brothers Grimm, Shakespeare, the Bible and Hopi Indian prophecies. Wilson likes to say that his images stand on their own and can be joined to any number of aural tracks, and in this instance it is literally true.

The design for the first scene of Act V, a series of fan-shaped bridge cables, was among the very first sketches Wilson drew in his journal back in 1979. By Freiburg the cables had been moved to outer space, perhaps linking together two spaceships; still later the scene became the background for a dance episode performed by a tribe of Hopi Indians. Yet another layer was added to the composition with the inclusion of the great Italian patriot and soldier Giuseppe Garibaldi, whose presence, di Niscemi says, was all but demanded by her cousin Gioacchino Lanza Tomasi, the director of the Rome Opera. "Garibaldi is the great patron saint of Italy's Communist Party and they are in power in Lazzio and that's where Rome is. Therefore if the Americans want a half million dollars to put on an opera in Rome, Garibaldi had damn well better be in it."

The Italian freedom fighter proved an auspicious choice, a hero worthy of taking his place beside Hercules and Lincoln who also had links to America and the Civil War. Garibaldi (born in 1807, the same year as Robert E. Lee) lived for a time on Staten Island and President Lincoln had even offered him a commission in the Union Army which he declined, refusing to accept anything less than a supreme command (he was also suspicious that the war was being fought more for commercial interests than the cause of abolition). Wilson eventually placed Garibaldi in a specially constructed opera box, midway between the audience and the stage, from which he presided over the performance. As the "Hero of Two Worlds" (he had gained fame and worldwide admiration fighting for the liberation of Uruguay as well as his homeland) he stood symbolically between Italy—the audience—and the New World, represented by Lincoln, Lee and the Hopi Indians who filled the stage during his big scene. "Bob said I need an aria for 'what's-his-name' so I wrote a lovely poem called 'Garibaldi a Caprera (1862)' which is all about water. Garibaldi was abstemious and in the battle of Milazzo—boiling summer of 1860—his boys were about to drink from a well when he tasted the water and spat it out. He told them there was a dead animal in the well and gave a dissertation on the quality of water in various parts of the world, which was most extraordinary in the midst of battle. After Victor Emmanuel was established as the King of Italy, Garibaldi went back to Caprera, a small island off Sardinia which is without water. And he sat sulking on this rock until at last he gathered his forces and moved on Rome crying 'Roma o Morte,' which became his motto."

Once again di Niscemi fashioned a collage of phrases and images drawn from history, in this case a kind of associational biography of the 'Hero of Two Worlds':

1	Acqua di anfora	Water of Amphoras
	acqua piovana	Rain water
	acqua vergine	Virgin water
	limpida	limpid
	pura	pure
	come tortura	as torture
	subìta per amore	endured for love
	e libertà. . . .	and liberty. . . .
	aspetto l'appello	I await the call
	Gloria mia	Gloria mia
	dove sei	where are you
	Calatafimi	Calatafimi
	Montevideo	Montevideo
	Tregua dannata	Damned truce
	isola secca	bone-dry island
	rocca arida	bone-dry rock
	erba bruciata	burnt grass
	amare cisterne	bitter cisterns
	Imbroglioni	Rogues
	mascalzoni	Con Men
	parlatori	Talkers
	traditori	Traitors
	ROMA	ROME
	o morte	or death

"Garibaldi was tortured in Uruguay but he didn't say anything. He was betrayed by politicians. He sat on his barren island dreaming of past victories and the day he would return and take Rome. It's all there. Every single line is true. It's also very much in the nineteenth-century heroic style like Garibaldi's own writings." Philip Glass took di Niscemi's text and created a stirring tenor aria which some critics compared to Verdi's "Di quella pira." (Glass composed much of the opera with a portrait of Verdi sitting before him on the piano. "I was consciously reaching," he says, "for a certain kind of dramatic singing you'd find in the history of Italian repertory opera. I very much wanted to make the piece my Italian opera.") To accommodate Glass's need for a longer text, di Niscemi expanded her poem to more than three times its original length: "I thought, 'What the hell—we have all these Hopi Indians dancing around on stage, we have to tell the people what's going on.' So I did some research on the Hopi legends and wrote a new passage from the perspective of the eagle, which is the Hopi's sacred bird—Garibaldi sees himself as an eagle mocked by lesser beings." A choral refrain of Lincoln's "Let poisons cease," this time in Latin, was also added, strengthening the identification of Garibaldi with the heroes of the prologue. Much of this work was accomplished during the summer workshop in Rome: "It was boiling hot and we all marched around the room and chanted the text, even the technicians joined in. Bob created the staging and Philip Glass timed it with the minicomputer he always carries around. In the fall he went to his cabin in Nova Scotia and composed the music to fit not merely the text but the staging, choreography and all the predetermined timings as well."

Early in 1980, Wilson created two speeches which together with the texts of Seneca form the nucleus of the opera's final scenes. The first of these is spoken by Robert E. Lee, seen earlier astride his horse Traveller, then dying in a military hospital, and who now appears through the porthole of a spaceship. The speech is another melange of broken thoughts and snatches of conversation intermingled with unidentifiable phrases in languages known only to Wilson ("Bob does fake French, German and Italian. He doesn't really like language. I think it's his revenge."), uncharacteristically unified by a single theme, the main social theme of the work itself: warfare. Wilson attached this text, which seems to have been largely drawn from contemporary television reports of military conflicts, to a moving letter di Niscemi had given him, which was written in 1865 by William E. Hatcher, a Baptist minister who began weeping uncontrollably when he saw General Lee ride past his front gate in a rainstorm after his defeat at Appomattox. The text of the letter, which describes the vanquished leader's "incomparable dignity, his majestic composure, his rectitude and his sorrow," is spoken by Lee in the third person, as though he were a dispassionate observer of his own tragedy. Mrs. Lincoln and a line of eight singers in triangular black robes move across the stage in the wake of an enormous charred tree, singing the words of the minister's letter and phrases di Niscemi extrapolated from Wilson's closing speech, which appears in its entirety in the next scene. The description of Lee's lonely journey home in defeat together with such utterances as "it must have been a terrible war" and "it's over it's over" create an unmistakable sense of the approaching end, not only of the war that is Wilson's ostensible subject but of the opera itself.

The final scene of *the CIVIL warS* opens quietly on an empty landscape. As an offstage chorus sings the final lines of *Hercules Oetaeus*, asking the now deified hero to watch over the world and protect it from evil (a passage reminiscent of the "Let all poisons cease"), a ladder descends from the sky carrying Hercules to earth. As the trees of the world's continents move across the stage, a spaceship appears in the sky and a small girl dressed as Mary Lincoln is seen through a window that opens in the craft. Her rambling, fragmented monologue, written early in 1980 before the themes of *the CIVIL warS* had coalesced in Wilson's mind, gains power and expressiveness through its acquired context; we might be listening to the incoherent outpourings of a shell-shocked survivor of the war that now seems to be at an end. A ladder again descends from the sky, carrying to earth a human-sized Lincoln who reaffirms his determination to combat the evils of the world, a passage first heard in the prologue. The chorus, now dressed as mythological figures from Hercules' past, sing "Our revels now are ended" ("I put it in because I love *The Tempest* and because the revels now *were* ended") and take up the final lines of Mary Lincoln, concluding with "it's over it's over." Alcmene, the hero's mother, presents her son with the Olympic torch, and in a brief exchange nearly identical to that of the Seneca original he tells her to cease her laments for he has once again triumphed over death. Finally, Hercules stands alone on the empty stage, after the forests of the world have reclaimed its battlefields and covered over the bodies of the dead, holding aloft the torch that heralds both the opening of the Olympics and the promise of a new age.

On a wall of di Niscemi's New York apartment, amidst mementoes of other Wilson productions, is a large framed drawing bearing witness to her role in the creation of his most far-reaching work, a scene from the Rome opera with the inscription "Thank you for *the CIVIL warS*. Love, Bob." The drawing is also a testament to her willingness to work for a small share of glory rather than money; it was accepted in lieu of a promised fee for the Rotterdam section when Wilson ran out of funds. More often, di Niscemi has offered her services without expectation of remuneration or public recognition; she has freely relinquished all rights to her texts and in many instances even paid her own travel expenses. While she ruefully admits that it can be "expensive working for Bob," there is no doubt in her mind that it is worth it, not only because di Niscemi believes passionately in Wilson's art, but because she believes even more in his genius, and genius is a quality she prizes above every other. Her comparison of Wilson, who exemplifies her romantic conception of the artist, and Philip Glass is telling: "Phil is a practical man. He's very nice, very straightforward and I like him very, very much. But he is just an ordinary guy, *un homme moyen*. If he were not Philip Glass, he'd be the head of the Dreyfus Fund. He has that kind of mind. He's organized, knows every single detail and doesn't waste a nickel. Bob is a

the CIVIL warS. Prologue to Act V. Brooklyn Academy of Music, 1986.

the CIVIL warS. Act V, b. Brooklyn Academy of Music.

the CIVIL warS. Act V, b. Rome Opera, 1984.

genius. And he always ends up in the hole. It isn't that he doesn't make money. He makes huge amounts of money but somehow he and his cat always end up eating out of the same can of tuna fish." She regards whatever sacrifices she must make as the fair and necessary cost of working with an authentic genius. "Bob lives in a world of his own. He lives in outer space and that's the most expensive place in the world to live. It costs him huge amounts of money to maintain this world and therefore my feeling is that he doesn't have to maintain me."

Although di Niscemi's research and suggestions continue to influence Wilson and shape his works, the final moment of *the CIVIL warS* provides a fitting conclusion to any consideration of their friendship and collaboration: Hercules stands alone on the stage of the Rome Opera, eight years after that first meeting at the ballet, and with the wondrous logic that is Wilson's signature, kneels down and touches the earth.

HEINER MÜLLER

A more unlikely and mutually contradictory collaboration could hardly be imagined than that of Robert Wilson and the East German playwright Heiner Müller. On the one hand, there is the engaged Marxist poet, hailed by some as the heir to Brecht, and on the other, the political naïf committed only to the furtherance of his own art and career. The American is a dreamer and optimist for whom no goal is impossible; the European is wary and pessimistic, his outlook shaped by a half-century of experience. The intellectual from Saxony possesses a vast knowledge of literature and history; the visionary from Waco has read at most a handful of books in his life. In appearance they also present a striking contrast: the lanky American and the small puckish German (the *Village Voice* observed that Müller's "pale eyes, tulip lips, Roman features, and skin the color of mocha cream could have been assembled from different faces") who moves in a haze of cigar smoke, not unlike that other venerated denizen of East Berlin to whom his work is frequently compared. Their work presents another dichotomy. One's theatre is jagged, dense and angst-laden, crammed with conflicting attitudes, self-destructing meanings and twisted shards of history; the other's glassy, graceful and self-reflexive, prompting one German critic to proclaim its creator "the genius of the aesthetic vacuum—of fascinating, beautiful emptiness."

Yet for all these differences a remarkable artistic bond and friendship developed between the two men, who found they shared a number of complementary views about the theatre, chief among them an abhorrence of interpretation and fixed meanings. Still, basic differences more than any common sensibility initially fueled the collaboration, and these remain a source of mutual fascination, especially for Müller, who tends to view the world in dialectical terms. Nothing illustrates the gulf between their respective experiences of the world more vividly than the earliest childhood memory of each man. Müller's first recollection is of Nazi brownshirts coming in the night to arrest his father, a Socialist Democrat, hours after Hitler had taken power, while Wilson remembers the layout of the neighborhood supermarket with its neatly arranged produce section, gleaming linoleum aisles and checkout counters (though as Müller points out this model of order and regularity was not without its own terrors). It is no wonder that Wilson found his collaborator's personal history so intriguing, for unlike his own youth which had as its background the uneventful life of a small farming community in central Texas, Müller grew up in the maw of history, which was to become the obsessive subject of his work. The playwright's youth and adolescence spanned the Nazi era, and at the age of sixteen he was drafted into the labor force and sent to the front, where he witnessed the last fighting of World War II. After being held briefly as a POW by American forces, he settled in Soviet-occupied East Germany, preferring this new society to what he regarded as the Nazi refuge on the other side of the border. (Ironically, his father was later expelled from the Communist Party after refusing to place Stalin's picture in his office and fled to the West, where as a minor government official he spent his declining years dispensing pensions to former Nazis and their widows.) Müller, who had no desire to pursue a university education ("too boring"), earned a living for a time as a librarian, eventually establishing himself in East Berlin, where he began writing plays and working as a dramaturg, first at the Maxim Gorky Theater, then the Berliner Ensemble ("I was mostly paid for writing plays but they didn't perform them") and finally the Volksbühne, where he is currently in residence. In the mid-1970s Müller also spent a year in the United States as a writer in residence at the University of Texas at Austin, where Wilson had studied business as a young man; the European's travels through the new world brought about a major change in his writing, which had previously focused on the problems of the German Democratic Republic and would subsequently take on broader social and political issues, bringing him closer to Wilson's universal vision.

Müller, who has always kept abreast of new developments in literature and the arts, became aware of Wilson's work several years before the two men met. He had seen *Network* in Munich in the fall of 1977 and again in Amsterdam the following summer, and attended a rehearsal for *D D & D* at the Schaubühne in Berlin. "I was very interested in how Bob worked with amateurs, nonacting people, it was really fascinating. I didn't notice the time factor immediately. It seemed so normal to have one time in this space, a different time than outside. It was so natural and the whole playing seemed so necessary that it was no problem getting accommodated to the time. I wasn't so interested in the visuals. My main interest was the rhythmic structures of the work and how the images changed in the same rhythm as the acoustic." A year earlier Müller had been asked to submit a paper for an MLA conference in New York on postmodernism, a term then new to him, and he chose as an example Wilson's theatre (cannily judging it to be "as naive as it is elitist"): "I tried to find a formula for the work or what it meant to me—something like a combination of mathematics and child's play." He also seized on Wilson's practice of using nonactors, calling it "a prospect of epic theatre as Brecht conceived it but never realized it." "You know, Marx said that in a communist society artists would not be special people, just people who are artists in their free time. Brecht said something quite similar in his discussion of the epic theatre, that there should be no difference between actors and nonactors, everyone should be able to act if he wants and as long as it's something special, you won't have epic theatre."

The two men finally met a few years later in Cologne after a performance of Wilson's solo work *The Man in the Raincoat,* and although Müller's memories of this first encounter are vague ("I was drunk, he was stoned"), he remembers with pleasure a moment in the show when the stage gradually filled with twenty-four figures in dark suits and glasses, all identical to Wilson. Their paths did not cross again until 1983, when Wilson was seeking a writer for Act IV of *the CIVIL warS.*

At that time the fourth act of the projected twelve-hour opera was to consist of a long film assembled from archival footage of civil conflicts and natural disasters by the Argentine documentary-maker Edgardo Cozarinsky, and what Wilson envisioned as a small play "depicting the family unit in stories of struggle and survival throughout history" which would be simply staged on a platform in front of the screen. Wilson had thought about approaching Botho Strauss, whose plays had been presented at the Schaubühne, which was considering sponsoring the German section, but the company's director Peter Stein told him he didn't think Strauss would be interested. It was Ivan Nagel, the director of the Württemberg State Theater in Stuttgart, who proposed Müller, whose work was barely known in the United States at that time (a suggestion endorsed by Susan Sontag, who had been invited to collaborate on the French section), and Wilson wrote him a letter describing the project and asking if he'd be interested in creating the text for the fourth act. The invitation came as a complete surprise to Müller but he accepted at once: "There was no question." The two men met that spring in Rotterdam, where Wilson was preparing the Dutch section of *the CIVIL warS,* immediately hit it off and talked briefly about how they'd work together. "We never discussed ideas or concepts, we never had discussions in that sense. What I like most is that when Bob says nothing, you understand what he means. He showed me some drawings and asked me what I thought about them. Was it right? Was it okay? Then he said this scene will be twelve minutes and this one should be eight minutes, forty seconds. And don't you think we need texts for this one? It was very free and I liked that."

While Wilson responded at once to Müller's intelligence, openness and curious personal charisma (as well as to his enthusiasm for the project), his attraction to— and indeed identification with—the German playwright went deeper. Wilson is essentially a creator of images and in Müller he found for the first time a writer who seemed to share the same visual impulse, someone whose language translates not into rhetoric or narrative but pictures of the mind. If Wilson was unwilling to wrestle with the contradictions and complexities of Müller's texts, he could respond immediately to the rich and striking imagery, found both in the dense, highly charged prose with its barrage of pictorial metaphors and the often hallucinatory scenes suggested by the stage directions, which are almost Wilsonian in their strangeness and grandeur:

> "A wall of fire, in front of a snowstorm. . . . The stage is changed to a ghost-ship, dead sailors are nailing the captain to the mast." *Gundling's Life*

> "The actor [playing Hamlet] steps into the armor, splits with the ax the heads of Marx, Lenin, Mao. Snow. Ice Age." *Hamletmachine*

We are very near to Wilson's own theatrical realm. In fact, the dramaturgy of Müller's recent works somewhat resembles that of the American artist. Like Wilson, Müller has taken to creating theatrical collages (or "montages" as he calls them) made up of disparate scenes, speeches and literary fragments, eschewing narrative, linear action, causal development and characterization. (Müller's translator Carl Weber suggests that the playwright may have been influenced by American experimental theatre techniques during his stay here in the mid-1970s.)

Müller wasn't present during the first weeks of the Cologne workshop so Wilson began work alone. (The GDR was boycotting the Los Angeles Olympics along with most of the Eastern bloc, but Müller ultimately obtained clearance to participate in the project.) While there was no script or even a formal scenario at that point, Wilson did have a model of the setting—an arrangement of wooden ramps and platforms situated before a large white scrim on which filmic images could be projected—a stack of material on German history, Cozarinsky's archival footage and two words, "family" and "war," which together would form the main theme of the act. The director began by assigning various family roles to the actors (father, mother, child, young woman and man, aunt and grandfather) and having them assemble one by one around a table, the basic action of the first scene. All these components came from earlier works—the family unit is central to *KA MOUNTAIN*, the television film *Stations* and *The Golden Windows*; the act of gathering around a table is another familiar Wilson motif, one that would reappear a few years later in his production of Müller's *Hamletmachine*. Many staging ideas were drawn from improvisations. Wilson would see an actor sitting in a corner reading a book and incorporate the activity into the scene, or pick up a piece of styrofoam lying on the floor, give it to another actor and lead him to the stage. At one point Wilson asked the actors "What do you want to do?" and a number of their ideas and inventions became part of the production. Typically, many of the scenes he devised consisted of everyday actions, such as sitting, crossing ("walk over there, stop, count to twenty-five and turn around"), painting one's nails or bouncing a ball. It was also Wilson's decision to interweave episodes involving this nuclear family (which was to appear in other parts of the opera) with real and imaginary scenes from the life of Frederick the Great, whose presence would provide the historical focus of the act. As is the custom in his workshops, drawings and other visual materials were posted on the walls of the rehearsal hall, and a number of these images, such as a painting of the German monarch on horseback or a portrait of his mother with a small dog in her hand, soon found their way into the production.

On the day he arrived Müller sat quietly beside Wilson, who described the work the company had been doing, made drawings of the main episodes and ran some of the scenes for him. From that moment on Müller became an active participant: "It was impossible just to sit and watch. Every three minutes Bob would turn and say, 'What do you think?' or 'What should be here?' It really was a full-time job just to sit with him." At Wilson's insistence the playwright became involved in every aspect of production—contributing ideas for images and sound effects, working with the actors and functioning as a dramaturg and translator—and all this was reflected in his program credit, which read simply "mit-Arbeiter."

Müller began by handing out a number of texts, most of which related in some way to familial relationships. Ann-Christin Rommen, one of Wilson's assistants in Cologne, remembers the consideration he showed for the actors, telling them to "try a textual passage and see how it goes and if you don't like it, we can find something else." But despite his amenable, reassuring manner, Müller's presence and the texts he brought with him initially caused apprehension and friction within the company. "At first it was a little tense," says Tom Kamm, one of Wilson's codesigners. "Bob respected Heiner so much and he wanted very much to use his brilliance but I don't think he knew how to do that. Bob also has a very specific process and I don't know if Heiner knew how to relate to it." Even Wilson has acknowledged that in the beginning the resulting union of texts and images "didn't work at all." "It was very strange," says Rommen, "because we had seen so many of these episodes in silence and they worked very well that way. All of a sudden there was a second thing coming in and it was difficult to see right away how these scenes connected with the texts. It took awhile but you gradually made a connection. In the beginning we all felt it wasn't working, especially the actors. It was very difficult for some of them. The words got in the way with all the situations they had made up for themselves. Even in the end there were some actors who didn't want to do some of the texts because they didn't think they fit. They also had an image of Bob's work not being political or literary. They thought of Heiner as someone putting something else on his work and they wanted to save him. Bob had to convince them that he didn't want to be saved."

Müller proceeded slowly and calmly by trial and error. "He kept looking at what I was doing," says Wilson, "and putting different texts with it and eventually we would find things that *did* work." Müller compares the process to a mechanism. "It was like having a machine and this machine needs texts so you put one in and wait until it comes out. If it comes out, it's okay. Sometimes it comes back or it gets stuck." Müller now believes that the writings he first brought to the work "had too much continuity." Gradually he came to realize that such passages, like Wilson's visual constructions, "should not be linear but like different gravity fields." Despite these difficulties, Müller found working with Wilson unexpectedly liberating. "There's this Brecht slogan, 'The lightest way of life is in the arts.' That's the way it was for me working with Bob in Cologne. No ideas and no concepts. Always it was like playing games. I had a feeling of not being responsible for my work. It was a space of freedom, like the attitude of children playing. It was a new experience for me and I liked that." Müller also found the absence of intellectual labor invigorating—"An art without effort, where the step [rather than the idea] creates the way," he would later write of Wilson's theatre.

Rather than imposing their own meanings on an audience, both men believe in giving the individual spectator virtual free play with the materials put before him. In an essay on *the CIVIL warS*, the critic John Rouse points out that like Wilson, "Müller is concerned with eliminating, or at least subverting, the authorial subject of his texts—that is, himself as the provider of a meaning around which a text can be centered." In Müller's case, authorial carries with it multiple meanings of author, authority and finally authoritarian. No one better understands how those who hold power can coopt literature and the arts and turn "meaning" to their own ends than a German writer who has spent his life under two totalitarian regimes. His recent assemblages are therefore constructed to resist the confines of verifiable content and escape what he has called "the prison of meaning." Though the motives of the two men might be very different—Müller's rejection of interpretation is both an aesthetic and political position, while Wilson seems more concerned with preserving a sense of mystery—both seek the same thing: an open-ended art. No answers, no statements and no resolutions. "I have no message," says Müller, "I just want conflicts, even between the audience and the text." For years he has been frustrated by directors who impose their own values and interpretations on his works as well as by the analytical nature of the German theatre. "I am now fifty-six or something and for the last forty years all they talk about in Germany is this year's concepts. It's so boring. I have them, it's no problem. There's no reason to talk about them. In the fifties I often watched rehearsals at the Berliner Ensemble. When an actor got an idea—'You know I think it should be, etc.'—Brecht would say, 'Show it, don't discuss it, show it.' There were no discussions. That's why I like working with Bob. He has a visual concept and it's compelling. He gives you something and you can deal with that and you don't have to talk concepts or ideas. It's stupid. It's theatre and theatre is not ideas. You shouldn't have to remember your ideas like in school, you just get the image and maybe in the next four weeks you work with the ideas you get from it in that moment." In Germany, he has complained, the text is not considered a reality but an instrument used to communicate about reality. Müller holds to Samuel Beckett's view that a work of art is not about something, it is something—an organic entity, not an armature to which a set of ideas has been attached.

Müller says that *the CIVIL warS* was the first time he ever clearly heard or even understood one of his own texts, and he attributes this to the simplicity and directness of Wilson's presentational method. "Bob treats a text like a piece of furniture. He doesn't try to break it up or break it open or try to get information out of it or meaning or emotion. It's just a thing. That's what I like about his way because a text can stand for itself. It doesn't need support, it doesn't need help." (In this context the artist's apoliticality and lack of analytic skills might even be considered a virtue.) Rather than attempting to x-ray, classify or reshape this object Müller calls the text, Wilson simply places it within an artful setting. In an interview published in the Cologne program book, Müller compared his texts for *the CIVIL warS* to stones lying at the bottom of a river, submerged in Wilson's imagery which flows around them without discoloring or obscuring them. "Bob leaves the text alone. He never tries to be interpretive and that's what makes it difficult for the audience. The actors do not try to explain the meaning of the texts or give their opinion. I'm not interested in the opinion of actors in that way. What they should do is just serve the text, not tell you how to read it or how to hear it. That's mostly what the German theatre does. It's very interpretive, very boring." Wolfgang Wiens, Wilson's production dramaturg, offers a corroborative view: "What the German theatre is about is: 'What does the play mean, what does it say?' And everything that's done on stage is to illustrate that meaning. Of course Heiner is interested in the way Bob does theatre—it's so removed from the way it's done in Germany." (Wiens has gone so far as to describe his usual role as "the little green man who whispers the meaning of the play in the director's ear.") Müller's open-ended texts in turn place few if any restrictions on the artist's imagination. Characters, action and settings are frequently unspecified, and the result is again increased "space." Extending Müller's geological metaphor, Wilson often compares Müller's texts (as he does Philip Glass's music) to rocks which can be "put in the snow, in the sand, in the ocean or in outer space and their state is not altered." Because they are a strong entity in themselves they can withstand almost any manner of presentation.

Of the early images and ideas that Wilson discussed with him, Müller was particularly impressed by his desire to make Frederick the Great the focal point of the Cologne presentation. "It showed a very good instinct for German history." As Jonathan Marks pointed out in his program essay for the American production, Frederick II is one of history's most contradictory figures: at once the champion of

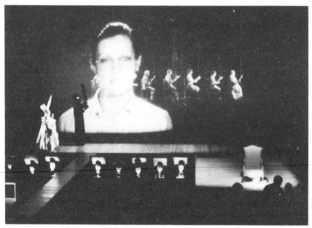

the CIVIL warS. Act IV. American Repertory Theatre, 1985.

the Enlightenment and the engineer of the eighteenth century's most brutal military machine, an advocate of free speech and religion and a despot who ruled his kingdom with an iron hand, a cultivated patron of literature and the arts and a butcher who brought death and destruction to much of Europe. Frederick would seem to personify the collective German spirit with its dual capacity for humanistic achievement and annihilation. As the progenitor of the Prussian principles of militarism, expansionism and obedience to authority, he has had a profound impact on the history of the twentieth century (Hitler marked his assumption of power in 1933 by placing a gold wreath on Frederick's tomb in Pottsdam and twelve years later committed suicide in a room where a portrait of the monarch hung.) As it happened, Frederick the Great already figured in Müller's writings, chiefly as the protagonist of his 1976 play *Gundling's Life*, from which he would draw liberally in constructing the text for this new work.

The figure of Frederick can be seen to embody the idea of civil war in all its meanings. The monarch's own internal struggle was itself a kind of civil war, as was his tormented relationship with his authoritarian father, a familial battle that shaped his character and ultimately his harsh policies, and would provide one of the fourth act's pivotal motifs. Finally, there was Frederick's obsession with national unification, itself the source of so much bloodshed and misery, which would ironically culminate with the partition of Germany in our own century. For Müller the term had application not only to history and the present world situation but to his own identity as an inhabitant of a divided city situated within a divided country within a divided Europe—a civil war in geography, whose symbol is the wall (a civil war in concrete). While Wilson originally defined his theme as "any kind of civilian struggle," Müller impressed upon him the belief that all wars are now civil wars because they directly affect the civilian population. In a telegram he sent to Wilson shortly after the cancellation of the project in 1984, he proclaimed that *"the CIVIL warS* defines the theme of our era; war between classes and races, species and sexes, civil war in every sense of the term." Indeed, to a dialectical thinker like Müller, nearly every polarity and social interaction can be seen as a civil war. (As he blithely told an uncomprehending audience at a postperformance discussion in Cambridge, "Bob drinks vodka and I drink Scotch. That's a civil war.")

Rather than creating an original script for the Cologne section, Müller set to work constructing an assemblage of fragments (not unlike di Niscemi's collages), cannibalizing his own works as well as selecting historical and literary texts that he felt in some way complemented or contradicted Wilson's visuals. Although there was an immediate need for texts and he is known to write slowly, Müller had other reasons for fashioning the book out of existing material. "It was like being given a melody. It's unnatural to write a text for a melody that already exists. Anyway, it wasn't necessary to write new texts—the frame was universal enough and I had so many associations.

And as long as you can use old texts, why write new ones? I would be happy if I could copy a whole act of Shakespeare for a play." (Müller created only one original text for the production, a description of a recent dream. Wilson, who was fascinated by his collaborator's ability to write backwards, filmed him writing the text on a pane of glass and projected the image on a screen during the first scene change.)

For the opening scene in which the family assembles at the front of the stage, Müller selected a letter that Frederick I wrote to his son in 1728 rebuking him for his lack of obedience and filial love. This was spoken without emotion by the actor playing the father of the family while behind him Frederick the Great was seen raising his cane toward his own father, whose head was projected on the large screen that filled the proscenium. This pivotal theme of father-son discord was amplified in subsequent scenes through a number of related texts. One was a recriminatory letter written by Franz Kafka to his father; as Dan Sullivan pointed out in the *Los Angeles Times*, "Two hundred years separate these communications, but they might have crossed in the mail." Müller also included recollections of three encounters with his own father—his earliest memory of peering through a crack in the door as the S.A. dragged him off into the night, watching from behind a barbed wire fence as he came down the path from the concentration camp where he was being held, and gazing at him through a glass wall in an isolation ward after the war; in each instance a barrier—not unlike the one running through Berlin—separates them. Texts drawn from world literature presented other aspects of familial strife, and these were often linked in some way to the Prussian king: a confrontation between Hippolytus and his stepmother from Racine's *Phaedre* suggested the forbidden love of Frederick II and his friend Hans von Katte (both of whom were played by women in this production, adding to the air of sexual confusion), while an agitated exchange between Hamlet and his mother ("O Hamlet, thou hast cleft my heart in twain") alluded obliquely to the genealogy of the monarch, who was descended on both sides from James I of England, the supposed model for Hamlet. (Müller: "James knew his mother [Mary, Queen of Scots] married the murderer [Bothwell] of his father [Darnley]—so Frederick could be Hamlet." Müller says that Hamlet always seemed to him more a German than English character—the tormented, blundering protagonist haunted by the "nightmare of history.")

The scenario and staging of the fourth act suggest that world conflicts have their origin in the tensions of the family, itself a kind of embryonic civil war. This theme of familial conflict is developed through simple acts (a grandfather knocking down a child's blocks, a scrimmage over a radio dial, a silent face-off) as well as various historical and literary texts, all of which are in turn linked to Frederick II, who presides over the action. "You can if you want see the Cologne section as being about Frederick the Great in hell. Now he's forced to see normal everyday life, to have all human experiences and learn what he missed learning in life. There's that Dante aspect." While Müller acknowledges that Wilson probably didn't conceive the piece in these terms, he says "it doesn't matter, it is in the structure, even in the images. Many years ago I wrote in a play—and I didn't know why—that the resurrection of the dead takes place in slow motion. Later I remembered that sentence and its meaning became simple in connection with Bob's theatre."

In selecting texts for Wilson's images, Müller—to paraphrase the American critic Gordon Rogoff—tended to seek "affinities" rather than "equivalencies." For a scene in a drugstore alluding to conflict and commerce, he chose Shakespeare's commentary on the corrupting power of gold from *Timon of Athens*, which he considers "the classical text on the function of money—it's quoted by Karl Marx in the first volume of *Das Kapital*." (In the original German staging, the passage was to have been recited by Peter Pilz, an actor in his late seventies who was about to retire. This idiosyncratic performer, whom Wilson adored, refused to deliver the speech and made up a different text for every performance. Wilson told him "Do what you want," an example of the enormous latitude he can allow an actor he trusts.) Often Müller's contributions were intended not so much to complement or heighten the visuals as put "an edge" on them. For a scene in which Frederick lay dying on a candlelit platform at the front of the stage, Wilson created a procession of Black Scribes, hooded figures on stilts with enormous black quills who moved through the auditorium and across the stage. He conceived of these phantom wanderers as the witnesses of history and Müller supplied a whispered litany of twentieth-century placenames, what he ironically describes as "a rough catalog of German goods": "guernica / coventry / auschwitz / oradour / buchenwald / dachau. . . ." Characteristically, Müller merely provided a "connective" between Frederick the Great and the horrors of our century, which audiences were free to contemplate or ignore as they chose.

Müller had considerable impact on the overall shape of some of the episodes that make up the fourth act. For its penultimate scene he chose the text of Goethe's *Erlkönig* and conceived the accompanying image of an eagle soaring through the sky. Goethe's poem, which every German schoolboy knows, tells of a child's surrender to death and of the beckoning "Elf-king" who appears before him as his father gallops helplessly homeward, holding the dying boy in his arms. In *the CIVIL warS* the poem is recited by a woman suspended in space (another of Müller's ideas) as Frederick rises on horseback from beneath the stage and his corpulent mother, Sophie Dorothea (who later mouths Schubert's setting of the text), sits chained to a sofa stuffing herself with chocolates. While the father-child relationship and the image of the night rider have links to Frederick, the scene also contains what Müller calls a "very hidden image": "For me Hitler is the Erlkönig, giving the young people a fascination for death and dying. This was the main force of the Nazis." Müller, who was familiar with Michel Tournier's novel about the Nazi youth movement (also titled

Erlkönig), had himself been forced as a child into the Hitler Youth, many of whose songs dealt with death, so this interplay of visuals and words—"Elf-king," hanging woman, Frederick and the eagle (a Nazi emblem as well as a romantic image of release and exaltation)—had very personal associations.

Müller also contributed a critical image to the exhilarating conclusion of the act, in which the company gathers silently on the main platform and simply smiles at the audience for an extended period before leaving the stage. The sequence, which as originally conceived was much like the building-train scene in *Einstein on the Beach* where cast members assemble one by one and then disperse in the same manner, is a striking example of the way in which the German playwright's contributions complicate or even subvert Wilson's own imagery. Müller had seen the Reggio-Glass film *Koyaanisqatsi* and remembered the episode showing the demolition of a housing project in St. Louis. At his suggestion this panorama of falling brick walls, together with German archival footage of a collapsing bridge, became the filmic background of the scene. As the company assembles at the front of the stage—their mouths slowly broadening into frozen smiles to the jubilant, pulsing strains of Philip Glass's accompanying organ music—building after building crashes to the ground on the screen behind them in a slow, continuous spectacle of destruction. Critics found varying and often contradictory meanings in this juxtaposition. For some it suggested man smiling in the face of the apocalypse or greeting the demise of the old order and the promise of a new age, for others it pointed to man's propensity for destroying the universe with a smile or the media-induced dulling of our senses. The channels of response are kept open. "I like showing this to an audience," Müller says, spreading his arms wide and then narrowing them again, "rather than this." The sequence, with its contradictory images of terror, joy and destruction, also suggests the apocalyptic vision which Wilson and Müller share. When asked what he found most interesting about this juxtaposition, the playwright laughingly replies: "That there were people smiling and total destruction. I like destructive forces, you know. I believe in them and the necessity of destruction. And I believe in Bob's fantasy there is a lot of destructive force and that's important."

Though the German section of *the CIVIL warS* was Wilson's first contact with a rich, allusive complex of texts—one that asks to be listened to and thought about rather than just heard—the artist was more interested in the sound of the language than what was being said. According to Ann-Christin Rommen, "He didn't want to know at all what was being said. He even refused to get translations at one point. He would say, 'Don't tell me what it is. I want to listen.'" Wiens recalls that he "always tried to tell him about the meanings of the German texts but he wasn't very interested. Bob really knows whether something is correct by the way it sounds. And if one of the German actors does too much or puts a wrong accent on a word, Bob hears it and is able to make corrections as if he knows the language." (Wiens estimates that nearly 80 percent of the material Müller contributed was eliminated shortly before the Cologne opening: "In the end Heiner realized it didn't make sense to have so much text. He had to respect Bob's way of working.")

Wilson saw Müller a number of times over the next two years and spoke with him regularly via the late-night phone calls that are his favored means of communication. During this period the playwright gave him the use of his *Medea* texts (which Wilson layered over the prologue of his operatic version of the Euripides tragedy) and contributed a prologue (*Description of a Landscape*) to his production of *Alcestis* at the ART in Cambridge. (While Müller was not directly involved in the development of that piece, Wilson sent him rehearsal tapes and they conferred by phone. The writer also recommended the Kyogen comedy *The Birdcatcher in Hell* which became its epilogue.) Wilson, who had been talking about staging contemporary works for some years, was also eager to produce one of Müller's plays, a prospect that pleased and intrigued the playwright. "Bob wants to do plays now and I'm really curious about this," he said during a visit to the United States in 1985. "I've never seen a production of one of my works that satisfied me and I'm interested in the way Bob will deal with a whole text. I don't know what will come out of it." That opportunity came in the spring of 1986 when Wilson accepted an invitation from New York University's School of the Arts to create a small-scale piece with a group of student actors in one of their studio theatres. The play he chose was *Hamletmachine* (1977), a six-page text the author has called "the shrunken head of the Hamlet tragedy." It is one of Müller's most dense and recondite works, a phantasmagorical meditation on the disintegration of Western civilization. Müller offers us a vision of the world as a Hamlet-machine (title and author share the same initials) turning out haunted protagonists blindly stumbling their way to extinction.

Although this time Wilson had the text in hand, he chose to proceed in virtually the same manner as before, creating an independent choreography made up of slow, ritualistic entrances and simple actions and gestures: a man hitting his head on a table, three women scratching their heads in unison, a man leaning over a wall, another hopping across the space on one leg, a woman turning in a swivel chair—all of which were activated by the sound of Japanese wood blocks (wielded in rehearsal by the director). Only after this sequence had been fully worked out and rehearsed in silence did Wilson consider how the staging would absorb the play that was its reason for being. One day he turned to the fourteen members of the company and said simply, "Now we have to figure out where to put the text." Müller's words were then distributed among the actors and layered over the existing pattern of movement, creating two independent tracks. (Wilson actually complained at one point that the staging—though separately conceived—related "too much" to the text.) In order to fill out the five-part structure of Müller's work, Wilson repeated the basic sequence of entrances and gestures four times. Each time the simple scenic enclosure he had designed was rotated and the actions seen from a different perspective, suggesting a kind of human mechanism or spatial timepiece—an appropriate if perhaps unintentional metaphor for the work's title. A contrasting film interlude, in which Müller's text appeared in rapidly moving print at the bottom of the screen, was placed at the center of the work to complete the formal structure.

Prior to leaving for New York, Müller told Wiens, who was again Wilson's dramaturg, that he couldn't imagine a production of *Hamletmachine* that would illustrate his texts in a conventional way. They agreed that what was necessary was not a literal representation but a "very clear structure so the audience would get the text" and when Müller arrived midway through rehearsals he found that this was exactly what Wilson had provided; Robert Brustein would later call the staging "a parallel reinforcing event." Müller's fantastic stage directions—a refrigerator oozing blood, Ophelia sitting in the deep sea in a wheelchair, a visit to the university of the dead— are among the work's most striking features, and doubtless some were disappointed by Wilson's decision to have the actors intone the descriptions as though they were part of the dialogue rather than try to realize them visually. His approach was entirely in accord with the aims of the playwright, who was to explain repeatedly during his American visit that these passages were intended more as "provocations" or "images to provoke the audience" than literal stage directions. In fact, when questioned about Wilson's seemingly antitheatrical solution he puckishly replied, "Why should he do the stage directions? It's in the text." For his part Wilson explained his spare, nonillustrative approach by saying that Müller's "texts have so many images in the words that one needs a certain amount of space in order to see the pictures. So I work the same way I've always worked."

Müller hadn't spoken with Wilson about the staging of *Hamletmachine* in advance so he couldn't have been entirely prepared for the glacial, ritualistically paced presentation the director had fashioned (despite the brevity of the text, the production ran nearly two-and-a-half hours). When asked if it took time to adjust to a staging so at odds with the tone of his play, the playwright simply replied, "Why should it?" His response was meant to be neither flip nor evasive. Müller constructs his texts of words and has no fixed conception of how they should be presented in the theatre. He also trusts Wilson's sense of theatre implicitly. While he offered an occasional suggestion at rehearsal and stayed up a number of nights with Wilson and his staff discussing the progress of the production, Müller seemed largely content to sit back and observe the fine tuning of the mechanism the director had set in motion around and alongside his text.

In shaping the text with his performers Wilson revealed just how deeply the German playwright had influenced his thinking and rhetoric, especially in the matter of interpretation. In what has become something of a stock speech, Wilson would tell his actors, "Take all your ideas, put them in a little black box and leave them on the side of the stage. Forget about them." After denouncing the traditions of interpretive theatre ("It's fascistic") and psychological acting ("It's lies"), on another occasion he declared, "We don't know what's happening. It's a mystery. We can't understand it. Sometimes it sounds like you understand what you're saying. You don't understand it. We don't understand it! We're saying 'What is it?' The reason we make theatre is to ask 'What is it?' That's why we invite an audience. To have a forum. We want to leave it open-ended. As soon as you say what it is, it's closed, it's finished." (The playwright once told Wiens that he didn't understand the meaning of *Hamletmachine* and "if he knew the meaning he wouldn't have had to write it.")

Müller was to call this *Hamletmachine* "the best production ever" of one of his plays, and in praising Wilson's work he made repeated reference to its "lightness," a curious encomium that becomes fully comprehensible only when one takes into account the emotion-charged stagings his texts usually receive in Europe. Just as he disdains directorial interpretation, Müller sees no need to have the angry, despairing words of his play reinforced by the actors or freighted with their psychological insights. Bernard Shaw once said that if the actors would pronounce his words properly, he would guarantee the results, and this precept might serve Müller equally well. He trusts the text to speak for itself. Dismissing every theory of modern acting with a sweep of the hand, Müller told the student actors, "Just read it as if it didn't matter." As with *CIVIL warS* Wilson urged on the cast a cool, flat manner of delivery ("too expressive" was a criticism they were to hear again and again). Since working with Müller, the director has spoken increasingly about the relative values of *hot* and *cold* in the theatre. He describes the playwright's texts as "very hot emotionally" and says that he prefers to present them in a cool objective manner, with the distance and formality that characterize his own work. Wilson believes that this seemingly contradictory mode of presentation enhances rather than diminishes their impact: "When you've got a hot text and you want it to be really hot, you have to be very cold. If you perform it in a hot way, what you're going to get is . . . nothing." Müller concurs, offering as an example the scene in *the CIVIL warS* where Frederick, after playing with a favorite dog, takes out a pistol and shoots it in the head: "It was a scene of terror in Cologne but not in Cambridge. The theatre is Cologne is much larger so you get more distance. You don't believe it close up but you do fifty meters away. Because it's colder, the terror is much more convincing."

Müller has probably exerted as much influence on Wilson as anyone in his career, and the kinship the artist feels with him is readily understandable. In Müller he finds not a political dramatist but a fellow poet, attuned to rhythms, intonation, nuance and color, who works in a similarly intuitive manner (though the playwright doubtless has conceptual reasons for everything he does, even if he doesn't care to share them—"Too boring" would probably be his explanation). To someone as isolated by success and scheduling as Wilson, the collaboration also offers friendship, a vital bond with someone he recognizes as a peer (i.e., genius) which can be accommodated within his work—virtually the only kind of friendship his life allows. Wiens has rightly observed that Wilson "is always curious about things he doesn't know about" and in Müller he has found a savant and guide (not unlike Edwin Denby, who died around the time their collaboration began) who will never dismiss his questions as stupid or irrelevant and will always have stimulating answers. Ann-Christin Rommen, who also assisted Wilson on *Alcestis* and *Hamletmachine*, offers a number of insights into their relationship: "Heiner has this great reputation but when you meet him he's very simple and friendly and has a very gentle manner. He's very respectful with other people's thoughts, he never gives you the feeling that he knows more than you do. He sits and watches and when he talks or proposes something he's always very quiet—and Bob needs that, someone who doesn't disturb him in seeing and listening. He's also very deep. You ask him anything and he tells you something about it. He's really a scholar and I think Bob is very attracted to scholars who are giving their knowledge away. Heiner also thinks of Bob as somehow a genius. And they both deal in fantasies. Bob can draw them and Heiner can write them."

The hold that Robert Wilson and his theatre have on the German playwright is even more fascinating, as it seems to touch on subtler, deeper impulses. Müller has gone so far as to call Wilson's the only truly communistic theatre. He is not, of course, speaking in terms of doctrine—which he has long passed beyond—but of affinities. In addition to its drawing performers from the ordinary public, thus meeting the conditions set by Marx and Brecht for true socialist art, there is the work's integration into everyday life: "The way Chinese theatre was in the past with people going in and out, eating and drinking for twelve hours a day, is the way of Bob's performances. It doesn't matter if you go out and have some food and come back in. It's a very relaxed way of reception." The playwright could also point to the highly collaborative nature of the work, its universal egalitarian spirit (animals, plants and stones have no less meaningful a place on his stage than humankind), and its rejection of private ownership: neither text nor images are the possession of any individual (not even their authors), they are the common property of the audience to make use of as they will. Müller likes to say that the dead far outnumber the living and one must write for a majority; and again his view is mirrored in Wilson's theatre, where the dead are liberated from history and transported into the timeless present (hence Müller's phrase "the theatre of resurrection"). Finally, there is the promise Wilson's works hold of a new age beyond the cataclysms to come—the hidden face of their shared apocalyptic vision (*the CIVIL warS*, *KA MOUNTAIN* and *The $ Value of Man* all end with a metaphoric return to Eden). Müller describes his utopian ideal as "a society where there's no need for politics or ideologies anymore" and in Wilson's theatre he finds the artwork of that uncertain future. As he wrote in his 1984 telegram, "When panthers walk between the counters of the World Bank and eagles in their soaring flight tear to pieces the flags that separate us, the theatre of resurrection will have found its stage."

Müller, who has traveled through the Southwest and Mexico, often speaks of his fascination for the vastness of America, and quite possibly he finds in the vistas of Wilson's theatre a complementary expanse of space and possibility. These open landscapes may also offer a theatrical escape from the constricted, overdeveloped, divided topography of Germany (which finds its scenographic equivalent in the *Raum,* the boxed-in scenic enclosure so often seen on the German stage during the past decade) and even a way out of the dead end of the European literary tradition. Müller has said he doesn't know where their collaboration will lead or what it will produce, and perhaps that is its greatest appeal. Like the new world, Wilson's theatre offers the promise of the unknown, untapped energy, a certain amount of adventure and, of course, space.

When asked in what way he thinks of Wilson's work as specifically American, Müller immediately replies, "The primacy of design and images. My negative experience of that is Walt Disney's *Fantasia,* good music and good orchestras and the stupid images. The children who see this movie will never be able to hear this music without seeing those images. That is for me the horror of the American experience, the colonization of fantasy by images and the production of clichés that zap your brains out. And Bob's theatre is the positive aspect of this power of images." At the same time Müller observes that "the kind of fame he gets now is something like a Three Penny Wagner and there is a danger in that, if he becomes popular in a cheap way. When Bob's theatre is popular, it's getting near to kitsch and that's a danger." He feels, however, that Wilson has shown an increasing awareness of this and is resisting the fall into empty beauty: "With Bob himself, he felt at times it was too nice. He was afraid of being too nice." (Since working with Müller, Wilson has even spoken disparagingly of his "pretty pictures," something almost inconceivable a few years before.) When asked if he finds the hypnotic Wagnerian element in Wilson's work and the passive, even rhapsodic response it can evoke at all problematic, he replies: "I think that's okay but there should be some edges to it. It shouldn't lose its edges. And it won't now, I'm quite sure because Bob's very interested in the edges. What is also necessary now, I think, is the confrontation of this power of images with history and the European experience. You can see the Cologne *CIVIL warS* as a coming together of the American subconscious and the German subconscious. It's an interesting explosion and we're just at the beginning." It must be said that this "explosion" is viewed with misgivings by a number of Wilson's coworkers who find Müller's dramaturgy incompatible with the artist's imagistic theatre (some see the collaboration as a kind of Frankensteinian brain transfer by which the monster has acquired a mind without having to think). It is unlikely, however, that Müller would find these criticisms troubling. When discussing their work together he speaks of differences and collisions rather than shared values or common goals, taking us back to our point of origin—the oppositional nature of their union: "The first thing in our collaboration was that there was Bob's frame, which is sometimes in danger of becoming a hollow frame—just design. And then there is my material, my texts resisting this frame, and there's a conflict between images and language and this conflict is drama. And so our collaboration can change my idea of theatre and his ideas too. There's a drama here and it's not finished."

Hamletmachine. NYU, 1986. "Photograph of the author."

ANNETTE MICHELSON

The converted factory building where Annette Michelson lives in lower Manhattan gives an indication of the close community that existed in SoHo in the late 1960s and '70s when Robert Wilson was making a name for himself. Directly across the street is the loft of another major theatre artist, Richard Foreman; next door is the Paula Cooper Gallery, where Wilson has exhibited his drawings for the last ten years; and a few blocks to the south is the gray cast-iron structure at 147 Spring Street that was for many years the home of the Byrd Hoffman Foundation. Michelson, a professor of film at New York University and the co-editor of the magazine *October,* has been a close observer of the avant-garde renaissance that had its genesis in the surrounding industrial buildings and warehouses. Her interest in Wilson's work dates from 1970, when she saw *The Life and Times of Sigmund Freud* at the Brooklyn Academy of Music, a production praised in the *Village Voice* by Richard Foreman, whom she has long admired and championed. "For a very long time in my life I took more than a casual interest in the theatre. I had worked in the theatre and I had been witness to a considerable theatrical renaissance beginning in the 1950s in Paris, where I had followed very closely the work of Genet and Beckett. Coming back to this country, I found my interests shifted very quickly from theatre to film and performance, the theatre here being what it is, and I pretty much abandoned the notion of any kind of interesting work being done, except in the the the theatre of Richard Foreman. So when I went to *Sigmund Freud* I saw for the first time a theatrical work that engaged me in some of the same ways as Foreman's. Here were two people in the process of redefining the categories and coordinates of theatrical spectacle, that is to say they were involved in a radical redefinition of spatial and temporal modes of performance and the relationship of text to gesture. They also seemed to me particularly interesting to look at together, though I know how artists themselves detest this. What's always interested me is the way Bob, in a sense, works out of a vision of abundance and Foreman within a vision of, not scarcity but extreme economy."

Michelson was first introduced to Wilson in the early seventies by Bénédicte Pesle, an old friend who was later to become the director's European representative. While she continued to follow Wilson's career throughout the decade, the prospect of contributing to one of his productions never occurred to her. "It started with a phone call from Bob in December of 1980. He said, 'I want to hire you. I'm supposed to do a production of *Parsifal* for the Kassel State Opera and I'm scared and I want to hire you as my dramaturg.' And I said, 'Don't be silly. Come and have a drink one day and we'll talk about it.' Why me? For one thing he knows me and knows I'm very sympathetic to his work. He knew I had been to Bayreuth in 1978 for the centennial *Ring*, which was in many ways one of the supreme experiences of my life. He knew, largely from Bénédicte, that I'd lived with music all my life and was extremely interested in Wagner. We live in a milieu here in which musical experience is primarily concentrated on rock and its derivatives; there simply aren't many people within his circle who spend a great deal of time thinking about Bach, Wagner or Boulez and I guess he knew that I did. Bob came over and we talked and it became clear that he was truly in need of someone with whom to develop this project, because it wasn't just his first entry into traditional opera; he was making contact with a whole musical tradition. There was also the shadow of Wagner and Bayreuth. If I can put this as nicely as possible, he needed a guide. He needed someone to help him enter that world and that tradition. He needed a teacher." Wilson, of course, is keenly aware of his limited knowledge of literature and history and has always had people around him to advise, counsel and otherwise put their learning at the service of his imagination. While preparing *D D & D* at the Schaubühne the previous year he had worked with a dramaturg for the first time and perhaps Wilson realized that he again needed the services of such a scholar-critic. Although Michelson had never acted in such a capacity, she accepted his invitation for a number of reasons. "I sensed immediately that he genuinely needed me and I realized that it would give me a chance to renew my acquaintance with *Parsifal* and that having to think about it in an organized way would be interesting. Finally I thought it would be a terrific opportunity to observe the way a major artist of our time works."

While the Kassel production was to be his first attempt at Wagnerian music drama, and one of his first stagings of an existing work, Wilson's exposure to Wagner actually dates back to his student travels of the mid-1960s when he spent a day in Bayreuth and saw Wieland Wagner's staging of *Tannhäuser* (which did not seem to make a great impression on him). A decade later he was introduced to Wolfgang Wagner and his mother Winifred in Spoleto at a performance of *A Letter for Queen Victoria*. After praising the beauty of the staging, they asked him if he would be interested in directing at Bayreuth, to which Wilson replied, "Well, possibly, but do

you ever do new works because I'm really interested in creating *new* works."
According to Wilson, Gian Carlo Menotti began kicking him under the table as the
Wagners replied, "No, no, we don't do new operas, Mr. Wilson. We only do Wagner."
Although critics were already drawing comparisons between Wagnerian *Gesamt-
kunstwerk* and Wilson's own fusion of dance, music and spectacle, the possibility of
directing a Wagner opera was not something he seriously considered until late in 1979
when he once again met with Wolfgang Wagner, who invited him to come to the
Bayreuth Festival as a guest the following summer. That August Wilson attended the
celebrated Cheréau-Boulez *Ring* (sitting through two complete cycles) as well as
performances of *Lohengrin, Der Fliegende Holländer* and *Parsifal,* which he saw for
the first time. (Wilson apparently came in contact with the story elements of the opera
as early as 1978 when Maita di Niscemi sent him a synopsis of the original legend and
an article on Monsalvat in connection with her research on Rudolf Hess, whom Karl
Haushofer's son had referred to as "the motorized Parsifal," a fool-redeemer out to
save mankind in his airplane.) He toured the backstage area of the theatre, met with
Pierre Boulez, and had preliminary conversations with Wolfgang Wagner and his
wife (who acted as interpreter) about producing the centennial *Parsifal* in 1982 or
possibly a *Tristan* later in the decade, though no formal offer was made. (While
Wagner's final opera seems ideally suited to his own theatrical preoccupations and
temperament, Wilson was much more interested in doing *Tristan,* which he envisioned as a project for Jessye Norman.) The following month he met with Giancarlo
de Monaco, the controversial director of the Kassel State Opera, who proposed that
the artist's first operatic production be under his theatre's auspices. Wilson told him
that he was only interested in the two Wagner works; as a director had already been
engaged for an upcoming production of *Tristan,* they settled on *Parsifal.* Immediately Wilson set to work filling the pages of his journal with ideas and comments
relating to the opera. One of those entries was a note to meet with Annette Michelson.

Having agreed to work together on a concept for the production, Wilson and
Michelson arranged to hold regular weekly meetings, though the artist was in the
middle of several other projects, among them an early version of *Medea* for Kennedy
Center and a video adaptation of the murder scene from *Deafman Glance.* Michelson
remembers visiting Wilson's loft on one occasion and being shown his work schedule
for the next five years. "I found this an absolutely fascinating document. It was rather
like a musical score in that it was contrapuntal with many different representations of
linear development. It was an extraordinary demonstration of the way Bob can
simultaneously keep unrelated projects in his head. Painters can do this and it may be
that Bob's extremely painterly approach to spectacle equips him to work this way."

The first five or six weeks of their work together were largely pedagogical in
nature. "I was to initiate Bob into this work but to do that I had to initiate him into
Wagner's method of composition and the structure of Wagner's work in general. That

also meant doing something I had not anticipated, initiating him into some of the basic principles of music, because it became evident that Bob was not what we call musically literate. At our second or third meeting he asked me with a certain charm and candor to explain the difference between a baritone and a bass. Essentially, our work involved a very close reading and analysis of this text, both musical and dramatic. Bob presents himself as someone who doesn't spend a great deal of time reading so we worked act by act toward a basic comprehension of the structure. I also suggested to him that this was not an isolated text, that there were allusive threads to tie it to other works in the Wagnerian canon. Lohengrin, for example, presents himself as the son of Parsifal and in an early version of *Tristan* Parsifal encountered the dying knight during his travels. [Wilson says that at one point they even talked about presenting *Tristan* and *Parsifal* together as one work.] We used the Boulez recording, which I think is the most beautiful and translucent, and particularly interesting for someone like Bob because the extreme clarity of Boulez's interpretation makes it easy to hear the layered composition of the opera. I found that it's difficult to convey the full power and complexity of Wagner's musical structure to someone who has little musical education. In order to make clear that a leitmotif is more than a calling card for a character you have to show the way they are used to construct a musical fabric and that's not so easy on any kind of grand scale. There was perhaps a greater concentration on the libretto than on the score. I don't know how Bob hears musically, I'm not quite sure what he hears."

While Wilson was making his way through the opera with Michelson, other people were supplying him with historical and visual materials. From Kassel came photos of past productions, programs, clippings and pictures of monumental architecture (Masonic temples, medieval cathedrals, public buildings of the Third Reich). Wilson hired Ann Wilson to provide additional visual research, character précis and an elaborate scene-by-scene analysis suggesting images, themes, colors and references to other works of art (much as she had for *KA MOUNTAIN*). They studied the designs of Wagner's original Bayreuth staging, the drawings of Adolphe Appia and Wieland Wagner's famous postwar production to learn what other directors and designers had done with the opera. From time to time Wilson would take pieces of this research to Michelson, who would express her opinion or even tell him that "now was not the time to think about it. Perhaps when we get a conception." That search for a theatrical concept marked the second phase of their work together, and for Michelson it offered the real dramaturgical challenge of the collaboration: "Here's the score and here's the text. Here's the work. Now what are we going to do with it?"

That process of discovery and development had actually begun several months earlier in Wilson's journal. There he registered his first intuitive thoughts about the opera and created a series of preliminary sketches. His first entry on September 27, in which he considers putting the singers "on the side of the stage with pictures in the background" (it may be that he thought the physical exertion involved in operatic singing was antithetical to his style of acting), was followed by such brief thoughts as "maybe forest on tracks," "various activities in forest," and "stage in layers," and a quotation from Thomas Mann's essay on Wagner that someone must have shown him: "It is a work full of sounds which linger in our consciousness in constantly disquieting curiosity and enchantment." In late October Wilson produced his first sketch: a lake framed by two large cliffs with an enormous swan falling through the sky.

The scene shows how Wilson recycles or reformulates imagery and folds certain images over from production to production until he has found a place for them. The use of two huge rocks as a framing device had its origin in the red desert scene of *D D & D* from the previous year, and though the design shown above was soon discarded, the basic configuration found its way into Act II, c of *the CIVIL warS*, in which a small boat is seen simultaneously carrying a giraffe to China in the fourteenth century and Admiral Perry to Japan in the nineteenth century. Wilson's next sketch for the opening scene consisted of a hill with a lake behind it, an enormous tree and an empty expanse of sky.

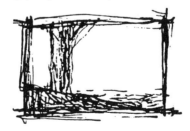

The design, which adheres to Wagner's basic scenic instructions, is traditional enough to suggest a prewar Bayreuth setting. (Michelson recalls that Pierre Boulez asked Wilson at their first meeting, "What kind of *Parsifal* do you want to do? Do you have some new approach?" and having no specific ideas at that time, he answered, "I guess I want to do a traditional *Parsifal*.") Other images that went through his mind at this time included a panorama of moving clouds, a curtain of light to facilitate scenery changes (this was eventually incorporated into the design), a temple floating in water and a landscape of icebergs, possibly meant for the transition scene in the first act.

This drawing bears a remarkable resemblance to a sketch Wilson had made for *Great Day in the Morning* about ten months before, and though both scenes were deleted early on, the image of an iceberg would eventually find a place in *Parsifal*. If there was a single visual motif running through Wilson's first sketches and ideas, it was water. The forest lake, which is only glimpsed at the back of the stage in Wagner's scenic directions and omitted entirely from most contemporary productions, had seized Wilson's imagination (rather than the shadowy wood that traditionally dominates the opera's outer acts). "Bob immediately had an idea which was opaque to me for about five minutes. He said, 'Well, I want it to take place under water. I want the audience to be sort of under water from the time the curtain goes up.' I had no idea what he meant until I remembered he lives in a loft on Vestry Street facing the Hudson River and when he looks out the window he sees the water. It seemed to me that the notion of the healing bath had somehow become associated in his mind with this expanse of water. The first thing Bob wanted the audience to see was a curtain of water because that's the first thing he sees when he wakes up." Ann Wilson recalls that the artist spent countless hours listening to *Parsifal* in his loft, during which time he would have seen the expanse of water outside his windows under changing conditions of light and weather—at sunrise, by moonlight, in the brilliance of noonday and in mist—a great reflective surface undergoing continual transformation, much like Wagner's music. It is likely that the music of *Parsifal* and this landscape of moving water became entwined in his imagination, and at some point he decided the audience should experience the opera as he had experienced it from his window.

Although his scenic realization of the opera's prelude was not to be finalized for several months, its elements were already taking shape in his mind. The audience would enter the theatre to find a luminous curtain, made up of vertical beams of light.

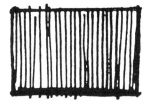

A wall of water appears in the background, with ripples of light which cross the vertical beams.

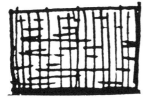 

As the curtain of light dissolves, the expanse of water begins to recede, creating first a horizon line, then an empty sky and the edge of a lake where Gurnemanz is seen saying his morning prayer. Ann Wilson recalls that Wilson originally wanted to create a huge wave out of scrim which would slowly sweep over the heads of the audience during the prelude, enveloping them in the watery world of the opera as he then envisioned it, but the restrictions imposed by traditional theatre architecture made him reconsider.

In addition to this great lake on and around which the drama would take place, Wilson brought Michelson at least two other images from his journals. The first of these impressed her as "brilliant and totally Wilsonian. There's a long monologue in the first act just before Parsifal kills a swan and Bob's idea was to have a very large swan falling very, very slowly through the sky. It's ordinarily something that happens offstage or is produced unsatisfactorily."

His other early idea was for Klingsor's castle in Act II. "He wanted a tall structure rising out of the water in which Klingsor would appear. It might be the periscope of a submarine. He wasn't sure what it would be. The basic image, however, was very clear in his mind."

What Wilson did not have at this point was an idea for the great temple where the knights of the Grail perform their eucharistic ceremony. This was to prove the chief stumbling block of the evolving production and the artist struggled with its realization as he had rarely struggled with any image or scene. Part of the problem lay in the work's intractable Christian doctrine and its troubling synthesis of religion and theatre. "*Parsifal* is a work toward which I have a great deal of ambivalence and I think Bob cannot but feel somewhat distanced from it. As a text it presents a complex of ideas that are difficult to deal with and for which few of us feel any tremendous affinity right now. In that sense it may be that *Parsifal* is a rather impossible work." Michelson recognized Wilson's need to secularize the opera and at the same time felt that it could never be fully secularized. "The work turns—and when I say turns, I mean there's a little pivot in the middle of the work—on Kundry's kiss and the kind of agonized guilt that it awakens. It seems to me that apart from the presence of the Mass, there's a whole Christian ethos of sex and guilt which can't be expunged. When Kundry talks about the source of her damnation she tells us she has been damned because she laughed at Him on the cross. How are you going to secularize that? The whole ethos of guilt and redemption is central to the work."

Perhaps this problem was not so insoluble for Wilson, who has always been more attuned to the sound of a word than its meaning and whose production was to be more of a response to the music and its resonances than to dramatic issues. Wilson did not consider it his responsibility to explicate the text in the manner of Chéreau or Syberberg or reconcile it to contemporary views but rather to create a physical space in which the audience could experience the opera's music and its mysteries. While scanning the research that had been assembled for him at the start of the project, he paused over an article describing Wagner's music as "opening the way to depths unilluminated by the word" and stopped to underline the phrase "one is moved beyond any explaining by meanings not yet understood." It was this sense of mystery, of the inexplicable and the wondrous, that Wilson sought to convey in his visuals, especially those for the temple of the Grail. His viewpoint was not so different from that of Wieland Wagner, who wrote at the time of the Bayreuth Festival's reopening in 1951 that a staging of *Parsifal* "requires mystical expression of a very complex state of the soul, rooted in the unreal and grasped only by intuition."

Although Wilson would eventually secularize and radically transform the iconography of the Grail (which could be secularized, unlike the text), his first sketch for the temple scenes was entirely conventional, a semicircle of pillars which reflected both the traditional designs he had studied and the columnar arrangement he had recently devised for a workshop production of Euripides' *Medea*. After hastily discarding the idea of using columns from various periods of history, he envisioned each column having a crown of live flame. (At this time he also considered showing the moon in a different phase in each scene.) Next Wilson added a circular platform similar in shape to the refectory table seen in most productions of the opera. (Another variation on this basic scheme involved a square platform surrounded by pillars which descended to allow the audience an unobstructed view of the Grail ceremony.)

After Michelson entered the project, Wilson also played around briefly with a number of cruciform platforms and even a pyramid, which had figured in such works as *Deafman Glance, Overture* and *The Life and Times of Joseph Stalin.*

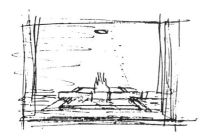 

At some point Wilson realized that creating an impressive setting for the Grail scenes would not be enough; the real problem lay in the eucharistic ceremony itself. Michelson feels that "Wagner's fabrication of a kind of religious order, bastard invention though it may be, is nevertheless grounded in something very Catholic." The obligation to present a theatricalized Mass, complete with glowing chalice and kneeling knights, made Wilson uneasy. "The most complicated problem to solve," he now says, "was how to present a work that's very religious with a sincere religious attitude. It never seemed right to me to have this fake church service with these knights standing around singing and passing this holy Grail. It was somehow sacrilegious, everything the work was supposed not to be. When I listen to the music here in my loft it's a religious experience but when I go to the theatre and see this temple-church-whatever and these klutzy knights walking around with this cup, it's ridiculous, it's disturbing and it's all wrong." Wilson wanted the audience to experience the Grail as the boy Parsifal first experiences it — not as a Christian ritual but as an intense and unfathomable mystery.

In time Wilson was drawn back to the image of the floating disc, adding at one point a small iceberg (or castle) that rose from the lake into the sky.

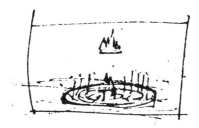

He showed his designs for this floating disc—which would increasingly come to dominate the production—to Michelson, who told him she thought he was "to some extent consciously or unconsciously reproducing antecedent versions of *Parsifal*. I don't know if it was very helpful but I also told him about Bresson's film *The Grail (Launcelot du Lac)*. There are two things especially remarkable about it. One is the modesty of the production: the film is not about reconstituting the Middle Ages with studio resources, in fact almost every object you see in it is still an object of common use in France. Then there is an extraordinary scene in which a number of knights are walking and pass a small curve. If you're paying attention you realize that what you're seeing is a fragment of the perimeter of the Round Table. It's the only time you see the Round Table in the film. There's a magic about that metonymy, the use of a tiny part for the whole. Now, obviously, you can't do that on stage. I told Bob, 'You've got to find some way of doing the Round Table and dealing with the knights and that is the real problem of this production.'"

Although his own solution owed nothing to Bresson, Wilson would similarly discard the worn trappings of medieval pageantry and religious ceremony, freeing himself to create a new kind of theatrical magic—and one wholly his own. While he did not yet have that solution ("It took so long to get this scene right," he would later say) it would soon be synthesized from his past work, a few of the images he had already sketched in his journal and a suggestion made by Michelson.

During this time Wilson would bring images and ideas "he was thinking about but hadn't yet thought through" to Michelson, who was careful not to "question him too closely until he was ready for discussion," though it seemed to her that most of the artist's images did not need to be justified. While she took care not to impose her own concepts on him, Michelson felt that part of her function should be to introduce him to new materials and ideas. "I was very interested in the Boulez-Chéreau production of *Lulu* and I talked about that and showed him the Louise Brooks film, which he had never seen. Lulu is a kind of Parsifal, an unformed person. In the first act of Wagner's opera, the old man asks Parsifal who he is and where he comes from and his answer to all of this is 'Ich weiss nicht.' He knows nothing. Curiously, in the libretto of Berg's opera and I think in the original Wedekind play, Lulu is asked by the artist, 'Who are you?' 'Ich weiss nicht.' 'Where do you come from?' 'Ich weiss nicht.' There are people who are not knowing and achieve a kind of redemption while working for that knowledge. I was very interested in the relationship of these two characters." In the kind of coincidence one frequently finds in Wilson's life and work, the small boy in the kitchen scene of *D D & D* (who might be Rudolf Hess, "the motorized Parsifal") responds again and again to his mother's queries with the same words, "Ich weiss nicht." It is likely that this episode was based on an actual incident in which Wilson repeatedly asked Christopher Knowles "Who is Einstein?" and each time received the answer "I don't know." (Wilson has always associated Knowles with the unknowing Parsifal—an example of how the themes and concerns of Wagner's opera conjoin with those of his own work.)

While the Louise Brooks *Lulu* had no direct effect on his *Parsifal*, Wilson was deeply impressed by the film and Michelson felt certain that some aspect of it would eventually appear in his work (in fact, the young woman in *The Golden Windows*, which he created in Munich the following year, was modeled on Brooks'). "I also showed Bob some of the first films ever made. We looked at a very early version of *Parsifal* made by Edison's company, which was really of little use, and also several of Méliès' films, in particular one called *The Palace of the Arabian Nights* (*Le Palais des Mille et Une Nuits*, 1905), which is the transcription into cinema of the magician's spectacle, the figure of the magician being central to *Parsifal*." Wilson, who had already decided to set the Flower Maidens scene in an underwater garden, was fascinated by the film's two-dimensional scenery and magical transformations as well as its enchanted grottoes, fantastic plants, deep-sea vistas and Jules Verne spaceships. One wonders if he did not feel some special kinship with Georges Méliès, an artist who similarly reinvented nineteenth-century stagecraft and created a world of his own imagining. Wilson's design for the flower garden would eventually incorporate a number of scenic elements from these films, and at one point he even considered having Klingsor appear with his spear in an underwater spaceship, similar to the one seen in Méliès' *A Trip to the Moon*. (Although deleted from the final version of the opera, the same spaceship would reappear in *the CIVIL warS*.)

By now Michelson defined her job as "essentially thinking about the general shape and structure of the production, at the same time knowing that it was not mine to fashion. In a sense that's what was wonderful about it. I was free to have these very interesting ideas and then perhaps this master of stagecraft would make use of some of them. It was a little like having a fantasy realized without the labor." One of those ideas (or "possibilities" as she calls them) would have considerable impact on the final design. "I had seen the centennial *Ring* at Bayreuth, which was a post-Brechtian production. The dragon, for example, was a wonderful Godzilla-type creature on wheels moved about by little men in black suits, like Bunraku puppeteers. That was brilliant and charming and it sparked another thought in my mind. At the end of the 1978 *Ring* I stayed on a bit in Bayreuth and spent some time with Boulez, who had never visited the Wagner house and museum. One of the things on display there was a little etching of a nineteenth-century stage machine for the Rhine Maidens and I found it quite remarkable. To some extent what had happened in the trajectory between 1876 and 1976 was that stage machinery had moved from backstage to out front. That led me to think about modes of representation in the theatre and how they had changed. It seemed to me the really big change that had come about in that period was the invention of the cinema, another mode of representation. I showed a number of examples of machinery for the Rhine Maidens to Bob. I thought it might be interesting to somehow make use of not just Méliès' imagery but the actual stage mechanisms of that time, and of different modes of dramatic representation. In *Parsifal* you have a somewhat symmetrical structure. You have two worlds, a world of black magic and a world of the Grail. It seemed to me that these two worlds required two different registers: one could be of stage mechanics—that is, stage machinery at work—and the other could be that of light." (The structure of *Parsifal* is itself similar to the arrangement of mirrored scenes one finds in a Wilson opera: Wagner constructed two parallel episodes—each moving from the forest to the temple of the Grail—around a contrasting section set in Klingsor's realm.)

Though it is difficult to say if Wilson consciously set out to put Michelson's suggestion into operation, her concept of contrasting modes of theatrical representation was subtly incorporated into the design. While there was to be no visible stage machinery in Klingsor's domain, Act II would be characterized by nineteenth-century stage effects and the two-dimensional painted scenery he had seen in the films of Méliès, a contrast to the luminescence of the surrounding acts, at this point envisioned as the play of light on water. (In this sense Wilson seemed to bring together, if not exactly reconcile, the contrasting traditions of Old Bayreuth and New Bayreuth.)

Act II would begin like the prelude, with vertical beams of light and a curtain of water that descends to reveal the lake, now seen by moonlight. A riveted metal tower rises up out of the water, in a sense piercing this luminous realm, and a door opens revealing Klingsor and Kundry.

At the conclusion of their scene, the tower sinks beneath the lake and the action moves underwater for the flower garden scene.

The stage is filled with rocks, two-dimensional plants, and painted flowers which open and close in the manner of Méliès. "It's like Chinese flowers that open in the water," says Wilson. To further underscore the contrast between Klingsor's realm and the kingdom of the Grail, this scene is multicolored, while the outer acts are largely blue and bluish-gray. (Wilson's underwater garden was to reappear in a slightly different guise in his drawings for *the CIVIL warS*, where it would be seen through the window of Captain Nemo's Nautilus.) Another nineteenth-century element that Wilson incorporated into his *Parsifal* design at Michelson's suggestion was the swimming mechanism used to propel the Rhine Maidens in the first production of the *Ring*. While Michelson had the idea of making the apparatus visible at one point, possibly when Parsifal catches the spear and the magic garden is destroyed, Wilson is by nature an illusionist and preferred to keep the mechanism concealed. The effect he eventually devised for the collapse of the garden, however, was to illustrate Michelson's initial concept far more effectively than any sudden revelation of stage machinery. With the triumph of the Grail, the power of light would reassert itself; Klingsor's painted world would vanish not in a mechanical earthquake but in a burst of radiance. "At the end of the act," says Wilson, "Klingsor throws his spear at Parsifal. Here it's a rod of light. The scene is all back painted and at the moment Parsifal picks up the glowing rod, we turn on all the lights from behind and everything appears in cold black-and-white light like a skeleton. Parsifal takes the rod and draws the outline of the chalice in light." The scene then dissolves behind the curtain of light seen at the beginning of the act. Michelson remembers that while Wilson was interested in the oppositions of cinema versus stage representation and light versus stage machinery, he was most attracted to the idea of a world defined by "the irradiant, diaphanous play of light and the diffusion of luminous energy," and this was to prove a key to the realization of the Grail scenes.

At this time Wilson still envisioned the temple of the Grail as a large ring-shaped disc, perhaps silver colored, floating in the middle of the lake. (For the transformation scenes between the forest and the temple he had created a series of mountain ridges in the water across which Parsifal and Gurnemanz would travel; he considered having rocks rise out of the lake for them to walk on.) Then in mid-April, after nearly four months of struggle with the Grail image, he suddenly transformed the existing design in a manner so Wilsonian as to seem almost inevitable. The disc would be not a stationary platform floating in the lake but an apparition of sculptural light moving through the sky. There would be no great hall, no knights, no bread and wine, only Wagner's music and "a singing temple of light." Wilson could discard his design for the transformation scene (which was stylistically out of place anyway) since the appearance of the disc of light would itself be the transformation.

"The idea is to make this mysterious temple of light. It's as if one were to see this big ring of light floating out here in the middle of the Hudson. It's all about light." Wilson had found his solution. Not by illustrating the story but by creating a mystery that could exist almost independently within Wagner's own mystery, each magnifying and clarifying the other. By clearing the stage he also hoped to create space, not merely physical space but space in which to listen and experience authentically.

Although Wilson's disc of light (a literal illustration of Debussy's famous comment about the music of *Parsifal* being "lit from within") evolved in part from his earlier designs and his discussions with Michelson, its real origin is to be found in *Einstein on the Beach,* whose subject is in a sense the power and mystery of light. While the shape of the disc was anticipated in the ringlike spaceship that travels across the sky in the field scenes, for true correspondence one must look to the cold white bar of light that rises from the horizontal to the vertical in the final act of the opera, ascending slowly into the flies to Glass's shimmering organ accompaniment and a haunting, wordless melody. It is one of the most hypnotic and beautiful moments in twentieth-century theatre: the luminescent bar gradually escaping the atmosphere of earth, its ghostly white light suffusing the auditorium and incorporating the hushed audience into its mystery, then disappearing from sight, leaving behind an afterglow but no explanation. In creating his "temple of light," which was to be similarly constructed of Plexiglas and fluorescent light, Wilson was seeking another such encounter with the sublime and the unknown. Perhaps he even thought of *Parsifal* ("Here time becomes space") as somehow opening onto that Einsteinian universe.

As the glowing disc moves through the sky, a crystalline iceberg, illuminated from below, begins to cross the lake. (Icebergs also appear in *Stalin* and the German section of *the CIVIL warS*; like so many of Wilson's recurring images—spaceships, volcanoes, dinosaurs, planets, pyramids—they are objects that hold special fascination for children.) As the disc reaches the center of the sky, it tilts backward and slowly descends into the lake, completely surrounding the iceberg.

It is at this point that Amfortas appears. He walks onto the brilliant white disc and takes from the iceberg a gold Egyptian box. Inside is a clear glass chalice which he holds aloft. The process of secularization is now nearly complete; the spear that pierced Christ's side has become a rod of light and the holy Grail is transformed into a shining glass sculpture whose shape (two conical sections joined by an ovoid) is a mirror of the production itself. When Parsifal catches the spear in Act II, he does not make the sign of the cross but instead draws the shape of the chalice in the air in laser light. Christianity has given way to the religion of light.

Through all of this, Parsifal stands speechless and transfixed downstage, watching the luminous spectacle in the sky "the way the audience watches it. . . . At the end, Gurnemanz comes into the ring of light and asks Parsifal, 'What have you seen?' And there's just the light, the whiteness." This scene has a number of counterparts in Wilson's work, where time and time again we witness a boy dreamer observing a succession of magical visions, usually from a great height—the mute black child on the floating bench in *Deafman Glance*, the boy on the tower in *Einstein*, the little man in the tree in *the CIVIL warS*, the young Christopher Knowles flying through the air crying "Sky, sky!" in *Queen Victoria*. While the beholder in *Parsifal* is on the stage and the vision in the sky, the sense of encounter and revelation is the same. (The opening of *Deafman*, in which the black boy stands with his back to the audience watching the murder of the two innocents, struck dumb by the spectacle before him, provides a nearly identical scene of witness.) While studying the text of *Parsifal* with Michelson, Wilson must have been surprised to find that Wagner's holy fool shares many qualities with his own protagonists. Like Knowles and Raymond Andrews, Parsifal is a youth judged to be injured or deficient by the world—though these disabilities are also the source of a special knowledge. Like Freud, Einstein, Edison, Lincoln and even Stalin, he is someone seemingly ordinary who changes the world. Finally he is a passive figure, like nearly every performer in Wilson's theatre.

Wilson devised a striking variation on his flying ring of light for the final scene of the opera. The disc that appears in the sky is now black with hard white edges, reflecting Parsifal's appearance in black armor, the state of disuse into which the Grail has fallen in his absence and the death of the aged Titurel. Wilson also decided to bring on the knights for one brief moment as they demand that Amfortas perform his duty and unveil the Grail. He envisioned the male chorus suddenly rushing on stage in chain mail and forming a wall of bodies downstage. Parsifal now approaches the disc, which turns white the moment he steps on it.

Parsifal again takes the chalice from the iceberg and holds it aloft before leaving the stage. The iceberg disappears and fire rises in its place from the center of the disc. The end of the opera, from which all performers have been banished, is given over to Wagner's music (Wilson would like to have the sound of the chorus coming from around the auditorium) and a spectacular display of light drawn from the artist's most cherished effects.

Fire. Moon. Stars. Light. By eliminating the potentially clumsy human element from this scene, Wilson returns Wagner's music to the realm of pure radiance from which it emanates. There is nothing to stand between the miracle of the Grail and the audience's experience of it.

About the time he was completing his revised designs for the Grail scene, Wilson added a number of scenic effects to the final act, some of which refer back to his earlier works. When he was in Munich he happened to see an article on Loch Ness monsters — "just thought of the lake and these ancient sea creatures" — and decided to incorporate the mythic creature into the opera before the entrance of Parsifal. (As Ann Wilson explains, "Practically every one of Bob's works has a monster in it.")

Wilson's design for the Good Friday scene again reveals his predilection for mirror imagery and reinforces the opera's symmetrical structure. In the absence of a meadow, he created an enormous tulip that falls slowly from the sky into the lake, mirroring the descent of the swan in the first scene. Michelson liked the correspondence but wondered if "it would work as a sign for the audience."

Wilson also found a picture of a man frozen in a block of ice and decided this was how Titurel should appear in the final scene. Rather than being carried on in a coffin as Wagner specified, the body of Titurel would float across the lake, entombed in glistening ice. The image has antecedents in *Deafman*, where the Pope was carried across the stage in a frosted glass coffin, and *Einstein*, where two time travelers moved through space in Plexiglas boxes.

Though Wilson spoke with Michelson about some aspects of characterization, his approach to character was almost entirely visual: Parsifal would appear in a simple white robe; Amfortas would be entirely covered with dots of blood (an image taken from a religious drawing he had seen); Gurnemanz would be a bearded old man "like Moses" or the bent pasteboard figures that lined the path to Ka Mountain back in 1972; Klingsor would look somewhat like Eisenstein's Ivan the Terrible ("Only not so terrible"), a figure who had previously appeared in *Stalin*. It is only natural that Wilson conceived the characters in this manner since the performers in his works—though given a specific physical attribute or appearance—have always been allowed to retain their own personalities. "I can only tell you that it won't be psychological acting," he says. "It will be the opposite of what Chéreau did with the *Ring*. I never understood why they called that naturalistic acting. It's the most artificial way of behaving on stage that I've ever seen in my life." "He thought that Chéreau's *Ring* was too busy," says Michelson. "Bob didn't want too much motion on the stage. You know, there's a curious way in which the rhythms and pacing of Bob's work are fairly consonant with the ritualistic manner in which *Parsifal* is usually presented. One could almost say that his staging fits into a traditionalist approach to the opera."

The shape and design of *Parsifal* were now clear in Wilson's mind. A scale model had been constructed and costume plates were nearing completion. In June of 1981, however, barely three months before the scheduled premiere, Wilson's contract with the Kassel State Opera was suddenly terminated by Giancarlo del Monaco, who charged the artist with unprofessional behavior and failing to submit working drawings on time. Wilson denounced the action as "immoral and illegal," and charges and countercharges flew back and forth in the ensuing weeks. Perhaps del Monaco sensed that the production was beyond Kassel's resources and technical abilities and decided to cancel while there was still time to mount another opera for the opening of the fall season (ironically, the disc of light which had given Wilson so much trouble became a major object of contention, the theatre claiming that they would have had to tear out a wall to realize the design). The resulting lawsuit was settled in arbitration court a few years later with Kassel withdrawing their charges and Wilson agreeing to drop all claims against the theatre. While he has had discussions with other companies about staging the opera, among them La Scala, Bayreuth, the Lyon Opera and most recently the Hamburg Staatsoper, the production has yet to be realized. Nearly ten years after it was conceived, this *Parsifal* continues to occupy Wilson's thoughts and fitfully inhabit his imagination; he has made countless graphite studies of its imagery as well as a series of lithographs, and tiny storyboard sketches still fill page after page in his journals.

The imagery of *Parsifal* and the materials Wilson studied during its development were to weave in and out of subsequent works and will doubtless continue to make their presence felt. *Great Day in the Morning,* the evening of Negro spirituals he created with Jessye Norman in 1982, was drawn from the same body of images— lake, moon, flowers, fire—and shared in its "sincere religious attitude." (The holy forest which he had omitted from his *Parsifal* also found a place in this work.) A projection of the original Grail temple appeared in *Curious George,* his 1979-80 collaboration with Christopher Knowles; Titurel's floating glass coffin was seen in *Alcestis* (1985), where it bore the body of the Euripides heroine along a river to the underworld; the falling flower in the Good Friday scene reappeared as an enormous lily in *Le Martyre de Saint Sébastien* (1988). In the fall of 1987 Wilson also created a very different, nonoperatic treatment of the Parsifal legend with the playwright Tankred Dorst, and Christopher Knowles got his chance to play the fool-redeemer, the role with which the artist had always identified him. (By this time Wilson was creating paired productions—usually a play and an opera—on the same theme: a *Medea* based on Euripides and Charpentier's *Médée* in Lyon in 1984; Euripides' *Alcestis* and Gluck's *Alceste* in Stuttgart in 1986-7.) Finally, an upcoming collaboration with Philip Glass, *The Palace of the Arabian Nights,* was inspired by the Méliès film of the same name—another legacy of his exchange with Michelson. Wilson sometimes compares his body of work to a tree that puts out new branches yet remains the same tree and the analogy holds true even for *Parsifal.* In creating this production he has given up nothing of his own vision and iconography. "It's all one work," he says of his many creations. Wilson's *Parsifal* and *Parsifal's* Wilson.

DESIGN

Deafman Glance. "The Forest." 1971.

The Life and Times of Joseph Stalin. Act V, "The Temple." Brooklyn Academy of Music, 1973.

FRED KOLO

Fred Kolo brought to Wilson's work the traditions of perspective scene painting and the heritage of nineteenth-century spectacle. Kolo, who was to become the first of his scenic designers, met Wilson in 1967 shortly after the aspiring artist-performer moved into SoHo. "I don't remember how it happened exactly. It was the late sixties and you met people then. The city was like that. I liked Bob and his work was terrific. *Baby*, the first piece he did in his loft, was just brilliant. It was one of the best things I'd seen in New York up till that time but the audience was awful, they didn't know what to make of it. Then there was the piece at midnight at the Bleecker Street Cinema with dummies scattered through the audience. Totally entertaining in a lofty kind of way. At that time I was studying at Lester Polakov's Studio Forum of Stage Design and doing my primitive little sketches for class. Somehow Bob got interested in what I was doing and he came to me and talked about *The King of Spain.*"

Wilson has said that the setting for that piece, a large Victorian drawing room, came to him one day in Grailville, Ohio while he was building his outdoor sculpture "Poles": "It was all gray and musty and also I kept hearing drinking glasses and people; people like at a cocktail party and chairs moving. And the next thing I kept seeing were these enormous cat paws." While Wilson had great faith in his vision he didn't know how to realize it, and here Kolo's skills and knowledge proved invaluable.

"Basically Bob wanted a room with a slit cut out of it, a negative space in a positive space." Kolo created a single perspective scene, based in part on photos of Sigmund Freud's study. Its most prominent feature was a gap—a missing strip of wall that ran from floor to ceiling through which could be seen a distant field based on a Corot landscape, and a runner in red shorts who raced by at regular intervals. Many of the visual elements and activities in the production were taken from Wilson's previous pieces—mounds of hay, lighted candles, a row of oversized brass rings (which were suspended on a cable high over the heads of the audience and continually repositioned during the evening), people leaning against a wire, sitting or engaging in other simple acts. In fact, *The King of Spain* was much like the other performance pieces and happenings Wilson had presented in lofts, movie houses and at outdoor sites during the previous few years, only this time the action was placed on a proscenium stage (that of the Anderson Theater, a dilapidated vaudeville house on Second Avenue which he rented for two nights) within an illusionistic setting—something wholly new to his work. It was really through Kolo that Wilson came to realize the potential of traditional painted decor and the magic-box stage, which together made possible the wondrous living pictures that were to be the basis of his art.

"So much of what I did was *trompe l'oeil* painting. Old-fashioned scene painting. Lester has a good school and he taught that kind of thing. There were things in *The King of Spain*—paintings on the wall, architectural details—that were convincingly three-dimensional. You don't see that in any of the photographs but there was a great quality of illusion. Everything had a certain presence and you kind of believed the painted detail. The trees in *Deafman Glance,* for example, really looked real within the conventions of painted scenery. I think one of the reasons why the look of those shows had a profound effect on people was that nobody had seen anything like it on stage for eighty years or something. No one then was doing true illusionistic painted scenery. It was new by being very old." To understand the impact of these magic pictures one must also consider the "poor theatre" aesthetic of the times, embraced by such companies as the Open Theatre, Performance Group, Manhattan Project and Living Theatre, which rejected scenic spectacle and illusionistic effects outright. (Wilson himself often talks about a retrospective exhibition he saw at the Whitney Museum in the late 1960s called "Art against Illusion" and how his theatre seemed to fly against the prevailing spirit of the decade.)

While Wilson's early works were rich in scenic detail, they were realized with extremely limited resources, and it was again Kolo's skills—and his initial willing-ness to work for little or no pay—that made this possible. "There was no money in the beginning but canvas and paint weren't very expensive. You got a drop sewn up for a hundred and fifty dollars and then went and painted it. Maybe it was another fifty dollars for a day in the shop. In Pittsburgh I designed six big musicals over a summer for the Civic Light Opera, one a week, and I learned there how to make a drop count. The furniture was mostly found on the street but then I painted everything to tie it all together. Props were made at Bob's loft. Everyone chipped in and built things—there was a real commitment at that time. I personally painted every stitch of scenery through *Deafman.* The shows looked great but they didn't look slick. There was a certain homemade quality about them. It was an interesting combination of the rudimentary and some very sophisticated techniques."

The King of Spain also introduced the first of the spectacular visual effects for which Wilson would become known: the appearance just before the final curtain of a

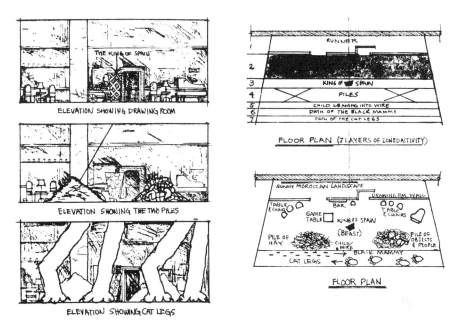

The King of Spain. 1969.

cat so enormous that only its legs could be seen. No one could initially figure out how to rig and animate such a huge object and many of those around him urged the director to forget the whole notion (Kolo, preoccupied with the design of the setting, chose to stay out of the matter entirely). But Wilson refused to surrender his vision. He went out and purchased a hundred feet of imitation fur and some giant slinkies to shape the towering legs, and eventually found someone to construct a system of pulleys and ropes that could be manipulated from the wings. The legs descended into the painted salon on cue and then moved majestically if somewhat unsteadily across the stage, their passage virtually unnoticed by those in the room.

In *The King of Spain* Wilson also divided the performing area into lateral zones for the first time. Each of these horizontal pathways, about seven in all, represented its own distinct time zone and moment-to-moment reality. By slowly filling the parallel paths with unrelated images and activities, Wilson created an everchanging three-dimensional collage, establishing a preference for horizontal movement and independent visual layers that continues to this day.

The settings Kolo created for Wilson might best be characterized as dream environments, magical spaces in which anything could and usually did happen. Such designs are not unlike one of those cardboard panoramas treasured by generations of children in which windows and doors open onto unexpected vistas, figures pop up, and flaps and tabs pull out or turn over to reveal further surprises. In *Deafman*

Glance, Wilson's richest work of this period, we are presented with a visual environment continually in the process of transforming itself. The curtain rises on a simple forest scene in which virtually every inanimate object comes to life: a little girl rises from a mound of earth piled on the floor by some workmen a few moments before; an amphibian creature slowly makes its way along a river of red linoleum; a gray rock nearby suddenly cracks open and a gossamer scarf escapes from its center; a small hut covered with skulls and antlers catches fire and collapses upon itself while a palm tree a few feet away grows to a great height; the moon rises and travels across the sky; an eye at the apex of a distant pyramid lights up and flies away; stars fall from the sky and smoke rises from the earth. The eye of the viewer had to keep moving over the stage to take in the action which might occur in any zone at any moment.

Unlike Wilson's current designers, Kolo says he never worked from the director's sketches, only from discussion and exchange. "I don't think Bob was any more specific in what he wanted than O'Neill or Shaw are in their scene descriptions. Basically I had to design something of my own. The process was not a very intellectual one. We kind of communicated in shorthand, we both had a sense of what something should be and reached agreements quickly. Bob is very responsive to good work." The imagery for these pieces came from every conceivable source — photographs, postcards, pictures Wilson found in art books, his dreams, the drawings of Raymond Andrews, suggestions from the company. One of the scenes in *Stalin* was even inspired by a drop Kolo had created for "The Street Where You Live" scene in *My Fair Lady* at the Pittsburgh Civic Light Opera. "Bob saw it and it set his mind going, that's the way things happen. You don't invent images, no one does. These things all came from somewhere. I don't believe in originality. I believe in absorption."

All of Wilson's early proscenium pieces were eventually incorporated into *The Life and Times of Joseph Stalin,* a twelve-hour, seven-act spectacular jointly designed by Kolo and his former teacher Lester Polakov. Wilson created three new acts for *Stalin,* drawing on the nonproscenium pieces the company had presented in the intervening years. Each of these was conceived as a kind of "mirror," reflecting the setting and spatial characteristics of an existing section of the work. An empty sand-covered planet in Act VII recalled the sand-strewn beach of Act I (instead of filling the stage with waltzing black mammies, Wilson now offered thirty dancing ostriches). The Victorian drawing room of Act II corresponded to the Victorian bedroom of Act VI (in Act II votive candles burned on a ledge on the left side of the stage, in Act VI a row of lanterns hung on the right-hand side). Act III was set in a cave, Act V in a subterranean chamber within a great pyramid (perhaps the one seen in the previous act). The mysterious forest of *Deafman* (Act IV) became the core of the cumulative work from which all other parts radiated outward.

The new entr'actes that divided the main sections of the opera provided further

Cave. *The Life and Times of Sigmund Freud*, Act III. Richard Foreman in the *Village Voice*: For me the last act was most powerful of all. Wild animals slowly enter a cave one by one and lie down in the straw. Beyond the mouth of the cave, in the sunlight, half-naked boys and girls run, exercise, and play. As the animals enter, iron bars slowly fall over the cave opening, separating animals from the world outside. Finally Freud enters, and sits at a little table amidst the resting wild beasts, and a small boy cries at his feet. This takes half an hour or so, and it is slow and gigantic and wonderful.

correspondences. A drop of a large Victorian house suggested an exterior view of the rooms of Acts II and VI; this great facade was seen twice during the opera, first with its windows bursting into flame as the carriage of Queen Victoria passed (an oblique reference to the burning house in *Deafman*), later boarded over and abandoned. A new drop for the murder scene pictured a vast wall of stones, the pyramid seen close up; the background for another entr'acte, a desert drop, reappeared in miniature on either side of the central doorway in the bedroom scene. This network of visual correspondences soon became the most basic organizing principle of Wilson's theatre.

Stalin also represented the zenith of Kolo's illusionistic stagecraft and he points with particular pride to the final scene with its craters and volcanoes and a vast sky in which appeared all manner of cosmic wonders, from a glowing nebula and a winged horse to a miniature Moscow in flames. "There was a black drop with tiny holes filled with clear vinyl for the starry sky and a platform above the burning city with a bride and groom on it. The illusion that the couple was floating in space was total. I had friends in my end of the business who asked, 'How did you do that?' The theatrical techniques we used were very primitive but they were dynamite."

The Life and Times of Joseph Stalin was followed by *A Letter for Queen Victoria*, their final collaboration. The production, which premiered at the Spoleto Festival in the summer of 1974, marked another turning point in Wilson's evolving scenography. "First of all, the designs were created for a tiny nineteenth-century theatre where no one is more than fifty or sixty feet away from the stage. You're working with a totally different space. *Trompe l'oeil* painted drops that may work in a large opera house don't work here." Wilson and Kolo began by thinking about corporate architecture and contemporary office design (in fact the ubiquitous "Victoria" chairs seen in the first act, with their heavy wooden beams and embedded headlights, were originally conceived as lounge chairs in the style of Mies van der Rohe) but later settled on a series of unadorned wall panels not unlike those of Edward Gordon Craig. Each setting was arranged on a raked floor transected by perspective lines or seams that merged into the walls as in a Renaissance or Baroque stage plan. Though in no way painterly, these sets were still to a degree illusionistic. "Everything was executed in perspective. The illusion was very subtle. Instead of painterly *trompe l'oeil* it was structural, architectural. Every scene was based on the floor in some way." The asymmetrical arrangement of scenery determined the movement patterns of the performers, which for the first time tended to be diagonal rather than horizontal. The use of color was also severely restricted, with most scenes painted shades of gray, a color to which the designer had always been drawn: "Bob really didn't want the set for *Victoria* covered with gray but I fought for it." (Kolo notes with some amusement that Wilson's subsequent productions—*Einstein, Patio* and *D D & D*—were almost entirely gray.) Despite this initial disagreement, Kolo feels that with *Queen Victoria* the two were still "very much at one" and he was "as influential in how that show looked as anything."

Kolo's design, however, was to undergo a major transformation after the Spoleto premiere, with many of the scenic elements (the raked floor and most of the structural walls) gradually disappearing as the company moved from city to city during the European tour. The spare, minimalistic settings that New York audiences saw the following year bore only passing resemblance to the intimate perspective pictures seen in Spoleto. The white stucco walls, red tile roof and blue sky of the final act, for example, had all been discarded, leaving only an enormous louver window, now set in a scenic void. "I didn't involve myself in the Broadway version because I didn't feel enough of the production was left," says Kolo, who was no longer credited as designer. While Wilson says these changes had more to do with logistical and budgetary considerations than aesthetics, the resulting designs pointed the way to *Einstein on the Beach* and the cool monochromatic elegance, severity of line and abstraction of what might be called his mature style.

"The end of our collaboration came when Bob asked me to work on *Einstein* but told me that he wanted to design it himself. I said, 'Well then you don't need me. If you want to design it you should design it, there's nothing for me to do.' Basically he came to me with a deal I could refuse and I refused it. We were good friends but there were always certain tensions in working together and in a way I feel my work was never properly credited. Now, as I understand it, he sees himself as designing his shows, he gets designers to execute his vision. I suppose the fundamental change in his work was to slowly take command of every element. He didn't do that in the early pieces. He was too swamped or he didn't realize his own power." Wilson's designs for *Einstein* (realized by the scenic artist Christina Giannini) were seen by many as breaking with the past. As Andrew Porter wrote in the *New Yorker,* in place of the "rich colors and textures and the visual elaboration of *Deafman Glance*" one now found "simple, largely geometrical scenes," a work "precisely organized, tautly patterned, economical in its sources and austere in its decor." Although the production came to be regarded as one of the great theatrical spectacles of the decade, Philip Glass has pointed out that "when *Einstein* was first seen there was general disappointment over how it looked. Bob chose grays, whites and blacks and it was considered a rather drab-appearing work, which is funny because no one speaks of it that way now. I remember people remarking how unspectacular they thought it looked in terms of Bob's *oeuvre*. Bob was experimenting with a very different sensibility." (Ann Wilson has observed that "like all artists, Bob went from romantic to classical.") This shift in Wilson's scenography can also be seen as a desire to be part of the art of his times, in particular the world of art that was all around him in SoHo. He had moved into that bustling artistic community during the heyday of minimalism, and many of the drops and sculptural elements in *Einstein* reflected that movement's seeming impersonality, repetitive structures and preoccupation with mathematical precision, though even at its most austere his work lacks the systematic rigor of true minimalism, for Wilson never embraced the tenets of the movement—nor was he really capable of doing so—only its stylistic motifs.

Kolo, who had some early discussions with Wilson about designing the production, visualized the settings of *Einstein* as "real places—something altogether more romantic and illusionistic," and when he finally saw the opera at the Met he felt "it was merely an indication of what it could have been." Stefan Brecht wrote that "the stage in *Einstein* has lost the depth Wilson gave it in his earlier pieces, and the stage sets are now just that—and stunning—instead of being, as earlier, mental environments." It was exactly this sense of atmosphere or "place" that Kolo found lacking in Wilson's sleek, artful compositions. "Now scenery is just what it is. Like the train in *Einstein,* there's no sense of a train, there's no magic, it's just a graphic thing." The designer is especially critical of the setting for *Patio,* perhaps the most consciously "artistic" of Wilson's creations in the 1970s: "It was a wonderful text but I thought the design work was appalling, it looked like a window at Bloomingdale's—chic and empty. Part of the richness of Bob's work was that nothing about it was abstract, nothing was just invented. It all had foundation in the real world and that's what gave it its impact. I think the work has become less interesting as it's become more abstract. *Victoria* was the turning point, though it was wonderfully accomplished originally. That was the beginning of Bob moving into something different." Wilson had set his sights on the contemporary art world while Kolo remained of the theatre. "I suspect," he says now, "we were headed in different directions from the very beginning."

Kolo, who has given up designing to pursue a career as a producer, continues to have strong feelings about what made Wilson's early productions so memorable. "I've always felt that Bob's brilliance at that time was very much as a director. It was the quality of the performing more than anything else that made those works riveting. There was a true sense of life and that's why those works were great. They weren't great because they looked a certain way—it was important to me that they did, but it's not what made them great." Wilson's current goal may be perfection in all elements but Kolo says that at the time the work had "to do with something much more specific and real, it had to do with people. There was nobody onstage doing anything false. Bob had a way of working with people that was very rigorous and totally got rid of their self-consciousness. He would take people off the street and find a way to make them astonishingly the same on stage. They all had such concentrated and focused energy. When I saw the revival of *Einstein* at BAM it looked as if it had been taught to a second-rate opera chorus, it had nothing to do with the performing qualities that made those early works so absorbing. There were great performers in those pieces— like Mary Peer. She was incredible, hilarious. You couldn't believe what that woman did. She'd sit at the piano and ramble on and then she'd lie on the floor and play the piano upside down and talk and talk and talk. Her performance was different every night, you never knew what she'd do. She was bizarre and totally wonderful. Andy de Groat's solos in *Stalin* brought down the house. It was as spectacular dancing as I've ever seen. People would continually walk onto that stage and take your breath away. There was also something very edgy about the early work. There were people who *hated* it because it had life. A lot of people don't like life on stage, they get uncomfortable.

"I think a lot of the change in Bob's work came from the critical response he got in Europe. Wilson's theatre came out of an American sensibility, out of his own roots. It didn't have anything to do with European avant-gardism or surrealism, that was a total misapprehension on the part of European critics. But when you're the talk of the town in Paris and you're not getting support at home it's hard to say, 'No, you're wrong, that's not what I'm doing.' I think he fell for what the Europeans were saying and the Europeanization of his work has made him less interesting. More and more Bob's been taken into an avant-garde aesthetic. That's not what the work was, it was not created to have an attitude of any sort. It didn't really refer to anything beyond itself. It had nothing to do with ideas or concepts, and it was in no way an intellectual puzzle, which is how the work has come to be seen. It was just about what was happening in front of you. Back then people were simply doing the work they were compelled to do. When you're forced into describing and explaining your work, you're forced into taking aesthetic positions. That's the horrible thing that's happening as a result of public funding. People are forced to verbalize what they're doing and then do what they've said. We did some wonderful things back then but they weren't a prescription for the theatre. I don't think anybody has been able to learn anything from them and when it's tried you end up with something as mannered as *Satyagraha*, which is just empty gestures. Bob's theatre didn't have anything to do with moving art ahead, it just was what it was. I don't look back on those times and that work as some kind of Shangri-La or Camelot. It was as valid and as interesting as anything being done in the theatre at the time. The theatre, of course, is ephemeral; it exists in the moment and Bob's work did extraordinarily exist in that moment. I don't know if it does now."

The final moments of *Deafman Glance*.

TOM KAMM

It was as a student at UC San Diego in the mid-1970s that Tom Kamm became aware of Robert Wilson's work. "I saw the spread in the *Village Voice* on *Einstein* and it sounded really interesting so I did some research to find out what else Wilson had done. At the time I was experimenting with combining sound and movement and design into some kind of imagistic theatre and it was fascinating to read accounts of someone who had matured in that work and gone so much further than I had. Five years later I was living in New York, working Off-Off Broadway as a designer and director, and I got a call from a friend who said Bob was looking for someone to help him design the video version of *Deafman Glance*. Like so many things in the theatre, it just happened. It's not something I pursued at all." Beginning in 1981 Kamm worked on a number of Wilson projects in rapid succession, realizing the scenic designs for not only *Deafman* but the television film *Stations, The Man in the Raincoat* (a one-man show presented at the Theater der Welt festival in Cologne) and finally the Dutch, Italian, Japanese and French segments of *the CIVIL warS*, which he would oversee as coordinating designer.

Unlike Fred Kolo, Kamm came to Wilson's work after the director's visual style and mode of presentation had been established and was initiated into an already existing scenography, one which requires a little more elaboration here. With few exceptions Wilson's theatre is the proscenium theatre, a predilection that for many years ran contrary to artists and directors of his generation. "I work in a form that's almost obsolete," he has said. "I work in a nineteenth-century tradition. I've never been afraid to use elements of the past. I like the formality and distance of a proscenium theatre. My work is usually conceived in terms of a two-dimensional space where one side is hidden. You don't see the ropes or the lights. [In stagecraft as in acting, he prefers that the labor not be visible.] I can't see in other kinds of spaces, my eye goes all around and I can't see the actor for someone scratching in the audience." When asked some years ago what kind of a structure he would erect if he had the money to build his own theatre Wilson immediately replied, "Oh, one just like Bayreuth. It's the best theatre. I don't know why more people haven't copied that house. It's fan-shaped for greater visibility and the orchestra is hidden—the musicians can be the most interesting people to watch so there isn't that distraction. And the sound just comes out at you." The Bayreuth Festspielhaus is the ultimate illusionistic theatre of the nineteenth century; and its submerged orchestra pit, unobstructed sight lines, enormous stage and recessed proscenium perfectly suit his aims, which are distance, focus and mystery.

Wilson's designs are conceived on a flat plane as simple line drawings and even in their final form retain something of their two-dimensional origins. "Bob is a pictorial artist more than a sculptural artist and there is this context in which everything exists: you have a black box with black wings and everything happens within this frame as it does in ballet. It's a picture within a frame. It's the same thing with the drawings he makes for galleries. He begins with a sheet of paper and masks each edge, then he makes his drawing and tears away the mask so there's a clean border and a very sharp edge to the picture. In a way, he does the same thing with the stage frame." (Fred Kolo, in contrast, looked upon the absence of decorative wings and borders as a deficiency necessitated by budgetary limitations. It may be that the sides of the stage do not really exist for Wilson since he rarely moves from his seat dead center in the orchestra.) "There are three basic things that Bob does. There's the back wall, the floor and then the elements within that. It's a very classical use of stage space. Very horizontal, integrated, lack of decoration. Wing and drop, very little departure from that."

While this arrangement resembles the traditional ballet stage, there is also a sense in which Wilson might be considered a landscape artist; many of his settings—like those for ballet—are open expanses or vistas. ("I was born in Texas," he has said. "So much space there. I think it's still in my head.") Since *The Spaceman* in 1975 Wilson has thought of stage space in terms of the three traditional ways of defining painting: portrait, still life and landscape. In *Einstein* the "knee plays," performed in a white rectangle at the front of the stage, were conceived as portraits; scenes on the main stage featuring static groupings and large sculptural elements as still lifes; and the dance episodes which occupied the full depth of the stage as landscapes. These terms have always been rather loosely applied, and landscape, which so often provides "the space for seeing" essential to Wilson's aesthetic, is perfectly capable of containing the other two.

Within the usually unbroken rectangle of the stage floor Wilson tends to place just a few carefully chosen scenic elements, among them the wood and metal furniture pieces that have figured in his work since *Queen Victoria* and reflect his early background in interior design. (These pieces can later be removed from their scenic

the CIVIL warS, Act I, b (Dutch section). TOM KAMM: Bob wanted bright colors for this section. It was like a picture postcard with a bright green groundcloth and bright red tulips, very different from what Bob usually does. It's the only scene that's designed naturalistically— cabbages, tulips, snow, wheat, winter skies—and that was something of a problem for the Dutch audience and the press who thought it was a stereotypical postcard view of Holland. It's the only scene in *the CIVIL warS* that has a horizon line, others just have bare floors with groundcloths. We built a long fluorescent light box behind the horizon with plexiglass cut to the angle of the landscape so that light reflected outward. There was also a fluorescent strip inside the tree intended to create a hard, focussed line of light, again to undercut the naturalism a bit. [The stretched-out cinemascope stage opening and spare disposition of scenic elements also brought the essentially nineteenth-century scene into the twentieth century.]

In a way the little house is one of the central characters in the piece. We watch it being taken apart scene by scene until at the end only the foundation is left. The bridge came from Breughel. We needed a way for the actors to cross the canal and yet they also had to skate along it so we devised this little drawbridge that went up and down. We played around a lot with scale. In fact, the Civil War soldier on the horizon can be seen as being as large as the big lady. There's also the little house with full-sized people next to it.

As in Wilson's early productions the stage is divided into lateral zones: downstage a thin strip of garden, covered first with snow (and then, as the seasons change in reverse, haystacks, cabbages and blood-red tulips), a narrow canal, a graceful slope and finally a gently contoured horizon against which a lone soldier slowly makes his way homeward.

context and displayed in museums or sold in galleries. A number of copies, sometimes constructed of more costly materials, are often made for such purposes.) Typically the space terminates in an open sky or a finely delineated, though essentially flat, painted drop. In recent years the artist has also employed blowups of his abstract graphite drawings, injecting a new element of spontaneity into his tightly controlled scenography. Most settings are characterized by a subdued use of color; as Kamm says, "It's not a highly chromatic palette. Mostly grays and natural woods."

Juxtaposition is an essential feature of Wilson's *mise en scène*. Placing a beer can next to a piece of pre-Columbian pottery, he once told an interviewer, "The two things are more interesting than just the one because they're so different. They're out of context, but they help you to see. My works are like that." While his stage pictures are frequently made up of contradictory images, Wilson will sometimes create a special zone or area at the front of the stage to contrast with what is happening on the main stage—the sand-strewn extension over the orchestra through which the chorus stuck their heads in *Stalin* or the "dead zone" in *Victoria* where he isolated a different object (a head of lettuce, a pile of cherries, a rock, a fish tank) in every act. Often Wilson places a small white rectangular platform near the proscenium to delineate a separate performance space, as in *Victoria*, his 1985 *Lear* workshop and *Médée* (where two women in modern dress contradicted the mythological scenes behind them). In recent years he has broken through the proscenium, constructing a runway out into the auditorium (similar to the *hanamichi* of Kabuki theatre) for the German section of *the CIVIL warS* and *Salome*, and a stunning multistage environment for *D D & D II*.

Wilson's imagery, like his texts and audio scores, aspires to the condition of music: motives and themes are introduced, return in different forms and undergo further modulations and metamorphoses. A large part of the pleasure of his theatre is in recognizing these reappearing forms. His is a theatre of transformation, like all spectacular theatre from the Jacobean masque to the popular entertainments of the nineteenth century (and even such twentieth-century works as Strindberg's *Dream Play*). In a sense this is the subject of *the CIVIL warS*, which chronicles the transformation of a single tree, which is felled and then becomes a log cabin, a boat that travels around the world, a book, a forest, and finally turns back into the lone tree seen at the beginning. Sometimes we witness the metamorphosis of a simple geometrical form such as the rake held by Hess in *D D & D*, which later becomes a cane, a glowing rod, a sword and a baton. In *the CIVIL warS* a series of triangles— always one of Wilson's favorite shapes—appears in numerous guises: a group of icebergs (I, a), a row of tents (III, e), enormous shark fins (III, a), sailboats floating over the ruins of Richmond (III, c), even the mosquito netting that covers the cots in a Civil War hospital (III, c). Transformation is, of course, also the basis of the parallel scenes and mirror images around which Wilson has organized most of his

Alcestis (1986). TOM KAMM: Bob was in Delphi the spring before we starting working on *Alcestis* and he was very taken with the surrounding mountain and the way it engulfed the landscape. So when he came back from Greece he knew he wanted to have a mountain running across the back of the stage. Rather than treating the stage as a two-dimensional space—which is what Bob most usually does—we ended up creating a three-dimensional environment, the entire back of the stage being a relief sculpture. Bob talked about wanting the set to be a mask and in a way it is since it's masking the open sky you usually see at the back of his stage. A number of objects from antiquity are embedded in the mountain. You can see the prow of a Viking ship on the left side and five Chinese terra cotta figures mirroring that on the right. There's also a big stone head at the top of the mountain that slowly rolls down a ridge. It reappears as a larger head and then at the bottom of the valley as this huge head. They're all done in scale so it looks like the stone is getting closer. Boulders also appear on the floor during blackouts—we start with a bare stage and by the end of the play it's littered with boulders.

In front of the mountain there are three cypress trees and in the course of the play they become three Corinthian columns and finally three smokestacks. It made me think of the passage of time suggested by the antiquities in the mountain. I carried the idea of these three

different epochs over to the stage floor — in front of the mountain there's a zone of dirt and grass corresponding to the trees, then stone and tile which suggests ancient paving, and at the very front of the stage a modern asphalt road with a dividing line down the center. Bob knew from our first meeting that he wanted a river to cut across the stage. It's actually a long trough filled with about a foot and a half of water. The stage was raked so the women of the chorus could walk across on their knees and it looked as though they were wading up to their waists. Death first appears on the river on stilts so he seems to be walking on its surface and later he leads the funeral procession of Alcestis, whose glass coffin floats along it.

On the left side of the stage is a huge black scrim box set at an angle to the main stage containing a giant Cycladic figure from pre-Greek antiquity. The idea was that if the stage were a book with the cover opened up, the main stage would be the body of the book and the inside cover would be this shadow stage which is meant to be the world of death. Embedded within the Cycladic figure is a actor wrapped like a mummy — in a sense he's the heart of the figure — who recites the text of the prologue (Heiner Müller's *Description of a Picture*).

The lighting in the play moves from sunup to sundown and the color is quite heightened, even romantic. The whole visual palette was much richer and warmer than Bob's pieces usually are. When Alcestis returns from the dead at the end of the play, a laser shoots out over the heads of the audience and starts tracing an eye in the mountain. Again, it's like a mask. The laser moves faster and faster until we see the shape of the eye break away from the mountain as though an eyelid is opening. Intense white light streams from the aperture and smoke starts filling the stage. Then the horizon turns red, the eye turns red, and the smokestacks glow and seem to crack from the inside.

The production ends with an epilogue based on the Kyogen play *The Birdcatcher in Hell* which is performed in the style of Japanese theatre. There's a white groundcloth downstage and a white curtain with a black hole in it cut in the shape of the big eye. The idea was that if you turned the stage around and looked at it from the other side this is what you'd see. Everything was intended to contrast with the main play; the lighting was flat, bright white and the costumes were rich and brightly colored — red, blue, green, yellow.

works since *Stalin*. Very often this transformation involves a shift of perspective; in *Edison* we are shown different views of a white clapboard house (the structure of the piece is also that of a house: two "exterior" acts surrounding an "interior" act); in *Medea* four columns stand before a small building and as the structure grows larger in each act one of the columns disappears, as though a camera were slowly zooming in on the scene; in *The Golden Windows* a little house on a hill appears in different positions at different times of the day; in *Hamletmachine,* a single setting is seen from four different angles.

Wilson effected a number of transformations in *the CIVIL warS* by means of scale and trick perspective. In the Dutch section an enormous black woman towers over the stage, holding in her outstretched hand a dwarf who later becomes the giant in a film episode based on the Jack and the Beanstalk legend. Frederick the Great hovers over a miniature reconstruction of eighteenth-century Berlin in the German section where live performers appear in and out of scale with their film images. In the Rome act a 20-foot-tall Lincoln crosses the stage during the prologue only to reappear in human scale at the end of the opera.

As originally envisioned, *the CIVIL warS* would have constituted the greatest theatrical spectacle of our time. In the course of the twelve-hour performance Wilson planned to put before his audience magical vistas, fantastic animals, a battery of natural effects—wind, snow, sea, moon and stars—and a cavalcade of man's mechanical creations, from sailboats to spaceships. The opera was to be not only the culmination of the scenic theatre he had been developing over the previous fifteen years but a kind of apotheosis of nineteenth-century stagecraft with all its flying machines, traps, scrims, artificial mists, fire and water effects and engines of transformation. (Wilson once claimed that the reason twentieth-century artists do twentieth-century art is that nobody will give them the money to do nineteenth-century art.) "When I was first exposed to Bob's work it seemed to me that the closest parallels were the big spectacles presented at the turn of the century where scenic effects were more important than story line. *the CIVIL warS* has more magic in it than any other project Bob has done, perhaps more than any theatrical project in this century. Every scene has some sort of strange technical dilemma. I mean, a lot of people laughed when they first saw the storyboards. They said it's ridiculous, you'll never do all this." Since Wilson "very rarely has a technical solution in mind" it has always been incumbent on his designers to find a practical method of realizing his visions, which in this case included an enormous map of a continent that split into pieces, the sinking of the Monitor and Merrimac, a beanstalk that rose through the earth and a descent by balloon into the Grand Canyon.

"For the most part the technology—like theatre technology in general—is not much different than it was in the nineteenth century. I think the most spectacular technical feat in the opera was the panorama in the final act where trees of all nations

The Forest (1988). Wilson's retelling of the Babylonian epic *Gilgamesh* received its premiere at the Freie Volksbühne in Berlin and was later seen at the Brooklyn Academy of Music.

ACT II. TOM KAMM: We meet Gilgamesh in his room overlooking his factory. In this version instead of being a king, Gilgamesh is a genius inventor and mogul of industry and his kingdom is the factory he's created. The only entrance into the room is a high door at the back that slides open and shut mechanically. On the right side of the stage there's a pipe organ that slides out of the wall and downstage an aquarium filled with live fish—a kind of metaphor for a caged existence or nature in civilization. The interior room is essentially a box set which is a big change for Bob. It's the first time he's used side walls and that meant the actors couldn't be lit from the wings, a Wilson trademark.

The arched opening at the back is meant to be a window onto another world. I submitted a number of proposals for the factory vista, one of which featured three sets of steam turbine wheels and a series of ceiling pieces going back in forced perspective. We later threw everything out and came up with the idea of a grid and moving ladders. The first thing that happens is the curtains at the back open and a catwalk descends, creating a horizontal division of the space. Five ladders then track on from the sides with workers on them. There's also two huge steam engine wheels that turn and a little tram that crosses overhead. The back wall of the factory is made up of panels that open and close and at the end of the scene smoke pours down. It's like steam is pressing against the boiler plate and things are about to explode. Originally a section of industrial pipe was carried on by an enormous hook, but Bob decided to cut it just before opening night.

ACT III. TOM KAMM: The third scene is a cave where we meet Enkidu in his own environment. The shape of the opening at the back is virtually the same as the window in Gilgamesh's room. We go from sitting in Gilgamesh's room looking out into his world, which is the factory, to Enkidu's cave which looks out into the natural world—so it's the manmade versus the natural world.

moved slowly across the stage. What was so amazing was the scale. There were two separate panoramas—one was two hundred and fifty meters long and the other was one hundred and fifty, which is about the size of two-and-a-half football fields. They were all covered with beautiful trees which had been painted on canvas, cut out and hand sewn onto black scrim. It took several months for three Italian seamstresses to accomplish the task. The stage opening was about seventeen meters wide so there were a total of about eight pictures that rolled by." Kamm employed a typical nineteenth-century technique to animate Wilson's vision, a long rolling drop stretched between huge mechanized drums in the wings. "It's a method that's been used in opera and dance and even in the early silent films. Making the panorama move was incredibly difficult because there's all this fabric which has to be kept taut. It's like a tape recorder—you have a small amount on one reel and a large amount on another which means that the small reel has to spin that much faster to keep the tension. In the beginning I went out and assembled a virtual arboreal library and found the most ideal trees. I even did an animation on two acetate scrolls like you would do in film. The trees were pretty much arranged by country and geography. At the beginning of Act V, b there is an empty stage with a spaceship wall at the back. The first thing you see is a series of bare winter trees moving across. Then a giant charred tree—a fully dimensional tree trunk with a stagehand inside—rolls across the stage followed by the octet in their black robes, and the sculpted hedges and trees of Versailles. The next scene begins with the American desert—scrub and different kinds of cactus roll by—and then the front panorama starts to move and a huge sequoia appears. All of this was on scrim thirty feet high. Small Mediterranean trees are now followed by huge ones, then a grove of fruit trees and the pines, cedars and eucalyptus trees of Rome, which you could see all around the city. Finally the foliage grows denser and denser and we're in the jungle with two stage-pictures' worth of tropical trees. It was beautiful to watch it move. The trees came to a stop twice and every time I watched it I felt like I kept moving."

Though scenic wonders were certainly accomplished in Rome, as in Cologne and Rotterdam, the initial assessment of those skeptics who said such a work couldn't be realized proved to be at least partially right. Many scenes and visual effects fell victim to cost-cutting, technical problems and what Kamm calls "simple realism about getting the production on in L.A." Two major segments of the Japanese section, Act I, c and Act II, c, were eventually conjoined into a single episode and one of the most charming scenes (Act III, d), in which a small boy journeys in a hot-air balloon over the continent of Africa and then to the moon before descending into the Grand Canyon for a picnic, was scrapped entirely: "We didn't get very far with that one. Everyone always asked, 'How is this ever going to be possible?'" The French section, which contained some of the opera's most stupendous effects, bore the brunt of the cutbacks. "In Act II, a, Bob wanted to have a number of escalators moving up and down at the back of the stage. Originally there was going to be a mechanical escalator which people could actually ride, then we devised a system of mechanical shutters that looked like an escalator, then a film of an escalator, and finally it was cut altogether. In the big underwater scene, Bob wanted to have a Second Empire Ball on the staircase of the Paris Opera with the guests swimming across the stage and Marie Curie riding her bicycle in mid-air. That would have been really difficult to do." Another casualty was a scene in which various figures from literature, myth and history—among them St. Joan, Don Quixote (with windmill), two giant parrots and an angel—were to rise up into the air from holes in the stage floor. "While all these people were going up and down there was supposed to be a World War I biplane traveling across with a pilot and a dog inside. There were eighteen figures who were all supposed to be independently rigged. According to union rules you need three men to fly one person so it would have been very expensive. At one point we considered making half of them mannequins but that also proved beyond our budget and abilities." (Kamm says that even with these deletions a lot of scenery would have had to be rehung while the show was in progress: "There's only so much space up there.")

the CIVIL warS originated with the tiny rectangular sketches that Wilson habitually draws in his journal in the middle of the night and early in the morning. These are redrawn over and over as a new production takes shape in his mind (he once told a correspondent for the *International Herald-Tribune*, "I doodle constantly, I doodle [a design] so many times it's in my body") and it is from these sketches that Kamm typically begins his work. With *the CIVIL warS*, the freedom he was allowed varied greatly from section to section depending on the available time and the clarity of Wilson's vision. "There were some scenes where Bob knew exactly what he wanted and others that were really unclear in his mind. Sometimes he's so pressed because of other commitments that he can't take the time to think it through. I will do what looks right to my eye and then take it to him and he'll say 'That's perfect' or sometimes 'No, that's not exactly what I had in mind.' We go back and forth that way."

Kamm's full-time involvement with *the CIVIL warS* began at the Freiburg workshop in 1982. Working with the embryonic designs created in Munich the previous summer, he constructed a complete set of small-scale white paper models and a large maquette for the final presentation. "What Bob does is stage a performance for guests in the rehearsal hall with makeshift props and a scale model of the scenery. So you look at this model and then you look at what's going on and then you have to put the two together. And that's what people did, they figured out who the performers were on stage and then put them into this imaginary setting. It's a fascinating way to work." A developmental workshop (Stage A) preceded the final rehearsal period for each section, and during this stage the designs were refined and finalized. "Bob is fond of doing what the Germans call a technical rehearsal or a trial

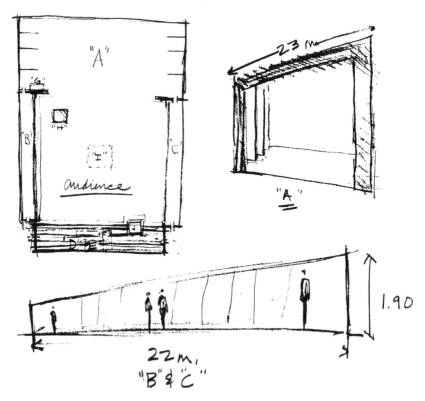

Death Destruction & Detroit II (1987). Wilson describes the multistage theatre he created for his sequel to *D D & D* at the Berlin Schaubühne, his first environmental design since *The $ Value of Man* in 1975.

ROBERT WILSON: In the beginning I had the idea that this room should be like a tomb, a labyrinth of the dead. Heiner Müller had told me about a form of Mongolian torture in which a man was buried up to his neck in the desert with skin from the neck of a camel sewn tightly to his shaved head. As the sun beat down and the skin began drying and shrinking, the hair would grow inward. In four out of five cases the man would lose his life. In the fifth case the man would lose memory. And I thought this work which in a poetical way was about Kafka could also be about this fifth man and his loss of memory. And this room could be that memory.

With that in mind I designed a theatre which had a formal proscenium space (Stage A) at one end and two long, narrow side stages running perpendicular to it (Stages B and C). Opposite Stage A was an enormous stepped wall nine meters high (Stage D), not unlike the giant steps of a pyramid or maybe a Mayan temple. There were various ways the performers could climb it—I had knotted ropes hanging down and there were steel handles you could use to step up to the next ledge. This was my favorite stage. There was a balcony near the top (Stage E) and in the prologue I had a Chinese Emperor sitting there—so in a way it might be the great wall of China. Within the wall I created an interior chamber (Stage F) and at one point you could see into the room which was occupied by the father of the Chinese Emperor, an enormous figure. I placed another performing area within the outer wall of the proscenium

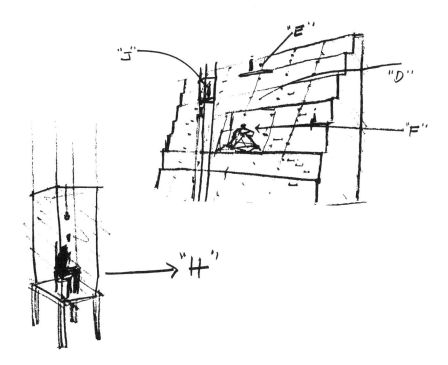

stage (Stage G). Then I had a little platform, like a table, out in the audience (Stage H). Most of the time it was covered with a semitransparent black box and inside Kafka or the man losing the memory was sitting under a light bulb. I always felt that that's where we would have someone reading Heiner's text about this Mongolian torture but Heiner never wrote the text. Then within the wall here (D) I had a clear glass box that could travel up through the floor and into the ceiling (Stage J). Rudolf Hess was inside most of the time because they had just built a glass elevator for him at Spandau. In the introduction I had Kafka rising up on a trap here in the audience (H) and then the black box started coming down while diagonally across the room the glass box rose up through the fog with Hess: "Ladies and Gentlemen, Welcome to *Death Destruction & Detroit.*" I also had a kind of surprise stage over the heads of the audience (Stage I). At one point the ceiling suddenly opened up and this messenger fell out and hung there in space while tons of letters fell down on the audience.

So we had ten performing areas and the audience sat in the center on triangular seats. Sometimes something would happen with one actor on the balcony here (E) and another actor here (A)—a dialogue over the audience. Sometimes there'd be an actor on this long, narrow stage (B) and another one over here (C). Sometimes they'd be here (G), here (H) and here (J), a diagonal line through the audience. Sometimes they'd be all around. To me it was a little bit like a child playing with an old radio, switching from station to station. In the first scene I had everything going at full blast, building and building. It's totally confusing and you're in the middle of it all. At the end of the first act, stone walls come down on all sides of the room and completely close off the space—the audience is suddenly enclosed inside this stone vault. (August 19, 1988) setup. It's a very extravagant process. He likes to go into a theatre and do a full scale mock-up with platforms and cardboard cutouts so he can begin to understand what the proportions and the scale should be. Remember, he conceives the stage picture before he conceives what will happen in it so there are always adjustments to make. In fact, the further down the line you can make design decisions with Bob, the better off you are."

While scenic elements are often carefully modeled on existing photographs or historical materials, it is not uncommon for chance or improvisation to play a role in the evolution of a design during the workshop phase, especially when Wilson is uncertain as to what direction it should take: "The way Bob always works in the Stage A workshop is to take whatever's available and make believe what it's eventually going to be. The rehearsals for the knee plays were held in a warehouse near the docks in Tokyo and they took all these cardboard boxes that were lying around, cut the centers out, stuck them together and began to make various shapes out of them. In this case that's what the design eventually turned out to be, modular boxes that could form all these different objects. Bob uses elements of chance a great deal and when he sees something interesting he can adapt it to his vision. During the Tokyo workshop we were using a cherry picker [a telescoping mechanical lift] for the theatre box that Lincoln was supposed to fall out of after being shot. Bob liked the way it looked and since we were short on money for L.A. he said let's just use that. By the time Stage A is finished so are the major set details. Of course when Bob gets it all on stage he always shifts things here and there to get the composition right." Months often separate the various rehearsal periods, with different projects sandwiched in between. What might be an inconvenience for others is all part of Wilson's chosen method for developing new pieces. "I like to work intensely and then forget about it," he has said. "That way I can come back and look at the piece fresh. I make drawings. Usually after a year or two I know if they're any good or whether to throw them away. It's only by living with them that I really know and it's the same with making a work. I like to work very carefully on a piece then put it aside—live with it—then come back and work. That way it becomes etched in my mind and head."

Since Wilson took full command of his productions in the mid-1970s one of the hallmarks of his theatre has been its exceptional visual refinement. As Christina Giannini, who realized the designs for *Einstein,* once said, "Wilson does not treat his drops as theatre drops, which only have to look good from a distance. He sees them as paintings. He wants them to look finished. He wants someone to be able to come up to his drops and stand ten inches away—even if nobody does—and still see a finished painting." Kamm confirms this: "You could have the furniture from the German part of *the CIVIL warS* in your house. It's built as well as anything you can buy in a store. The joints in the main acting platform and the facings of the corners were all dovetailed and mitered and beautifully done. I think Bob's been very influenced by the trips he's taken to Japan. All of that theatre is perfection, even to the way you put on your mask backstage." Wilson's pursuit of perfection also has a pragmatic basis. His designs are intended to be looked at for long periods of time and any flaw would at some point become readily discernible (his scenes also lack a central focus so the eye is free to wander around every corner of the stage). In the main, however, perfectionism is the rule simply because Wilson's obsessive eye demands it. (In the 1984 revival of *Einstein* he made the actor who carried a briefcase and balanced on one leg in the trial scene wear slippers over his shoes until he reached the wings to preserve the clean surface of his soles.)

It goes without saying that Wilson's coworkers must share his preoccupation with the kind of tiny details that usually go unnoticed in the theatre. As Beverly Emmons, a frequent collaborator, has pointed out, "He's a real perfectionist and he surrounds himself with perfectionists bar none—and if they're not, they don't last." Like many of his colleagues Kamm acknowledges that the collaboration makes heavy demands on his life. "The work is all-consuming. You really have to give yourself over to Bob's world and even more to his schedule because in order to make a project work you need to be there all the time. The people who work with Bob are generally pretty levelheaded people and flexibility is very important. You can't go in with a fixed vision. It takes a certain amount of giving up myself to work with Bob, I think that's true for everybody. There's always Bob's stamp on everything he does and that's the way it should be because it's really his work. But you can also see the imprint of his scenic collaborators. Actually, our visions and sense of aesthetics are very similar. I lived in Japan when I was a kid and I think a lot of my visual sensibilities came out of that experience. I'm not interested in decorative design. I care about strong architectural statements and a strong, clean composition—no extraneous details. That's something we share, though I tend to be more sculpturally oriented. My conceptual world is very close to his—if it weren't I don't think we would be able to work together so well. At the same time I don't want to work exclusively with Bob and I don't think he wants to work exclusively with anyone either. It's better for everyone if they can go away and do things and then come back and bring him new ideas."

THOMAS WOODRUFF

Robert Wilson's recent entry into video production has behind it two separate objectives. One is a concern to preserve his work in a living and enduring form, both transferring his ephemeral theatrical creations onto film and creating wholly original pieces for the medium. (This preservationist instinct also reveals itself in his meticulously maintained archive, where every document, tape and photograph relating to his career is carefully catalogued and stored.) The other is a desire to extend his creative reach and personal fame, attracting new audiences to his work and gaining the wider popularity he feels his creations merit. Implicit in this is the realization that though the stage may be the medium for which Wilson has the deepest affinity, it is of the past while television, as he often says, "is the future." Of the dozen film and television projects he has initiated since 1978, ten have been developed in collaboration with Thomas Woodruff, a young New York artist whose storyboards constitute the works' visual blueprints.

Woodruff, an accomplished painter and commercial artist with a pleasantly mocking smile, slicked-back hair and a large tattoo of a venomous snake on one arm, entered Wilson's circle of friends and coworkers in the spring of 1977. "I met Bob on the street right after seeing *Patio* and we started to talk. It was a very hard time for him because he had sort of exhausted all his friends. I was going to an art camp in Maine and as it turned out he was coming up later as a visiting artist so I started sending him postcards." (Much to Woodruff's surprise, a number of these old postcard scenes became settings in Wilson's next production *D D & D*.) "That's sort of how it started. There was a time in the mid-seventies when I took off from college and went to see everything in New York. I'd go to the Whitney every free night and see every new film that came out and all the work of Richard Foreman, Andrei Serban, Meredith Monk, Lucinda Childs, Trish Brown. It was a very productive time in terms of visual theatre. I saw *Queen Victoria* during this period and I was thrilled. It was so

Scenes from *Stations.* 1982.

spectacular. I really enjoyed figuring out his visual structure as it occurred, there were all these recurring triangular shapes—it could be a triangle of light or a dress or a piece of scenery. Creating a visual rather than narrative structure is still what Bob's best at in the theatre. Through the long, boring pieces I would fall asleep and have my own dreams about what was going on and then wake up and something else would be happening on stage. I loved that. So I would go hang out with Bob but I had no intention of working with him. What happened was he had these projects and he needed someone who could draw very quickly and facilely and I do that. He had also seen the video work I was doing in college. So he said, 'Okay, can you do this for me?'"

From the outset Wilson seemed to realize that the kind of prolonged time he usually deals in was not compatible with this new medium. "Television," he has stated, "is a very different way of structuring time. One second becomes crucial." In fact, after working in video for a few years he would say that thirty seconds now seemed like an eternity. "Television's scale is so different from theatre's. The space, time, texture, color—everything is different. . . . In the theatre I can spend half an hour walking five feet. In a performance in Belgium I did almost that and seventeen hundred people sat and watched. On TV they never would have. TV is about closeups, the movement of the eye, impact." While he was known for making long— sometimes very long—works in the theatre, he decided his video pieces had to be short. The first of these, which also began his collaboration with Woodruff, was *Video-50,* a fifty-minute work made up of nearly a hundred miniature scenes and episodes. It is Wilson's most modular work, without beginning, middle or end, a kind of cumulative picture gallery, the pieces of which could be rearranged in any order without significantly changing the whole. (The idea for *Video-50* may have grown out of the artist's first experiment with video, *The Spaceman,* a 1976 media installation mixing live performers with television "portraits" that appeared simultaneously on a wall of monitors. These were arranged architecturally in real space while those in *Video-50* are mathematically distributed over time, in blocks measuring thirty seconds rather than sixteen inches.)

As in Wilson's theatrical pieces, theme-and-variation (as well as repetition) constitutes the basic organizing principle, with objects, people and actions reappearing in different forms and configurations. Early in *Video-50* the camera isolates a

white telephone which is ringing unanswered. The image returns several times and later we see a girl lying in bed with a telephone spotlighted on her night stand. In another episode a large, furry hand reaches for the receiver. Later a black telephone is seen ringing off the hook and still later an old man (the surrealist writer Louis Aragon) appears on a bed, yet another telephone at his side. Similarly, we are shown a grouping of chairs, then a single chair floating in the sky and later a group of glasses filled with milk (another recurring image), arranged exactly like the chairs we saw earlier. Some of the scenes are evocative or theatrical—curtains blowing in the wind, a starry sky, a closeup of a human eye opening—yet more often the camera focuses on the most ordinary of human actions: a man turning on a light bulb, a shoe being tied, teeth being brushed, a mouth blowing a gum bubble, polish being applied to a fingernail. These episodes are leavened with unexpected moments of humor, often resulting from the sudden explosion of television illusion: a woman being robbed at gunpoint suddenly breaks into a smile for the camera, a man sits in his library and after a moment a large fish swims by (the scene has been photographed through an aquarium). *Video-50* is also something of a retrospective glance at Wilson's theatre career, excerpted and reconstituted in miniature. An isolated wine glass and the telephone ringing off the hook recall *Patio*; the hairy paw, the monster in *King of Spain*; a pane of glass shattering, *Theatre Activity* and other early works; a man balancing with a briefcase (in this instance Wilson), *Einstein*.

   "With *Video-50* we began by making lists of all the things that could happen, things that would be interesting to see. Then I would draw them real quick and we'd go through them. We had to come up with a hundred episodes and we were going crazy. Bob thrives on tense situations. You end up working at three o'clock in the morning because the thing has to be off by courier the next day." *Video-50* also typifies Wilson's rather idiosyncratic manner of developing new pieces. "Bob usually figures out some kind of structure and then it's sort of like picking up pebbles on the beach. He's a great stylist and a great detailer but the subjects are pretty much arbitrary." Woodruff gives as an example a sequence from Wilson's planned video portrait of Konrad Henkel, a German industrialist and art patron. "There was a gap in the cave scene, a fantasy sequence, and I was reading a lot about German romantic painting during the same time, so I showed Bob a book that I thought might help us. He felt the images were overused but then later he sat down and chose every other

plate. That's the major section of the video. *What if I didn't bring the book?* There's this completely arbitrary way of determining the imagery. Once it's chosen everything is precisely detailed and fine-tuned but initially it comes out of nowhere." (This approach may reflect Wilson's early training in interior design, where one must take given spaces and the arbitrary demands of clients—again chance elements—and make them into something of one's own.) Woodruff says that for the most part the work progresses through discussion and interchange and that Wilson rarely puts pen to paper except to correct something. "What generally happens is that after the visual structure is figured out, we spit out ideas and the piece gradually takes shape. In going through the material together he believes me as an editor and I function as one." For his part Woodruff has never been afraid to make his opinions known, even if it means telling his collaborator-boss, "'You can't do that, it's just too stupid, that doesn't make sense, that doesn't fit visually.' I don't think there are people in the theatre telling him these things. Then I draw the scenes and we put them up on the wall and tape them together because Bob has a very hard time reading anything. It all has to be visual. If there's a problem with something I'll redraw it but at this point I understand the aesthetic so well, I know what it should be."

Wilson has likened the medium of television to "another window in the room" and "a window to the world" that has "changed our lives." In *Stations* (1982), the most ambitious and technically complex of his produced video works, a window almost literally becomes a television screen, changing the lives of those within and the world without. As in so many Wilson pieces, a child stands at the center of the action, a small boy who lingers before a window in his family's suburban home looking out at vistas which change like images on a TV set being switched from channel to channel (hence the title). The familiar green lawn of everyday life gives way to television static, then a bridge collapsing in a hurricane, a small pyramid, a brick wall and a giant bee which descends into the empty window frame. Wilson says the work was partially inspired by Christopher Knowles, who used to visit him at his loft and stare out the window for hours, and by his own childhood self who spent "hours locked in his room, looking out the window." If *Stations'* subject is its medium, it is also imagination and the power of internal seeing possessed by child and artist. The action is presided over by a "mystery man," a distinctly Wilsonesque figure in a black suit and dark glasses who gives the boy a wristwatch which moves backward,

activating the fantasy. (Wilson once visited a clock factory in Milan with Knowles, who asked if they could make such an object). This mystery figure intermittently monitors the boy's adventures on a television screen from the back seat of his limousine, another way in which the medium asserts its power and presence.

Like *Video-50*, this playful fantasy shows Wilson's tendency to subordinate content to structure. *Stations* is divided into thirteen sections, each of which has a separate title indicating its setting or visual theme:

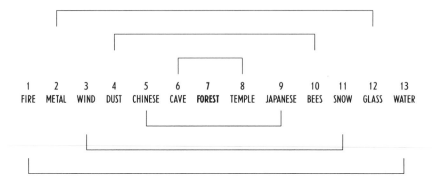

This structure is modeled after *The Life and Times of Joseph Stalin*, from which a sizeable portion of its imagery is drawn. Once again Wilson creates a series of corresponding episodes. The first scene ("Fire") in which the boy's parents are consumed by flames while sitting at their breakfast table is mirrored by the final episode ("Water") in which they are washed down a river and over the falls. In the third section ("Wind") the hurricane rages just outside the window, blowing the family around the room; in the corresponding sequence ("Snow") penguins cavort on ice and snowflakes fall in the kitchen. As in *Stalin*, "The Forest," that mythic realm of the imagination, stands alone at the center of the piece (its rising pyramid and banquet scene come right out of *Deafman*). In keeping with the theme of each section, the interior of the house and its occupants undergo fantastic transformations and face a multitude of trials and dangers, a vivid contrast to the dull complacency of everyday domestic life. The home is threatened by lightning, space creatures invade the kitchen and wrap their wire tentacles ("Metal") around the mother and father (who had gone up in flames only a scene before), a passing elephant makes its way

through the room, its inhabitants are submerged in a sea of dust ("Dust") and a fireball streaks through the house. Having survived its perilous trip over the falls, the family is reunited in the final episode for the obligatory happy ending and walks off into the dappled sunlight together. Taken as a whole, *Stations* is an engaging and good-natured if somewhat uneven work, suffering from uncertain pacing and uncharacteristically hasty execution necessitated by Wilson's limited budget.

Six of the storyboards Woodruff has created are adaptations of existing stage productions. "The storyboards for *Patio* were done several years after I had first seen the show in New York. We worked in Lucinda Childs' loft and she went through her movements very slowly. We'd both walk around looking at her and trying to figure out things that could be visually interesting in terms of television. Then I would have to draw it. Working with Bob is good in a way because it keeps you in real good shape as an artist. You become like an athlete. You have to be able to draw eight people playing croquet from overhead in two seconds and have it read, which is one of my skills. Bob added a new section with a cube falling from the sky but the movement structure of the stage play was basically maintained. I always thought of it as being like *Playhouse 90*, the piece could have almost been done live. With the *Deafman* video we worked in a similar way with Sheryl Sutton in his loft. Bob set the scene up and we would go through it over and over again. He'd figure out what would happen in terms of movement and I would figure out what would happen in terms of the camera." (Woodruff sees *Deafman* as the most powerful and accomplished of the video works Wilson has created to date; with its Hitchcock-like camera angles and carefully framed compositions, it is certainly his most successful assimilation of the grammar of film and use of the camera.)

The television storyboards for both *Edison* and *Dialog/Curious George* were created concurrently with the stage productions. "With *Curious George* Bob would rehearse from eight to twelve with Christopher Knowles and then I'd work from twelve to four, taking what he'd been rehearsing and seeing how it would work in terms of video." In the case of *D D & D* Woodruff worked from Wilson's ideas and a dim archival tape of the Berlin production. "For *Great Day* I was pretty much on my own. Basically, we trust each other at this point. And I understand the aesthetic." When produced the videos have tended to follow the storyboards closely and this has proved a sore point with Woodruff, who feels his contributions have never been

properly credited. "The one that really got me nuts was *The Murder* (*Deafman Glance*). The storyboards had to get done so I was drawing quickly and not really figuring things out that specifically and then virtually every shot was followed to the last detail. I was told I was doing the storyboards for budgetary reasons and I assumed Bob's creative prowess would come into it later but he followed them to the letter." This has always been Wilson's way—to refine and embroider but not significantly alter a set of actions and pictures which have been quickly put together early in the process, sometimes without a great deal of thought.

Woodruff thinks an important part of what he has brought to Wilson's video work is a greater knowledge of the medium. "I understand television better than Bob does. There are certain decisions he insists upon that make for not-that-interesting television. I think it's a mystery to him. In a lot of ways I have to be quiet. Actually, I think one thing that's interesting is that the television work looks very primitive. I sort of like the idea that it's primitive but it's not what he intends." With their rudimentary special effects and no-frills technology Wilson's videos offer a striking contrast to his stage works, which represent the ultimate in theatrical craftsmanship. "Bob hasn't been able to do enough work to completely understand the process of how things get done. And in a way that's exciting. What he really needs is to have a studio for a year where he can just play around and figure out what the medium can do. He knows about edges in the theatre but not in television or film." Whether Wilson will be offered that opportunity is unclear. (Only four of his thirteen video projects have actually been produced.) He has always been dependent on private patronage and public subsidy and while the mechanism for such funding doesn't really exist in film, it is not inconceivable that some producer-enthusiast might one day appear to underwrite productions on a grander scale than anything attempted so far. Wilson's development in this arena will also depend, as it always has, on his future collaborators and what he learns from them. It seems unlikely, however, that he could ever have the impact on the medium he has had on the theatre, if for no other reason than that his aesthetic has already been absorbed by a generation of media artists (the creators of rock videos and TV commercials in particular) who have grown up on his work and whose use of increasingly fantastic imagery and visual disjunction bears witness to his influence. It may be that they can already beat him at his own game. Woodruff also offers the intriguing observation that "perhaps he would be smarter

not to make the films and videotapes at all because the whole ephemeral quality of his work—with such relics as chairs and photographs—would be much more mysterious and potent."

While Woodruff continues to admire isolated aspects of Wilson's theatre, he no longer finds his eye interesting and says the work has long since ceased to fulfill him creatively. "I can do a Wilson production in my sleep at this point. It's such a specific aesthetic. What happened was I stopped learning from it. I understood it so well. It's almost like talking with a knee-jerk liberal, you always know what the response will be. I always know the way Bob will see it." Woodruff can reel off the aesthetic and organizational principles of Wilson's work in a few phrases: "It's this minimalist thing that's all about details. It runs in parallel lines generally and specific diagonals. Everything is graphically organized and very stylish. It's all designed color. He favors minimalist palettes, mostly grays, and then he'll put in a color. In terms of structure, he'll have very dark scenes and then a bright one or all gray, and then a bright color. It's all very figured out. The work is increasingly about technique. In the early pieces he was using these nonperformers but he's not interested in that anymore, now he wants professionals. It's become all about counting. He should do something at Disney World with robots." Woodruff also feels stagnation has set in. "He's reusing too many of the same things. I do illustrations for magazines and I'm very aware of the gimmicks of making imagery. Bob has a certain set of stock images, it's like a vocabulary and he just reworks it. If it's a theatre of images it's time to come up with some new imagery. The furniture can be made out of wood or out of pipes but it's basically the same design. I saw *the CIVIL warS* in Cambridge and it just drove me crazy. He's doing bratty things now like having a boy bounce a ball over and over again and making you listen to a dog barking continuously. Why put people through that? And I think the use of all those texts and historical documents is a mistake 'cause he doesn't understand them and they don't add up. It's not communicating anything to me—I'm an educated person, a bright person and I'm completely turned off by it. It'll be interesting to see what he'll do with whole texts because he can watch something and not understand the story, it's like he just doesn't get the narrative. He was trying to tell me the plot of *Medea* at one point but he couldn't get it straight—and he's worked on that production for such a long time. One of the things that makes him interesting as an artist is that he just doesn't understand."

Despite such views Woodruff has considerable respect for some of Wilson's accomplishments as a theatre artist. "If Bob were to die tomorrow he would be sitting at the right hand of Marcel Duchamp in terms of history. Why? He's doing something up there that no one else is doing. He's playing the role of artist to extraordinary lengths. Some people fall for it, some people don't. He's better at it some times than at others. Look at Robert Longo, Laurie Anderson, David Byrne, David Salle—all of these people have been extremely affected by Wilson's aesthetic. You see pictures of his work in books and it's just so amazing. Wow! College kids are going to be stumbling upon these pictures for years to come and they'll be fascinated. What he's done in terms of lighting for the theatre has never been accomplished before. You sit there and you can't believe it. Ultimately, he's a good artist. He works to get things done."

In the end this collaboration might be characterized as an uneasy alliance, even a mismatch. While Woodruff's impudent, offhand manner is refreshing, it is obviously disconcerting to Wilson, who has come to expect a certain deference from those around him. ("I heard at one point Bob was working with somebody else because I was just too impossible. I actually used to be much more arrogant than I am today.") Most collaborators work with Wilson for the honor of such an association or out of devotion, but not Woodruff. "My reason for doing this is not any deep-seated love of the work. It's for money. At this point I find magazine illustrations a much more fulfilling method of exploration. My work for Wilson is 'work to order.' I have a certain amount of expertise and I expect to be compensated for it. When I was first working with Bob I just absorbed it all—'Oh yes, oh yes, hmm, I see'—but as soon as you start saying, 'No, wait a minute, I don't believe that,' you start running into brick walls. More and more I don't understand his intentions. There were a number of clashes during our last project. It had become so clear where we had diverged in terms of our aesthetics. I think the whole experience helped me to become more confident about what I believe in and the things I find important in terms of emotionalism and communicating. And I wonder about Bob's whole aesthetic and what it is he wants to communicate other than a technique."

CHRISTOPHE DE MENIL

O ver the years Wilson has cannily encouraged his patrons to participate directly in his productions. Stefan Brecht, the son of the German playwright and poet, appeared as a performer and contributed texts to a number of works in the 1970s; Isabel Eberstadt, a socially prominent New Yorker, briefly turned actress in *Edison*; Michel Guy, the founder of the Festival d'Automne, was seen in *Overture* and *Video-50*; and Jerome Robbins, Wilson's earliest mentor, took to the stage as Sigmund Freud on several occasions. The most recent addition to this circle of wooed and conscripted benefactors is Christophe de Menil, the chief costume designer and coordinator of *the CIVIL warS*. De Menil, who is the granddaughter of Conrad Schlumberger, the founder of the giant multinational oil field service corporation, comes naturally to the role of patron and artist as a member of a family known for its collecting skills and philanthropic activities. Her mother Dominque recently built a new art museum in Houston to house the collection she amassed with her late husband; her brothers and sisters are active collectors; and she herself has quietly supported the work of a number of avant-garde musicians and performers over the years, among them Philip Glass, Trisha Brown, Twyla Tharp, Terry Riley and Robert Whitman.

De Menil lives in splendid luxury in a converted Manhattan carriage house designed by the Los Angeles architect Frank Gehry and the light artist Douglas Wheeler. Its spare, elegant interiors reflect her own fastidious tastes and modernist preferences. Virtually every object the eye encounters is an art object. Everything is designed, nothing left to chance, nothing purchased ready-made. The vast light-filled spaces, white walls, ash-gray carpeting and minimalist furniture might have sprung from Wilson's own aesthetic—and in some ways the design values suggest his New York loft, though one is luxuriously high-tech, the other very low-tech. A tall and graceful figure, de Menil herself would not seem out of place in a Wilson landscape though she is nowhere near so cool or impassive as most Wilson heroines. On the contrary, she radiates warmth, generosity and intelligence, as well as an amusing self-absorption that puts one a little in mind of the socialite millionairesses found in 1930s screwball comedies.

"I came to know Bob through insiders like Jerry Robbins and Paul Lepercq and most importantly, my cousin Bénédicte Pesle, who is an agent for American performing artists in Europe and said you really have to go and look at what he is doing. I was especially taken with *Queen Victoria*, which was really a knockout. I met Bob at a dinner party at the house of Menoush Yektai, an Iranian painter, and it was Paul Lepercq who introduced us. He had his little pad of paper and he was very fascinating, making lots of drawings. I liked Bob immensely and I liked his work immensely and so it kept on." Along with her brother François and a cousin, Pierre Schlumberger, de Menil became one of the principal backers of *Einstein on the Beach*, and she has remained one of the artist's most steadfast friends and benefactors. It was not until 1981, however, when Wilson was preparing a new piece for the Kammerspiele in Munich that he encouraged her, much to her own surprise, to take on a creative role in his work.

"Bob had done a lighting installation for my Paris apartment and in exchange he wanted me to help him with the costumes for *The Golden Windows* in Munich. We used to go see performances and discuss them and talk about different things but I had never done anything like this before. I was scared, of course, but I thought that I would be more scared not to do it. I also realized—though I'm sure I didn't tell Bob—that I would just go out and buy the dresses if I couldn't do it. But Bob gave me lots of faith, he was a hero. There were two costumes, one was for the young woman who I saw as very innocent in white or cream and the other for an older woman who would be in dark gray or black since Bob really prefers these colors above all others, though he will now use blue and sometimes a bit of red. I began by looking at Bob's sketches and going to rehearsals so I could see how the performers moved. Then I would check with Bob and ask what do you think about this? I'd ask him about swatches. 'Is this too cream?' 'How do you like this weight?'" The costume for the older woman, a "very feminine columnar figure," proved the more difficult; it took de Menil five months to arrive at a design she considered satisfactory (during this time she went through seven seamstresses). "I kept redoing the dress two or three times a week. It took me that long because I was learning as I was thinking about it."

A few months after the Munich opening, Wilson invited her to attend the final run-through of *the CIVIL warS* in Freiburg. Although she was scheduled to leave for Houston on family business, de Menil quickly changed her plans. "When they first called me I said no, I couldn't go. But then I thought, 'This is really so much more exciting. It's my life and I want to be there.' So I called back and said, yes, I'll come and I'm very grateful I did. The presentation was fabulous. I arrived the same day and was having a hard time staying awake but it was extraordinary. Hildegard Behrens was so moving reading the letters of Marie Curie that we all cried." One thing led to another and de Menil became the chief costume designer and coordinator for the massive project. She began work with the Dutch section, making lists of all the characters and compiling research materials to supplement those already assembled by the production staff. Since Wilson is always notoriously difficult to reach, and never more than during the multinational chaos of *the CIVIL warS*, de Menil typed out elaborate questionnaires with little boxes marked "yes" and "no" which were forwarded to him so he could answer in transit. As work progressed she also sent him photographs of costume mock-ups for his reactions. In some instances Wilson had specific ideas for a costume or provided a historical character whose image and dress he wished to reproduce. On occasion he would give her an indication of a basic geometric shape, "very often a triangle," as he did with the black-robed gospel singers who appeared before the spaceship wall in the Rome section. More often, however, his designers provide the stimuli. As John Conklin, who created the costumes for *Alcestis*, has said, "At first I was trying to have him tell me what to do. But he wants you to do something and then he'll react."

the CIVIL warS is a historical collage and de Menil did extensive research on its many characters, consulting fashion magazines at the Metropolitan Museum to find a suitable "execution coat" for Mata Hari and even conferring with art historians at the Frick Collection about the probable court dress of William the Silent. Considerable time and effort were expended in the search for authenticity. When she became fascinated by a picture of a little jacket worn in Axel but was unable to determine how it was made, one of her staff was sent to the Dutch town to track it down. "I think historical exactitude is very important to Bob. Sometimes it's just underlining, you don't even see it but it's been included in a way of thinking. He might have rejected the jacket or said we don't need it, and I wouldn't even have asked him why."

De Menil's working process is unlike that of most costume designers. "I don't sketch. I think from the body and the historical material and from the movement. Is the actor going to move sideways, is he going to dance or crawl?" Costumes were often taken directly from a photograph or painting or improvised on the bodies of the actors during rehearsals. (An early design for the enormous Snow Owl seen in the Act IV epilogue was constructed in origami after a trip to Japan with Wilson.) Since Wilson conceives the visual elements of his operas in flat, cartoon-like drawings, it is not surprising that the line or silhouette of a costume tends to be uppermost in his mind. "Bob is always saying that the thing that really counts for him is the line. He wants that to be very strongly delineated. So if an arm is to be extended out from the body, you have to lay the sleeve in horizontal rather than vertical. I think he's really looking for a poetic effect." Costumes for a Wilson spectacle often embrace a vast span of time and history and the subdued, even monochromatic use of color is an important factor in reconciling disparate elements. "Color is used very sparingly. In the Dutch section Mata Hari was in white and silver, the country people in browns and grays, William the Silent was in black, the bear was white, and Queen Wilhelmine and her attendants were in flowery colors with tiny flecks of red, which was a departure. In design, Bob has this very romantic side—lush, almost tropical— and then he has this very austere side that balances it. It's our diet, sometimes we have a lot of cream, sometimes salad."

De Menil's collaboration with Wilson has brought major changes in her life. Seized by what she calls "a keen interest in wrapping, binding and decking the body for different occasions," de Menil set up shop as a couturier not long after her return from Rome, selling a number of paintings from her collection to finance the million-dollar venture. "Thinking that much about clothes, I got interested in the body. There were so many things I wanted to explore more." (Wilson himself designed the lighting for a number of her showings, among them a spectacular presentation at the French Embassy in New York where he covered the walls with changing patterns of colored light—"all very carefully timed and very beautiful"—and sent a brilliantly lit cascade of dry ice down the grand staircase for the bridal-gown finale.) After so many years of supporting the work of other creators, de Menil has stepped boldly—and expensively—over into their world, a development she fully credits to her collaboration with Wilson: "Bob really gave me the idea and I don't think he even knew it."

Sheryl Sutton has said that one of Wilson's "most amazing abilities is to see people in a way they can't see themselves." He has always had a gift for recognizing talents people didn't know they possessed, sending them in new directions and on occasion changing the course of their lives. Christophe de Menil can confirm that these powers remain undiminished.

the CIVIL warS. Act III, e. American Repertory Theatre, 1985.

BEVERLY EMMONS

"Light," declared the Swiss theatre visionary Adolphe Appia, "is the supreme scene painter, the interpreter, the most significant plastic medium on stage." With the exception of Wieland Wagner, who revolutionized the staging of his grandfather's works at Bayreuth in the 1950s, no theatre artist has taken Appia's pronouncement as much to heart or devoted such energy to exploring the properties of light as Robert Wilson. In Wilson's theatre, light is as much a metaphysical force as a design element, and its transforming powers are felt everywhere, from the star-filled nightscapes and glowing interiors to the luminous sculptural forms which seem to grow out of his imaginary vistas. "For me light is the essential element in the theatre," Wilson often says. It is a primary component of composition, as integral to a piece as text, music or imagery. In a theatre that counts perception among its chief concerns, it is, says Wilson, "what helps us to see and even to hear" (he believes if the audience cannot see properly it's difficult for them to hear as well). It is also a tangible expression of the Manichean forces loosed in his work and of the encompassing mystery at its heart.

It is no coincidence that Wilson has sometimes taken for his subjects men whose lives were spent exploring the nature of light or harnessing its powers: *Edison* celebrated the one-hundredth anniversary of the incandescent light bulb and the inventor who singlehandedly illuminated his era, while *Einstein on the Beach* focused on the life of the great physicist and humanist who changed our understanding of what light is. (As John Rockwell wrote in the *New York Times* when the work was revived in 1984, "Above all, *Einstein* is about light: its beauty, its relation to energy and power, and ultimately its mystical connection to love.") In *The Golden Windows* light assumed the role of actor, an inanimate yet very real protagonist in a cosmic drama: observing, isolating, stalking, suddenly suffusing the human figures that crossed Wilson's lonely landscape in a luminous glow, then just as suddenly leaving them in darkness. When the earth cracked open at the play's climax, blinding white light poured out of the fissure as though the core of the planet were made of radiant energy. In what was perhaps the most remarkable scene in *Einstein*, light displaced the actor altogether and became the action: for nearly half an hour, spellbound audiences watched a bar of cold white light tilt upward from its horizontal position on an otherwise empty stage and rise into the sky. It would be no exaggeration to say that Wilson's works exist as much in the dimension of light as they do in time and space.

Many of these visions have been realized by Beverly Emmons, Wilson's chief lighting designer for the past twelve years, who has collaborated on such productions as *Einstein, Patio, Death Destruction and Detroit, Great Day in the Morning, the CIVIL warS* and *Salome*. An articulate and candid woman of Wilson's generation, Emmons also established herself during this period as one of New York's leading lighting designers, working regularly with such dance and theatre artists as Joseph Chaikin, Andrei Serban, Martha Graham and Trisha Brown as well as Meredith Monk and Lucinda Childs, who were classmates at Sarah Lawrence College, where she studied dance composition in the early 1960s. Since 1975 when she first came into Wilson's orbit, relighting his production of *A Letter for Queen Victoria* for Broadway in a single day, Emmons has seen his designs grow progressively more complex, his lighting rehearsals stretch into weeks and "his demands increase in direct proportion to the speed with which I could solve them."

"What Bob does with light which is extraordinary and difficult and unusual is to separate all the elements from each other and control them independently. In the theatre we have what is known as area light which lights the entire stage and the actors' faces at the same time. Its purpose is to enable two people to walk around a living room and look the same everywhere they go. Bob never uses that kind of light. Never. He wants the floor treated as a whole unit and separately painted with light. He wants the background treated as another whole, with maybe one color shaded into another, but what's happening on that drop shouldn't affect anything going on on the stage. Then he wants the human figure separately etched out with light, and very often he wants the head or even nose of that figure separately lighted." (In lighting, as elsewhere, the principle of independence prevails.)

Wilson usually begins with the backcloth — a painted drop or cyclorama — and the stage floor, which together form a kind of scenic envelope. Unusual care and effort is lavished on the latter, which is envisioned as a pure and even plane, and keeping stray light off this surface has become one of Wilson's obsessions. "Any light that hits the floor should not have any texture at all. He doesn't want to see any splotches, spills, hot or cold spots. He lights the floor so it's all one — very dim, smooth, and calm. That's one of his signature ideas. The floor is one thing. The levels at which he works are also extremely unusual. For the dance scenes in *Einstein*, we hung a battery of lights and brought them up to a reading of eighteen out of a hundred. So the stage is a hazy, murky glow that isn't a color. Lots of instruments putting out very dim light is typical of Bob. One normally selects equipment to read between half and full on the dimmer. He makes careful distinctions between the way a lamp looks at seventeen, twenty-two and twenty-eight; by the time you get up to thirty-two, that's bright for him."

Because Wilson "likes light that has only one source, like daylight," he sometimes uses a high-wattage German instrument called a "Flüter" which can illuminate the entire stage, producing a calm, even light with only a single shadow. Occasionally, he will pick out and isolate objects on the floor in rectangles of light—a row of alarm clocks in *Curious George,* a lone seashell in *Einstein*—though he tends to be "suspicious of anything on the floor" that has not been specifically conceived as part of the stage picture. He also uses the floor as a prepared canvas for the interplay of light and shadow, creating diagonal pathways of light or luminous shapes that reflect other elements of the design, such as the brilliant shafts of sunlight that poured through the rectangular archways in *Patio.* In contrast to contemporary stage practice, the forms and patterns of light that strike the floor are carefully conceived and controlled, never random or inadvertent. "Bob is a painter and as a painter he wants to decide all the parts. He doesn't want anything to happen by accident." The backcloth, which is frequently backpainted onto a translucent surface, constitutes another luminous surface. "Bob tends to like the light coming from below so there's usually a place at the horizon line where the light is hotter. He always says it keeps his eye focused toward the bottom of the scene and doesn't distract you upward."

Against these two subtly lighted planes, Wilson places the actors and a number of carefully chosen scenic elements. "What Bob likes to do is create a rather dim overall background and then etch out with light those things he wants to attract the eye." The method is not unlike that of a jeweler who places a gem on a dark velvet background to heighten its brilliance and intensity. "It's extremely high-contrast lighting. The figure in space is always sharply lit with low side lighting coming from the wings. But this isn't like side lighting for dance, which is used to flatter the body and comes from up in the air, filling the entire space. Light travels in straight lines so as soon as you put any lamp more than a few feet off the floor it's going to hit the stage floor. In Bob's pieces, the instruments are always placed low—usually under five feet—and focused to sharply strike the body and then disappear into the wings. So the light really etches the figure in space. Zap."

The performers in Wilson's landscapes often seem to glow as if they had somehow absorbed the light into their bodies; the human figure itself becomes a luminous object. "The lighting from the wings is mostly dead straight on and if the actor is looking directly forward it makes a dark line down the face, though this happens very seldom. Bob doesn't like the face obscured and generally wants it beautifully lit in addition." Sometimes a part of the face is lit with a cold light and then filled in with a warmer one, creating an image that is simultaneously hot and cold (like Wilson himself). "There are also moments when he wants different parts of the performers etched out. Sometimes the hand is brighter than the rest of the body. Again, Bob is the painter. He's sitting out front looking at the whole picture and if he were painting, he'd put a little bit of white around the hand. Not that you're supposed to see only that hand, but it often completes the focus of the composition for that particular moment. In *Einstein* we used lights to sharply etch the stenographers' hands in the trial scenes because that's what Bob wanted to see. They did hand motions and they all had hand specials." For Emmons such lighting is as much an aid to "seeing" as an element of design since "in *Einstein* what you're given to interest yourself in is the minutest of details." (Wilson first experimented with lighting different parts of the body when he was a student in the mid-sixties; while assisting with a children's program in San Antonio he helped create a tiny theatre where a nose or an eye could be isolated with a pin spot or a flashlight.) Stage lighting this precise and detailed poses an enormous challenge to the actor, who must hit his marks exactly, and it is probably no coincidence that Wilson's ever-increasing demands for precision and split-second timing coincided with the growing complexity of his lighting designs.

Sometimes it is an object that Wilson seeks to delineate and enhance. In *Patio* he wanted the outline of his brushed aluminum furniture to glow and cried repeatedly for more light, though this did not have the desired effect. Emmons hit on the idea of placing a thin strip of white tape on the edges of the furniture, which caught the light and provided the definition he was looking for. Wilson used this trick again in *D D & D* to highlight the black canes of the shadowy figures who moved across the stage in the prologue and even placed a white line down the shoulder and hand of one of the performers in another scene. Because he lights each part of the stage independently Wilson is also able to cross-cut between the different areas. Emmons offers as an example the prologue of the Rome *CIVIL warS*, in which the various elements of the stage picture are revealed piece by piece until the design is complete. "When the curtain rises, there's a crash and all you see is a brightly lit hand in the darkness. Then the sky lights up with stars and the stage lights come up on a tiger's carcass glowing slightly in a pool of light from above. There are side lights that follow two vultures who flap their wings and fly off the carcass and up into the wings. Then a snow owl appears in the branch of a tree and at the same time a light comes up on the Earth Mother, whose hand is still brightly lit, and a follow spot on the baby in her arms." In recent years Wilson has also become fond of suddenly extinguishing all the lights on the performers and throwing them into silhouette against the illuminated backcloth.

In contrast to general theatre practice, enormous time and effort is often spent eliminating recognizable effects rather than creating them. "The audience isn't aware

I Was Sitting on My Patio . . . . 1977.

D D & D. "The City." Berlin, 1979.

of what craziness is involved in making something that looks so simple and pure."
Because a beam of light focused on a performer becomes smaller and more intense as
he approaches the wings, for example, Emmons has sometimes put instruments on
wheels and pulled them slowly back to guarantee uniform consistency. In the trial
scenes of *Einstein* a large white bed dominated the stage and great care was taken to
make certain that the surface was smooth and clean by lighting it from a single
source. "You see, Bob's eye is perfect. If he sees a tiny line or a slight difference in the
light, he hates it. With most directors it wouldn't matter but Bob doesn't want
something he didn't design as part of the overall image."

Wilson's lighting demands have not always been so complicated or exacting.
Though he had been exploring the plastic values of light since his student days (it was
during an apprenticeship with Alwin Nikolais in the early 1960s that he seems to
have discovered its possibilities) and his lighting had steadily grown in expressiveness over the years, it was not until *Death Destruction and Detroit* in 1979 that
Wilson's present methods crystallized. Never before had he had the technical and
financial resources of a European state theatre at his disposal or the time to
experiment and indulge his tastes. At the Schaubühne Wilson discovered just what
was possible (though in the end he exhausted even their largesse). "Bob finished
D D & D several months before it got lit so he really had time to figure out what he
wanted. He screamed and screamed and carried on and had to verbalize it." Even so,
the chief electrician at the Schaubühne could not understand what Wilson wanted —
"he wasn't being technically precise enough for them" — and Emmons received an
emergency telephone call from Wilson's European representative, Bénédicte Pesle,
asking if she could be on the next plane to Berlin. Two days later she arrived at the
theatre, attended a run-through, conferred with the staff and in a single night created
a light plot that enabled Wilson to realize his vision. Emmons feels that *D D & D*
marked a turning point in their collaboration as well as in Wilson's own approach to
lighting. "What happened for me and I think for him is that we realized we
understood each other, deeply understood what he was trying to accomplish."
Something else also happened. Wilson would never again be satisfied with the more
casual and conventional solutions of past productions. In the future his formidable
lighting requirements would be carefully specified in all his contracts.

Light assumes many forms in Wilson's works. While primarily a transforming
force that travels unseen through the air from concealed sources, it may also take
more solid shape. Many of the scenic elements in *Einstein* were actually made of light
and the interplay of luminous objects and surfaces was as much a part of the drama as
the choreography or Philip Glass's music. Audiences entered a lambent world of
glowing globes and clockfaces, phosphorescent briefcases (an image that would
reappear in *The Golden Windows*), light-emitting missiles and lollipops, solar
eclipses, stars, and flashing spaceship lights. Most memorable of all were Wilson's

fluorescing light sculptures—solid shapes of white light that appeared throughout the opera in various guises, first as a coldly glowing vertical band that descended three times in the opening scene, then as a horizontal bar which was later halved and finally tilted back to a vertical position, disappearing into the flies from which it had first appeared. "One thing about Bob is that he's able to get something so spectacular out of the simplest means. The strip of light that came down in the first scene was just a little box eight inches wide, four inches deep and thirty feet long with fluorescent tubing and a Plexiglas skin, but it looked like a white, crystalline sword." While *Einstein* might be regarded as the most comprehensive expression of his scenography of light, Wilson has continued to seek out new ways to surprise and mystify the eye. *D D & D* saw the appearance of phosphorous walking sticks, green neon cactus plants and light-emitting Lucite shoes. The darkness in *Edison* was pierced by glowing windows and blazing incandescent bulbs; in *The Golden Windows* a comet streaked across the cyclorama and at one point the moon and stars disappeared from the sky, only to reappear a moment later on the floor.

During the past ten years Wilson has also become interested in what he calls "architectural light in the air"—the outlines of light traveling through space as held in mist or smoke. Such radiant light forms are usually triangular—"since light comes in triangles"—and often mirror other elements of the design. In *Einstein* these phantom triangles could be found nearly everywhere one looked: streaming from the lamp of a steam locomotive or the headlight of a bus, falling down upon the great bed in the courtroom scenes, shooting out in long compressed shafts from the wings and beneath the stage in the final spaceship sequence. (While these light forms appeared in Wilson's 1976 line drawings for *Einstein* it was not until the opera's revival at BAM in 1984, when smoke was diffused into the air at Emmons' suggestion, that his original conception was fully realized.) The artist's experiments with visible beams continued in *D D & D*, where, inspired by photos of the "Cathedral of Light" Albert Speer created for the 1938 Nazi Party Day in Nuremberg, he produced a radiant wall of light with forty-one spotlights set in the stage floor. Another manifestation of light's power and presence—though not actually within Emmons' purview—is fire, which has long held a special fascination for Wilson. Open flames and banks of lighted candles were often seen in the early works (one of the most memorable images in *Deafman Glance* was Marie Antoinette slowly crossing the stage with her parasol aflame) and pyrotechnics continue to provide some of his most spectacular effects. In *The Golden Windows* a small planet in the sky burst into flames; in *Great Day in the Morning* flames suddenly leapt up inside a large glass box suspended from the flies ("Like a fire in an aquarium. Very scary."); in the opening scene of *the CIVIL warS* the advance of Frederick the Great's troops was traced on an enormous map by tiny red lights which literally exploded as row after row of soldiers fell dead on the stage below ("it was like watching the battle from outer space").

While Wilson has boldly explored most of light's properties, color is one element he applies with restraint. "There's no color in Bob's lighting in the sense that he doesn't use red or green or yellow the way some designers do. He takes white light and treats it as different shades of white. It's extremely subtle." Intense color is for contrast and dramatic effect; on occasion he may highlight an object in blue, turn the cyclorama to red for a few moments or even etch out different parts of the body in rainbow hues, as he did when he wanted Lucinda Childs "to look like a flower" in *Patio*. Interestingly enough, highly saturated colored lighting was often seen in Wilson's work during the early 1970s. This may be attributable to youthful tastes (psychedelic colors were in vogue at the time) and the fact that with little money or time for detailed technical rehearsals decisions were left in the hands of others; the day when Wilson would take control over every aspect of production still lay in the future.

Like Wieland Wagner, Wilson often says that he paints with light. During his lighting rehearsals, which can last several weeks, he sits out in the darkened auditorium like an artist before a canvas, detailing his composition moment by moment. "Again, Bob's a painter. He deals with what he's looking at. He sits halfway back and center and only cares what it looks like from there. If you moved him over fifteen seats he'd want it to look perfect from there. And then if he moved back to center, you'd have to change it all again. So you can't let him move." Emmons, who is usually to be found beside Wilson at a computer monitor (their designs are the product of electronic memory, which makes such precision, detail and consistency possible), sees herself less as a creative artist than a technician who implements his vision. "What you're always lighting for Bob is the picture in his head, not the one in your own. He does not ask my design opinion and I'm not supposed to supply a concept—art is Bob's department."

When asked if the lighting design for any Wilson production would have been different had she not been involved, Emmons replies, "No, and that's the point. It wouldn't be any different. It would have just been whether he could have gotten there or not. If a lighting designer starts from another perspective, Bob will bang them around until they arrive where he is. If they're resistant to his vision or their plot doesn't work, he'll sit in a scene and scream and scream to get what he wants and make them run around and move everything. If he's working with a designer who— from bitter experience—already knows his taste and has anticipated his needs, he can get further in his vision. The collaboration comes in my understanding what the fuck he's talking about and that's a very special skill." (Some friends say that Emmons is entirely too self-effacing about her contribution to Wilson's productions and that her own sensibility is very much in evidence.)

While Wilson has learned more and more about lighting in recent years, he still lacks the tools to realize his own design. "Bob himself does not know technically how

Jessye Norman in *Great Day in the Morning*, "The Lake." Paris, 1982.

Salome. La Scala, 1987.

to accomplish things and he doesn't know all the implications of his actions. For example, he often wants a zone of light that stretches across the stage from the wings. He thinks of this as a solid mass of light. Of course, light doesn't work that way. While he's getting better at it, he doesn't fully realize that in order to create a completely flexible and solid area of light you need a battery of different instruments. That's why he has to work with a lighting designer. Then, he sometimes wants what light doesn't naturally do. He develops the work with pen and ink and I think he tries to bend the reality into looking like the drawings. Just because you can draw it on paper doesn't mean you can make it happen on stage."

Because he doesn't formulate his lighting design prior to rehearsals, Wilson also needs someone to anticipate his wishes. "This is an area where I get angry with him. It's not fair to say he's lazy because the man works very hard, but the way he uses his time before a performing period doesn't include thinking about lighting in any detailed technical way. Since he doesn't tell me in any detail what he wants in advance—I get the feeling that he thinks I read his mind and therefore he doesn't have to take the trouble—my light plot is really a bunch of suggestions based on hints he's given me and what we've done before. And the success or failure of that plot is the success or failure of my guessing where his head is at the time. There's a lot of things I could do if only I knew in advance what he wanted. 'Oh, I wish I had known that. It's a beautiful idea, Bob. I don't know how to do it now, it's too late.'" While Emmons makes a point of "not saying 'no' to Bob too often," such last-minute requests and inspirations tend to go unrealized. "A week before the opening of the Rome *CIVIL warS* he suddenly announced that he wanted the outline of the bridge in the second scene reflected on the floor in rainbow colors. In *D D & D* he wanted to have one of the actors stand perfectly still while his shadow grew larger and larger on the wall behind him. With so little time left it was impossible." While these eleventh-hour proposals make life difficult for Wilson's collaborators, Emmons ultimately accepts them as part of the process. "No one in the theatre thinks of everything in advance and besides you never exactly know what light is going to do. Bob thinks of things as he goes along and quite often he doesn't know just what he needs until it's all there in the theatre."

Wilson's failure to share his ideas and his research can also present problems. "In *D D & D* he was yelling he wanted a branch on the prison wall. Then one day a book with a photo of Hess in the prison yard fell open. Very often he's trying to duplicate an image and all he would have to do is hand it to me and say 'This is what I want.' But he doesn't. I don't know if that's because he wants to keep it a secret—after all, the genius is not the picture but what he does with it—but there's a part of him that isn't sure that he should let that be known. Maybe it doesn't occur to him that anyone's interested in his process or that I would find it useful. But Bob knows what he wants and that's one of the things I love about him. There are directors who say they want A.

You make 'em A and they say, 'I don't like A. Make me B.' You make 'em B, 'I don't like B, let's go back to A.' Bob never goes back to A. He goes from A to B to C to D to E. Refining and refining, as long as they let him work." There are moments, however, when he does reach an impasse and though Emmons may suggest options or alternatives, Wilson usually insists on finding his own way. "If he truly doesn't know what he wants then he's desperate to hide the fact. He won't let me help him and he can be exceedingly stubborn. When he knows what he wants he's much more relaxed. It's only when he's uncertain that he insists on desperate solutions. I think what makes him a little jumpy about me is that I'm faster than he is. Sometimes that's good, sometimes it's bad. I can go very quickly and rough it all in but often if I get too far ahead of him and he doesn't know how it's all been put together or he doesn't have it all in his head, he'll get nervous, stop me and make me take it all out and bring each light on one at a time. Sometimes we get right back to where I had it. We could be much faster as a team if he would let go of it a little."

Emmons also sees herself as a mediator who must reconcile the needs of the artist with those of the producer. "I work for two people in the theatre and I try to keep both happy, not only the man but the man paying the bills. There are two things that make Bob an expensive proposition for a producer. First, he wants the scenery to be museum perfect. As far as he's concerned, the drops are paintings. In the theatre, we accept things much sloppier than he does and one of the things I love about working with Bob is his demand for real purity and real quality at every step of the process. At the same time I think it's a little irresponsible to cover a dress with jet black beading if you light it so nobody ever sees it. That gets into a compulsion to be perfect for its own sake, regardless of theatrical use. But Bob can make compromises when he needs to—and has to. Mostly it's going to show in his mind so you've got to be able to examine every element with a microscope and it has to be just as beautiful as it is from sixty or seventy feet back. That's both extraordinary and expensive. It's also expensive because he doesn't articulate this in advance. So he'll approve a drawing, the shop will start building and then he'll make them rebuild it six times, each time making it more perfect. Partly it's the fault of the theatre system which is to knock these things together and throw them on stage. When I'm there in time I try to get to people building the show and say, 'Don't make it a schlock job, make it perfect because he'll make you do it over.' And very often he won't know the degree of perfection he needs until everything's on stage and once you get into production time it's extremely expensive. It's a real challenge for any theatre to produce his work. If they expect him to compromise they can forget it."

Wilson's perfectionism also means he is unable to set priorities since every detail is of equal importance to him. "People like the Germans, who are trying to do exactly what the Master says, go berserk because they don't know what to work on first. The technical director of the theatre in Berlin came to me the day after I arrived and said,

'Tell me vat to do about the wrinkles?' And I said, 'Have you done everything you can possibly think of to do?' He said, 'Yes.' Then I said, 'Forget about it. Go on to other things.' Now I don't know whether that makes me disloyal to Bob but he just won't give them permission to go on. Every bit of our training is so violently opposed to his way of working. You've got to understand that what Bob does isn't theatre, it's art."

No matter how many weeks have been set aside for technical rehearsals, time always runs out before Wilson has fully achieved his aims or satisfied himself. Always there remain the unrealized possibilities. "For *Great Day in the Morning* Bob created a show curtain with a view of a little house in the forest. When it came to the lighting, he wanted it to change. He wanted morning and evening and all the seasons of the year. You could have spent a month on that drop. We had two hours. In *D D & D* he wanted the kid in the dinosaur costume to carry a fire extinguisher, battery pack and light bulb so that when the creature opened its mouth it could breathe fire. Well, that dancer could barely stagger across the stage with the weight as it was. The costume was sixteen feet high and they had to hang it up in the air to get him into it. Bob just wants more and more." Inevitably, Wilson exhausts his coworkers long before he does his own imagination. "But I don't want to emphasize the problems and the struggle rather than the respect I have for him. He's very frustrating to work with but he makes beautiful stuff. It's hard to do and it's expensive to do but it's worth doing, and that's why I'm involved with it. Actually, one of the things I love about Bob is that he'll never give up his 100-percent vision. People in the theatre would quit at 40 percent and tell him that the rest can't be done. Since he won't let them quit, he probably gets 80 percent. No matter how much anyone gives him, what he wants is always just out beyond their limits. That's the nature of the artist, he's a man who's very interested in limits and he goes out there all the time. Bob demands the best of everybody. The two little German electricians backstage during *D D & D* were sweating blood. Being good Germans they wanted it to be perfect and they were killing themselves. It was wonderful, just wonderful what they managed to accomplish. I had to reassure them because there were things Bob was asking for that were impossible and I'd tell them, 'Yes, it's impossible. And we're going to try and do it.'"

IV
SOUND
AND
MUSIC

The opening scene of *Deafman Glance*. 1971.

ALAN LLOYD/IGOR DEMJEN

Alan Lloyd was the first composer in Wilson's theatre, an odd, gentle, humorous and gifted artist whose death from AIDS in 1986 deprived American music of a distinctive voice. Unlike Wilson, whose theatre reflected its times and the downtown art scene, Lloyd was a child of the classical tradition. Gene Rickard, a personal friend and the vocal coach for the original production of *Einstein*, wrote some years ago that his was the kind of music that "might have been heard wafting from salon or drawing room. Lloyd's music could be Beethoven or Weber or Schubert but for an abrupt cadence, a long pause or an extended sequential figure to throw the musicologist off the track. Perhaps Lloyd derives his candor and impetuosity from contemporary America, but the shifting colors speak of an earlier, brocaded era, lit by candlelight." Delicacy, elegance, lyricism and irony are the distinguishing qualities of his music, and are reflected in the intimate instruments he favored—piano, clavichord, flute, strings and the human voice. Long before the term came into popular usage, Rickard identified him as a "new romantic."

During the early 1960s Lloyd attended Antioch College, where he studied composition and collaborated with the dancer Kenneth King, then a philosophy major. "King had a piano and he would let me come over and practice while he danced. It taught me how to build up my endurance and energy and it was very good training for theatre and dance work." It was through King that he met Wilson in the summer of 1968. Lloyd, who believed Wilson "could talk anyone into doing anything," was soon drafted into the upcoming production of *The King of Spain*. He spent several days sewing the famous cat's legs and appeared as the title character ("no one else would take it"), a grotesque red-haired creature who sat through the performance with his back to the audience, turning and revealing himself only moments before the curtain fell. About this time Lloyd also began providing incidental music for Wilson's productions, sometimes from an onstage piano, at other times from the wings. Selections included his own compositions and fragments from his sketchbooks as well as interpolations from the classical repertory—a Schubert impromptu, a Brahms intermezzo, a Bach prelude (repeated over and over in the drawing room scene) and music by Couperin, Mozart and Scriabin. "Atmosphere is the key to writing for Bob. If he likes the atmosphere of a piece he likes the piece. Once he had a scene on stage, Bob would say 'Oh, I need something here.' Mostly, though, he would find his own music. He had no musical education but such musical imagination. I walked into his loft once and he was playing a record of *Tosca* and singing back into the speaker. He loved music." Pieces were typically chosen for color or mood and drawn from divergent sources without regard to stylistic consistency: the Pachelbel canon, the pop song "Alley Cats," Strauss's "Blue Danube" to which the fifty black mammies waltzed in *Freud*, "Old Man River," Otis Redding's "I've Been Loving You Too Long to Stop Now" to which Wilson performed his signature dance. Lloyd put it simply: "Bob used anything he wanted."

For *A Letter for Queen Victoria* in 1974 Lloyd created the first performance-length score heard in Wilson's theatre, a delicate yet sensuous group of interlocking chamber pieces for string quartet and flute as well as a short aria (consisting of a single line, "Seven o'clock and the general's not here," followed by a scream). Lloyd's music, which was supplemented by ostinato violin interludes by Michael Galasso, received a Tony nomination when the production came to New York a year later. *Queen Victoria* was followed by *I Was Sitting on My Patio . . .* (1977), in which the composer once again sought to reanimate the musical language and sensibility of the early nineteenth century. In creating the score Lloyd worked with the production's sound technician, who read the script to him for several hours every morning as he improvised on the clavichord. While the score was created in conjunction with Wilson's text, and was in a sense inspired by it, it also remained an autonomous musical statement; as *Le Monde*'s theatre critic Jacques Lonchampt wrote, the "music floats above the action, not making it more explicit but collaborating in its mystery." Like Philip Glass's score for *Einstein* the previous year, Lloyd's composition mirrored Wilson's theatrical structure. *Patio* was divided into two parts with the same text spoken in succession by the two performers; Lloyd similarly created two versions of the same music—in the first act the basic piece was played on a sourish piano while in the second, with the order somewhat rearranged, it was heard on a dry, almost percussive clavichord. Together the two sections, which were classically organized in terms of introduction, statement, improvisation, inversion and trio, constituted a modified sonata.

Lloyd's collaboration with Wilson was by no means always easy or amicable. In contrast to Wilson, who seemed to whip up new pieces overnight, Lloyd found composing slow and difficult, and he felt that the director showed little concern or sympathy for his process. "Bob doesn't understand how long it takes to write music.

He thinks you just sit down and it all comes out magically. It was always 'I need this—do it in two hours' or 'You should have had the music written before I asked for it.' Finding what he wanted was usually a matter of guesswork." Even more troubling to Lloyd was Wilson's failure to respect the integrity of his compositions. "He'd get music from you before it was ready and if he liked it, he'd become committed to it and you wouldn't be. That happened a lot. If he decided he needed more music, he would repeat a phrase over and over. Then he'd get used to it and you couldn't get him to change it. Very often he used recordings in the early productions and I think he preferred them because he could turn them on and off as he wanted. Bob tried not to change my music around but he just . . . I wrote a string quartet for *Queen Victoria* and he wanted to have it rearranged for two voices. You just can't do that." It was during this time, Lloyd says, that the relationship went sour. "There were lots of terrible times, mostly having to do with money. Music was not a high priority with Bob. There was a day-to-day fight over everything, over musicians, over just getting a rehearsal piano. Bob could be very difficult and after a while I needed to get some distance. I think he also needed to move on and work with other people. I really didn't want to work for him after *Victoria* but he persuaded me to write *Patio* and then *D D & D*," their final collaboration. This time Lloyd made it as difficult as possible for the Byrd Hoffman Foundation to meet his demands, "thinking they'd have to turn me down." Much to his surprise he received everything he wanted—an orchestra, a recording studio and complete freedom. But the eight orchestral movements he created left him as dissatisfied as they did Wilson, who had wanted a full theatre score with recurring motifs such as Glass had provided for *Einstein*: "I got everything I wanted and it didn't turn out to be anything so you never know. You can't predict."

Although Lloyd looked back on their collaboration with ambivalence, he continued to regard Wilson with gratitude and admiration. "Bob was a very generous person yet he could also be quite frustrating. He was terribly encouraging, terribly proprietary and formative. He gave me so many opportunities. He cultivated me. He had a gift of cultivating people in some mysterious way and he provided a protective wing. Of course, there were fifty people competing for that protectiveness which made for some lively scenes. There's a lot to be said for him. He gave work to so many people and made so many friends—and so many enemies. He really is a person on another plane."

It would be difficult to find two composers more different than Alan Lloyd and Igor Demjen, who also worked with Wilson during the years of the Byrd Hoffman School. If Lloyd was heir to the classical tradition, Demjen was the committed son of modernism, for whom looping, splicing and synthesizing had far greater relevance than counterpoint and harmony. Demjen was studying music and art at the University of Iowa (where his father, a Czechoslovakian émigré, was a visiting professor) when he met Wilson, who had come to Iowa City to stage *Deafman Glance*. "At that time I had a big Oldsmobile and a friend of mine had a tape recorder which I wanted very badly for some reason. So I gave him the Oldsmobile and he gave me the tape recorder. I started doing things like dropping pieces of metal and glass and recording the sounds. What I did was very similar to *musique concrète*, splicing things together and making different sound patterns. Then I started adding synthesized sounds and got interested in how white noise and musical or natural sounds go together but with no particular idea in mind. I think Cage was really the fundamental influence on me with one simple sentence: everything is music. One night I was at a bar and I met Bob. We talked for a while and suddenly he said, 'I'm doing this play and I need someone to do the music. Would you work with me?' I looked around. Who was he talking to? 'No, no, no,' I said, 'I don't know anything about music'—I had only started studying—but finally I said yes." A month before the premiere of *Deafman* Wilson also persuaded Demjen to appear in an on-site presentation called *Handbill* at the New Museum: "Bob asked me to be an usher and stand naked at the door of the museum. I agreed but when it came to taking off my clothes and standing there—and when I saw the president of the university walking through the door—I said, 'No, I can't do that.' So I just watched the performance."

As music coordinator for *Deafman Glance*, one of Demjen's first tasks was to try to interpret "a piece of yellow paper with ten notes on it" which the unpredictable Lloyd, sometimes known as "Crazy Alan," had left behind when he took off for Ohio in the midst of rehearsals. The two musicians eventually became friends and for a time Demjen acted as a "chaperone," making "sure Alan didn't get lost" and prodding him to compose: "I was the catalyst, but if I hadn't been around there probably would have been someone else. One reason Bob invited me to work on *Deafman* was that Alan was incompetent in terms of large structures, though very competent in terms of particular compositions." With the exception of piano passages, usually provided live by Lloyd, and a string quartet in the Brazilian version of *Stalin*, the audial scores for Wilson's shows were entirely on tape, which Demjen assembled and mixed in performance.

"With music Bob was concerned with something very logical—that nothing went out of context. With so many different elements coming into his work, a harmony had to be created to sustain them all. It's like a painting where everything has to fit into the composition. What we were working with was rhythms. You must remember that because of the silence every step was audible. The crux of the performances was quiet, attention and mutual respect. Every sound, every noise, every single uttered syllable became part of the work's rhythmic beat. So a lot of musical things had to be toned down so they didn't draw attention to themselves. In *Deafman Glance* there was a piece of music which I don't think anybody ever noticed. It was a synthesized tape, which I called 'Tape,' and it made a sound like

'EEEeeeeEEEEeeeeEEEEeeeeEEE' with deep rumbles underneath. It played almost throughout the whole act. A lot of the music in the productions was subliminal. There was a very rich, almost inaudible context. A lot of what I did was meant to enhance the silence, to focus the ears in a very subtle way. I remember once when we were in Paris, Pierre Cardin's agent who was managing the company came into the sound booth and started banging on my back and hissing, 'Turn up the music, turn up the music! Nobody can hear it!' I said, 'Get out, get out!'"

The potent silence of these early works was often augmented by natural sounds — bird cries, the roar of the ocean, animal noises such as the bleating of sheep or the distant mooing of cows, human breathing and humming, wind and rain. Although Demjen was unaware of it, he was actually expanding on the work of a teenager named Hamp Sailer, who created the original sound designs for *The King of Spain* and *The Life and Times of Sigmund Freud* (and was nearly killed when the giant cat's legs and the steel tracks from which they hung came crashing down onto the stage the day of the premiere). As Wilson explained in his notes to *Freud,* those early sound scores were "based on the same principles as the stage activities in that different sounds at different times were in full register and other times they were dissolving or building." Often noises and musical fragments would be layered one on top of another, creating a fabric of shifting sound not unlike the work of Terry Riley, which Demjen greatly admired. Perhaps Demjen's most arresting construction in this vein was "Watermill," a layered tape piece inspired by the Fauré Requiem which lasted as long as three hours in some versions. "There were nine notes at the end of the requiem that struck me for some reason and I started working with them, just those nine notes. That single phrase repeated without changing for the first fifteen minutes of the piece. It was a device to get people out of their expectations and it was very hard on a lot of ears. It sounds almost cruel but at the time I thought that's what it took. Then I made a lot of loops and added harmonic drones underneath and modulated the sound. I had about five tape recorders with all these loops going simultaneously. Over the years the piece became the national anthem of the Byrd Hoffman group. Eventually there were about fifteen different tape recorders so everything became densely overlaid. In the final part I took some voices from a Wagner opera and built them to a crescendo and then there were drums from another part of the requiem and some harps that defused everything." Although Demjen originally mixed all the tapes on the spot so that each performance was a little different, he created a permanent version at the Xenakis studio in Paris during the 1971 *Deafman* tour which became the accompaniment for the dance section in *Prologue* and was later integrated into the fifth act of *Stalin*. "After one performance in Paris an older man came back and told me, 'This is wonderful.' I didn't know until later that it was Aaron Copland."

Demjen stresses the collaborative nature of his work with Wilson, especially when speaking of the creation of the musical continuity for the productions. "Bob and I would sit down together and I'd pull tapes out of a box which I thought might interest him. I never imposed anything on him. Bob was the judge and he would say 'Oh, that's interesting' and one of us would decide where to put it. We would spend nights in the sound studio pushing buttons and playing with pieces of sound. It's very hard to say whose ideas were whose. It was a collaborative effort and to attempt to determine who did what is not to see the nature of the work. Bob and I were usually in total agreement and we very, very rarely discussed anything. It was fantastic how we were able see things as one all the time. From the beginning, after an initial period of not being able to stand one another, we had a method of working that was not a method, it was love."

Demjen created his most massive audial score for *KA MOUNTAIN* in 1972. During the weeklong performance "every single sound that I ever recorded got played somewhere" (he estimates that by that time he had collected as many as five thousand tapes). These recorded sounds and musical fragments were augmented by a wealth of natural noises provided on-site by the zoo at the bottom of the hill, wind, thunder, the city below and the chants of the local inhabitants, all of which Demjen considered an intrinsic part of the work's aural continuity: "Since I believe that everything is music, I was never aware of any interruptions. As Cage would say, when I listen to Beethoven with the window open the sound of the trucks passing by outside enhances the music for me."

The 24-four hour *Overture* presented at the Opéra Comique in Paris the following November can be seen as the culmination of the composer's work with the Byrd School. For this performance Demjen created a continuous, densely layered mesh of music, noise, sound and speech over which he presided from a glass-enclosed booth in the orchestra pit. "This underground room was filled with tape recorders, synthesizers and microphones. The concept was like Cage's 'Fontana Mix.' There were a lot of natural sounds and excerpts from opera and radio music. From time to time I would also pull someone from backstage and bring them to a mike and ask them to read or say something. Then there was a texture of sound from a long row of tape recorders which kept slowly building up—the only time the sound level was ever overpowering. For me the whole thing was a big game. You were allowed to do anything you wanted." A new musical element was provided by Michael Galasso, who would become another of the Byrd School composers: "Michael used to play the violin in the Paris subways and he hung around the theatre. He came up to me one day and said, 'I can play the violin.' I said, 'Can you do this—go into that room and play the same note for five hours?' And he said 'Sure.' He stayed there for about two hours playing the same note nonstop until that note became so beautiful I came in and said, 'That's great, that's great. Now add another one.' Then another. He came up with this very plaintive piece and we put him at the front of the stage where he stood throughout the performance."

Demjen continued to work with Wilson until 1974, when he became "the first to leave the company from the so-called inner core" after an engagement in São Paulo. "Bob was always being put into the coordinating role, especially by the critics for whom egotism was the main standard of judging. In Brazil this came to a head. We kept saying, 'What is this? Why Bob? Bob is just sitting around doing what everyone else is doing.' The great thing about the Byrd Hoffman Foundation was that it was so deeply collaborative. On the inside this was well known but on the outside it was always Robert Wilson's work, which it never was."

Demjen's years with the Byrd Hoffman School were to have a lasting effect on his music, though he credits Alan Lloyd rather than Wilson with bringing this about. "Meeting Bob didn't do anything for me. Bob never understood anything about music at all though he had a great sensitivity and that makes up for everything. Meeting Alan changed me entirely. At the time I was very much involved with *musique concrète* and Terry Riley—things that titillated my ear—and I believed that melody and counterpoint were passé. Alan said to me, 'What nonsense, these things are eternal. Look, you either want to create beauty or you want to convey all these modern precepts of behavior and aesthetics.'" At a time when everything was music, Demjen came to realize that music was also music. "Alan encouraged me to sit down at a piano and slowly I taught myself to play and was able to introduce classical arabesque into what I was doing. Basically what Alan said was look for a voice within. I would say that the only way Bob has done anything for me is by being my friend— which is the biggest thing—and by being totally nonjudgmental. I remember a particular incident at the Opéra Comique. I was opening with a piano piece and before the performance I rehearsed and rehearsed upstairs until it was total perfection. Then I got behind the piano before the curtain opened and I was playing and playing and I was really playing fantastically and then suddenly I hit a wrong note and I froze. And the audience went 'Ohhh.' I wanted to continue but I couldn't. I tried again but finally I got up and walked away, feeling terribly guilty about having spoiled the whole thing. I was backstage and Bob came up to me and said 'Igor! That was beautiful!'

"And that was the thing about Bob, he really only looked at the crest in people. He never bothered with anything else. And this, I think, provided us with the power to do what we did. You know, a lot of my friends accuse Bob of doing this or that to them but as far as I'm concerned it was their own egos that did it to themselves. Bob just said, 'Do what you want to do.' A lot of people went mad, they couldn't stand the responsibility of being up in front of two thousand people and having that kind of freedom. A lot of people also get mad at Bob because he's so single-minded. He does what he wants and people get hurt because they've got their hopes, they come in with 'I want to do this' and by the time they finish thinking about it, Bob is in Rome. What I want to say about Bob's work is this. Many people think it went downhill after

Program Prologue Now. Espace Cardin, Paris, 1971.

Stalin. I myself think there was a period when he was trying to do new works but he was still using the old elements, and it became repetitious. On the other hand, Bob moving in new directions has remained just as fascinating as he ever was." Inevitably, Demjen's view of Wilson's work reflects his own interests in metaphysics and religion. "In my opinion Bob's vision is foreboding and apocalyptic. There are two facets of Christ, one is where he says if you do this you'll get into trouble and the other is if you do this you'll see light. Bob is still dealing with the foreboding side of Christ. I saw *The Golden Windows* at BAM recently and it was set on this planet and there was a watchtower with light coming out and these lonely characters who spoke of their life experiences. Bob is still involved with this struggle between life and death, light and dark. The whole vision is rather scary. I hope that at some point he'll get to the part about seeing the light and it won't be coming from a military watchtower — it will be coming from all over."

PHILIP GLASS

Over twelve years after the premiere of their epoch-making opera *Einstein on the Beach*, Philip Glass remains the collaborator with whom Wilson is most closely identified. In a sense that historic collaboration, the first time Wilson was to work on an equal footing with an artist of his own stature, had its beginnings in 1974 at the final New York performance of *The Life and Times of Joseph Stalin*, when Glass saw Wilson's work for the first time and immediately sensed the possibilities of such a partnership. "I thought *Stalin* was a wonderful piece. It's important to note that though it was the first Wilson piece I'd ever seen, I had worked with the Mabou Mines since 1965 and had an in-depth familiarity with the new theatre. I had been following the Living Theatre since 1958 or '59 and I knew Richard Foreman and Meredith Monk's work. This kind of theatre was a natural for me. Very often when people come to Bob's work from the traditional theatre experience, they're impressed because it's something they've never seen before. But if you've grown up in New York in the sixties and lived in the world of the theatre, you know about this work and what kind of work it is. What was remarkable about what I saw wasn't that it was so new but that it was so individualized, so particular and refined. I was especially impressed with the lighting, which must have been fairly primitive compared with what Bob can do today, but was still—shall I say—light years beyond anyone else. I knew that we would do a piece. I hadn't even met him but this was obvious. First of all, the weak area of the work for me was the use of music, which was sensitive but had no pronounced character. *A Letter for Queen Victoria*, which Alan Lloyd did in association with Michael Galasso a few years later, was a much more coherent piece of music and superior in its way. While *Stalin* had a great sweep to it, a great sense of space and time and scale, it seemed to me that Bob needed something more. I just thought I would be able to work with the man." At the end of the performance, Glass went backstage and met Wilson, who invited him to a party immediately afterwards at his

Spring Street loft. "I told Bob I liked the work and he said he knew mine, though I wonder whether we knew each other's work very well at that point." They talked for a while and agreed to meet for lunch several days later. "We eventually decided to meet every Thursday when we were both in New York at a little restaurant in SoHo. We talked in a general way and didn't press ourselves too much about coming up with a work. We gave ourselves time to get to know each other. There's no doubt that we liked each other as artists and people."

Although the two men were a study in contrasts—the reserved, laconic Wilson and the down-to-earth, outgoing, well-educated Glass (a child prodigy, he entered the Peabody Conservatory of Music at the age of eight and received his undergraduate degree from the University of Chicago in philosophy and mathematics at nineteen), they found that they shared many of the same interests and values. "We both came out of the world of the theatre and, certainly, the community we lived in was a common community. We shared a great admiration for Cunningham and Cage—dance was more important to Bob than theatre, I on the other hand related more to Cage and had spent a little time with him—and also within that circle, Jasper Johns and Robert Rauschenberg. These were the older generation for us and the people we looked up to. While they were not exactly our mentors, because neither of us did work similar to theirs, they expressed in their lives and work a kind of authority that was completely admirable. They gave a whole sense of how an artist lives in American society and how he expresses himself and communicates to a younger generation. People always remark that one of the things Bob and I have in common is that we work in the same time sense, and of course that's obvious, it's something I already knew. In 1974, I was completing a six-hour piece called *Music in Twelve Parts*. It had taken me three years to write and was performed in New York, Paris and Houston. This was a continuously evolving piece of music, unlike Satie's *Vexations* which is the same thing over and over again, though there are people who may fail to see the difference. Before that I had done an evening-length piece called *Music in Changing Parts*, which lasted two hours without intermission. So an extended time sense was something I was already working in."

That summer Wilson flew to Italy for the premiere of *Queen Victoria* and then toured with the production through Europe. When he returned to New York near the end of the year the two men resumed their weekly meetings. "I had just finished a major work and Bob had just finished a major work. We were not exactly at loose ends but I think we were both ready for a new project." After another couple of months of "'idling'—not in the sense of useless or inactive conversation but discussion that isn't in gear," Wilson and Glass finally committed themselves in early 1975 to creating a work together. They did not begin with a subject or a theme but with two elements common to their respective arts: time and structure. "We decided at the beginning to do a four-hour work. There would be four acts and each would be about an hour long." Next they needed an idea around which a series of images and scenes could be organized. Most of Wilson's previous pieces had focused on the life of a historical character—Sigmund Freud, Queen Victoria, Joseph Stalin—who had changed the world and would be immediately recognizable to any audience. Wilson again chose to employ this organizing principle, initially envisioning another work to be called *The Life and Times of* . . . ." "What's important," says Wilson, "is that we come into the theatre sharing something. In a sense, we don't have to tell a story because the story's already been told." Glass was in full agreement: "It's very much in line with the idea that the audience brings something real to the experience, that the audience completes the work. That's a generational belief and something I grew up with in the theatre."

In an article that appeared in the *New York Times* the day *Stalin* opened in 1973, Wilson said that he could have chosen Chaplin, Hitler or Einstein as his title character; and each of these was in turn suggested to Glass. "Einstein wasn't the first idea. Bob initially proposed Chaplin and Hitler. I didn't want to do Chaplin because I didn't see how a man who was such an incredible performer could be portrayed on the stage, you'd need a Chaplin-like person. It would immediately create a problem because you would be comparing the performance to something outside the work and I didn't want that. Hitler I just didn't want to think about for two years. I suggested Gandhi, which Bob didn't want to do and of course that became my second opera, *Satyagraha*. I was very keen on Gandhi but Bob wasn't interested and I never inquired why. It just didn't make his mouth water. The thing I've discovered is that our instincts were very correct at the time. In order to commit to a piece that's going to take two years, you have to be passionately involved with the ideas and subject matter. Our feeling was it had to be something we both cared about and that could sustain our energies for that period of time. At one of these meetings Bob said, 'How about Einstein?' And I said, 'Great.' It was simple, it was done. I had read a lot about Einstein as a kid growing up in Baltimore after the Second World War. I was born in 1937 and by the time I was eight years old the nuclear age had begun. As a young adolescent, like everyone else in America I was suddenly bombarded with books on relativity and articles on Einstein. He was the perfect hero for me." Einstein was also a congenial subject for Wilson, who envisioned the great physicist not merely as another legendary figure but as a fellow dreamer, mystic and time traveler. (His simple humanity and "ordinariness" must have impressed him in the same way that Sigmund Freud's had a few years earlier.) As Wilson said some years later, although Chaplin and Hitler were rejected as subjects, Einstein was someone who could encompass both: the comic tramp (Einstein was in fact viewed as a rather Chaplin-esque figure by many of his contemporaries) and the little man who unleashed new terrors on the world.

"Coming back to Einstein at the age of thirty-seven, the first thing I did was get the

Clark biography (*Einstein: The Life and Times*). I offered the book to Bob a number of times but he would never take it. We had a lot of discussion about that and it became a kind of joke between us. I said, 'Bob, this book's real interesting' and I would show him pictures in it. But Bob has his own way of doing research which is quite different from mine. His way was to collect photographs of Einstein and to talk to people about him. He said to me once, 'I don't want to know any more than what everyone knows about Einstein. I just want to know what the man in the street knows because that's what they'll be bringing to the work. If he snuck off and read a book about Einstein he never told me, but I don't believe he did. In order for me to do a portrait of a person—and I've done a number since then—I have to totally immerse myself in their work and life and at a certain moment I form a subjective image of the person which has a musical context. Then I can write the piece. I've done it with Gandhi, Muybridge (*The Photographer*, 1982), Akhnaten (1984), and Mishima (1985). *Einstein* was the first time I'd attempted this. Reading about him and thinking about him was the only way I knew how to begin. It often meant that the two of us were not working from the same source. I was working from a literary-historical base and Bob from a populist idea of Einstein."

Having agreed on a four-act structure, a length of four hours ("as you know we missed") and a subject, the two men began discussing possible visuals. While some composers would have been uncomfortable creating an opera out of associational imagery rather than from a story or scenario, Glass found it "the most natural thing in the world. My experience in theatre had not led me to approach opera in the traditional way, which is to take a text and set it to music. I really grew up in the tradition of nonliterary theatre. Beginning in the early sixties, there was a whole generation of people who did not work from a literary base—it never occurred to anyone to take a play and set it to music, no one ever did that. I'm only doing it for the first time now. With the Mabou Mines, the inception of a work could be a drawing, a gesture, it could be a word or a title. Very often the text came last. It seems to me that in the 1960s, the designers, directors and composers—all those who had been the secondary people in the theatre—somehow usurped the role of the author and become the authors themselves. My connection to the theatre has always been strongly visual. During the first Mabou Mines tour in 1970, I was one of the people who put up the set and the lights. I was also the adopted child of the art world and consider myself part of a generation of visual artists. So it was quite easy for me to work with Bob. I didn't say to him as some composers might have, 'I can't write. Where's my text?' And in a way the character of Einstein replaced the plot or story. I felt that the historic context gave the work a terrific focus."

Wilson and Glass began "circling in" on their subject at their weekly meetings. Like Einstein, who was known to scribble diagrams and equations on tablecloths and scraps of paper, Wilson covered every available surface with his sketches. "Bob began thinking about trains and courtrooms. We looked at quite a number of ideas before we settled on three. The way we worked was that Bob proposed images to me and I would say, 'I like that' or 'No, nothing.' What we were trying to do was arrive at a group of images we both felt we could work with. We had agreed to work on things we both felt strongly about. To me the biggest problem in the theatre is always what the piece is about." Stefan Brecht has written that in Wilson's early works, images are neither shaped nor ordered "by logical principles, concepts or ideas"; they appear to metamorphose "according to their own nature," without the "interference of a conscious artist." With *Queen Victoria* Wilson began to choose and structure his material with far greater rigor and economy, and he was to move even further in this direction with *Einstein,* the first work in which every major image related in some way to the life of its protagonist. Although Glass isn't certain, he feels he may have been inadvertently responsible for the opera's more coherent network of imagery. At one point, for example, Wilson proposed a barroom scene with a cowboy in a ten-gallon hat. "There was a saloon and some guy with a gun. I couldn't see how I could make that part of the work, I didn't see what it had to do with Einstein. If it doesn't have an emotional sense for me the music won't work. Perhaps I was also troubled by Aaron Copland's pieces dealing with the American West. I may not have felt like dealing with that kind of musical imagery." One of the main images actually evolved out of Glass's early suggestion that they create a science-fiction opera: "Bob wasn't so interested in that but he said, 'Let's put some spaceships in it.' So this also became a part of the opera."

A few weeks into their discussions Wilson had a tentative title. "Bob wrote down *Einstein on the Beach on Wall Street* and I just laughed. I thought it was a great idea." (The director had recently completed *The $ Value of Man,* a work interwoven with images of commerce and capitalism.) The last part of the title was quickly discarded, "probably because Bob didn't feel like writing it out." Although mention was never made of Nevil Shute's apocalyptic novel *On the Beach* (Glass says he has never read it), Wilson later revealed in an interview that he had seen the film, but said that he chose the title because "I found it beautiful. I liked it, that's all." (It may simply be that the title was inspired by a photo he came across of Einstein standing at the seashore.)

Wilson and Glass finally settled on three basic images—train, trial and space-ship—which would be seen in various incarnations and from varying perspectives in the course of the opera. The train and the spaceship both relate obliquely to the life of Einstein, who was born in the age of the steam locomotive and died on the brink of the space age which his pioneering work helped bring about. Together the two images trace the trajectory of the physicist's life and both were bound to appeal to Glass, who at the time associated his music with motors, engines and modern machinery. The remaining image, a courtroom with an enormous bed at its center, did not seem to have any basis in the life or work of Einstein, though its associations are perhaps the most powerful in the opera. "Bob and I never really knew what the trial was. When Bob suggested something to me I never asked, 'What does it mean?' I think that's why Bob likes working with me. He would draw something and say, 'This is the trial,' and I'd just watch him draw for fifteen or twenty minutes. I wasn't sure what it meant but it didn't matter very much to me. I was able to work easily in a theatre where image turned to image and the rules of causality were suspended. What was important was that the trial came after the train—the dramatic sequence was crucial." Glass's concern as a composer was that a scene of propulsive energy generated by the image of a steam locomotive would be followed by the static and controlled tableaux of the courtroom, which would in turn yield to the free and rapid dance sequences of the field/spaceship scenes. Glass was interested in the contrasts of density, motion and tempo and the associational power of the images themselves. "To me what something meant wasn't important. What was important was that it was meaningful, and that's a very important difference. If you're looking at the haystacks of Monet, what do they mean? You don't know. You can look at a portrait by Rembrandt and be overwhelmed by its meaningfulness and not be able to tell exactly what it means. The conviction of meaningfulness is all that was necessary for me. Even if I had needed to ask what the trial was, Bob couldn't have supplied a proper answer. So those questions didn't come up."

The trial in *Einstein* is an example of Wilson's ability to create images that lack specific meaning yet fill the mind and imagination. What crime had been committed and who is being judged? Wilson was later to say that he always felt the bed itself was on trial. Is the dreamer, whose capacity for discovery and creation may yet bring the world to the verge of destruction, the defendant? Is it imagination or science or human knowledge or time (which Einstein redefined) or the universe itself? The questions are never answered nor can they be. Like the title *Einstein on the Beach*, which may refer to humanity brought to the brink of annihilation, man on the shore of the unknown or—as one critic jokingly suggested—that "we're all washed up" (or perhaps only a man standing by the ocean), Wilson's image evokes many responses and resonates many meanings, but yields no certain answers. "It's not a question of what *Einstein* means," as Glass says, "it's that it's meaningful."

The two men next finalized the structure of the opera and agreed on the time lengths of the various sections. Wilson also devised a series of short, intimate episodes called "knee plays" (K 1-5) to punctuate the major scenes. Just as time served as a denominator of their respective arts, the language of numbers now provided them with another common principle to organize the work (and one likely to appeal to Wilson, who had become interested in simple mathematics as a result of his work with Christopher Knowles). The scenic and musical development of *Einstein* would be controlled by permutations of the number three: there would be three basic images—train (1), trial (2), spaceship (3)—and each would appear three times. The nine episodes were then distributed over four acts so that every possible numerical combination (1,2; 3,1; 2,3; 1,2,3) was made in the course of the opera:

K 1

    ACT I SC. 1 TRAIN [1]

        SC. 2 TRIAL (BED) [2]

K 2

    ACT II SC. 1 FIELD (SPACE MACHINE) [3]

        SC. 2 TRAIN [1]

K 3

    ACT III SC. 1 TRIAL (BED)/PRISON [2]

        SC. 2 FIELD (SPACE MACHINE) [3]

K 4

    ACT IV SC. 1 BUILDING/TRAIN [1]

        SC. 2 BED [2]

        SC. 3 SPACE MACHINE (INTERIOR) [3]

K 5

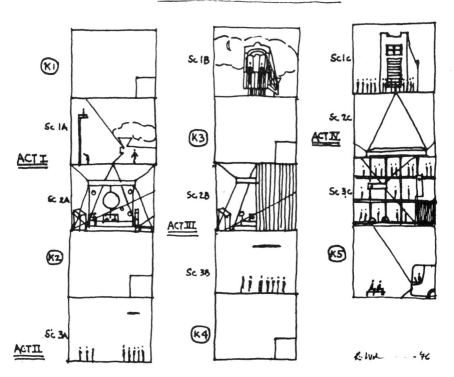

EINSTEIN ON THE BEACH AN OPERA IN 4 ACTS

"The numerical scheme is an important conceptual part of the work's structure. What we're doing is taking two three-part structures and spreading them over three two-part structures. Consider for the moment the first three acts—each of those acts is in two sections (sc. 1, 2) and against that I'm putting two three-part structures (1-2-3, 1-2-3). That's something we do in music all the time. The fourth act is 1-2-3 all together—it's actually a recap of the first three acts. What we have is a musical idea that works as a dramatic idea, and that's why it appealed to both Bob and myself. It gave us a common structure."

Having reached agreement on the form, length and thematic content of the opera, Glass set to work on the score while Wilson continued to refine his drawings. Although they worked independently for several months, Glass believes "that we're so much in the same place and understand so well what the other person is doing that our work is not really independent." In fact, Glass worked directly from a notebook filled with sketches that Wilson had sent him from Paris. "I put it on the piano and composed each section like a portrait of the drawing before me. The score was begun in the spring of 1975 and completed by the following November, and those drawings were before me all the time." Although Glass knew the time length for each sequence and what might happen on stage, he and Wilson never discussed the mood or emotional content of a scene. Like so many of their contemporaries, they "felt the emotional content would be the result of our work, not something we would try to do but something that would arise spontaneously." The one musical request Wilson made was that there be singing throughout the piece. "I think Bob had a bug up his ass about opera. He had always called his pieces operas and maybe he thought that with me he could finally do a real one. He was much more interested in *Einstein* being like a real opera than I was. Bob wanted as much singing on stage as possible and he was very pleased that there was a duet in the night train scene and an aria for the flying bed. Even though Bob had little interest in traditional opera, he encouraged some of its trappings. I always thought of *Einstein* as a music-theatre work while Bob thought of it more as an opera, maybe it's an equivocation of what those two things are. It didn't really matter to me though later, of course, it became rather convenient for me that people viewed it as an opera."

Like Wilson, who considers all of his plays and spectacles part of a greater evolving work and often carries over scenes and images from one piece to another, Glass conceived *Einstein on the Beach* as part of an ongoing project dealing with problems of rhythmic and harmonic structure (and even incorporated material from his recent "Another Look at Harmony" into the new work.) The musical idiom in which *Einstein* was composed had its beginnings in the mid-sixties, when Glass was studying with Nadia Boulanger in Paris and was asked to work with the Indian sitar player Ravi Shankar. "I discovered that a piece of music could be organized around the idea of rhythm rather than harmony and melody as I had been taught." He began working with simple harmonic progressions, steady driving rhythms and the expansion and contraction of short, repetitive musical phrases, fostering with a number of other New York composers a style that came to be known as "minimalism." In "Music in 12 Parts" (1974) Glass had "developed a vocabulary of techniques (additive processes, cyclic structure and combinations of the two) to apply to problems of rhythmic structure" and in "Another Look at Harmony" the following year he turned to problems of structural harmony. Now in *Einstein* he attempted to link harmonic structure directly to a base rhythmic structure, reversing the traditional priorities of Western music. "What I was trying to discover was a function between rhythm and harmony. We have what's called functional harmony but I wanted to find a rhythmic structure that was functional in terms of harmony. Everything in *Einstein* is about that, there's practically no note in the piece that doesn't conform to that idea. The opera is rather obsessive in that way." (While Glass and Wilson may both enjoy the challenge of filling in arbitrary time structures of their own making, the idea of taking on an artistic or intellectual problem and attempting to solve it in a work of art is alien to the director.)

Glass also set out to underscore and reinforce Wilson's visual structure with various combinations of the number three. "It isn't enough just to write music that's effective or descriptive — it's not, for instance, very hard to make music that sounds like a train. What you need is a structure that pulls you through the piece. What I tried to do in *Einstein* was follow the visual structure through the musical structure. Bob is always very conscious of staging a work so you can hear the music and I've always been conscious of writing the music so you can see the images. What makes *Einstein* a uniquely collaborative work is that we're both looking at each other's work through our own. For example, in the very first scene of the opera the train comes on three times and that immediately gave me the idea of a three-part structure. In the first train scene, you hear all three parts or themes of the train music. Then in the night train scene we have just the the first theme, in the building scene we have the second theme and in the final spaceship scene the third theme":

ACT I, SC. 1 (TRAIN)	ACT II, SC. 2 (NIGHT TRAIN)	ACT IV, SC. 1 (BUILDING)	ACT IV, SC. 3 (SPACESHIP)
THEMES 1 ——————————— 1			
2 ————————————————————— 2			
3 ———————————————————————————————— 3			

"Each appearance of a theme is a further playing out of that theme. To say that the scenes mirror one another isn't accurate, what we have is more like an extrusion. Each time you come back to the train music you're further along, you're in a different place." The trial music is similarly made up of three sections which are distributed over corresponding scenes:

ACT I, SC. 2 (TRIAL)	ACT III, SC. 1 (TRIAL/PRISON)	ACT IV, SC. 2 (BED)
THEME 1 ——————————————— 1	————————————————— 1	
	THEME 3	
THEME 2 ——————————————— 2	————————————————— 2	

Where Wilson had taken three images and distributed them over a two-part structure (Acts I-III), Glass took a two-part musical structure (train, trial) and distributed it over three images (train, trial, spaceship). His decision to give the spaceship the third train theme rather than a theme of its own emphasized the correspondence between the two machines and the opera's progression from the age of steam to the age of space travel. The two earlier sections in which the spaceship appears in the sky above a field filled with dancers were largely created from independent material, though once again the number three figured in Glass's conception. "I thought of the dances as two pillars that were equidistant from either end of the opera, dividing the piece into thirds—the first third is before the first dance, the second third between the two dances and the last third after the second dance. It's a very musical idea. The first and second dances are actually different versions of the same piece. It's as if you took the same exact materials and built two different houses."

Although Glass spent a great deal of time thinking about the shape and musical content of *Einstein,* the actual process of composition was accomplished very quickly, most scenes taking no more than two days. Last to be completed were the knee plays (each composed in two to three hours), which draw on themes from the main scenes and "represent an almost epigrammatic presentation of the ideas of the opera." Glass scored the opera for his own ensemble of amplified keyboards and winds, to which he added voices and a solo violin part to be played by a musician dressed as Einstein, who had been an amateur violinist. "I immediately knew when we chose the subject that we would have a violinist who was Einstein and he would be the link between the stage and the pit, and in fact Bob literalized this relationship by having him sit halfway between."

One of the most striking passages in the score is the electrifying musical climax of the final spaceship scene, with its blasting chordal shifts and soaring organ runs: "At one point I said, 'Bob, what about a big finale?' and he said 'Okay' and that was the end of the conversation. It was the only moment in making the piece that either of us talked about a conventional theatre formula." At the time of the opera's revival at the Brooklyn Academy of Music, Glass told an interviewer that "I wrote a piece I hoped would get people up on their feet, and by God it worked! I said, 'Bob, I'm almost embarrassed at how well it works, because it seems somehow so *calculated.*' But in a way, that's what theatre is all about, and it would be false to pretend we aren't conscious of the dramatic flow of an evening. We're both theatre people and we had to

Einstein on the Beach. Act IV, sc. 1C (Building). 1976.

embrace the strategies of the theatre. Verdi did it, so did Mozart, so did Wagner." Glass also admits to having employed harmonies "right out of Berlioz," especially evident in the rapidly moving chromatic bass lines of the finale. Like Wilson, he isn't afraid of making use of elements from the past: "What makes a piece new isn't a new harmony or a new kind of tonal organization; it's a new perception."

While Glass was completing the score of *Einstein*, Wilson was finalizing his scenic designs, which had evolved from the dark expressionistic drawings in Glass's workbook to the cool, geometric pictures audiences would see at the Avignon Festival the following summer. Unlike such theatrical compendiums as *KA MOUNTAIN* and *Stalin,* the new opera was to make only the most general use of visual motifs from previous pieces. The gyroscope that descends almost imperceptibly across the proscenium in the trial scenes brings to mind such "timepieces" as the hanging chair and crossing tortoise in *Freud.* The row of prison bars that splits the stage in two in Act III, sc. 1 has antecedents in the bars that close off the cave in *Freud* and the descending grill in *A Letter for Queen Victoria.* From *Queen Victoria* also come the triangles that appear in nearly every scene of the opera, another incarnation of the number three. ("Once you start looking for triangles in *Einstein*," Wilson has said, "you find them everywhere.") To these Wilson added other simple geometric shapes—circles (clocks, compasses, moon, eclipse, sun dial, lamps, the disc-shaped spaceship), lines (various bands of light) and rectangles; as April Kingsley later wrote in the *SoHo Weekly News,* the artist "honors Euclid while depicting his demise."

From the life of Einstein Wilson also took the image of the 1919 solar eclipse, in which the appearance of two stars on either side of the sun demonstrated the curvature of space, supporting the theory of relativity; the example the physicist offered of a man lying in a box with a clock traveling at the speed of light; and his offhand comment that if he had his life to live over again he'd just as soon be a plumber, which led Wilson (so he says) to construct chairs and tables out of ordinary piping materials. While the visual environment of the opera was now very clear in his mind, Wilson had at best only a sense of what might happen within it. What Glass calls "the libretto," the fabric of human exchange that most operas and plays have as their starting point, had yet to be created.

The final developmental phase of *Einstein* began in December when a company was selected and daily rehearsals (which were to last nearly four months) got under way at Wilson's New York loft. "It's interesting how few of the old performers were in this piece. The only person he carried over was Sheryl. He had done a number of pieces with one group and now he wanted to work with new people. Our rehearsal day was divided into three parts: one for dance in the morning, one for music in the afternoon and one after that for the staging. We didn't have a rehearsal pianist so I had to play through all three rehearsals." Although Wilson often says that the visual and aural content of his works are independent and he could replace the score of *Einstein*

Einstein on the Beach. The Trial. 1976.

with Wagner or Haydn if he chose, Glass sees the two as closely bound together. "Although certain parts of the work were done independently, we didn't follow the model of Cage and Cunningham very closely. In fact, there were no staging rehearsals without music. Those rehearsals often began with our listening to the music and looking at Bob's drawings. Then people would get up and improvise things to the music, which Bob would select from and refine. You see, it's not independent at all. The music shapes the action in the same way that the visual structure does. It shares with it a full authorship role. Now with *the CIVIL warS,* Bob completely staged the piece and then I wrote the music. So it turns out you can do it either way."

Although Wilson and Glass had talked often and at length about nearly every aspect of the opera in the preceding months, once rehearsals began they observed a respectful silence. "What we do is look at each other's work and not say very much. I remember the only comment he made in maybe a year and a half of working together was, 'Isn't that piccolo a little shrill?' I said, 'Maybe you're right,' and changed it to a flute. And the one comment I made was in Venice when Bob was thinking about the waiting platform he had built for the night train scene and said to me, 'I hate this piece of scenery, I think I'll throw it into the canal,' and I said, 'That's a very good idea.' I was reluctant to make any comments about what Bob did and he was reluctant to make comments about what I did. On the other hand we watched intently what the other person was doing all the time." Even when he didn't think the evolving staging complemented his music, Glass refrained from comment. "I was already well instructed in the collaborative and improvisational process through my work with the Mabou Mines and I knew that a lot of times you have to wait and see what happens. What you're watching at that moment isn't what you're going to end up with. I also didn't want to disturb the process by intruding and saying 'I hate it,' which can have exactly the wrong effect. I didn't like everything I saw but I saw things evolve. It seemed to me that the best way I could support Bob's work was to sit there and play the music and watch everything. And I think it might have been important for him to have me to talk to when he needed to. Anyway, there were very few things we disagreed about. Bob really has an excellent musical ear. While he can't exactly articulate what he's hearing in musical terms, he's a careful listener and an accurate listener and I think he understands music in the best sense that a listener understands music."

During rehearsals Wilson continued to introduce dislocated elements from the life of Einstein into the work. Photos of the scientist at various stages of life were inserted in the knee plays, as were his last page of calculations, the phrase "Bern 1905" (the city and year in which his first paper on relativity was published) and the image of the great man sticking his tongue out for photographers. Wilson was fascinated by the curious way Einstein held his thumb and forefinger together in the photos he had examined and this gesture became a motif in the performance choreography.

(Eventually, all the performers would be outfitted in Einstein's habitual costume of shirtsleeves, suspenders, wristwatch and tennis shoes.) Glass remembers how the trial of the newspaper heiress Patty Hearst for armed robbery also provided an unexpected source of inspiration: "Bob would show me articles in the newspapers every day and we would discuss what was happening. I probably wouldn't have taken a great interest in the trial otherwise. Sometimes he would read something in the morning and try putting it into rehearsal that afternoon." The story of Patty Hearst eventually found its place in the trial/prison scene where the featured performers, Lucinda Childs and Sheryl Sutton, each acted out the young woman's transformation from socialite to gun-toting revolutionary to prisoner.

While Glass himself made only small musical changes during rehearsals ("I don't do a lot of rewriting"), he still had to resolve the problem of what the chorus would sing, since he had composed the opera without a text. "I knew there would be singing but what would be sung wasn't decided. Since we didn't have any words for the chorus I began teaching them with solfège syllables, which I had previously used in my work. With rhythmically complicated passages I found that the easiest way to teach the music was with numbers. I had the company singing numbers and solfège for about a week and then I invited Bob to come to a rehearsal and said, 'I think we have the text.' Bob heard the numbers and said, 'That's wonderful.' So the way I taught the singers became the text. It's also a description of the music: the solfège are the names of the notes—do, re, me, fa, sol, la, te, do—and the numbers are the rhythmic structure; for example if I want to do a ⅞ measure I go 1-2-3-4, 1-2-3, 1-2-3-4, 1-2-3." (Numbers were, of course, the language in which Einstein reasoned and through which he changed our understanding of the universe.) "Another reason this idea was so appealing to Bob and myself back in 1975 was that we knew the work of Jasper Johns. If you look at Johns' paintings, for example the alphabet paintings, the painting is not the depiction of the thing, the painting is the thing. And so I was doing in the words what other people were doing in the visual arts. I think Bob could respond to this because it connected to a world of culture we were both part of. Though it came up accidentally through the process of rehearsal, it wasn't just a goofy idea. It was an idea which had roots in the practice of contemporary art."

During rehearsals Glass also followed with considerable interest the creation of the spoken texts that would weave through the opera. "Bob asked various people to contribute parts. He got Lucinda and Mr. Johnson [the 77-year-old black patriarch of the company] to write speeches. He got Christopher Knowles to write by shouting "Einstein, Einstein, Einstein" at him—and the stuff just came out. Back when we were first discussing the possibility of doing a work, Bob began appearing at our weekly meetings with Christopher. I think Bob was hoping that I would strike up some kind of working relationship with him but that wasn't really possible for me. In fact, I told Bob at one point that though I'd be happy to work with Christopher's words, I couldn't work with him because it was simply too strange for me. Looking back on it now, one of the minor — or maybe major — miracles of *Einstein* is how right those texts turned out to be. That's part of Bob's special genius. Not everyone would have gotten those words out of Christopher. His relationship to these people is not passive, it's catalytic. They're writing a piece for Bob and they write to the level Bob is living on."

Glass was particularly impressed by Mr. Johnson's speech at the very end of the opera, a soppy yet oddly touching description of two lovers on a park bench which recapitulates many of the themes and images of the piece (moon, sun, stars, beach, silence, calm, infinity). "It's a perfect speech and we accepted it. But how do you account for the fact that neither Bob nor I gave him any hint of what was required. Mr. Johnson just appeared one day with that text. It's amazing. When people work with Bob they tend to write things he wants. Actually, it's not as strange as it sounds. I remember working as an assistant to Richard Serra and whenever anyone came into the studio to work on a piece whatever they did ended up looking astonishingly like one of Richard's pieces. I said to Richard one day, 'Why is it that when people come into your studio they always end up doing work that looks like you?' He said, 'Because I make the rules in the space and they come into my space and play my game and whatever they do is mine.' I think that's very much true for Bob. He sets up a rehearsal situation and creates such a strong sense of his own space that people automatically do what he wants. One of Bob's great qualities, of which he may not even be fully conscious, is his way of drawing contributions from people that are appropriate to his work. He does it instinctively and people respond instinctively."

Rehearsals ended in March and that month Wilson and Glass previewed parts of the work at various venues in Manhattan: a run-through of the entire opera at the Video Exchange, the knee plays at the Museum of Modern Art and musical selections performed by Glass's ensemble at The Kitchen. The *Einstein* company reassembled in Avignon early in July and rehearsed for the first time with Wilson's scenery, which had been constructed in Milan. The world premiere on July 25 was followed by a triumphal tour of Venice, Belgrade, Brussels, Paris, Hamburg, Rotterdam and Amsterdam, culminating with two sold-out performances at the Metropolitan Opera House in November. Glass says that up until that first performance in Avignon he had no idea that they had created one of the major theatrical works of the decade. "I was totally unprepared for the reaction *Einstein* received and I think that's true for Bob also. Theatre is often like that, you really don't know what you've done until the audience is there. Especially when you've worked on the piece for nearly two goddamn years. The very first night in Avignon I was dimly aware that we had been present at an event. I could tell from everyone else's reaction that something extraordinary had happened but Bob and I were still too involved with it — we were still worried about sets being stretched properly and people coming in at the right places in the music. My memory is that it was an instantly acclaimed work, especially among young people. Of course we were also younger then, I was thirty-eight and Bob was thirty-four or thirty-five. But a lot of our audience was in their twenties and some of them followed the work all over Europe. Jerry Robbins saw the piece in Paris. Bob and I visited him at his hotel and I remember him picking up the phone and calling the Met and saying, 'Get someone over here. Someone must come and see this work.' He was very insistent. The next thing we knew Jane Herman [the company's director of presentations] came to Hamburg and saw two performances. And Bob said, 'I can't believe this but it looks like it's going to go to the Met.' Bob and I were worried about two things. Could the Met set the show up in the allotted twenty hours? And would anyone come to see it? It seems absurd now, but we were worried about an empty house."

Although *Einstein* ended its run in a blaze of glory and publicity at the Metropolitan Opera (a cultural fortress that must have seemed all but impregnable only a year before) and brought them their greatest popular and critical success, Glass and Wilson would not work together for another seven years. "I think for one thing Bob and I wanted to have successful works that were not done with each other, we did not fancy becoming some kind of contemporary Gilbert and Sullivan. We considered that we were successful people before we met and that our success didn't depend on each other. The main thing you have to remember is that we had spent roughly two years together and were sick to death of seeing each other. And when I mean together I mean from morning to night, it was a very close working relationship and I think we really needed to get away from each other."

Glass feels that the reports of tension and bad feeling created by his unwillingness to assume a major portion of Einstein's nearly $150,000 debt have been exaggerated. "Of course there were financial problems but I think there was some confusion between the natural disinclination to be together and the unnatural pressure of the debts and how to deal with them. There was never any long period of time when we didn't talk to each other. We often talked about designers and directors. I would ask him about people to work with and he would ask me about composers [David Byrne and Laurie Anderson were among those Glass suggested]. I think we were generous with each other in that way. If Bob had a show of drawings I would go to it and he came to Holland for the premiere of *Satyagraha* in 1980—and as I recall there was no seat so I gave him mine. We were in touch with each other but we weren't ready to do a new work. In fact, we both felt we ought to wait five or six years."

Although Glass was back earning his living behind the wheel of a cab only a week after standing before a cheering audience at the Met, *Einstein* was to change his life. As one commission followed another over the next ten years, he established himself as America's foremost opera composer, a position to which he had never aspired. "It happened that *Einstein* fit into an opera house, in fact that was the only place you could put it. As a result, directors of opera houses came to see it and one of them, Hans de Roo of the Netherlands Opera, offered me a commission. Had I not done *Einstein* it never would have occurred to me to write an opera and more importantly I never would have been given an opportunity to write one." After *Einstein* Glass gravitated increasingly toward large operatic and theatrical works. "Like Bob I've made my living in my chosen field and it hasn't been easy. One of the keys has been to find an audience that will support the work without my having to change it, except in the natural way things change in themselves. One of the reasons I'm attracted to the theatre and do so much of my work there is that generally speaking the theatre audience is so much larger. I can do a run of *Einstein* for two or three weeks but I can't do a concert for that length of time. The difference in audience size is vast." This desire for popular acceptance is something shared by both men, who now move restlessly through the world juggling projects and overloaded schedules: "It's very easy for us to understand how the other person works since our habits are quite similar in certain ways. Bob can be thinking about two or three different pieces at the same time and I'm doing the same thing. It's the way I like to work. I never take vacations, I just change projects. It's effectively the same thing."

Today, more than a decade after its creation, *Einstein on the Beach* is recognized as both a landmark in American musical theatre and a kind of summation of the minimalist movement. While it is hardly a reductive or analytical work, its repetitive structures, minimalist-based score and simple, geometric forms (which a number of critics have compared to the work of Robert Morris, Sol LeWitt and Dan Flavin) constitute a virtual catalogue of minimalism. Glass, however, rankles at the very mention of the word. "I think the whole thing has been overplayed and besides it doesn't describe what you hear in the piece. My other problem with minimalism is that the work I do is collaborative, it involves dance, visual and directorial elements. Minimalism is a reductivist aesthetic, so the two things are going in different directions." When pressed Glass admits that the opera might be considered "the end of minimalism. It's like the king is dead, long live the king. It may be the end of minimalism but it's also the beginning of something else which is musical works fully conceived for the theatre." Indeed *Einstein* gave impetus to the large-scale collaborations of contemporary musicians, artists and directors that have come to characterize the 1980s, and signaled the emergence of a real audience for such work. (Glass believes that the great age of American opera is only now beginning.) Returning to *Einstein* in 1984, the composer found that the style and idiom of the opera had been nearly fully absorbed: "The piece was truly more radical in 1976 simply because the language was not generally known—the visual language, the dramatic language and the musical language. Coming back in '84, it didn't present such daunting problems. There was an *ability* to hear it, not just a willingness. In just ten or fifteen years we begin to find a way to listen, to hear, to see—and it becomes simply the language of our time."

While Glass and Wilson have each worked with many other collaborators since *Einstein on the Beach,* neither has found a partner whose work so complements and enriches his own. While they share many aesthetic views and shape their pieces by means of somewhat similar additive principles, each usually attributes the success of the collaboration to a mutual ability to give each other "space in which to work." The same may be said of their music and visuals. Both are powerful entities in themselves yet neither attempts to wholly occupy the mind or make the other subservient; each offers the other a complementary expanse of space and time. When asked outright why his music and Wilson's images go so well together, Glass brings the discussion back to a favorite subject, the commonly held generational values of the downtown cultural scene in the late sixties and seventies. "I think it has a lot to do with the community of experience we come from, which is very much a shared community and a shared experience. It has to do with growing up under the influence of people like Cunningham and Jasper Johns and knowing about the Living Theatre, Grotowski and Peter Brook. Bob and I were also very much the adopted children of the art world and our ideas came from them. What we had in the late sixties and all through the seventies was an authentic community of people who were working

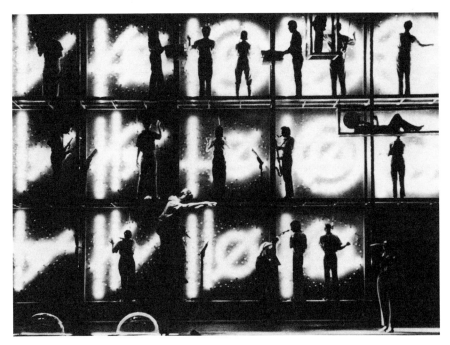

Einstein on the Beach. Act IV, sc. 3C (Space Machine). 1976.

together. Artists, dancers, architects, musicians and performers. It was a little like what people said Paris was like in the 1920s. A Saturday didn't go by that you didn't go to the galleries with all your friends. You couldn't do that today. In fact the last time I was in SoHo on a weekend it was like being at a shopping mall. Why would you go to a shopping mall on a Saturday unless you wanted to buy something? So that world doesn't exist anymore. But in the SoHo of the early seventies I would do programs and benefit concerts with John Cage and Laurie Anderson and David Byrne and Bob Wilson. I could walk down the street and run into these people. It would have been almost surprising if my music and his theatre didn't fit. We were experiencing the world of contemporary art, theatre and performance at almost the same time, we were almost having identical experiences. I can remember very clearly going to see a Richard Foreman play called *China Hotel* in 1971 and sitting with Yvonne Rainer, Richard Serra and Michael Snow—a dancer, a sculptor and a filmmaker. It was a completely ordinary thing to be in constant contact with people that way. I think that's what was strongest about the period. It made these collaborative theatre works possible, they wouldn't have happened if that community of people didn't exist."

HANS PETER KUHN

While Wilson's stage pictures glow alluringly at one end of a darkened auditorium, rarely breaching their frame, the sonic drama that accompanies them knows no such boundaries. If his stagecraft is firmly entrenched in the proscenium tradition, sound is environmental, claiming as its territory the entire theatre. It ricochets off the walls and ceiling, moving instantaneously from stage to audience, dispersing bits of memory, data, noise and music into the darkness. To sit out in the auditorium is to be adrift on an ocean of sound, which like deep water can turn suddenly from calm to turbulent, lulling us one moment and buffeting us the next. Wilson may extol the values of distance and restraint in design and performance but audially his is a theatre of total immersion.

These sonic environments are the brainchild of the German sound designer and composer Hans Peter Kuhn, one of Wilson's most frequent collaborators. Kuhn, who grew up in the small West German city of Kiel, studied at the University of Berlin in the mid-1970s but dropped out and took a job at the Schaubühne am halleschen Ufer, at the time Germany's most important theatre. In a few years he progressed from third assistant to chief sound engineer, overseeing the audio designs of several legendary productions. One of these was Peter Stein's *As You Like It*, in which the audience followed the actors through a foliage-covered labyrinth over 250 meters in length into the forest of Arden. A network of concealed speakers filled these winding, dimly lit passageways with the elemental sounds of wind, rain, storm and finally a polyphonic chorus of bird calls as spectators emerged into a sunlit clearing. While Kuhn was excited by the possibilities of such a conception, the experience itself was less than satisfying. "Peter Stein is a very different kind of director than Robert Wilson. *Auch* God. He's very straight. He tells you what to do and that's it. It's really his design. He knows exactly what music he wants, he even tells you the band of the record. It was fun to do, of course, but if you always have someone who's standing behind you, you can never play the game you like. You always have to cut your ideas to the man giving the orders. The thing about German theatre is that it's not very interesting to make something with sound. People don't care about lights or sound or scenery, the only thing they're interested in is the actors and the director." His most rewarding experience was working with Klaus-Michael Grüber on *Die Winterreise,* which was presented in Berlin's enormous Olympic Stadium in the dead of winter. Kuhn put a body microphone on the central character and broadcast his voice and breath over the public address system as he ran around the playing field. "It was a beautiful atmosphere. Usually what we try to do is make high fidelity. Here it was the opposite, we had low fidelity."

That same season Stein, the chief director of the Schaubühne, saw *Patio* in Paris and decided to ask Wilson to create a new work for the company. "Wilson came right after we did *As You Like It* and *Winterreise,* it was a big year and we were all a little exhausted. The manager of the theatre appeared one day and said Robert Wilson is coming from America. He's a very strange guy and he will do something very strange, but he's very important so do what he wants even if it's strange. He also said we should go see *Patio* when it comes to Berlin and we did that." Kuhn, who knew nothing of Wilson's work or reputation, was at a loss as to what to make of that initial encounter. "I never saw anything like that before. It was really a shock. We were always working on political stuff at the Schaubühne and here was this guy on stage talking I don't know what. There were some visual things I was really amazed by but I couldn't figure out what the whole thing was. My reaction was almost—'What is this?'"

Kuhn was soon assigned to Wilson's project, the now legendary *Death Destruction and Detroit,* but their initial attempts at collaboration were neither harmonious nor productive. "Wilson came and I tried to work in the same way as with Mr. Stein but no matter what I did he didn't like it. He couldn't stand it. It was always shit. I couldn't figure out what he wanted and he couldn't make it clear to me. And he was always changing things—you do something one day and you appear at rehearsal the next day and it's already gone. If you're not used to that, it can be very difficult. He shouted at me and we had big fights. I can't stand it when people shout at me, I get really mad and shout back. He was telling me that I was a bastard, a shit. He was like a little child not getting his way. I was just trying to serve him well and do what he wanted. We had one very serious fight and I said that's it and switched off everything and left. But Wilson's good at that. You can fight with him one day and he's able to work with you after that the same as before. Then one night I was sitting in the studio working on some tapes, I was very dissatisfied and I said to myself, 'Whatever he says tomorrow I don't care, I'll just do now what I want.' He had to have some music for a dance scene so I got out this Keith Jarrett record: 'I'm going to play this tomorrow because that's what I want. I don't care what he wants.' So I took it to rehearsal and it was exactly right for the scene. From that moment on there were no real problems. I realized the way to work with Wilson was to try to please myself first. Before, I was always thinking of how to make it the way he wanted it and that didn't work because what he needs is people to add ideas." As it happened, Kuhn was to leave the Schaubühne soon after the opening of *D D & D*, in part because he had grown tired of the long hours and felt he had learned all he could at the theatre but also because after collaborating with Wilson he never wanted to go back to the old way of working.

Wilson made two initial requests of Kuhn: the principal performers should all wear body mikes and their voices should seem to come from somewhere other than their own mouths. This started Kuhn thinking. "I felt if that was what Wilson wanted we must do something more. Just separating the voice from the performer is not very interesting. It's like having a TV with the speakers on the side, after a while you hear the sound coming from the images anyway. It's an acoustical-psychological phenomenon, your brain switches it over. So I said why don't we make something more complicated, something that makes a complete other space." The design Kuhn created for the Schaubühne production—a kind of sonic cocoon—was to become the model for all his work with Wilson. "We had a line of 10 little speakers grouped around the sides and back of the auditorium. There were nine separate spots in the house, four for voices and five for taped sound effects. We also had speakers in the ceiling, the proscenium and backstage. So you were completely covered by sound." Although Kuhn believes that this was the first time such an environment had been created in a European theatre, something similar had been prophesied over twenty years earlier by John Cage, who called for the dispersal of orchestral players throughout the auditorium and envisioned a "total sound space" (made possible by magnetic tape, splicing and multiple speakers) in which a sound at any given point could move instantaneously to any other point. The use of numerous low-level sources which impart a sense of immediacy and an even spread of sound throughout the auditorium is a key feature of Kuhn's design. "There are lots of speakers around the house putting out the same signal rather than one big speaker so you don't have a situation where one person hears something faintly and another gets blasted." (Although no money was available to implement his plan, Kuhn had hoped to go one step further with *the CIVIL warS* and mount a small speaker on the seat in front of each spectator.)

The audio score itself is made up of two basic components. The first of these is live sound—usually just the voices of the actors—which is amplified and transmitted to various speakers in the theatre. Body miking has been an essential part of all Wilson's productions since the mid-1970s and its use is a logical extension of his performance theory, which stresses relaxation and interiority. By obviating the need for conventional voice projection, microphones make it possible for actors to speak without strain or effort. ("Not only is it different here in the vocal cords," says David Warrilow, "it's a different mind-set. The sensitivity of sound puts you in a different psychic space. It's like talking to yourself.") By miking the actors and then dispersing their voices through the theatre, Wilson and Kuhn have radically altered the relationship of the speaker to the audience, the text and his own body. No longer are the actor and his voice a single entity; as a French reviewer wrote, "The voice accompanies the body from a distance without getting caught up in it, without submitting to it and without violating it." A number of critics immediately seized on the implications of this initially disorienting realignment. In a long essay on *DD&D* the German commentator Wolfgang Max Faust wrote that "the person becomes 'Persona.' The speech rings out as if through the mask of an ancient theatre actor. The electronic alienation, connected with a neutral, emphasized speech, allows for the appearance of a person as a medium, as a placement of speech and gesticulation. Thus an impression is being created that it is not the person who speaks the language, but that the language is using the person to be spoken by it." Andrzej Wirth, who reviewed *DD&D* in *Theater heute,* similarly observed that "the speaker is accompanied by, but never identical with his voice. His statements are produced by him, but do not belong to him; they belong to the space. . . . Separated from the actor, language and speech are elements of a spatial, not written, text." This disjunction can be somewhat unnerving to the performer who must surrender some of his natural authority to a new collaborator—the sound designer, who now stands between him and the audience.

Each performance is controlled by a single sound technician seated at a console who modulates the various sonic elements like the conductor of an orchestra, making adjustments for nightly fluctuations in performance and in the noise level of the audience. "Everything is processed through a sound mixer which controls the levels of the various signals. We also have a computer that enables us to separate voice signals and send them to different speakers around the house." This capability has made possible some of Kuhn's most arresting sonic inventions. The voices of the actors may occupy different areas in the theatre or jump suddenly from one spot to another. In *The Golden Windows* an actress's disturbingly prolonged laughter issued from the stage while simultaneously bouncing back at her across the chasm of the audience. Perhaps most extraordinary of all was the moment in the Dutch *CIVIL warS* when the tiny figure of William the Silent sat in the hand of the world's largest woman, reading the Edict of Nantes while his voice traveled in a nearly perfect circle around the perimeter of the auditorium.

In addition to dispersing speech within the space, Kuhn can extend the actor's speech through looping and playback or juxtapose it against a recorded double, creating internal discourse and counterpoint from a single voice. As the critic Judith Gershman has written, through the medium of tape "monologue becomes dialogue with self, solitude becomes polyphony." (A somewhat less sophisticated form of instant replay occurred in Wilson's collaborations with Christopher Knowles; in *The*

$ Value of Man the youth taped bits of the spoken text with a cassette recorder and then played them back during the ongoing dialogue.) With the aid of a harmonizer Kuhn is also able to change the pitch of a performer's voice or transform its dimensions. In the first scene of the German *CIVIL warS*, for example, the voices of the two astronauts seen floating on ladders in outer space occupied a vocal space unlike that of anyone else on stage, as though their words were reverberating within "a empty cathedral." On a few rare occasions an actor's voice may even be heard in its natural state—an often startling occurrence once the ear has become attuned to the prevailing sonic milieu—as happened for a brief moment in the same scene: "One of the astronauts had a line 'Stefan und Suzanne verstehen sie wieder' [Stefan and Suzanne are back together again], and at that moment the cathedral effect went off and for the one sentence he was live. The audience laughed. That was Bob's idea." Sometimes live sounds (such as a bouncing ball in Act IV of *the CIVIL warS* or a fist banging against a door in *D D & D II*) will also be amplified and sent into the auditorium, a carryover from such early major works as *The King of Spain,* in which a hidden microphone picked up the creak of a chair and the sound of ice cubes being poured into a glass. The greater part of the audio score, however, is made up of taped material, from which the designer fashions a vast and often densely layered tapestry of prerecorded speech, music and sound effects. Sometimes there are as many as a dozen different tapes running simultaneously. (Although the playing time of *D D & D* was about five-and-a-half hours, Kuhn estimates that it would have taken almost 150 hours to play all the tapes end to end.)

Wilson believes that all these independent layers of sound and language replicate the workings of the mind, through which simultaneously pass random, often extraneous pieces of information and stimuli (such as street noise, half-overheard conversation and Muzak) as well as one's own thoughts and mental images. The audio is a kind of metaphor for the way we think and experience the world; to sink into its contours is to enter a mental realm where the interior and exterior screens merge. It is also Wilson's contention that the spectator is capable of processing and making connections between these simultaneous layers of information if they are clearly presented.

While the sound environments Kuhn creates are often subtly atmospheric and subliminal in the manner of Demjen's earlier work, he is also capable of launching an outright assault on the audial nerves of the audience. (Indeed, some critics have chosen to see in his audio landscapes the chaos of modern life and the technological nightmare of static and sensory overload.) Kuhn offers as an example the New York rooftop scene in *D D & D* in which eight different earsplitting tracks—explosions, shattering glass, a clattering typewriter, machine-gun fire—jumped around the auditorium. "It's the loudest thing I've ever done for Bob. Pretty disturbing." The powerful visual and audio disjunction of this scene made a great impression on

Eugène Ionesco, who wrote that he had never before seen or heard so vivid a presentation of the approaching apocalypse of which "most of humanity is not yet conscious." He related how a young couple in bathing suits lay on modernistic beach chairs calmly exchanging meaningless phrases in English and German while "around them machine guns, bombs, shells, the noise of our death leaves them completely insensible. How can we continue to live? We are beyond menace, we are already in the realization of menace."

Kuhn created another kind of sonic onslaught for the spectacular climax of *The Golden Windows* in which the earth splits apart and giant boulders fall from the sky. "Wilson told me, 'We need something beautiful for Miss Nicklisch [the distinguished German actress who played the older woman]. She's so great, we need something beautiful.' That was what he wanted. It was funny." Rather than attempting to reproduce the reverberations of a literal earthquake, Kuhn fashioned fragments of spoken text into a powerful and disturbing sonic collage. "I took a piece of text and made two recordings, one in a normal voice and the other in a whisper, with a lot of repetitions. I put the whole tape on a multitrack system and recorded it six times with a random delay and then played it back on six speakers in the house. I also created a loop of Miss Nicklisch saying 'buzzard' and made it beat like a drum. The play is very calm and this section really jumped out of it. It's really like a piece of a cappella music." The spiritual father of such "music" is again John Cage, who championed a new kind of music based on discontinuity and "the coexistence of dissimilars" rather than harmony, and urged in the manner of Varèse (of whom Cage wrote, "he fathered forth noise—that is to say, twentieth-century music") the acceptance of "all audible phenomena" as its proper material.

Kuhn's work can cross over into many areas of the production—technical design, music, performance and on occasion even text. For *The Man in the Raincoat,* a one-man show seen in Cologne in 191, he made a tape of Wilson reading about ninety phrases. Kuhn then took these brief recorded fragments and fashioned them into an audio score, becoming in a sense coauthor of the text. He began with Wilson's recitation of a group of words starting with the letter *b* which were then manipulated, rearranged and distorted electronically. "I cut the tape in very small pieces and overlaid the sounds, making loops with lots of repetition. I just put it all together and made something that sounded good to me." What resulted was a kind of rhythmic audio mural or word construction which he dispersed through the auditorium:

        black black black black black black black black
        black black black black black black black black
        black black black black black black black   lack
        black black black black black black black black
        black black black black black black black black

black black black black   lack black black black
black black black black black black black black
black black black black black black   lack black
black black black black black black black black
black black black black   lack black black black
black black black black black black   lack black
black black black black   lack black black black
black black black black   lack black   lack black
black ball black ball black ball
bath sent bath sent
black black black black
black ball black ball black ball

As with the writings and tape constructions of Christopher Knowles, words were broken apart and redistributed to form an abstract quasi-musical language. (Much to Kuhn's amusement, Wilson later published the studio-created text: "Someone actually sat down, listened to the tape I made and wrote down all the words. It's so crazy.") The visual scheme Wilson devised for *The Man in the Raincoat* was characteristically made up of mirror images, and Kuhn decided to reflect this structure in his sound score. "There were six sections, three pairs of mirrored scenes, so I made audio mirrors. One had a lot of repetitions, one had lots of space. One was very reverberated, another was clear and sharp. I also used different combinations of speakers for different scenes."

In most cases Kuhn's audio score evolves slowly during the workshop stage through a process of trial and error. "We always work with music and sound from the very first rehearsals. I look at what he's doing with the actors, make proposals and find the recordings we need and then I try out a lot of things to see how he likes them." As elsewhere in Wilson's theatre, the principle of independence prevails. "If he has an image which is very dizzy you first try dizzy music and see what happens. But the audio is pretty much separate and I try to keep it that way because I don't want to illustrate. The things I do should be another world." Kuhn also prefers not to study the text in advance or even listen to the words once rehearsals have begun. "I don't illustrate the text so it doesn't matter. I prefer not to understand the text, it's easier for me. If it's in English or another language, I just listen to the sounds. If I hear it in German I get too much information."

Although Wilson is "more interested in sound than he was in the beginning," Kuhn says he still has a greater degree of freedom than many of his colleagues. "Wilson is most concerned with the visual side of his work—the sets, the lighting, the movement of the actors. He's very, very careful about all of that and he knows exactly what he wants. He's careful about the audio too but it's not his thing. I can do much more on my own ideas. The visual people sometimes have to fight for their ideas which is not easy."

There are other reasons theirs is a mutually satisfying collaboration. Kuhn provides skills the director does not have and an abundance of ideas on which to draw, and Wilson in turn offers him the opportunity to try them out and a theatrical form capable of accommodating them. The two men also share a common passion for the strange and beautiful, and a wholly instinctive method of working. In spite of a mutual debt to John Cage (to whom Wilson dedicated the 1973 Copenhagen performances of *Stalin*), neither is interested in aesthetic principles or concepts or the implications of what they do; they care only for the immediate and the concrete, for sounds, atmospheres, textures and the excitement and gratification of making something, and making something happen.

D D & D II. Berlin, 1987.

V

BUSINESS

AND

ART:

THE

PRODUCERS

SoHo Weekly News, November 15, 1973: Robert Wilson is looking for 32 dancing ostriches, over one hundred sleepwalkers (experienced and nonexperienced), bears, mammies, fishing ladies, apes, a pregnant woman, a Wilhelm Reich and an Alexander Graham Bell lookalike for his latest piece, *The Life and Times of Joseph Stalin,* slated to run from dusk to dawn (for 12 hours, beginning at 7 p.m.) Dec. 14, 15, 21 and 22 at the Brooklyn Academy of Music.

Perhaps even more remarkable than Robert Wilson's theatre is his almost unfailing ability to make it happen, often against considerable odds. While some have argued that Wilson's visions are no more extraordinary than those of Rousseau or Magritte, their scale sets them apart, and the fact that they occupy real space and time, which are, among other things, expensive. Money and intensive labor are essential to the creation of such works and, from the beginning of his career, Wilson has somehow managed to find a regular supply of both. Even in those early days, friends and associates marveled at his business acumen, organizational skills and above all his "genius" for finding money. As Fred Kolo has said, "Bob was a master of funding. He created it in a certain way, that's the second of his creations"—and it's true that the emergence of organized funding for the avant-garde coincided with Wilson's own rise. "He knew early on he wanted to work with the big brush and he was very smart about knowing what he had to do to accomplish that. Other people weren't able to work big until much, much later." David Warrilow has recalled that many in the SoHo community were baffled by Wilson's ability to bring off these spectacles while others were envious, even resentful, at his always getting what seemed to them a disproportionate share of exposure, grant money, foreign invitations and publicity ("many reviewers seem to vie for the number of times they could call him a genius," Stanley Kauffmann once wrote in the *New Republic*).

Much of Wilson's early support came from a circle of private patrons (chief among them Jerome Robbins) who were as attracted to his personal magnetism as his art. The persuasive powers of that subtle, low-key personality have always been considerable. Ross Wetzsteon has written in the *Village Voice* of how Wilson's "combination of elegant manners, conviction in his work and ability to make its dreamlike abstractions accessible—always interspersed with uncannily charismatic silences—seems as hypnotic as his work" and of his ability to "exert his almost-passive charms on rich art patrons, quietly sucking money as if into a vacuum." Ann Wilson, as usual the voice of candor, puts it more bluntly: "He knows how to get people to part with their money." Part of his effectiveness has to do with his gift for making whoever he's talking with feel that no one and nothing else matters—a quality as useful in directing an actor or conducting a newspaper interview as it is in raising money. In the early years, of course, the Byrds provided an almost inexhaustible source of labor and talent, making it possible for him to get a great deal more for the dollar than anyone else. He also managed to attract people like Kolo who could create remarkable settings for a few hundred dollars, inventive costume and property people who literally dug things out of ashcans, and admirers willing to do the paperwork for subsistence wages. (While putting together *the CIVIL warS* a decade later he would look wistfully back to these years and wonder "Why can't we do it the same way?")

For all his entrepreneurial talents and money-raising abilities the history of Robert Wilson and the Byrd Hoffman Foundation has been—until quite recently—one of big losses, lingering debts, weary creditors and even in the best of times barely making ends meet. But no matter how deep the debt or dire the predicament or unrealistic the goal Wilson remains one of those people who simply refuses to give in or be held back. No known force of man or circumstance is allowed to defeat him for long.

The $ Value of Man. Brooklyn Academy of Music, 1975.

HARVEY LICHTENSTEIN

For nearly twenty years Robert Wilson's work has found a home across the East River at the Brooklyn Academy of Music. Since 1967 BAM (as it is popularly known) has been run by Harvey Lichtenstein, who is credited with transforming a moribund institution in the borough's depressed downtown area into the country's leading center of new dance, music and theatre. The Brooklyn-born Lichtenstein, a shrewd businessman with a sure instinct for promotion and marketing, began his career as a dancer, studying with Martha Graham and appearing with Pearl Lang's company and the New York City Opera Ballet. By the mid-1960s he had moved into arts administration, starting as a Ford Foundation intern with the New York City Ballet, where he initiated the company's first subscription program, and then taking up his present post at BAM, the nation's oldest performing arts center.

Upon assuming his duties as executive director, Lichtenstein decided that instead of duplicating the attractions that could be found in Manhattan or catering to the borough's own residents as had been the existing policy, he would try to attract new audiences by presenting experimental companies whose work couldn't be seen regularly across the river. In the years that followed he revitalized the Academy, sponsoring Merce Cunningham's first major season in 1968, bringing the Becks' Living Theatre back to New York after their four-year European exile the same year, introducing Peter Brook's International Center for Theatre Research and Jerzy Grotowski to American audiences, and later providing a showcase for the early work of Steve Reich, Laura Dean, Twyla Tharp and countless other emerging American artists. His efforts to present such innovative work culminated in the creation of the "Next Wave" festival in 1983, a two-month program of experimental music and performance that established BAM's president as the premier impresario—some would even say power broker—of the avant-garde.

Lichtenstein, a genial, paternal figure who might pass for a middle-aged dress manufacturer, was one of those present at the Anderson Theatre in 1969 when Wilson presented his first work on a proscenium stage, *The King of Spain.* "I think a friend of mine was involved with the show and he mentioned it to me. My reactions? It was surprising and difficult and absorbing and boring. What made it work was its visual beauty and sense of humor. Bob's work has grown on me a lot since then. I do think the fact that I had a background in the visual arts and had grown up with abstract expressionism sort of saved it for me in terms of seeing it." While Lichtenstein had no immediate desire to claim Wilson for Brooklyn, he says "it would have been clear to me that this was the sort of work I not only liked but which could make the reputation of BAM." Eventually it was Wilson, in need of a large proscenium house for his next piece *The Life and Times of Sigmund Freud,* who approached the Academy; and after some preliminary scheduling problems and hesitancy on the part of the management (the fact that he had managed to have the drops for the two outer acts painted seemed to reassure them) BAM agreed to give him the main auditorium for two nights, providing, as he wrote a few years later, "I would assume all the costly cost and I did. I did. I did. I did. I did." Lichtenstein puts it succinctly: "In the beginning Bob was financially on his own."

Actually, Wilson had already gained a good deal of experience as a producer and fund-raiser, roles he would come increasingly to dread in the years ahead. *The King of Spain* was just one of several shows he had organized over the previous two years by marshaling his limited resources and his friends, then begging or borrowing the additional means needed to realize his plans. During that time he had presented pieces (each a little more ambitious in scope or scale) at various venues — his Spring Street loft, a movie theatre in Greenwich Village, Robbins' atelier on West 19th Street and an alley in the East Village. With a budget of over three thousand dollars, *The King of Spain* had been his most elaborate and costly project to date, most of the monies coming from Jerome Robbins, the New York State Council on the Arts, members of his group from the Summit Art Center and his own meager savings — "every cent I had in the whole world." Even then Wilson had to resort to such eleventh-hour tactics as writing bad checks to make up the existing shortfall.

Though *Freud* was presented in cooperation with BAM, Wilson was again obliged to act as his own producer, agreeing to bear not only the cost of the production but all backstage, box office and publicity expenses (though he eventually received a 50-percent reduction on the Academy's rental fee). The total budget was in excess of ten thousand dollars, with the lion's share going as usual to the union crew backstage. While the resulting spectacle, with its fifty waltzing black mammies and majestic tableau of animals bedded in the hay, left Wilson several thousand dollars in debt, it marked his emergence as a major figure of the American avant-garde. Writing in the *Village Voice,* Richard Foreman declared the production "one of the masterpieces of the 'artist's theatre' which exists almost in secret in this country," adding that his readers "had better keep their fingers crossed that the Byrd Hoffman Foundation will somehow be able to find the backing to mount another of these gigantic performances." This is just what happened. Word got around and a return engagement followed a few months later, underwritten largely by the New York State Council on the Arts in the hope that the second run would enable Wilson to repay his debts from the first. This time BAM waived its rental fee, taking instead 20 percent of the box-office gross, a nominal return at best. With each subsequent production Lichtenstein and the Academy took a more active role, by 1973 assuming most of the house costs and offering some assistance with fund-raising. "In essence the productions were brought in by Bob, who dealt with the expenses of the company itself—the actors, dancers, musicians, sets and costumes—and we took on the expenses of the theatre, publicity and so on. So it was really like a coproduction."

By *Deafman Glance* the following year Wilson's budget had risen to nearly twenty-five thousand dollars, part of which was again contributed by Robbins' foundation, NYSCA and the group of private donors he had developed (the production itself, created in Iowa several months before, had been made possible by a grant from the Rockefeller Foundation). As always there were the impassioned last-minute appeals for money and as always Wilson managed to get it. Although promotional efforts were limited and often primitive (Lichtenstein remembers him sending a member of the company to the New York Public Library in a bear suit to hand out flyers), the spectacular nature of his productions captured the imagination of the press and Wilson began to receive considerable attention from publications not known for their regular coverage of experimental theatre, among them the *New Yorker* (literally becoming "The Talk of the Town"), the *New York Times, Vogue,* the *Post* and *Variety*. By this time he had also acquired a small but devoted following. "Bob's audience was very much a downtown audience. It was very dedicated and very specific—artists, young people, some Europeans—where today you see a mix of people, the Lincoln Center crowd as well as the artists." While Wilson probably would have preferred having his work seen in Manhattan, the relationship with BAM endured. "Bob needed a proscenium theatre and he needed a large stage. Both those things were crucial and I don't think that anybody else who had a stage that could accommodate those works would do them. Of course, Bob could have rented a theatre like he did with the Anderson but that's disastrous. The two big things he produced in New York were *Victoria* and *Einstein* and both times he ended up losing his shirt. At BAM he had to invest a lot of money and he didn't make anything but at least his losses were limited."

Lichtenstein says he was taken aback when Wilson brought him plans for his next project, a twelve-hour compendium of all his work to that point. "It's hard to recall how stunned I was. The cost of putting on something like that at a place like BAM is kind of outrageous. I couldn't take the idea very seriously in the beginning. We had already done *Freud* and *Deafman* and originally I think I said why not just do the new work, but then hearing about how it was going to be put together I got more and more intrigued with the idea — I'm a sucker for something that's a little strange like starting at seven at night and ending at seven in the morning — and eventually we agreed to do it." *The Life and Times of Joseph Stalin* was given four performances in December of 1973 with Byrd Hoffman and BAM again sharing costs, Wilson being responsible for the production and the Academy for backstage staff, house services and promotion, with the box-office take to be split fifty-fifty. (The total budget, Wilson's largest to date, was estimated at $120,000, about a fifth of what it cost to mount a Broadway musical at the time.)

"There were five hundred in the audience a night, maybe six hundred at most, and that dwindled to two or three hundred by morning. I spent most of the night roaming around. We turned the Lepercq Space on the second floor into a canteen and people could buy soup and sandwiches throughout the night. It looked like something set up by the Salvation Army. I remember going up there at three o'clock in the morning and having a smoke, some black coffee and very earnest conversation in quiet tones. Then I'd go up to the balcony and sit with my feet over the railing or go back down to the mezzanine where people would be watching or sleeping, it was really quite an incredible sight. I stuck through the whole thing. The show was wonderful and exhausting and it was great to lie back and get a nice little nap in the middle of the night. This was December and you could hear the wind whipping around the building and gradually the light came up outdoors. I remember that the first performance was supposed to end at 7:00 A.M. and 7:00 came and the show wasn't finished and I went backstage and said, 'What's going on?' And Bob said, 'Oh, we still have a little way to go yet.' The opening performance didn't end till 9:00. It went fourteen hours and I was furious. I mean it was costing a bloody fortune. It's tough enough to be committed to doing something like that in the prescribed time and I was very upset at Bob, who said, 'It will be all right tonight,' and sure enough the rest of the performances were twelve hours. We lost a lot of dough on those shows. Stage costs were phenomenal. An arm and a leg. How we survived all that I don't know."

Wilson returned to BAM in 1975 for *The $ Value of Man*, a much smaller work that was staged arena-style in the Lepercq Space, originally the Academy's ballroom. "That was the one time the house was packed. Of course, we're talking about an environmental situation with a few hundred people. It was quite a chaotic production, kind of fun, and I enjoyed it but I think Bob's great pieces are those that take place on a proscenium stage where he's able to create a panorama." *The $ Value of Man* marked a low point in Lichtenstein's relationship with Wilson, who never has made things easy for his producers. Shortly after the run Lichtenstein sent the artist a strongly worded letter, taking him to task for his outbursts during rehearsals and abusiveness to coworkers, and reminding him that the Academy had lost a good deal of money on *Stalin* and couldn't meet its payroll. Yet for all this, Lichtenstein, who had initially decided to let their relationship lapse, offered the theatre's continued collaboration because of his respect for Wilson's work. (The president of BAM says that "even today, for a guy who appears to be very held in and controlled, there's a moment in every show where he goes absolutely wild and starts screaming at everyone.") As it happened Wilson would not return to BAM with another production for eight years, though his absence had more to do with circumstance and scheduling problems than any residual tensions.

Wilson's commercial ambitions and desire to reach out to new audiences led him to look beyond BAM to Broadway and eventually Lincoln Center. Lichtenstein, who admits that possessiveness toward the artists he has sponsored is one of his worst failings, says he had ambivalent feelings about these outside ventures. "There was a part of me that felt, 'How dare this work be produced anywhere other than BAM,' which is totally ridiculous, but there was another part of me that felt, 'Well, thank God I'm not going to have to go into debt for this.'" And debt did indeed dog Wilson's steps when he strayed from Brooklyn. Acting as his own producer, he managed to put together a limited run of *A Letter for Queen Victoria* at the ANTA Theater on Broadway in 1975. While he might have taken this production to BAM after its European tour (though a smaller theatre was desirable), Lichtenstein says the artist hungered for mainstream success—"I think he was really intent on wanting to be a Broadway star." But destiny had other plans. *Victoria* played to tiny houses and closed after three weeks, losing its entire investment. Then came those two legendary performances of *Einstein* (which Wilson had originally planned to take to BAM) at the Met the following year. If as Stefan Brecht has written, "*Freud* had established him where it counted, in SoHo; *Deafman* had gained him admiration among the Parisian intelligentsia of both banks; *Stalin* media-ted his name about 14th Street"; and *Victoria* put him briefly on Broadway; *Einstein*'s appearance at the Met crowned Wilson's rapid ascent, making him the indisputable superstar of the American avant-garde. It was not only a personal triumph but also a victory of sorts for the SoHo community, in the words of the *New York Times* "a sensational one-of-a-kind event in which the downtown art world occupied a temple of uptown establishment culture for one brief moment."

Despite a sizable grant from the French government, European bookings, funding from the National Endowment for the Arts and his usual private sources, Wilson's money-raising efforts for *Einstein*—which the *Village Voice* called "the largest avant-garde fund-raising project in history"—fell short of the goal and he had to resort to some old ploys to make up the difference. Philip Glass recalls that he got the company over to Europe by charging plane fares on the foundation's American Express cards far in excess of their credit limit: "I think Byrd Hoffman had three cards and they sent people to buy tickets at various agents in such a way that it wouldn't all appear on the record at the same time. So American Express became — without meaning to — our corporate sponsor. They were very angry about that but eventually they got paid." *Einstein*'s appearance at the Met left Wilson deeper in debt than ever and brought Byrd Hoffman close to bankruptcy. It also marked the beginning of a period when the main focus of his activities would shift to Europe, where opportunities and subsidies were more readily available and state theatres and independent producers better prepared to meet his increasingly exacting demands. Although smaller pieces such as *Patio* and *Curious George* were produced in this country in the interim, American audiences would not see another major work until 1984.

During these years Wilson would speak with some bitterness in newspaper and magazine interviews about his country's failure to support his work, a failure made no more tolerable by the favor shown him in Europe. He would regularly decry the United States' lack of "an educated theatre public," its pervasive profit motive (on one occasion even denouncing the officials of Lincoln Center as "capitalistic pigs") and the "populist" predilections of NYSCA and the NEA. Despite his broadening European base of support Wilson continued to find himself in the role of unwilling producer (especially when he attempted to mount his work in the U.S.) until the mid-1980s, when his alliances with major opera companies and repertory theatres relieved him of the responsibility of raising money for his projects, though the overhead of the Byrd Hoffman Foundation would continue to drain his resources.

While Wilson's designs and lighting for Lucinda Childs' *Relative Calm* were seen at the Academy in 1981, he did not return to BAM with one of his own productions until the end of 1984, when *Einstein on the Beach* was revived for that year's Next Wave festival. As a producer Lichtenstein has spanned virtually the whole of Wilson's career and he has seen his works evolve from the homemade efforts put together by a group of dedicated volunteers to the most accomplished and costly theatrical creations of our era. It was on terms befitting his stature as America's most celebrated avant-garde creator that Wilson returned to the house where in a sense his career began. *Einstein* was not only an entirely professional undertaking but one of the most expensive attractions ever presented by BAM (and the ticket prices reflected this, with top seats costing forty-five dollars, the equivalent of a Broadway musical). "With *Einstein* we paid for everything. It cost us around a million dollars not counting overhead. With overhead — in other words figuring in the theatre and our staff — the cost was between a million and a million and a half. And this wasn't even a new work. Most of the money went into labor. We had two full months of rehearsal during which the cast was being paid. Bob's lighting is so much more precise than it used to be and those technical rehearsals were fiendishly expensive. Everything now costs a lot more. But we worked fairly efficiently and I don't know if there's a way of producing that work for any less money. At a time when conventional opera is very often produced in a sloppy way one of the things that's wonderful about Bob's work is its beauty and consummate professionalism. The problem is that you have to figure out a way to do his pieces as economically as possible but you can't do them sloppily, you can't skimp."

Lichtenstein, a man who must always keep his eye on the balance sheet, views the escalating costs of presenting Wilson's work with a certain apprehension. "The cost is almost prohibitive right now. A legendary work like *Einstein* took eight years to get revived and if we hadn't developed the Next Wave festival, with the kind of funds it generates, we probably wouldn't have been able to do it. It's not a commercial work that can pay its way back in two or three months so you damn well better have your money up front. As much as an audience is beginning to develop for this kind of work, there's still not enough to pay off the cost of this extraordinary process. In direct cost we lost about $300,000 with *Einstein* but that's what we budgeted, we were prepared for that. We had taken a calculated risk that we would do 90-percent box-office capacity and we did. Anything below that would have caused problems. Again, what's important to me is to be able to produce the work and not go broke." One solution is to share the costs with another producing organization or bring in productions that have been created elsewhere (as Lichtenstein has done with *Einstein, The Golden Windows* in 1985, the Rome section of *the CIVIL warS* the following year and *The Forest* in 1988), thus eliminating the slow and costly developmental process. "At this point it may be too expensive for any single organization in this country to take a work all the way from the first workshop to performance." (The only producer to have managed this professionally is Robert Brustein, who presented Wilson's *Alcestis* at the American Repertory Theatre in 1986. Such a commission was possible because the ART is a true repertory house with a permanent company and staff, and because the theatre was able to augment its normal production budget with special funding from outside sources.)

Given the times and economic climate, would it be possible for a Wilson or another experimental theatre artist inclined toward working on a grand scale to emerge today? "Well, I don't know. Even in the early days we lost a good deal of money. There wasn't a big audience. We're talking about a 2,000-seat house and a few hundred people that came to see the pieces. I don't know what I would do now frankly. Bob needs a theatre the size of the opera house, it's part of the way he works. Now he can draw an audience to fill it, then he couldn't. At the time we did a lot of important work and it played to very few people which is rather demoralizing. I don't know if I'd want to go through that kind of experience again. Obviously putting on those productions today would be much more expensive. BAM still takes lots of chances but, I think, in a more sophisticated and professional way. And Bob himself has changed, now he works with a company of professionals, back then he was working with friends and people who were attracted to him for one reason or another.

Those shows were very homemade. We don't present things like that anymore. The sixties was the heyday of the Judson Church and Rauschenberg's performances and a lot of those pieces had a very amateur air about them; that was part of the aesthetic, that anything can be art. It was a different time. Now everybody is more professional, even younger artists. I'm sure if you saw some of those productions today they would look very tacky, though there were extraordinary moments like the cave scene with Freud coming in and sitting down among the animals. Today Bob is able to realize his vision in an extraordinarily professional way yet I'm sure those amateur, slap-dash, put-together things had to be quite amazing. It's a whole different ball game now." (Meredith Monk, whose 1971 opera *Vessel* featured a hundred volunteer performers, has stated flatly that such work is no longer possible: "Today people either perform professionally or don't perform.")

"I think Bob is a great artist but his work isn't easy to comprehend. It isn't narrative theatre and it doesn't follow in established traditions where most people can get it. It's very much a visual experience in which he develops his own sense of time and rhythm and the ways things happen. I find his theatre quite extraordinary and beautiful and contemporary, much more so than most theatre work that's being done today. I also think Bob is so unexpected. Given the kind of work he does when you see him he's such an unexpected presence. I remember one thing that was very indicative of the intense but held-in energy you sense from him. We had a memorial for Ninon Karlweis some years ago and several of us spoke and reminisced. Bob got up and read a psalm from the Bible, I think it was "The Lord is my shepherd," and it was absolutely terrific. That's a quality he shares with his work, of being both surprising and very apt—once you get over being surprised your sense is that it's perfect, it couldn't be any other way. I love the work. At the same time it's difficult theatre to get to the stage both because it's not easy to comprehend and it's extremely costly. In a way, Bob is a very special case. I don't think there's any other theatre artist who's able to do all the things he can in terms of conception and writing, design and lighting. Laurie Anderson approaches that kind of total theatre but she's a much more commercial product. Laurie will never have trouble getting produced, Bob will always have trouble. But you've got to remember that despite all the problems somehow or other Wilson gets his work done and as people sort of catch up to it and assimilate it some will get their eyes opened and begin to see theatre in a different way. It's been a passion of mine to give the work an opportunity to exist and to find its public. Yes, it's more than just putting on a show. It certainly doesn't exist for making profit, right?"

BOB WILSON IN FRANCE:
PIERRE CARDIN/BÉNÉDICTE PESLE/MICHEL GUY

While Wilson's talents had not gone unrecognized in New York it was in France that his reputation and fortunes were made. The appearance of *Deafman Glance* (or *Le Regard du Sourd* as it was titled) in Paris in May of 1971 created a sensation, gaining him such admirers and enthusiasts as Eugène Ionesco, Louis Aragon, Peter Brook, Roger Planchon, Mme. Georges Pompidou, Max Ernst and Jean-Louis Barrault. Wilson experienced not only the critical praise and cult recognition he had attracted in New York but packed theatres, genuine popular acceptance and his first taste of celebrity. At the age of twenty-nine Wilson had taken Paris by storm and was launched on an international career. These times are recalled by three individuals— Pierre Cardin, Bénédicte Pesle and Michel Guy—who have played key roles in the artist's European career, as well as by a number of other witnesses to his early successes in France.

Wilson's first European odyssey began with an invitation from Jack Lang to the Festival Mondial du Théâtre at Nancy, which presented an adventurous program of experimental and student theatre work every spring during the university holidays. Wilson withdrew his savings of three thousand dollars and begged and borrowed the additional money to purchase one-way plane fares to Nancy. (Many of his performers paid their own way; in those days one's financial means often determined how much of one's expenses were paid or sometimes whether or not one went along on the tour.) Wilson's ambitions were once again in inverse proportion to his means. It was his plan to combine *The Life and Times of Sigmund Freud* and *Deafman Glance* into a single work lasting seven hours.

ROBERT WILSON: When I was first thinking about going to Nancy I asked my agent Ninon Karlweis, "Do you think the French will sit for something that's seven hours long and silent?" And she said, "Yes." And I said, "I'm not so sure. The French are so verbal, I can't imagine them sitting so long for a work that's silent. Why will they do that?" "They will do that because it will seem very mysterious to them." And she was right.

The two-performance engagement, which Wilson would later call his "passport to the theatre," attracted the attention of critics and theatre professionals, who were dazed and dazzled by what a festival publication called his "unclassifiable, unjustifiable and unbearable" spectacle.

PASCAL ORTEGA (stage manager of *Deafman Glance*): I had no sense it would turn out to be such a success. The first performance started almost two hours late because we weren't ready and when we finished I looked at my watch and assumed that the theatre must be empty. But it was still half or three-fourths full and there was a standing ovation. People just couldn't believe it. *Deafman Glance* was exactly what the French—whose theatre is all logic, rationality and language—could never have conceived.

Jack Lang: After the howling and confusion, here is the rehabilitation of silence, after the theatre of gesticulation here is the theatre of images. . . . A show that resembles no other: it irritates some, induces delirium and rapture in most. Never before in Western theatre has a play lasted so long. At the end of the show, the public, dazed and put out, wandered in the Place Stanislas, already steel blue in the light of morning, with the feeling of having witnessed un spectacle sans pareil.

PIERRE CARDIN: The play caught the truth of time, the reality of time. It was infinite, interminable. The movement was so slow you almost couldn't see it. I was very pleased with this idea. It was the movement of the time. Many people used drugs and with drugs people like to sit, to be quiet, to stare. You are in a different mood of yourself. You can sit hours looking. Bob took the time to look the sun, to look the river, to look the rain, to look the animals, to look the beauty, to look everything in peace and quiet. In contrast to this there was a runner—shssssss—always rushing across the stage or a dancer turning—zzzzzzz—never stopping. A symbol of the crazy people, of the life. We were very excited. We discovered Bob.

BÉNÉDICTE PESLE: One day I was called by Jean Rigg, the administrator of Merce Cunningham, and she said we know a group of people who go to Nancy absolutely unprepared. They do not have a penny, not a penny and we give them your name in case they get into trouble. The Festival de Nancy is at Easter time during the university holidays and everyone was going—in those days that was really *the* festival to go to—but I was working in the Gallery Iolas in Paris and had no time. Two other girls from the gallery decided to make the trip and they called me and said you must come, you cannot miss this. So I took a 7:00 P.M. train and arrived in Nancy just as the performance was starting. I thought it was something amazing! It was so new for the French. You know in France theatre is text and here was a big piece of theatre just filled by images. It was stunning. I was stunned by it. At that time *Deafman Glance* was seven hours and it ended about 4:00 A.M. I had to be at work in the morning so I did not meet Bob then but I looked at him and I was very intrigued by the way he walked and held his arms. He has a very strange way to stand. You know, most people favor one side over the other, they are totally left-handed or totally right-handed, but Bob is really *ambidextre*. And his face is totally *symétrique*. With most people each side is slightly different. I was very impressed with this balance. Maybe it was all in my head, I don't know.

Immediately after the show finished its run in Nancy the company traveled to Rome for a brief engagement at the Teatro Eliseo. Wilson was running out of money and his situation was fast becoming desperate. One Byrd Hoffman employee in New York remembers receiving a grim overseas phone call from the director, who lamented, "I've got thirty people over here and I've no money to feed them and no way to get them anywhere." But a few days later Wilson's fortunes turned. Pierre Cardin, who had gone to Nancy in search of attractions for his recently opened theatre complex in Paris, came to the rescue and brought the company back to France. Since his own theatre could not accommodate such a large and technically complex production, Cardin leased the Théâtre de la Musique (Gaîté-Lyrique), a large music hall off the Boulevard Sébastopol where *Le Regard du Sourd* opened on the night of May 14, 1971. (Wilson also created a three-hour companion piece for the empty Espace Cardin.)

PASCAL ORTEGA: The first night was a smashing success. The word was out and everybody was there. From the very first night we knew it was a hit.

PIERRE CARDIN: All of Paris came. *Tout Paris!* Many intellectuals, actors, directors, important people. Some only stayed three hours, some fell asleep, many stayed because it was so different.

DOMINIQUE BOITEL (director of Espace Cardin): The first night the show finished at five o'clock in the morning. The audience was *so* surprised. The stagehands could not believe it.

ROBERT WILSON: I left before the end of the first performance because I thought it was a disaster. I had worked for a long time to get the piece just right and I was very upset so I went back to my hotel. Ninon Karlweis came to the hotel which was just around the corner from the theatre and said, "You won't believe this." She took me back and the audience was still applauding. That night she told me, "You've had a phenomenal success and, if you want, for the rest of your life you'll be able to work in the theatre." I still didn't believe her, I thought she was just saying that to make me feel better but she said, "You wait and see, if you want you can have a career in the theatre."

The critical reaction was nothing short of sensational. *L'Express* called *Le Regard du Sourd* "the most extraordinary theatre piece of the season" and *Le Monde* hailed it as "a revolution in the plastic arts such as one sees only once or twice in a generation." As the *New York Times* later reported, "From the conservative *Figaro* to the extreme-left *Lettres françaises* (which devoted five articles to the event), from middle-France's *L'Express* to the intellectual left weekly *Nouvel Observateur*, the praise was near-unanimous."

Bradley Winterton in the Guardian, *June 22, 1971: I have hardly room to do more than signal the arrival of the most brilliant and revolutionary theatre with Robert Wilson's Byrd Hoffman School of Byrds from New York. The greatest art cannot be described, only suggested, so imagine the worlds of Magritte, Traherne and Fauré united in a spectacle that suggests the elimination of the very boundaries of art itself. . . . Here, if anywhere, is the theatre of the future, of a consciousness struggling for recognition—a post-schizophrenic, post-materialist world, relaxed, liberated, meditative and visionary. It's the prodigal soul returning to drama. Since the old theatre died we've had darkness and anguish. Here is the light.* (Winterton was "so overcome" by *Deafman* that he persuaded Wilson to let him appear in its companion piece, *Prologue.*)

Eugène Ionesco in Khjitevne Novine, *September 16, 1971: . . . after I saw Wilson's performance I was both happy because it was extraordinary and unhappy because I was jealous. Wilson succeeded in creating a miraculous light. I've tried to do something like that several times but have never succeeded . . .*

Eugène Ionesco in Belgrade Literary Gazette, *September 16, 1971: Beckett has succeeded in creating a few minutes of silence on the stage, while Robert Wilson was able to bring about silence that lasted four hours! He has surpassed Beckett in this: Wilson being richer and more complex with his silence on the stage. This silence is a silence that can speak. However, what is interesting about both Beckett and Wilson is the fact that they are above politics. They are interested in the existential — not social — destiny of man. In this, Wilson has gone further than Beckett, for in his play* Deafman Glance, *despite silence, he conjures up the whole tragedy of man and his history. Wilson speaks of the metaphysical defeat of man. The whole of existence has been condensed here into four hours which bring us to an apocalyptic end; but this end, at the same time, announces the arrival of a new Adam and a new Eve who will start again a new cycle.*

But what made all Paris take notice was the response of Louis Aragon, the grand old man of French surrealism, who had been invited to the opening by Cardin. On the front page of *Les Lettres françaises*, the Communist weekly of the arts and literature, readers found the words "HAVE YOU SEEN *DEAFMAN GLANCE*? YOU CANNOT MISS IT" followed by a rhapsodic appreciation in the form of an open letter to fellow surrealist André Breton, who had died five years before and with whom Aragon had not spoken in forty years.

Louis Aragon in Les Lettres françaises, *June 2, 1971: . . . the miracle was produced, the one we were waiting for, about which we talked . . . the miracle came about long after I stopped believing in them. And this happened today. In a theatre which was the old Gaîté-Lyrique, and do you remember the time we spent in the square in front of the Gaîté, one day in May, 1918 before we were separated? It must have been a Sunday, the silence was absolute. Not a horse-drawn car, not a coughing taxi. You said to me, 'Listen to the silence.' And we laughed for all the horses who weren't there to neigh at that idea of listening to silence . . . all of a sudden, in deepest seriousness, you continued, 'It's because we have become deaf that we think Paris is mute.' Well, that's precisely the miracle. The play they did — but was it a play and were they acting? who? — was called* Deafman Glance, *my friend. To get there you had to go through the hell of Paris, the tumultuous Boulevard Sébastopol, and all of a sudden one no longer needed or hardly needed his ears. The world of a deaf child opened up to us like a wordless mouth. For more than four hours, we went to inhabit this universe where, in the absence of words, of sounds, sixty people had no words except to move. I want to tell you right away, André, because even if those who invented this spectacle don't know it, they are playing it for you, for you would have loved it as I did, to the point of madness. (Because it has made me mad.) Listen to what I say to those who have ears, seemingly not for hearing: I never saw anything more beautiful in the world since I was born. Never, never has any play come anywhere near this one, because it is at once life awake and the life of closed eyes, the confusion between everyday life and the life of each night, reality mingles with dream, all that's inexplicable in the life of the deaf. . . . Bob Wilson's piece, which comes to us from Iowa, is not surrealism at all, however easy it is for people to call it that, but it is what we others, who fathered surrealism, what we dreamed it might become after us, beyond us. And I imagine the exultation you would have shown at almost every moment of this masterpiece of surprise, where the art of man exceeds at each breath of silence the supposed art of the Creator.*

Invoking the names of Douanier Rousseau, Magritte, Paul Delvaux, Dali and Duchamp, reviewers likened Wilson's work to such native movements as surrealism, the theatre of cruelty, the absurd and Dada. Wilson's theatre was seen as something completely new that at the same time had—or seemed to have—connections to their own art and cultural traditions. Alfred Jarry might almost have been speaking the prologue to *Deafman Glance* and not *Ubu Roi* when he announced from the stage of the Théâtre de l'Oeuvre in 1896, ". . . you will see doors open on fields of snow under blue skies, fireplaces furnished with clocks and swinging wide to serve as doors, and palm trees growing at the foot of a bed so that little elephants standing on bookshelves can browse on them."

ALAIN JOUFFROY (journalist): When I was very young I met Antonin Artaud and André Breton and I participated in the surrealist movement until I was twenty. I found the memory of these things again in the dream of this play. The spectacle of Bob Wilson was very new but with special roots in French art. We find this connection. Maybe it's not true but we find it. And we think, how is this possible? Astonishment.

MICHEL GUY: I happen to know that Bob didn't know anything about European art or surrealism yet strangely *Deafman Glance* was like the ideal surrealist theatre. It was a vision that didn't really look American except in the way that it couldn't be European.

GILLES ANQUETIL (journalist): Bob Wilson's theatre is a meeting of the new world and the old world, of American culture and European art. Bob doesn't create like European artists. He's very intuitive and not at all intellectual yet there's this memory of European culture in his work.

PIERRE CARDIN: Bob came and lived in my house for three months and he was always looking through my books on painting. He was very inspired by pictures. He would look at the work of Paul Delvaux and make a scene with a Delvaux look. He discovered, he was surprised. Bob was not really very cultivated but he was intelligent and sensitive. He came to Europe and saw so *many* different things. And he would take from everywhere and put into his shows.

GILLES ANQUETIL: I am part of the reason why Bob made such a success in Paris. I'm an intellectual, the literary editor of *Nouvel Observateur*. I was never theatre crazy. So many times I get bored and when you get bored at the theatre there's no place more boring in the world. Bob Wilson was the theatremaker for people who didn't like theatre. He didn't come from the theatre and neither did the people who were working with him yet the mixture made for the purest theatre work in the last twenty years. For me and my friends it was the end of 1968 — the roaring sixties — and the last expression of the theatrical revolution that had started with Grotowski and Luca Ronconi. Very special, very new, very magical. Even now people in Paris are crying when they remember *Deafman Glance*.

MICHEL GUY: It was one of the five or six most important things I'd seen on stage in my life. I saw it nine times and for months and months I continued to get the images in my head.

BÉNÉDICTE PESLE: In France you very often have this craze. People discover someone and he becomes like a magic person. That was Bob Wilson. I don't know if it's so true now, but at the time Bob was drawing young people like those who go to rock concerts. They were very passionate. They were getting an experience and would get high. Great excitement.

PASCAL ORTEGA: Patrice Chéreau was a big fan of *Deafman Glance* and saw it I don't know how many times. He came to the opening in Nancy and was really excited. I remember him saying it was great because you could go to sleep and when you woke up it hadn't changed yet all the same it was different. Chéreau came again in Rome where there was a big scandal. Bob set fire to the umbrella at the end of the performance although it had been strictly forbidden by the fire department. They almost closed the show. Chéreau was backstage and he said, "That's a real director!"

GILLES ANQUETIL: Bob was very *à la mode*. It was very very chic to like this kind of thing and it attracted many snobs.

MICHEL GUY: What was strange—and is still strange—was that you could see the very young and avant-garde people as well as mink ladies who arrived in their Rolls Royces. Oddly enough there was something easy about Bob's work at that time. It was very new, very personal, very beautiful and also very simple. No text so nothing to understand, really. Just things to watch and dream with. Anyone could enter it at some level. It took me about ten years to make Merce Cunningham successful in Paris but Bob was successful overnight.

BÉNÉDICTE PESLE: People in France are curious. They go see. They want to know. I saw is quite late in Paris but I remember the day I went the ground floor was like *parterre de roi*. So many writers and people from theatre. Genet was there with Roger Blin. Roger Planchon was there. The writer Henri Michaux was looking at the stage all through the performance without moving a finger. Later when I was working with Bob we always put Michaux in a box by himself so people could see him.

PASCAL ORTEGA: There were a lot of what you'd call hip people. We also attracted a real group of weirdos from Paris who attached themselves to the show. Some of the people were really spaced-out, you sort of had to push them onstage at times. All anyone who wanted to be in the show had to do was go speak with Bob. It was difficult to get paid but it was easy to get into the show. It got to the point where someone in the cast would say I can't come tomorrow so I'll teach my part to somebody else and suddenly I'd look out and there'd be another snakehandler or another glass carrier. People would come up to me and say, "I'm the black bear. When am I supposed to go on?" It used to freak me out in the beginning but it kept the show alive. For weeks afterwards people would say hello to me on the street and I had no idea who they were. I assumed they must have been in the show at some point.

Wilson, who had never been able to present more than two performances of any of his works in one place, played to capacity houses for more than six weeks. The world opened up to him. He received invitations from the Berlin Opera and the BITEF Festival and an offer from Michel Guy to create a new work for the first Festival d'Automne the following year. He also found himself in the company of some of the great creative figures of the century—Aragon, Max Ernst, Charlie Chaplin, Man Ray—who would pass from the scene only a few years later. Had Wilson, who brought his company over to France without return fares, any expectation of the acclaim, celebrity and financial rewards awaiting him? "No," he says today in his laconic way, "we were just hoping we'd find a way to get home."

DOMINIQUE BOITEL: *Deafman Glance* had nothing to do with what had been done before in France and that's why it was successful. Planchon, Chéreau—they all took inspiration from Bob Wilson. The work gave something to other people. It was beautiful and that beauty inspired people.

PIERRE CARDIN: Bob Wilson changed completely our idea of time, he changed all the concepts of the theatre in Paris for two or three years.

PASCAL ORTEGA: There were many imitations of Bob's work after that but what no one could ever imitate was the rhythm.

CHARLES DENNIS: The reviews for *Deafman* were incredible but even in Paris there were times when people would boo during the beach scene or yell, "What is this, this is not art!" or "This is not theatre!"

GILLES ANQUETIL: The first half-hour was always like that with Bob. People would grumble, "What is this?" "There's no story." "I don't understand." "Who is this crazy man?" But soon these people go home and those who remain are hypnotized. The images are so strong you get a kind of hallucination. Nobody had ever seen theatre so slow and images so precise, so intense. There is a resistance to this in the beginning but when people accept they can sit and watch for hours.

ALAIN JOUFFROY: I went with Aragon the first night and it was strange because by the third hour we thought maybe now it's finished. And we were surprised. No, no. It's not finished. No, no, just wait. This feeling of wait was very strong. Like life, you know. Life is a long wait.

PIERRE CARDIN: I say, Bob, I see tonight we are finished at three o'clock in the morning. I say, Bob, who can sit in the theatre seven hours? No one's brain can receive seven hours of theatre. Bob, it is not nice for you if people walk out. Please, Bob, please—cut! Finally, Bob says, "Okay, Pierre, I understand, I do for you." So he cut three hours. In reality he cut nothing. He just made everything go faster.

I've presented two hundred productions and the most expensive was Bob Wilson. There were eighty people and everyone was paid. I lost a lot. A lot! I lost too much. Every day he would change the show. I remember near the end I was very angry. At five o'clock Bob came to see Pierre and said, "I need six black boys for nine o'clock tonight." In Paris, you can imagine! I say, "Bob, I can't find six black boys in Paris at this hour, not for tonight." There were many things like that. I had to change the boa constrictor three times. It is not so easy to find a boa in Paris either. I say okay. He asks me for this, I say okay. Every day was something new. Okay, I'll buy. Okay, I'll buy. Then, he says "I want six black boys. If you don't do this, Pierre, I don't play tonight." I remember I said, "Bob, if you don't play you give me the best present I *ever* receive in my life." After three months I was exhausted. I am a designer and couturier and during the day I had my own business to run. I got so little sleep. When he asks me "will you, please, next year . . ." I say "ah, no, Bob, no." I helped him in many different ways. Okay, Bob. I will try, Bob. Yes, Bob. Yes, Bob. Yes, Bob. Yes, Bob. I was a saint.

MICHEL GUY: Bob Wilson is powerfully imaginative and intelligent and also a little mad. When he has something on his mind it becomes an obsession. The idea gets to be enormous and he thinks of nothing else. That's part of his genius. It's strange, rather amusing, sometimes stupid but it's also part of his genius.

BÉNÉDICTE PESLE: Meredith Monk was also doing big pieces at the time and she was invited to Nancy too but she didn't dare to ask people to come for free. I think she came alone and did a solo work. That is probably the big quality of Bob. He's daring, he's not stopped and when he has an idea on his mind his will power is fantastic.

This determination is illustrated by an incident—perhaps the most often told of all "Bob Wilson stories"—in which Pesle found herself a direct participant. During rehearsals of *D D & D* in Berlin, Wilson decided to suspend an enormous light bulb above the stage in the scene where Hess dances beside the cradle of his infant son. He described the object he envisioned to the technical staff of the Schaubühne but by then he had exhausted his budget and couldn't get anyone interested. Wilson, of course, would not give up so easily. He had some business in Paris and on his way back to Berlin the plane stopped over in Düsseldorf. Instead of getting on the next flight he found a young taxi driver who spoke English, explained what he wanted and asked, "Will you stick with me until we figure this out?" The taxi driver looked through the phone book and they found a firm that manufactured chemical flasks. The two drove to the factory where Wilson selected a flask of the proper shape and size—a credible bulb—and then continued on to a neon-design company where the artist described the filament he wanted. The driver then took Wilson back to the airport for the second leg of his journey, leaving the concerned parties to put the giant light bulb together. It was Pesle's task to pick up the unwieldy object on her way to the premiere and in this her determination proved equal to Wilson's own.

> BÉNÉDICTE PESLE: Naturally it was huge. At the airport they would not let it on the plane. I said, "Okay, I will buy a seat for it," and they said no. I said, "I will buy two seats," and they said no. I was ready to buy four seats, I didn't care. Finally they said, "You are really stubborn. We take it." And they ship it through with the luggage. So Bob Wilson got his light bulb. That's it. That is the power of Bob. He will go after what he wants. And he knows how to give people the feeling that he can succeed. He can give people the confidence to take a chance. Michel Guy was very courageous to give Wilson the Opéra Comique for *Overture*. It could have been a total disaster. What do you think of Guy being minister of culture and saying okay, two French festivals—the Festival d'Avignon and the Festival d'Automne—are going to sponsor *Einstein on the Beach*. Without his support, the work would never have been done. This is why I will never forgive Robert Fitzpatrick [the director of the 1984 Olympic Arts Festival]. Michel Guy knew how to get people involved and how to get the government to support and subsidize. Fitzpatrick didn't work to get that support. He was the first person to let Bob down and he was an American. It's easy to say in Europe you have money, in America you don't. It's not true. We don't have money—who has money? We fight to get it. And if it is found ultimately it is because we fight enough to make people do it.

Through the efforts of such influential and committed advocates as Guy and Pesle, Wilson has continued to find support for his work in France—and the French have continued to take an almost proprietary interest in an artist they can justifiably claim to have discovered. Wilson's situation exemplifies the frequent dilemma of the American performing artist, who is nourished by his own culture and anxious to take his place in it yet finds far greater opportunities and recognition abroad.

> MICHEL GUY: This is true for all American geniuses of the last twenty years. When I asked Merce Cunningham to come to France he was playing in university gymnasiums. Taylor, Nikolais, Twyla, Trisha, they were all very miserable playing in tiny theatres, more or less empty. Then I invited them and when they went back to America it was usually better.

> PASCAL ORTEGA: It was the same with Bread and Puppet. In New York they played in churches to a hundred people while in Paris they played to thousands every night.

GILLES ANQUETIL: This often happens with American artists. A lot of your jazz musicians are virtually unknown in America and here they are gods. In the States you have this incredible cultural vitality but also a nonattention to your artists. In cinema Jerry Lewis was derided but in France he was recognized as a real creator. The same thing for Bob Wilson. Europe is fascinated by American creativity. You also have a big problem with culture in America. If you don't make a hit you disappear. You don't have the right to fail. In Europe you have that right.

MICHEL GUY: It's always been a French tradition to invite foreigners to work here. Many Italian and Dutch painters spent their lives in France. Verdi and Rossini were commissioned by the Opéra. We have been doing this kind of thing for centuries.

BÉNÉDICTE PESLE: This is the difference between Europe and America. We support not only Bob but the Living Theatre and Richard Foreman. We had Diaghilev. It's a tradition to be open to new things from wherever they come and to welcome expatriate artists. I also think it comes from the deprivations of the war. I grew up in France during the war and we were starving for art. So when art started to come back in 1945, people of my generation would go everywhere to look at it. We would go to the museums, we would go to the galleries, to the theatres. We know maybe better that art is necessary to live so we must get from everywhere and make available to people. We had the Théâtre des Nations of Jean-Louis Barrault [the coproducer of *Overture*], which was part of the spirit to get work from everywhere. Now we have the Théâtre de l'Europe, which you can call an offspring of that, so all year round we have theatre in foreign languages coming to Paris. We also have the *maisons de culture* which in the mind of André Malraux were the cathedrals of modern times, the place where culture might be available to anybody. In France it is a tradition to support the arts, in America they think art should be paid for by the people who go see it.

ROBERT WILSON: I had a friend who lived a couple of houses away from Man Ray on rue Férou and one day she asked me if I would like to meet him. I saw Man Ray two or three times altogether and towards the end of his life he said to me, "I hope that you don't become an expatriate. I did and I've regretted it. I think it's important for you to keep roots in America." At that time it would have been quite easy for me to live in Paris because I had so much support there. Michel Guy, who was the minister of culture, asked, "Would you like a theatre? Do you want to make films? What do you want to do? We'd like to support you." Jack

Lang said the same things to me. Still, I knew what Man Ray meant. I didn't want to be an expatriate but all my work was in Europe. There was no work here.

Although Wilson continues to draw large audiences in Paris nearly twenty years after his first appearance there, time has inevitably eroded the critical consensus he once enjoyed.

DOMINIQUE BOITEL: *Pour moi Wilson, c'est tout passé.* It was of the moment and now the moment has past. His theatre hasn't evolved, it's always the same. But he still has an audience. The intellectuals aren't so interested anymore but some of the people who were there at the beginning continue to follow him. There are also young people who didn't see the early work and for them it's new. But he doesn't bring anything more to me. The performances have moved further and further from the life and what people want today is life.

PIERRE CARDIN: He couldn't do better than *Le Regard du Sourd* and he never has done better. Artistically it was fantastic. He put everything in that production.

PASCAL ORTEGA: I never found the freshness again that I had found in those early pieces. Of course, there's always a tendency to feel the thing you were part of was the best. Bob still has his followers and many people who did not see *Deafman* want to catch up with his theatre and be in on him. I think he can go on for a few more years.

MICHEL GUY: Most of the critics think that Bob has nothing to say anymore. They don't understand that his work is now ten times more interesting than it used to be. It's deeper, it comes from a much stronger personality. *Le Martyre de Saint Sébastien* was a masterpiece, *Hamlet-machine* was a masterpiece. The work he's doing with sound is among the most interesting in this generation. A lot of people liked *Deafman Glance* because it was beautiful — beautiful images and that's all. Now Bob's work is stronger, more difficult to see. People stay with the old ideas of Bob. Of course, for those involved in the early pieces it's pure *mélancolie*. People get used to the way an artist works and when he changes, they always regret it. When Picasso changed his way of painting every ten years, people thought always it was much better before. Now Picasso is dead for fifteen years and we know that his last works, which were very much despised during his lifetime, are masterpieces. I *always* thought they were masterpieces.

To me, Bob's work is more and more interesting. Not everything, because he is doing too much and he does things too fast. It's a kind of pity that he wastes his time doing things he shouldn't do. I've always told Bob—and still tell him—that he should only do works of his own. I think this is much more interesting than his doing the *mise en scène* of *Parsifal* or God knows what. But Bob has a problem. He's very snobbish. He likes very much publicity, he likes stars, he likes rich people, he likes big theatres. He likes, for instance, the idea of opening the Opéra Bastille on July 13 where he will do God knows what. With a lot of pieces you have the impression he should have worked two or three months more. He has a one-week workshop in one city and then flies off for a week workshop in another city. It's very amusing to read his schedule. It always makes me laugh. But when everything's right, his work for the theatre is pure genius. The problem now is that people are not very much interested in what is new and important in his work.

Bob Wilson has been a rather important adventure in my life. He has changed my own way of looking at the theatre, my way of listening and my way of looking. The mark of the great artist is to change you and Bob has done that.

BIOGRAPHIES

PIERRE CARDIN is an internationally known designer and the creator of his own fashion empire. He is also the author of *Fernand Léger: Sa Vie, Son Oeuvre, Son Rêve*. Cardin introduced some of America's most innovative performers to Paris (among them Wilson, André Gregory, Alice Cooper and Pilobolus) at his theatre complex Espace Cardin. (Paris. March 10, 1989.)

BÉNÉDICTE PESLE is the founder of Artservice International and has been a major force in establishing American artists in Europe, among them Merce Cunningham, Twyla Tharp, John Cage, Philip Glass, Meredith Monk, Karole Armitage and Lucinda Childs. She has served Wilson in a number of capacities—as agent, fundraiser, producer, lighting assistant and even performer, making a brief appearance in *Video-50*. (New York City. September 16, 1988.)

MICHEL GUY is the founding director of the Festival d'Automne, an international celebration of dance, theatre and music held in Paris each fall. Guy commissioned Wilson's 24-hour *Overture* for the first festival in 1972 and later initiated the creation of *Einstein on the Beach* as secretary of culture under Giscard d'Estaing. He has also commissioned the upcoming Glass-Wilson opera *Palace of the Arabian Nights*. (Paris. March 15, 1989.)

PASCAL ORTEGA was stage manager for the European tours of *Deafman Glance* and *A Letter for Queen Victoria*. He assisted Cheréau at Bayreuth and recently helped organize the July 14 parade for the French bicentennial celebrations. (Paris. March 13, 1989.)

GILLES ANQUETIL is book editor of *Nouvel Observateur*. He met Wilson while attending the Shiraz festival in 1972 and appeared as a performer in *Overture* later that year. (Paris. March 15, 1989.)

DOMINIQUE BOITEL is artistic director of Espace Cardin. (Paris. March 10, 1989.)

ALAIN JOUFFROY is an author and teacher. He was a close friend of Louis Aragon and contributed articles to *Les Lettres françaises*. (Paris. March 15, 1989).

ROBERT APPLEGARTH

Robert Applegarth, who would become the project coordinator of *the CIVIL warS*, was working as a stage manager for Peter Brook in Paris when he first heard the name Robert Wilson. "Bob was doing a workshop at Royaumont outside Paris in 1972 and we all drove out to see what was going on. It was in a castle of some kind and there were all these little environments set up that you could walk through. I didn't know who Bob was or what was going on. I'm reminded of the Bob Dylan song, 'Something's Happening Here and I Don't Know What It Is.' It was potent and it bothered me that I couldn't quite figure it out. Some months later I went to see *Overture*, the 24-hour show at the Opéra Comique which was more interesting for what was happening in the audience. The curtain went up and there was Madeleine Renaud crawling across the stage in slow motion. Every so often she'd turn quickly toward the audience, shake her head and wag her tongue and then go back to crawling. Well, the Parisian audience took about ten minutes of this and then started booing, hissing and throwing things. The piece is twenty-four hours long and they start this after the first ten minutes! And it got wilder and wilder. They love to organize into factions, the pros and the cons. There were fights breaking out on the grand staircase. I remember seeing a beer bottle someone threw rolling down the stairs. Everyone screamed and carried on for a number of hours and then things quieted down. The people who were into it were into it and the others left. I remember I went home and did my laundry and then came back for the last six hours which were quite extraordinary, so quiet and mesmerizing. During the curtain calls Marie France, this famous drag queen, came up on stage and threw herself at everyone's feet. She was just transported. Again, I really didn't know what was going on or what to make of it. It was so removed from anything I'd ever seen. Yet, like the song says, I had a feeling something was going on."

Applegarth returned to New York in 1973 and worked briefly as an assistant stage manager on *The Life and Times of Joseph Stalin* at the Brooklyn Academy of Music. "It was the first time I saw *Deafman Glance* and those images really blew me away. The lady in white with the flaming parasol, the frog playing the violin and at the end those gorillas with the red apples rising from their hands into the sky. The stuff was absolutely magical. From then on, I went to see all Bob's works." Their paths, however, would not converge again until nearly a decade later. By then Applegarth was the associate director of the Dance Theater Workshop in New York and Wilson, who was in the midst of preparing for the month-long workshop of *the CIVIL warS* in Freiburg, needed someone to organize the mammoth undertaking. Wilson's invitation to join the project took Applegarth completely by surprise. "I was floored. I had been introduced to Bob at Royaumont and remember thinking he was very weird, spooky even. Then I met him again when I got to New York and he was just kind of solemn and withdrawn. I always felt uncomfortable around him. Unless Bob's comfortable with you, he's very forbidding. I never really got to know him until he asked me to do *the CIVIL warS*. He didn't have anybody to organize the project and he saw that Dance Theater Workshop was very well run and a lot of people knew me. I think he chose me just on instinct."

Applegarth was excited by the prospect of working on such a spectacular project and somewhat daunted by the immensity of what had to be accomplished. "I remember Bob pulled out a piece of paper and began drawing the scenes. He said that it was going to be done in six countries and then brought together for the Olympics. There was never ever a moment's doubt in his mind that it would all happen, or if there was he never let it show. And everyone was hooked as soon as they heard about it. In terms of sheer excitement it was an offer that you couldn't possibly turn down. Nothing like it had ever been done before. The time factor, however, was very tricky. This was June of 1982 and the work was scheduled to be performed in Los Angeles in June of 1984. Just stop and think what Bob had to accomplish in that period of time . . . and at that point there were just those little drawings. We were really winging it all the way. To tell the truth I didn't know what I was getting into. I did not know Bob very well, I didn't know how he worked, I just knew that this was a terribly exciting project and I wanted to be part of it."

Although *the CIVIL warS* existed largely in the artist's imagination at the time Applegarth joined the production team, Wilson had been mapping out the project since late 1979 (his first sketches appeared in his journal in December of that year). When Robert Fitzpatrick, the dean of the California Institute of the Arts and director of the upcoming Olympic Arts Festival, approached him about presenting a work in conjunction with the 1984 Los Angeles Games, he saw an opportunity to create a huge multinational opera that would draw its performers from many nations, like the Olympics themselves. Work on this expanded conception officially got underway at the Bavarian State Opera in Munich in August of 1981. Wilson spent two weeks with a small group of performers, technicians and assistants, shaping the text, discussing the designs and blocking out scenes. Over the next ten months he met with individual participants and made an exploratory trip to Japan to familiarize himself with its artists and institutions, all the while continuing to work on other projects. In June of 1982, Wilson brought together over fifty participants from around the world—writers, choreographers, dancers, actors, musicians and technicians—for the next major phase, an intensive four-week developmental workshop in the small West German city of Freiburg-im-Breisgau. It was there that Applegarth got his first real look at Robert Wilson in action.

"Something happened in Freiburg that impressed me deeply. We were blocking the whole thing out and we began to realize that the work was going to be about twelve hours long and cost X million dollars and everyone got very depressed. I thought, we'll never be able to raise this money, we'll never be able technically to make this thing work. At that point we had no sponsors for any of the sections and no guarantees. All he had was a letter from the Olympic Organizing Committee agreeing to contribute up to 10 percent or $300,000 of the presentation cost in L.A. Everyone on the steering team agreed we had to convince Bob to cut the project back and make it more realistic because we didn't think it could be done. So we all asked him to come to a meeting. Sensing what was about to happen, Bob came in like an angry bull—you could see the veins in his throat—and said, 'I don't want *any* negativity! I don't want *anyone* saying it can't be done. It *can* be done. We'll make it happen.' He stopped any discussion of cutting back or making it more realistic right there. It would happen, we'd just have to use our brains. That's his big expression, 'Use your brain and figure out how to make it work.' No one could say anything. And that's what Bob does, he absolutely challenges you. He says, 'Don't say it can't be done. Make it work.' You have to be completely committed. That's it. If you don't operate that way, he's not interested in having you around. On the one hand, it's megalomania but—goddamnit—on the other hand if he hadn't had that attitude, no one would have worked the way they did and we never would have accomplished what we did." If Applegarth had any idea of Wilson as an innocent pursuing an impossible dream, he was soon to find out who the innocent really was.

On the last day of the Freiburg residency (which was funded by grants from the National Endowment for the Arts and BMW), a five-hour "final review" was presented before potential sponsors and donors in the rehearsal hall of the municipal theatre. "Bob made us get on the phone and call every theatre producer he knew in Europe and invite them to come for this final run-through. I found that astonishing. I can't imagine any other director saying, 'Hey, we're having a run-through, come to Freiburg and look at it.'" Among the invited guests were the directors of the various *maisons de culture* in France and state theatres in Germany and Holland, members of the press and even Madame Georges Pompidou, long an enthusiast of Wilson's work.

"They all came on Saturday, watched the run-through, stayed overnight and then attended a meeting the next morning at a little German restaurant. Everyone was sitting there waiting and I thought, 'Jesus.' This whole thing was new to me. And Bob leaned over to me and said, 'What'll I say?' And I said, 'Bob?' I was so scared — because he was serious. Then he just turned to them and said, 'You've seen the run-through, you know the scope of the work, you know what we want to do and what I want to know is what each of you can do for this project.' He put those people totally on the spot. And they found themselves saying, 'Well, we'll take this section, we'll try to do this.' It's not that they actually ended up doing it as much as they went back and spread the word about the project. I came away from Freiburg terrified. I had never seen Wilson or anyone else operate in that way. From that point on I just took my work from Bob, he called all the shots. If he said call so-and-so and ask them this, then that's what I did."

Apart from a few weeks spent rehearsing *Great Day in the Morning* in Paris, Wilson devoted the next ten months to the search for sponsors and support. "Bob was on the phone every minute, using every connection, every past working relationship and lead. He ran around Europe and the United States — you can't imagine how he ran around, I could barely keep up with him. He had to find sponsoring theatres for six productions, get the governments of those countries to agree to send the productions to Los Angeles, pay the actors, pay his staff, pay the fees, pay the per diems and then raise 2.6 million dollars in the United States for the performances in Los Angeles. And he started in Freiburg with absolutely nothing." Though Applegarth was stationed at the Byrd Hoffman Foundation in New York during this phase of the project, he spent a month traveling with Wilson in Europe. "It was a blur of running for moving trains — that's how I remember the whole trip. We were running for one train that was moving out of the station and Bob jumped on and pulled me on. There was this poor woman running behind with my bag and we were reaching for it but she just got farther and farther away. Finally she was left standing at the end of the platform with this bewildered expression on her face and Bob and I just fell on the floor laughing. My luggage never caught up with us. I had to wear the same clothes for weeks."

One of the ploys that Wilson used to entice prospective producers during these exploratory treks made Applegarth particularly uncomfortable. "Bob and I went to Holland and he said, 'Look France is doing this, Germany is doing this, Italy is doing this. Now Holland should do this.' So they said, 'Oh, well, then Holland better do something.' Of course, none of those other things were set. Then we'd go somewhere else and do the same thing. For me this was the worst part of the job. I didn't understand then that that's the way you make things happen. My natural instinct would have been to say, 'Look, we're trying to get so-and-so to do this and so-and-so to do that, will you come in on it too?' But people don't want to hear that maybe it's going to happen. Bob's attitude was to tell them, 'We have this one remaining section and then the whole thing will fall into place. If you act quickly we're going to allow your participation in this incredible, international Olympic project.' It worked. And it was the only method that would have worked. What I ultimately realized was that the theatres knew that none of these other places were set—they all talk to each other—but they were playing Bob's game so they could do it themselves. They didn't believe it for a moment but they needed an argument in order to go to their respective boards and say, 'We'd better do it.' Everyone was playing this little game with each other but Bob just did it with aplomb. He's a real Texas entrepreneur." In this Wilson would seem to be following in the footsteps of his paternal grandfather, a turn-of-the-century contractor who made and lost fortunes—and a family figure for whom he has always had a special affinity. (If Wilson is an artist and dreamer, he is also a businessman, and the three years he spent studying business administration at the University of Texas may have been as formative as his subsequent years at Pratt studying design and absorbing the contemporary art scene.)

Selling *the CIVIL warS* was not an easy task, as Wilson's requirements were liable to put a strain on the resources of even the most generously supported state theatre. In each case he asked for a workshop period (Stage A) to finalize the script, block out the scenes and draw up plans for the physical production. This was to be followed some months later by a lengthy rehearsal period (Stage B), culminating in public performances at the various theatres prior to the complete presentation in Los Angeles. "Bob's productions always cost more because Bob does more. His fee is probably the highest in Europe but then he works twice as hard as anybody else, and longer. But he is up front at the very beginning. When they work out a budget he sticks to it. So the theatres enter into it knowing what it will cost them and Bob enters knowing what he has to work with." The various theatres were also required to ship their productions to California and pay all fees, travel and living expenses of performers and chief technicians while in Los Angeles, though in most cases these costs were to be borne by the governments of the sponsoring institutions.

Despite the financial challenge and complexity of mounting a piece of *the CIVIL warS*, a number of European theatres soon began expressing serious interest in the project. In Holland, Wilson had the active support of Dr. Willy Hoffman of the Rotterdam Theater Council. Because Rotterdam's resources were limited, Wilson offered them a single scene and secured the coparticipation of the Munich Residenz Theater, whose chief administrator August Everding had made the facilities of the Bavarian State Opera available for the first workshop of *the CIVIL warS*. A number of state theatres in France were also exploring the possibility of presenting a section of the work, as was the Schaubühne in Berlin. While Wilson had not as yet found a primary sponsor in Japan, where he hoped to produce a sizeable portion of the opera (and where there was little government support to be had), grants from the Japan-

United States Friendship Commission, Pierre Cardin, Toyota and the Kajima Construction Company enabled him to hold a Stage A workshop in Tokyo, at which time he could look for additional funding. Japanese participation was essential; one of the chief inspirations for *the CIVIL warS* had been a series of photographs taken in Japan at the end of the Edo period and images drawn from Japanese history and art were to be incorporated into several scenes. Each of the other sections would also bear the imprint of the sponsoring country. "As early as Freiburg Bob had a feeling about what scenes lent themselves to what national color. He felt certain scenes were Dutch in character while others were delicate and Japanese. And it's remarkable how successful he was in placing them. The scenes based on Jules Verne went to France and the heavy, dramatic scenes went to Germany."

For the knee plays, the brief connective interludes that would be played at the front of the stage in Los Angeles to cover scene changes, Wilson enlisted the aid of Robert Stearns, the director of the Walker Arts Center in Minneapolis. Stearns was an old friend; he had commissioned Wilson's first video performance piece, *The Spaceman*, in 1976 and later organized a comprehensive exhibit of his work at the Contemporary Art Center in Cincinnati. The Walker did not have the resources to produce the piece by themselves, but when Applegarth learned that the neighboring Guthrie Theater had received a grant to stage *The Golden Windows* (the production had subsequently fallen through) he spoke with Stearns about the possibility of bringing them into the project. "It was difficult persuading the Guthrie to work with the Walker Art Center but they realized they could keep the grant if they applied it to another Wilson piece. It was the first time they ever coproduced a work. What was even more difficult was persuading these people to go out and actively raise funds to send the piece to Los Angeles. Can you imagine telling an American cultural organization that on top of their own fundraising, on top of their own deficit they'd have to raise X number of dollars? But they did it."

Wilson was hoping to enlist one of the world's great opera houses for the concluding section of the work. When none expressed interest, Maita di Niscemi persuaded her cousin Gioacchino Lanza Tomasi, the director of the Rome Opera, to come to New York to discuss the project, and an agreement was soon reached. Although the pieces of Wilson's epic were quickly falling into place, progress was frustrated by a series of setbacks. The first of these came in December of 1982 when the prestigious Schaubühne dropped out, citing cost and prior commitments. "Bob was crushed because he really felt they were going to do it. They had three big productions that year and they said they couldn't afford it. They knew it was going to be horrendously expensive." (Wilson was to express rueful amusement when the set design for Peter Stein's production of *The Blacks* the following year bore more than a passing resemblance to the first scene of *the CIVIL warS*.) A few months later the Cologne Schauspielhaus stepped in and assumed sponsorship, much to the relief of

Wilson and his staff. "Then August Everding suddenly backed out of the collaboration with Rotterdam, saying that the renovation of the Prinzregenten Theater in
Munich was consuming all his resources. Holland had entered the project with the
understanding that costs would be shared. Rather than abandon the section, Bob
decided to assume the risk himself, which was scary. It was a huge risk for Byrd
Hoffman." The situation in France, where Wilson hoped to create one of the most
spectacular and costly episodes, was also problematic. With the first workshop
scheduled for the coming fall and no producer in sight, Wilson and his team
hurriedly began to search for a European theatre, opera house or even an American
university capable of undertaking such an ambitious project on short notice.

"My image through all this was of plates spinning on sticks, and running from
here to there to over there to keep them up. No sooner had you got one going than
another would start to wobble and you'd have to run to keep it from falling. That's
exactly what it felt like through all of *the CIVIL warS*." Working out of his office at the
Byrd Hoffman Foundation, Applegarth was responsible for keeping everyone involved with the project (no matter where in the world they might be) abreast of what
was going on and what was required of them. "Basically, I was the clearing house for
the entire project. I worked with Bob setting up the productions at the various
theatres—budgeting, telling them what they needed in terms of actors and technical
requirements—and as liaison with Los Angeles, Fitzpatrick, the Olympics Committee and the press. I kept the information flowing." Applegarth was also on call
twenty-four hours a day in the not unlikely event that some unforeseen circumstance
should arise.

the CIVIL warS was a campaign that had to be waged on two fronts. In addition to
securing six separate productions in various parts of the world, Wilson was required
to raise most of the Los Angeles presentation costs, then budgeted at $2.5 million,
money logically to be raised in the United States, where the presentation would be
seen. The Olympic Organizing Committee had agreed to contribute up to 10 percent
or $200,000 (cut back from the original $300,000) of the final budget, specifying
that all other monies must be secured before their grant would be released. Although
Wilson had gone on record after *Einstein on the Beach* as saying he would never
produce another of his works, he was once again forced into the role of producer.
"Bob entered all of this knowing that it was his responsibility to raise the money. It
may have been impossible, but that was the deal and Bob accepted it."

To compound problems, a great deal of money had to be raised at a time of
economic austerity and worldwide recession, most of it in a city where—with the
Olympics a little over a year away—competition for any available funding was
already intense. Though preoccupied with the actual creation of the work, Wilson of
necessity became actively involved in fund-raising, making several flying visits to Los
Angeles to solicit support and make contacts. In addition to an international

committee whose honorary members included Merce Cunningham, Gloria Vander-
bilt, Jerome Robbins and Jerzy Grotowski, a small advisory committee was formed
in L.A. to approach local corporations, the art community and other private sources.
But the almost insurmountable difficulties they were facing soon became evident.
"L.A. said this thing should be a national effort and the rest of the country said,
'Look, it's happening in L.A., let L.A. pay for it.' L.A. said, 'Look, we can't be
responsible for all this' and everyone else said, 'Why are you asking *us* for money?'"
Major corporations and foundations were approached but the project often met with
scepticism and resistance rather than the enthusiasm its promoters felt it merited, a
reaction that Applegarth later came to understand. "When big corporations put a lot
of money into something, it's got to be pretty goddamn safe. This was a risk to say the
least. We're talking about a major corporation putting its name on a project and not
having a clue as to what it would turn out to be. [As Wilson was later to say, 'If you tell
them you're doing *Tosca* they know what that is.'] At that point the work didn't exist. It
could be a disaster. It could be offensive. The very title scared a lot of them. They
could end up with one-or-two-million-dollar egg on their face."

The most common objections in the beginning were the perceived elitism of the
opera and its limited visibility. "'How can we justify giving this kind of money for
something that's only going to play for three performances and reach X number of
people?'" Although Wilson was eventually able to counter this argument with the
prospect of BBC television coverage, he couldn't get around the fact that most
corporations simply weren't interested in funding avant-garde work. The resistance
they were encountering had another cause that neither Wilson nor Applegarth
anticipated. "You had between fifteen and twenty official sponsors of the Olympics
who had given up to twelve million dollars and they weren't interested in giving any
more, especially not to the Arts Festival. Other corporations were not interested in
coming in because they would get only the meagerest visibility. The Times-Mirror
Company [the publisher of the *Los Angeles Times*] had given five million dollars to
the Arts Festival and was credited as its sole sponsor — that was less than attractive to
many companies. It was a real conundrum. I think Bob initially believed that the
glamor of the Olympics would open doors. It just didn't happen." To complicate
matters further, Wilson did not have a contract with the Olympic Organizing
Committee, only a letter of interest; so to a number of potential sponsors it must have
seemed that he did not even have the committee's full endorsement.

Although he was to find his share of admirers in Los Angeles, Wilson was at a
disadvantage in raising funds; he did not know the community well, could not afford
to staff a local office and had no one to solicit support full time. (Fitzpatrick, the head
of the festival, was responsible for over a hundred other events and could not devote
much energy to the project.) Worst of all, Los Angeles did not know him. "No one
here seems to know of my work," he told *Theatre L.A.* in the spring of 1983. "I've

been running around talking to people all day and no one knows what I do." Even the names of opera singers Jessye Norman and Hildegard Behrens, major international stars who were scheduled to appear in the work, brought little in the way of recognition. Only the prospect of rock star David Bowie's appearance as Abraham Lincoln sparked immediate interest.

Armed with only a pen and sketchbook, Wilson made his way from reception to reception in pursuit of the movers and the shakers and the givers of the Southland, with variable and sometimes amusing results. One of Applegarth's favorite stories concerns their encounter with Lloyd Rigler, the president of Adolph's Corporation (best known for its meat tenderizer) and a well-known patron of the arts. "We found out that Rigler gives a lot of money to opera, particularly the New York City Opera. The reason he does that is that his dead lover Larry Deutsch was an opera buff and also gave money. Apparently Deutsch now communicates with Rigler in the form of a little bird who flies in the window of his house up on Mulholland Drive and tells him who to give money to. Bob heard the story—and this is a story we were told in L.A. by perfectly serious people—and said, 'We've got to find that bird!' We somehow got through to Rigler and a lunch was arranged. Rigler, who'd never heard of Wilson, met us at the door and said, 'So you're the genius, come on in.' We went in and had our little lunch and then he said, 'Now, tell me about this thing. So Bob started describing the work and about ten minutes into his presentation, Rigler said, 'W-w-wait a minute. You mean to tell me you're going to have David Bowie reciting the Gettysburg Address in Japanese?' And Bob said, 'That's correct.' And Lloyd Rigler said, 'If you pull this off, they ought to put you in *Ripley's Believe It or Not.*' Bob literally fell on the floor laughing and could not stop. It was such a typical response to what he was trying to do. This was the corporate mentality. Rigler thought it was the craziest and silliest and most impossible idea in the world and he went on record saying, 'You'll never get this done in L.A.' He was serious."

Another story drawn from Wilson's encounters with the power brokers of the West—one that he is particularly fond of telling—involves a meeting with Lew Wasserman, the chairman of MCA and a powerful figure in the entertainment industry. Wilson told him he needed to raise three thousand dollars to present *the CIVIL warS* in Los Angeles and then launched into his description of the work. He didn't get very far before Wasserman stopped him and asked, "How can you do all this for three thousand dollars?" Wilson paused for a moment and then blandly replied, "Oh, I'm sorry Mr. Wasserman. I meant three million." According to Wilson, Wasserman listened to his appeal and then said, "I wouldn't touch this project with a ten-foot pole."

Wilson was, however, warmly received in art circles and by a number of people in the film industry who seemed to understand, or at least have some feeling for, what he was trying to accomplish, among them David Wolper, Norman Lear and Doug

Cramer, the producer of the television series "Dynasty." They offered suggestions, moral support and some financial assistance, but the big-money sponsors he needed did not come forward. Wilson also tried to interest filmmakers George Lucas and Francis Ford Coppola, who might have felt a kinship for such a visionary venture, but they were in the midst of their own projects.

The spring and summer of 1983 found Wilson moving between Rotterdam, Tokyo, Cologne and Rome where *the CIVIL warS* was being developed in independent workshops. Fund-raising attempts continued in Los Angeles, and the artist returned for an optimistic two-day visit in April. In September, the Dutch section (Act I, b) played a week-long run in Rotterdam and then moved on to Paris, where it opened the city's Festival d'Automne. Although critical response was mixed and there were occasional longueurs, the show was an instant sellout and audiences were treated to such extraordinary sights as the "Largest Woman in the World," a figure in black twenty feet tall, moving silently through a changing landscape of snow, wheatstacks, blood-red tulips and giant cabbages. Most important to Wilson, a piece of *the CIVIL warS* now existed; he was no longer selling a paper dream. Although the scheduled premiere of the opera at the Olympic Arts Festival was less than nine months away and only a fraction of the presentation costs had been accounted for, Wilson now had photos, a sheath of enthusiastic reviews ("Wilson's *CIVIL warS* Wows Paris" read the headline in *Variety*) and at least partial proof that this wild undertaking was achievable. He had something to show Los Angeles.

Wilson's most immediate concern, however, was to find sponsoring theatres for the two remaining sections of the opera, the Japanese episodes and the scenes he had initially planned to stage in France. Though Fitzpatrick was continually urging reductions in the scale and length of the piece, Wilson steadfastly refused to give up his vision. "Now he really scrambled to complete the work. Whoever would do it, he let do it. The French section was the most peripatetic. From France to Bloomington to Stuttgart to Lyon and Marseilles—it was all over the place." When the University of Indiana, which had an ambitious opera program, expressed interest, Wilson and Applegarth flew to Bloomington to meet with the administration. They were impressed by the university's technical facilities, the equal of any theatre complex in the United States, but found production standards wanting. "We went to see a performance they were doing of *The Ballad of Baby Doe* and our hearts sank. We realized that they would never be able to pull it off and more or less told them it would have to be better than what we'd seen. Things fell apart pretty quickly after that." Negotiations were subsequently initiated with the Stuttgart Schauspielhaus and Opera, and Applegarth met several times with the staff and director Dennis Russell Davies. Although a budget was drawn up and an agreement seemed imminent, Stuttgart backed out in September, a few days before workshops were scheduled to begin. It was then that Jean-Luc Choplin, the director of the *maison de culture* in

Marseilles, entered the picture, enabling the scenes Wilson had conceived for France to circle back to the country that inspired them.

"As so often happened, Choplin became obsessed with the project and railroaded it through. His idea was to make the opera a joint project involving the Region Provence-Alpes-Côte d'Azur. There's a rivalry between Paris and the other regions and I think he was very pleased at the idea of bringing off such a coup. Because it was so late, the piece would have had its world premiere in Los Angeles and played in France afterwards. His main condition was that it go directly from the Olympics to the south of France. He wanted to beat out Paris." Eager as he was to participate, Choplin had only limited resources, necessitating a lean budget and the elimination of some spectacular effects. Wilson now showed an unexpected willingness to compromise and make do. "I don't know what goes on in Bob's head. One would never suggest compromises to him. They impose themselves and they're always, always financial. What I came to realize is that Bob maintains the vision. When a theatre says we'll do it but this is how much money we have, he'll start figuring out what he can do within those parameters. First he figures out another way to realize it scenically—he always says 'there are different ways to do a thing, just make it work.' When push comes to shove, he'll make the cut but he will never ever accept it until the final moment, and often he'll make everything happen with the amount of money that's available." In Wilson's original design for the underwater scenes, the audience was to witness a series of changing vistas through the window of Captain Nemo's Nautilus, among them the submerged grand staircase of the Paris Opéra. "Bob still had the drops from his old shows in a warehouse in Hoboken and he just said we'll use the forest from *Deafman Glance* and the cave and planet drops from *Stalin*. That's how he'll compromise to make something happen."

Even with these economy measures, Choplin had the money to present only one segment of the section. In order to salvage another scene—Act II, b in which Robert E. Lee appears astride his horse Traveller—Wilson resorted to an inventive ruse. He was scheduled to direct a production of Charpentier's baroque opera *Médée* at the Opéra de Lyon and simply arranged to substitute the episode from *the CIVIL warS* for the original prologue of the opera, a paean to Louis XIV, after making suitable alterations: Charpentier's music was relegated to background accompaniment, Traveller was modeled after an equestrian statue in Lyon's Place Bellecour and Lee was made to share his steed with Louis XIV. "Bob was very pleased with himself over that one. That was the old fox, the old masterful fox he is." Questioned later about the matter, Wilson blandly replied, "It seemed appropriate."

Cost-cutting and frugality were by no means restricted to the stage. *the CIVIL warS* may have been perceived as an extravagant and star-studded enterprise, but on a day-to-day basis it was decidedly short on glamor, with humble accommodations and low salaries. "I remember the morning after the opening of the Dutch section in

Paris we were summoned to a meeting at Bob Fitzpatrick's hotel room. Bob and I were staying at this fifty-franc-a-night affair, one step up from a pension. And there we were in Fitzpatrick's suite at the Ritz. The contrast was intense. Bob always traveled second or third class, taking a train rather than a plane and sleeping overnight. He just scraped."

Now Wilson had only to find sponsorship for the Japanese section, the most difficult to secure and the last to fall into line. Although "all the artists in the country got behind the project from the very beginning" (these included the director Tadashi Suzuki, the composer Toru Takemitsu, the celebrated Noh actor Hideo Kanze, Kabuki stars Tamasaburo Bando and Ennosuke Ichikawa III, and the designer Setsu Asakura), "Japanese businessmen didn't want to have anything to do with it." In a country where government support for the arts was virtually unknown, their participation was essential. Applegarth doubted that the money could be found in time but again Wilson refused to admit defeat. "Bob knows nothing but push, push, push. He won't give up until it's absolutely thrown in his face that it's over. Until that moment, it's going to happen. And I adopted that attitude. I simply had to, otherwise there was no way of living with him. You'd have to be constantly saying, 'Bob, give up. Bob, cut back.' And he wouldn't like that." Every lead was followed and every useful acquaintance or business contact enlisted in his cause. "Bob was relentless — relentless — in pursuing people. I've never seen anything like it. It was the greatest education in the world."

His successful pursuit of Hanae Mori, the Japanese designer and businesswoman, eventually turned the situation around. "Hanae Mori is the Coco Chanel of Japan. She's a big name internationally but especially in Japan, where it's particularly impressive when a woman rises to prominence. She knows everybody and she had the power and connections to put it together, and ultimately that's what she did. Bob got everyone in Europe who had business or personal connections with Hanae Mori to barrage her about *the CIVIL warS* and play on her sense of national honor. 'France is doing this and this for the project. What is Japan doing?' Madame Pompidou gave a big dinner party in France and surrounded Hanae Mori with people badgering her about Bob Wilson. The woman didn't have a chance! Eventually she said, 'I'm going to put this together for you.' And mind you, this is an individual, a private individual. She gave dinner parties, she raised money, she did an American Express commercial for Japanese television, something she'd never done before, with a caption at the end saying 'Proceeds from this commercial are going to support Japan's section of *the CIVIL warS*.' Tamasaburo did the same thing. The Japanese waited and waited and waited until they were absolutely sure that this was something that should be done and then they moved. It was incredible." Although economy measures were again necessary (two major scenes were conjoined into a single episode and an elaborate balloon journey in Act III was replaced by a dance solo for Tamasaburo), Wilson had enough money to underwrite final rehearsals and begin building the scenery. The pieces of *the CIVIL warS* had fallen into place to the amazement of everyone, except perhaps Robert Wilson.

Meanwhile, fund-raising efforts continued in the United States, though without the much-needed presence of Wilson, who could only spare the time for brief visits. With the clock running down, there was simply not enough of Robert Wilson to go around. While he was off securing the remaining sections of the opera during the last months of 1983, there had been a number of developments on the home front. Two major articles had appeared on the project in the November 6 "Calendar" section of the *Los Angeles Times,* an interview with Wilson by drama critic Dan Sullivan and a highly critical review of the recent presentation in Paris by freelance writer Robert Schneider, which enraged Wilson's supporters. "Then two months later Sullivan went to Cologne and didn't especially like what he saw. Martin Bernheimer, the *Times* music critic, would write snide remarks about it regularly. Negative reviews while we were trying to raise that kind of money? It was very damaging." *the CIVIL warS* was perceived by many not as a bold, unprecedented cultural event but as the calculated self-apotheosis of a willful and eccentric artist out to spend other people's money. (Wilson recalls being told by an executive at Warner Communications, "If Europeans think this is so great, let them pay for it.") In retrospect Applegarth believed it was a mistake to release an estimate of the total cost of the project to the press. "Early on we tried to figure out what everything would cost. The figure of twelve or fourteen million came up then and kept cropping up. It was unfortunate because the press seized on that from the start."

In December Wilson hired Carl W. Shaver and Company, a New York fund-raising agency, in the hope they could find new solutions to his financial predicament, and Applegarth finally announced that David Bowie had dropped out of the project. "Bowie, who's apparently a great fan, was hot to work with Bob and came to his loft to talk about playing Lincoln. It took forever to get their schedules to coincide. He invited Bob to his home in Switzerland where they talked further and then Bowie said, 'And now you deal with my managers.' That was really the end. They wanted to know, 'Do you have a signed contract in Los Angeles? How much are you going to pay Bowie?' I said everyone was taking nominal fees, this was strictly nonprofit and obviously we couldn't pay Bowie what he usually gets. It would be around, I don't know, say five thousand. And they laughed in my face. They said that with his expenses and retinue it would cost Bowie about a hundred thousand dollars a month to work for nothing. After that they didn't want to hear about *the CIVIL warS.* We couldn't even get a message to him. Finally after months of trying to get through, Bob tracked down a number in Australia and Bowie told him that he just couldn't do it, he had a film or something." Applegarth felt that Bowie's defection had little impact on fund-raising efforts since "we were going around telling everyone he was in it anyway."

Fitzpatrick, who always considered the original twelve-hour length of *CIVIL warS* to be unrealistic in terms of overtime costs and audience stamina, had persuaded Wilson to cut the presentation down to eight hours back in September and was now urging him to consider presenting the opera over several nights or doing only as much as his present finances allowed. (Wilson's plans for radio and television adaptations of the work had been scrapped some months before.) In mid-January it was announced that *the CIVIL warS* would be presented in two parts between June 5 and 8, and then brought together for one complete performance on Saturday, June 9. That same month Olympic Arts Festival order forms were sent out to prospective buyers with a note explaining that ticket information for *the CIVIL warS* would be provided "at a future date." Fitzpatrick felt that they could not ethically ask for money until details of the production were finalized. It was a bad omen.

The premiere of the German section in Cologne on January 19 was a triumph, bringing Wilson the brilliant press and unequivocal public response he had been seeking. "I sat there and felt relief that it was good and that we weren't lying to people, but more than that, I realized that I was watching the work of a great master. It was thrilling. And seeing it I thought, 'This is it. This is why I'm doing this.'" The financial situation in Los Angeles, however, remained unchanged, and by February Applegarth "was getting the signals from Fitzpatrick." One prospect still remained. They had been introduced to Jill Conway, a board member of Merrill Lynch & Company, who became excited by the project and went to the president of the company. "Merrill Lynch came very close to doing it. They give a lot of money to the arts and they have a very specific clientele. The names Jessye Norman and Hildegard Behrens mean something to them. And if it hadn't been for the fact that the first quarter of 1984 was the worst in the history of the company, we would have had a real good shot at it. In fact, they said if we had come to them a year ago, they probably would have done it. We had them on the line until late February-early March and when they said no I realized we weren't going to get the show on." On March 9 Applegarth phoned Fitzpatrick and told him, "We don't have any more ideas left for where to get the money, there's not a prayer left." Fitzpatrick suggested that they just present the knee plays and the Rome section but Wilson rejected the proposal outright. "Because he had made commitments in so many countries, it became impossible for him to take one section and not another. At that point, everyone was in too deep." As Wilson was to explain some months after the collapse of the production, "In Japan, schoolchildren and artists sent in contributions. The Germans spent so much on the production and the French. . . . How could I say to them, 'I'm only going to take this section?' These are the people who support my work. I couldn't do it. I couldn't choose one over another."

In Act III, c of *the CIVIL warS*, an angel materializes out of the ether and hovers over the bed of the dying Robert E. Lee. Applegarth realized that this was now the only thing that could save the project: the immediate appearance of an "angel" who would either put together a funding package or make good the deficit out of his own resources. Fitzpatrick had already granted Wilson numerous extensions in the hope that the money could be found but now a final deadline was set for April 1, by which time scenery and costumes had to be shipped to California. Of their current $2.6 million budget, $1.4 million had been accounted for through projected ticket income, sales of Wilson's drawings, a planned benefit, and individual contributions and grants (primarily from the National Endowment for the Arts, the Olympic Arts Committee and Schlumberger Corporation). On March 13, with time fast running out, Applegarth and Wilson "went public," announcing to the press that unless they could raise the remaining $1.2 million, performances in Los Angeles would be cancelled. Contacted in Rome, where he was preparing the final section of the opera, by *Times* reporter Morgan Gendel, Wilson shouted, "It's not fair. What people have contributed outside of America is outstanding: under $1 million by the Italians, just under $1 million from the Germans, 2 million French francs ($250,000), $300,000 from Japan. And in America we can't raise any of this money. They don't deserve it, baby!" (Applegarth also recalled Wilson telling a journalist, "Look at all they've done for us in Italy and they're practically a Third World country!") The eleventh-hour disclosure brought a flurry of newspaper articles and an impassioned editorial on the work's behalf in the *Los Angeles Herald Examiner*, but the kind of money they needed did not materialize.

"I really didn't think Bob was going to get Japan and I always had my doubts about the U.S. section but I did think the Olympic Committee would come through for us in the end if we didn't raise the whole amount. I thought the various countries involved would bring so much pressure to bear on Peter Ueberroth (president of the Los Angeles Organizing Committee) and his people that they would do whatever they had to do to get the money." Part of the decision to go public was no doubt based on the belief that the resulting publicity would force them to become actively involved. But the committee was not to be moved; in fact there is evidence to suggest that they didn't want *the CIVIL warS* to happen at all. "Robert Fitzpatrick ran the festival and he was a vice-president of the Olympic Committee but he reported to Peter Ueberroth and Howard Usher, the general manager who controlled the purse strings. He had work within his budget. Fitzpatrick told me that they did not want *the CIVIL warS* to come to Los Angeles and leave town with a million dollars in debts. They felt that even though they were the debts of the Byrd Hoffman Foundation, the committee would end up being responsible for them. The pressure was always to cut back, do less, do something manageable. Fitzpatrick understood but none of the others did. 'Why do all that?' was their attitude."

Perhaps what Wilson and Applegarth failed to consider was that Ueberroth and Usher had dedicated themselves to keeping the Olympics on a firm business footing and deficit free, and must have regarded *the CIVIL warS* as exactly the kind of wasteful and grandiose enterprise they were pledged to keep the Games from becoming. "The committee cried poor and said, 'We don't have the money.' And of course they ended up with a $250 million surplus." As Wilson later lamented, "They were out to sell hamburgers and tennis shoes, not present art. . . . Mr. Ueberroth and all the others who were out to make money had no feeling for this project and no understanding of it. They had no idea of how much time and effort had gone into it and how many people had worked to make it happen. They didn't care." Fitzpatrick, on the other hand, cared very much about the project but found himself powerless to save it. "He wanted it to happen, no question about that. But he wasn't the power there, the power is where the money is and he didn't control the money. Fitzpatrick was doing a balancing act. He wanted *the CIVIL warS* for the festival but he suspected that Bob couldn't raise the money to do the whole thing. I think he was secretly hoping that parts of the work would fall out and through natural attrition it would emerge on a smaller scale as something manageable. But that didn't happen because Wilson wouldn't let it happen. It was a funny cat-and-mouse game of let's wait and see, and as it turned out they played it too long. Bob pulled the thing off and Fitzpatrick was left having to play the ogre and kill it."

Nevertheless, Applegarth was left with considerable admiration for Fitzpatrick, who foresaw such an eventuality all along and did his best to avert it. Wilson was the first artist Fitzpatrick had approached about participating in the festival (he initially wanted him to stage a revival of *Einstein on the Beach*) and only his support and the prospect of an appearance at the Olympics could have made a project like *the CIVIL warS* possible. As he saw Wilson's creation grow from a five- or six-hour work to a twelve-hour international epic of unprecedented scope and ambition, Fitzpatrick came to view his role as a "reality therapist" (reality never having been one of Wilson's strong points either in or out of the theatre) and was constantly urging the artist to reconsider the work's length and scale as well as the gigantic theatre he had selected in Los Angeles. (Wilson wanted a venue as spectacular as the opera itself and his decision to present the piece in the 6,500-seat Shrine Auditorium was an early source of disagreement and added considerably to the cost of presentation.)

Although *the CIVIL warS* was now nearly lost, Applegarth found he was not as despondent over the prospect of imminent collapse as he expected to be. "Bob and the rest of us had done everything we could. I felt that there wasn't one stone we had time left to unturn and that, frankly, it was out of our hands. I wasn't depressed. The only time I was depressed was at the very beginning when the sheer enormity of the project overwhelmed me—and Bob knocked that out of all of us pretty quickly." Then, with barely a week remaining before the expiration of the final deadline, Wilson came up with a last-ditch plan to salvage the project—a satellite transmission of the opera. The European sections could be presented somewhere in France or

Germany and telecast live to Southern California, the Japanese scenes could be either prerecorded or similarly transmitted by closed-circuit satellite and *the Knee Plays*, which was to have its premiere in Minneapolis the following month, could be moved to a smaller theatre in Los Angeles. Wilson even envisioned simultaneous satellite presentations in Rome, Rotterdam, Cologne, Marseilles, Nice and Lyon so that all the sponsoring cities would have a chance to see the complete work. In less than a week he organized the project with the assistance of Volker Canaris, the Intendant of the Cologne Schauspielhaus, and managed to get commitments from French and German television. Then he flew back to New York two days before the deadline and explained the plan to Fitzpatrick, who immediately rejected it as impracticable at such a late date. Wilson later recalled the conversation: "I said, 'This is financially feasible! We have the monies to do this!' And he said, 'It's too late.' And I said, 'It's all rehearsed and ready to go. How can you say it's too late?' 'It's already been announced that it's going to be live.' 'Yes,' I said, 'but you'll still have something live—and you'll have the whole project! And what's more you'll have the respect of people who put millions of dollars into this creation!' And he said, 'It's too late. It can't happen.' It was clear that he had already made up his mind to kill it."

Applegarth came to think that Fitzpatrick was right in turning the idea down. "It's a great concept that probably wouldn't have worked. It would have been like watching an archival tape. It was so complex technically and there was not really enough time to pull it off well." Although the official deadline was not until April 1, at which time Wilson and Fitzpatrick were supposed to issue a joint press statement, John Rockwell called from the *New York Times* later that day to tell them that he had just received notice over the wire service of the project's cancellation. Unlike Wilson, Applegarth took the announcement calmly. "I almost felt, 'Okay, let's just get it over with.' Everyone was on hold and asking, 'What are we supposed to do? Do we put this thing on the boat or what?' To me, it was almost a relief. At least we didn't have to keep everyone hanging any longer. Bob is a much more spontaneous person than I am. I was gearing myself for that moment, but Bob would not accept it until it actually happened. So it hit him at that moment. He called Fitzpatrick and started screaming, 'You traitor, you traitor.' Bob was quite rightly upset because Fitzpatrick jumped the gun and didn't give us time to call everybody. It was awful. A lot of people who had worked on the project found out by reading about it in the papers." (Applegarth believed that Fitzpatrick rushed the deadline so that notice of the cancellation could be included in a major news story in that Sunday's *Times*. Perhaps he too was anxious to "get it over with.")

Wilson was also stung by Fitzpatrick's claim a week later in *Libération* that the project had grown increasingly out of control over the past three years. Not only had the opera adhered to its original five acts and fifteen scenes, Wilson maintained, but his budget had decreased from $3 million to $2.6 million. In the weeks that followed, Fitzpatrick, who has characterized working with Wilson as "impossible but worth it," took most of "the heat" for the cancellation of *the CIVIL warS* (*Newsweek* called it "a cultural embarrassment" and *L'Humanité*, the Communist daily in Paris, "a crime against humanity") despite the fact that he had been its catalyst and one of its most ardent supporters.

the CIVIL warS had now come to an abrupt end barely ten weeks before its scheduled premiere, an event that seemed destined, almost calculated, to bring Wilson his greatest celebrity. Choking back tears, he told a BBC interviewer, "It's really very interesting. It's the only time in my life that I didn't succeed. It's the only time it didn't work." Although *the CIVIL warS* had been lost, Wilson still had to fly to Minneapolis to prepare *the Knee Plays*, which was to have its world premiere at the Walker Art Center on April 26. It was there that Applegarth felt the full effect of the cancellation for the first time. "Someone turned to me and said, 'You know what today is?' Today is the day we were supposed to load into the Shrine. That's when it hit me. And then later when I was watching the opening ceremonies of the Olympics on television, it *really* hit me. I thought, 'We should be there.' I really was depressed for a couple of days." *the Knee Plays* opened to enthusiastic reviews in Minneapolis and even made a convert of critic Dan Sullivan, though too late to help *the CIVIL warS*. "Sullivan went to Cologne and didn't like it. He has since seen the same section at the American Repertory in Cambridge and has decided it's a masterpiece. The man had to be told it was great."

The various parts of *the CIVIL warS*, one critic wrote, now lay scattered around the world like the pieces of a colossus. Almost immediately after the cancellation, various organizations expressed interest in presenting the complete opera at a later date, among them the Brooklyn Academy of Music, the French cultural ministry and Frankfurt's Theater der Welt, but ultimately none could put together the necessary financial package. Some months later a consortium from Texas approached Wilson about staging the work in Austin in 1986 as part of the state's sesquicentennial celebrations, but once again the necessary funding failed to materialize and the project was shelved. In the fall of that year, the debt-ridden Byrd Hoffman Foundation, burdened by mounting warehousing costs, decided to destroy the scenery for the Dutch and Japanese sections (as well as for many of Wilson's past productions), effectively putting an end to hopes that the work might one day be seen in its entirety.

Applegarth, who went on to work for BAM and Peter Brook before his untimely death in 1989, looked back on *the CIVIL warS* with a mixture of exhilaration and exhaustion. "It's certainly the most exciting thing I've ever worked on. I had trouble physically keeping up with Bob although it gave me energy too. I mean, he's a galvanizing force. People end up working ten times harder for him than they've ever worked for anyone else in their lives. He just brings that out of people. What I got out of it more than anything else was the attitude 'We will not have any negativity.' You've got to be convinced you can make the thing happen and it's astonishing how much energy that gives you. Still, I couldn't keep up with Bob's nonstop running around and I don't think anybody could. It was wild."

Working at Wilson's side for more than two years, Applegarth had the opportunity to observe the artist's restless energy and frenzied lifestyle at close range. "It's scary. If his life isn't filled every single second with work, he starts to get crazy. If he works sixteen hours and goes home and is faced with eight hours of sleep, he will stay up for six hours and draw. I think he slept an average of two or three hours a night throughout the whole *CIVIL warS* period. I don't think I'm exaggerating. He has a phobia about having any spare time, even a few seconds. If he gets to the airport ten minutes before a flight, he starts making phone calls to everybody in the world. The only time he's forced to do nothing is on a plane or a train. In fact, he said to me that's the only time he relaxes. There's no telephone, no meetings, no rehearsals. He just sits there. I stopped feeling sorry for him early on in *the CIVIL warS* because it's his choice and he's obviously doing what he needs to do. And I think it feeds him artistically too. I think there's this absolute chaotic frenzy that churns out stuff for him and he needs that." Though some friends and coworkers have pointed out the potential hazards, both physical and artistic, of such a crazed, obsessive existence, Wilson gives no indication of pulling back or slowing down. In fact, he seems to have rebounded from *the CIVIL warS* with renewed vigor and redoubled activity. "Now what he does is to have ten projects going at once. It's frightening. When I was working with him I also got possessed, but now that I'm no longer intimately involved with Bob I can stand back and look at the way he operates and it's crazy. He's got so many projects and he so overbooks himself. He literally can't have a free hour. He's got to be on a plane going somewhere. The energy! It's obsessive, it's compulsive, it's demonic, it's unrelenting!"

At the same time Robert Wilson's best qualities would seem rooted in the American character, with its distinctive blend of innocence and cunning and its unshakeable belief that anything is possible. Finally, what impressed Applegarth most deeply was not the perpetual state of frenzy in which he exists or the obsessions that drive him but instead Wilson's singlemindedness, his refusal to recognize limitations and his almost unfailing ability to make things happen, even in the face of impossible obstacles. "I happened to be at an interview Bob did for the *Dallas Morning News* and the reporter asked him, 'What one word would you use to describe yourself?' And Bob gave one of his hmms, looked around and then looked at me. And I just said to him, 'Tenacity.' And that's what they wrote. Tenacity."

BACK
OF THE
BOOK

CHRONOLOGY AND WORKS

1941-1962

Robert Mims Wilson is born in Waco, Texas on October 4, 1941. First child of Loree (Hamilton) and D.M. Wilson, attorney and later city manager of Waco.

As a child of eight or nine, he presents plays in his garage with his grandmother and the girl next door. At the age of 17 he is cured of a stammer with the help of Miss Bird ("Baby") Hoffman, a local dance instructor, who teaches him to speak slowly and free the tension from his body through dance movement. During his junior high and high school years, Wilson appears in school plays and in productions presented by the Waco Children's Theatre (Jearnine Wagner, director) and Baylor University Teenage Theatre, and participates in speech contests and debates. He graduates from Waco High School in the spring of 1959.

Enters the University of Texas (Austin) the following fall, majoring in business administration. He begins working with brain-damaged children and children's theatre groups. In the spring of 1962, a year before his scheduled graduation, he drops out to pursue a career in design and the arts.

1962-1966

Moves to New York in the fall of 1962 and enters Pratt Institute (Brooklyn), where he studies interior design. He appears in a number of student productions (notably as the visionary Eilert Lovborg in Hedda Gabler*) and creates dance and theatre pieces with the friends and followers who gather around him. While at Pratt, he is exposed to the work of Martha Graham, Alwin Nikolais, Merce Cunningham, "happenings" and the New York art scene. He continues to work with brain-damaged and disturbed children.*

SLANT

A film by Robert Wilson. NET-TV, c. 1963. NOTE: Abstract film, approximately 10 minutes long.

Travels through Europe and studies painting with George McNeil at the American Center in Paris. Summer, 1964.

LANDSCAPES *(DESIGN ONLY)*

A dance by Murray Louis. Decor (uncredited): Robert Wilson. PREMIERE: Nov. 20, 1964. Murray Louis & Co. at Henry St. Settlement House.

JUNK DANCES (DESIGN ONLY)

A dance by Murray Louis. Decor: Robert Wilson.
PREMIERE: Nov. 27, 1964. Murray Louis & Co. at
Henry St. Settlement House.

[DANCE PIECES AT PEERLESS MOVIE HOUSE]

NOTE: Wilson and a group of friends rented a
movie house near Pratt for two midnight shows
(dates unknown). Wilson's piece, in which performers were seated in chairs, was first performed
as a solo and then, a few months later, with four
additional participants. A film of some kind accompanied the performance.

[DANCE EVENT AT NEW YORK WORLD'S FAIR]

A dance piece with film, performed at the New
York State Pavilion during the 1964-5 school year.

DURICGLTE & TOMORROW

A work conceived by Robert M. Wilson. Music:
Praetorius. Constructions and properties: Wilson.
PREMIERE: Apr. 9-10, 1965. Spring Dance Recital, Memorial Hall, Pratt Institute. NOTE: The
dance was performed by three men and eight
women to baroque music and the sound of a
banging hammer. The decor consisted of foil-
covered poles and floating mobiles on which colored lighting played.

AMERICA HURRAH [MOTEL] (DESIGN ONLY)

"A Masque for 3 Dolls" by Jean-Claude van Itallie.
Director: Michael Kahn. Setting: Robert Wilson.
Dolls designed by Wilson and Tania Leontov.
PREMIERE: Apr. 28, 1965. Cafe La Mama E.T.C.

*During the summer of 1965, Wilson returns to
Texas and teaches painting and movement in
Trinity University's "Ideas in Motion" Youth
Theater program (Jeannine Wagner, director).*

[SILENT PLAY]

PREMIERE: Summer, 1965. San Antonio. NOTE:
This half-hour piece, which Wilson says he hastily
substituted for the traditional play he had originally intended to present, featured some of the
visual elements and actions he would use in his
later works. Three actors in a white room (Wilson

among them) were seen performing simple tasks
in silence: walking, sitting, putting on a glove,
tracing a line across the floor with sand, leaning
against a wire. Wilson thinks the piece may have
been called "The House" (also the title of a film he
conceived that summer).

MODERN DANCE
Four dances by Robert Wilson

PREMIERE: July 29-31, 1965. Waco Civic Theater. Performed by members of the "Ideas in
Motion" Youth Theater program. NOTE: The program included a version of *Duricglte & Tomorrow*,
a pop art satire on the Miss America pageant, and
two other dances in the style of Alwin Nikolais.
(Two of these pieces had been performed at Trinity University the previous month.)

THE HOUSE

Uncompleted film featuring Jeannine Wagner.
Summer, 1965. San Antonio. NOTE: The story of
a young woman who tries unsuccessfully to communicate, set against the arid landscape of central
Texas.

*Lectures at Harvard on "Schools: A Laboratory
Situation," Winter, 1965. Invited by Jerome Rob-
bins to observe and teach classes at the American
Theater Laboratory, New York City.*

CLOROX and OPUS 2
Two dances (Entire production conceived by
Robert Wilson)

PREMIERE: Apr. 29-30, 1966. Spring Recital of
Dance Workshop of Pratt Institute. NOTE: *Clorox*,
an earlier version of which had been seen in Waco,
was performed by 11 dancers; consumer products
and Day-Glo triangles covered the stage. In *Opus
2*, seven performers appeared in two wooden
crates, one facing the audience, the other turned
toward the wings.

*Receives his BFA in interior design from Pratt
Institute on June 10, 1966. Travels to Arizona for
a six-week "apprenticeship" with the Italian-
born architect Paolo Soleri. He assists in building
the swimming pool and one of the domes for the
Arcosanti prototype community. Wilson is unable
to paint and suffers a nervous breakdown. After*

ALWIN NIKOLAIS

Wilson went backstage to meet Alwin Nikolais after a 1964 dance concert and soon began working for the choreographer. In retrospect the attraction Wilson must have felt for Nikolais' dance theatre is easily understood; here was a mystical fusion of light, movement, sound and decor, shaped by a single creator who controlled every element of presentation. The dance pieces Wilson presented at Pratt Institute and in Texas were closely modeled on Nikolais' kinetic dream theatre and featured such elements as black light, stretch fabrics, masks and foil-covered mobiles. If Wilson is a spiritual descendant of Edward Gordon Craig, who envisioned a synthetic theatrical artwork under the control of a "Master of Drama," it is through Alwin Nikolais that this lineage can be traced.

B ob was a student at Pratt and I needed someone to assist me with handyman tasks that required some aesthetic judgment. He came and worked for a year, maybe two, at the Henry Street Playhouse, down on the Lower East Side. We didn't have any money then so everyone pitched in and he was just another of the pitcher-inners. Bob was very quiet but he had a gentle, penetrating sense of humor and an enchanting kind of underground grin. While he was at the Playhouse he designed a set for Murray Louis's *Junk Dances* with a lot of wonderful things like broken toys, boxes, milk bottles, dolls and garbage cans. I was impressed.

Those days were very, very exciting from the experimental and exploratory point of view. Years later I saw *Einstein* in Paris and was fascinated by the compelling monotony of the piece—its absolute, vivid involvement in repetition. That was something we were involved in too. I created pieces called "fixations" where dancers were caught in a pool of light and simply did the same movement over and over. I remember experimenting with moving so slowly that you couldn't see the motion, only a changing aspect to the environment as the motion occurred. We were all into mimimalism and chance, though we may not have called them by those names and we may not always have carried it to the nth degree. After seeing Bob's stuff I always felt that something rubbed off from being at the Playhouse. I'd be pleased to believe so.

(New York City. June 26, 1985.)

attempting suicide he is committed to a mental institution where he remains for several months.

1967

Acquires the former Open Theater loft at 147 Spring St. in New York for his living and performing space. Works with children in Harlem as a special instructor for the Department of Welfare and the New York Board of Education. Also works with the terminally ill at Goldwater Memorial Hospital on Welfare Island where he organizes events for patients in iron lungs and wheelchairs using elements from his earlier dance pieces.

BABY BLOOD [AN EVENING WITH BABY BYRD JOHNSON AND BABY BLOOD] *(SOLO)*

PREMIERE: Nov. (5 performances). Spring St. loft. NOTE: Audience members climbed a staircase strewn with the bodies of dismembered dolls to the second-floor landing where a hooded figure (Andy de Groat) collected the admission. They were then led one at a time into the candlelit performing space. In the first section, Wilson traversed an elevated plank wearing only a t-shirt; in the second, he lay curled up like an infant under a miniature train track while a toy train passed overhead; in the final section, he appeared in black light, covered with strips of Day-Glo plastic which seemed to grow longer and longer. In between each episode, the hooded figure changed the position of the candles and the large metal rings which hung on a wire over the audience.

1968

Performs in two of Meredith Monk's dance pieces, Blueprint$_3$ *(Jan. 28, Colby College, Waterville, ME) and* Blueprint$_5$ *(May 10, The House, NYC).*

THEATRE ACTIVITY [1]

CAST: Robert Wilson, Andy de Groat, Kenneth King, et al. PREMIERE: Mar. 7. Bleecker St. Cinema, NYC. Presented by the Byrd Hoffman School of Byrds at midnight. NOTE: The audience entered to the sound of a Meztec Indian chant.

Several seats in the theatre were occupied by dummies and live performers with paper bags over their heads. A pane of glass hung above the stage. The piece was divided into four sections. Part I: "Ten people sitting in ten chairs [two rows of five] centerstage facing one another. Two people exchange places at undetermined time." Part II: "Ten people stand at edges of stage facing one another. Two people exchange positions at opposite side of the stage at undetermined time." Part III: "Ten people sit in an almost closed circle facing one another. At undetermined time clear plastic gloves are blown out of the mouths of the performers." Part IV: "One performer [King] runs to center stage and stops, holding position for four minutes. This action is repeated four times from each of the four corners of the stage. During the last four minutes a slide of a cat's face is superimposed over a film loop of grass. It takes four minutes for the slide to come into full focus." At the end of the performance, which lasted a little over an hour, the pane of glass fell to the floor and shattered.

THEATRE ACTIVITY [2]

CAST: Robert Wilson, Devora Bornir, Kenneth King, Hope Kondrat. Recorded talk by Buckminster Fuller. PREMIERE: Apr. 19. American Theatre Laboratory, NYC. Presented by the Byrd Hoffman School of Byrds. NOTE: The four performers constructed a four-sided wooden frame around a suspended pane of glass. After covering the structure with fabric, they entered the cube. A moment later, the glass fell and shattered. The performance lasted about an hour.

POLES

An outdoor sculpture commissioned by the Grail, a Catholic laywomen's organization, for their retreat in Loveland, Ohio. NOTE: With his friends Duncan Curtis and Kikuo Saito and members of the Grail community, Wilson spent two-and-a-half months erecting the massive sculpture (as well as an arched entryway of telephone poles) in a wheat field. During construction, Wilson danced every night in the nearby chapel. It was there that he conceived the character of the Byrdwoman, a strange figure in a floppy hat and long braids, who was to appear in later works. In the middle of August, Wilson presented a new piece (possibly

JEAN-CLAUDE VAN ITALLIE

The Belgian-born author of *America Hurrah* and *The Serpent* was playwright-in-residence at the Open Theatre from 1963 to 1968 and has collaborated with Joseph Chaikin on numerous projects.

A friend from Harvard called one day and said, "I know this young man who is trying to break into the theatre in New York. Is there some way that you can help him?" This was '64 or '65 and I was young enough and new enough to the theatre to be flattered by such a request. I remember Bob as being quiet, good-looking, a little bit stern. We became friends and a while later I asked him if he would make the giant dolls for my play "Motel" which was being done at Café La Mama. Bob was also interested in designing the setting for *America Hurrah* when it was produced off-Broadway a year or so later. He wanted to set the entire play in a yellow submarine — I guess from the Beatles' song. I've met a few really inspired people in my life, and I think I knew Bob was one of them from the start so I wanted him to be involved — but there was just no way I wanted the yellow submarine.

For a while we were talking about some kind of collaboration. Nothing came of it, but I did appear in *The Life and Times of Sigmund Freud* at the Brooklyn Academy of Music. I had a white leather overnight bag that Bob was quite fond of and I was supposed to carry that onstage and stand there for a while, and I did. I also got buried in hay which was sort of fun. I found Bob's work really wonderful at the beginning and the beginning went on for a long while. His transformation of time and space was in the most positive and considered sense mind-blowing. It was a theatrical experience of a dimension you couldn't find anywhere else and I just relaxed into it. Perhaps I'm growing impatient with age but I'm not turned on by his later work. It's too polished, too exquisite — too perfect really. Bob's refining the same thing again and again and I want something rough and new. Maybe that's asking too much. Bob's done a great deal in this one lifetime and I feel people ask too much of creators.

(New York City. May 12, 1988.)

entitled "Byrdwoman") with Grail members in the chapel. Another event was staged to celebrate the completion of the project. Upon entering the performance site, spectators found Wilson, dressed as the Byrdwoman, silhouetted against the setting sun. They then helped lay a bed of gray slag around the base of the monument and Wilson threaded a red rubber hose through the poles.

Working with children, creates a large outdoor sculpture out of scrap and found materials at Hemisfair in San Antonio. Begins conducting movement workshops and art classes at the Summit Art Center in New Jersey. Inception of Byrd Hoffman School of Byrds.

BYRD woMAN

CAST: Robert Wilson, S.K. Dunn, Kikuo Saito, Raymond Andrews, Hope Kondrat, et al. (Part One); Wilson, Robyn Brentano, Meredith Monk, et al. (Part Two). PREMIERE: Oct. 26. Presented by the Byrd Hoffman School of Byrds. NOTE: The first part of *BYRD woMAN* took place at Wilson's loft. The audience sat on bleachers facing the straw-covered performing space. A curtain at the back rose and Wilson was revealed on the fire escape in his Byrdwoman costume. The other participants entered and performed simple actions such as bouncing on wooden boards or leaning on wires. The audience was transported in two flatbed trucks covered with straw to Jones Alley for the second part of the performance. Many of the visual elements seen earlier in the evening reappeared in different guises: Byrdwoman figures could be seen on nearby rooftops; at street level a young boy bounced on a board and a woman leaned on a wire; another performer descended a fire escape. The audience was then taken around to the other side of the alley where they found nearly 40 Byrdwoman figures bouncing on wooden boards. At the conclusion of the performance, a rock band played and performers and spectators danced together.

ALLEY CATS
A duet performed in Meredith Monk's *Co-op*

CAST: Robert Wilson, Monk. PREMIERE: Nov. 3. Loeb Student Center, New York University.

1969

THE KING OF SPAIN
A play by Byrd Hoffman (Robert Wilson)

Scenery: Fred Kolouch. Lighting: Peter Egan. Sound: Hampton Sailer. Stage manager: Richard Nelson. CAST: Wilson, Alan Lloyd, Scotty Snyder, Mary Peer, Hope Kondrat, Raymond Andrews, Robyn Brentano, et al. PREMIERE: Jan. 30-1. Anderson Theatre, NYC. Presented by the Byrd Hoffman School of Byrds.

HAUCO - 1941
Performance • Lecture • Demonstration

PREMIERE: Mar. 29. New Providence High School, NJ. Presented by Byrd Hoffman School of Byrds. NOTE: Hauco is the Indian word for Waco; Wilson was born in 1941.

WATERMILL

An educational film documenting Wilson's seven-part movement exercises, demonstrated by students from Iona State College and members of the Byrd School. Filmed in Water Mill, Long Island during the summer.

During the spring and summer, Wilson teaches movement and creative arts at Far Brook School in New Jersey, Iona State College in New Rochelle and (as a Head Start consultant) Messiah Church in Yonkers. In the fall, he directs a creative workshop at the Ethical Culture Society of Essex County in Maplewood, New Jersey. The Byrd Hoffman Foundation is chartered in the state of New York.

Appears in a Kenneth King dance concert on October 24 at Loeb Student Center, New York University.

THE LIFE AND TIMES OF SIGMUND FREUD
A dance play in three acts by Robert Wilson

Direction: Wilson. Scenery: Fred Kolouch. Lighting: Rick Nelson. Sound: Hampton Sailer. Production supervisor: Peter Harvey. CAST: Byrd Hoffman School of Byrds; Wilson, Raymond Andrews, Kenneth King, Hope Kondrak, Cindy Lubar, Mary Peer, Jack Smith, Scotty Snyder, M. Sondak, Jean-Claude van Itallie, et al. PREMIERE:

Dec. 18, 20. Brooklyn Academy of Music, Opera House. Presented by the Byrd Hoffman Foundation. SUBSEQUENT PERFORMANCES: May 22-3, 1970. Brooklyn Academy of Music, Opera House. NOTE: The second act was a shortened version of *The King of Spain.*

1970

During the winter Wilson conducts a six-week seminar at the University of California at Berkeley, followed by a two-week visit to Yucatan.

GEORGE SCHOOL ACTIVITY
Lecture • Demonstration

Spring. George School, New Hope, PA. NOTE: "Part I - Walton - Audience seated. Part II - Construction site - Audience follows the white path to the exhibit in the construction site. There the individuals are free to move or stop as they wish while examining the garden, both down and up."

HANDBILL

Music: Alan Lloyd, Julie Weber, Verdi, Strauss. Taped text: Kenneth King. CAST: Mel Andringa, S.K. Dunn, Lloyd, Carol Mullins, Robert Wilson, et al. PREMIERE: Nov. 13. New Museum, Iowa City. Presented by the Byrd Hoffman Foundation in association with the University of Iowa Center for New Performing Arts. NOTE: *Handbill*, a site-specific work presented during the rehearsal period for *Deafman Glance*, was divided into four sections: the first taking place in the museum's lower sculpture court, the second on the main floor where the audience moved about viewing a number of independent activities and scenes, the third in the lower gallery and auditorium where spectators viewed Wilson's film *Watermill* while listening to a recording by Kenneth King, the fourth back on the main floor. Many of the visual elements in *Handbill* were drawn from earlier works such as *BYRD woMAN.*

DEAFMAN GLANCE

Director: Robert Wilson. Music: Alan Lloyd, Igor Demjen, others. Scenery: Fred Kolouch. Lighting: Richard Nelson (Johnny Dodd, NY; Laurie Lowrie, European tour). Costumes: John D'Arcangelo. Film: Franklin Miller. CAST: Byrd Hoffman School of Byrds; Wilson, Raymond Andrews, Sheryl Sutton, Andrew de Groat, Demjen, Cindy Lubar, James Neu, Carol Mullins, Mary Peer, Jerome Robbins (Paris), Susan Sheehy, Scotty Snyder, et al. PREMIERE: Dec. 15-6. University Theater, Iowa City. Presented by the Byrd Hoffman School of Byrds in association with the Center for New Performing Arts, University of Iowa. SUBSEQUENT PERFORMANCES: Feb. 25, Mar. 5. Brooklyn Academy of Music; Apr. 22-3. Grand Théâtre de la Nancy, VIII Festival Mondial; Apr. 27-8. Teatro Eliseo, Premio Roma '71; May 14-30, June 11-July 3. Théâtre de la Musique, Paris; July 6,8. Holland Festival, Stadsschouwburg Theater, Amsterdam. NOTE: The length of the performance varied from city to city. In Nancy, Amsterdam and Paris, *Deafman* and *Freud* were combined to form a single work. "Overture for a Deafman," an eight-minute black-and-white film depicting the murders seen in the the prologue, was shown during the performance. Wilson shot the film in an empty house in Iowa City with Sheryl Sutton as the Byrdwoman. *Deafman Glance* received the Drama Desk Award for outstanding direction and the Prix de la Critique Française for best foreign play.

1971

WATERMILL
Performance • Demonstration by the Byrd Hoffman School of Byrds

Music/Sound: Melvin Andringa, Igor Demjen, Alan Lloyd, Pierre Ruiz. CAST: Robert Wilson, Andrew de Groat, Cindy Lubar, et al. PREMIERE: Mar. 16. Morristown Unitarian Fellowship, NJ. NOTE: "Audience is free to come and stay or go anytime during the five hours of performing time. Audience is free to join in group moving."

Conducts workshops at Newark State College, NJ.

PROGRAM PROLOGUE NOW: OVERTURE FOR A DEAFMAN

CAST: Sheryl Sutton, Raymond Andrews, Ann Wilson, Andrew de Groat, et al. PREMIERE: June

8. Espace Cardin, Théâtre des Ambassadeurs, Paris. Produced by Pierre Cardin and ALPHA. NOTE: Wilson's prologue, a theatrical mass in three sections, was performed before an audience of 100 spectators and lasted approximately three hours. "Part One. April 5, 1986. Rectangular Space. Actors and audience at each end." The audience was admitted to a large candle-lit room and seated on bleachers; they witnessed a procession of white-robed performers, free-form dancing and movement. "Part Two. April 5, 1964. Square Space. The spectators surround the actors on four sides." The audience moved onto the playing area, kneeling or sitting around a large wooden square, above which a pane of glass was suspended. The ritualistic murder of a doll was enacted by a small girl, after which a four-sided wooden pyramid was constructed around her. The *Deafman* film was shown on all four sides of the structure and finally the pane of glass fell and shattered. "Procession." The audience was led downstairs through the foyers and backstage corridors of the theatre past strange and often macabre tableaux vivants, some arranged out in the surrounding streets and gardens and viewed through windows along the route. "Part Three. May 5, 2000. Spiral Space. The spectators surrounded by the actors." The audience was seated in the main theatre, the boxes and balconies of which were adorned with candles and icons. A black fire curtain rose on the interior of the pyramid, a smoke-filled operating room where surgeons clustered around the dead. Small panes of glass were hung on wires and drawn upward.

[DEMONSTRATION • LECTURE • PRESS CONFERENCE]

Sept. 14. Atelje 212, BITEF Festival. NOTE: Wilson's performance seems to have consisted mostly of incomprehensible mumbling and humming delivered into a microphone while he slowly peeled two onions. A discussion followed during which Wilson concealed himself behind a curtain and answered most questions with the word "dinosaur." This encounter may have lasted as long as 12 hours.

Recipient of Guggenheim Fellowship, 1971-2.

1972

OVERTURE [NEW YORK]
Overture for KA MOUNTAIN AND GUARDenia TERRACE

CAST: Robert Wilson, Stefan Brecht, Edwin Denby, Andy de Groat, S.K. Dunn, Alma Hamilton, Cindy Lubar, Carol Mullins, Jim Neu, Sue Sheehy, Scotty Snyder, Ann Wilson, et al. PREMIERE: Apr. 24-30. Spring St. loft. Presented by the Byrd Hoffman School of Byrds. NOTE: *Overture* marked the culmination of the first preparatory phase of *KA MOUNTAIN.* Two presentations were given daily. From six to nine in the morning, activities included readings, music and dancing. A more formalized presentation was offered each evening from six to nine. During the day all three floors of the recently renovated Byrd loft were open for inspection, with exhibits on the main floor, a reading room upstairs and a dining area in the basement where lunch was served each afternoon. Evening performances were held in a long room lined with cushions on the ground floor. A four-sided wooden pyramid stood at the far end of the space and above it a large egg and turtle were suspended in the air. Performance activities included processions, readings, storytelling, chanting and such simple acts as slicing an onion or pouring water; visual effects included a cardboard city that burst into flames, a large dinosaur curtain and painted pink flamingos that rose through slits in the floor.

[ROYAUMONT RESIDENCY]

May 11-June 14. A four-week workshop at Royaumont Abbey (40 km north of Paris) sponsored by Jean-Louis Barrault's Théâtre des Nations and the Festival d'Automne. NOTE: Wilson worked with Byrd School members and a dozen actors from different countries developing material for the upcoming *KA MOUNTAIN.* On Saturday nights, presentations were given before invited guests and friends.

In July, Wilson is imprisoned on Crete for possession of hashish. He is released on bail and flies to Iran where rehearsals for KA MOUNTAIN are in progress.

MEREDITH MONK

The composer and performing artist Meredith Monk was gaining a reputation in the avant-garde dance world when Wilson moved into SoHo in 1967. The two became friends and appeared in each other's pieces over the next twelve months before going their separate ways.

In June of 1967 I was at an artists' colony up in Woodstock called Group 212. On my first night there Kenneth King came up and did a piece, and all of a sudden this guy in a madras jacket and tie—which was pretty strange in 1967—walked up to me and said, "Are you Meredith Monk?" I said, "Yes." And he said, "You're a star! You're a star!" Of course, it was Bob. That summer I needed a studio and Kenneth suggested I ask Bob if I could use his place on Spring Street. I went to see him and I remember passing a table; on it were a slinky, a doll, an ultraviolet light—exactly the things I had been working with the year before. It was a bit uncanny. We started performing together that winter when I needed a last-minute replacement for an engagement at Colby College. A few months later we did some of the same material in New York in my piece *Blueprint₅*. At that time I was interested in creating different audience-performance relationships. I lived above the sculptor Julius Tobias and in the piece we did the audience was free to move back and forth between an exhibit of people arranged in huge white boxes on his floor and my loft one flight up. At one point Bob and I sat side by side in two white chairs, blindfolded, with long sleeves that opened to reveal four hand puppets with white heads and black fingers. It was almost like giving birth to this group of little people. I'm very short but I have a long waist and Bob is very tall with a short waist so we looked like we were the same height until we stood up and then he grew and grew while I stayed the same height. We had a good laugh about that. I also did a piece called *Co-op* at NYU where the audience walked around looking at exhibits and booths that continually changed. There was a little stage where different things happened and one of them was a piece Bob created. He put a board across two chairs and we wore these big fur coats and floppy hats and just bounced up and down to a funny pop record called "Alley Cats." That was it but it was rather witty and fun.

The idea of stillness was something that all of us were working on at the time—like sitting still for an hour in *Blueprint* with the audience just looking at a silent image. Many of us were working in very slow time. At a certain point I realized that movement as a structural continuity—real out-and-out choreography—was limiting what I could do, so I started dealing with images and music as my main concerns, and slow motion became the purest way of moving from one image to another.

(New York City. June 15, 1985.)

OVERTURE [SHIRAZ]
Overture for KA MOUNTAIN AND GUARDenia TERRACE by the Byrd Hoffman School of Byrds

CAST: Byrd Hoffman School of Byrds; Robert Wilson, Andrew de Groat, Cindy Lubar, Jim Neu, Scotty Snyder, Sheryl Sutton, Ann Wilson, et al. PREMIERE: Aug. 31. (Two performances: 12 midnight and 3 A.M.) Narenjestan Garden, Khaneh-E Zinatolmolk, Shiraz, Iran. NOTE: Both *Overture* and *KA MOUNTAIN* were dedicated to Wilson's mother, who had died in May.

KA MOUNTAIN AND GUARDenia TERRACE:
"a story about a family and some people changing" by the Byrd Hoffman School of Byrds

Directors: Robert Wilson, Andrew de Groat, Cindy Lubar, Jim Neu, Ann Wilson, Mel Andringa, S.K. Dunn, et al. Authors: R. Wilson, de Groat, Jessie Dunn Gilbert, Kikuo Saito, Lubar, Susan Sheehy, A. Wilson. Music and Sound: Igor Demjen. Scenery: R. Wilson, Andringa, Saito, A. Wilson. Costumes: John D'Arcangelo. CAST: Byrd Hoffman School of Byrds, et al. PREMIERE: Sept. 2-9 (One continuous performance beginning at midnight Sept. 2 and lasting over 168 hours). Haft Tan Mountain, Shiraz, Iran. Presented by the Byrd Hoffman School of Byrds and the Shiraz-Persepolis Festival of the Arts.

OVERTURE [PARIS]
Overture for KA MOUNTAIN AND GUARDenia TERRACE by the Byrd Hoffman School of Byrds
(A two-part presentation lasting seven days)

Part One: Gallery Presentation
Design: Robert Wilson, Melvin Andringa, Kathryn Kean, Kikuo Saito, Ann Wilson, et al. Music and sound: Igor Demjen. Nov. 6-11 (noon to midnight). Musée Galliéra, Paris. Presented by the Festival d'Automne and Théâtre des Nations. NOTE: The visitor walked through seven rooms containing the work of Byrd School artists before coming to a central hall where the *Overture* chair stood in a rectangular pool of water, its bronze side-torch aflame. A number of performances, some of them unscheduled, took place during the six-day exhibition and every night a discussion and demonstration were held.
Part Two: Theatre Presentation: "CYNDI"
Director: R. Wilson. Texts: R. Wilson, Cindy Lubar, A. Wilson. Music and sound: Demjen. Dance: Andrew de Groat. Scenery: Paul Thek. Costumes: John D'Arcangelo. CAST: R. Wilson, Lubar, Sheryl Sutton, Madeleine Renaud, Edwin Denby, James Neu, Carol Mullins, Scotty Snyder, de Groat, A. Wilson, Stefan Brecht, et al. PREMIERE: Nov. 11 (midnight to midnight, 24 hours). Opéra Comique, Paris. Presented by the Festival d'Automne and Théâtre des Nations.

1973

king lyre and lady in the wasteland

CAST: Robert Wilson, Elaine Luthy. PREMIERE: May 12. Spring St. loft. Presented by the Byrd Hoffman School of Byrds (Last evening of "Solos").

Wilson conducts workshops at Le Centre de Développement du Potentiel Humain Atelier de Travail in Paris in March and the following month lectures with Mel Andringa at Ohio State University. He also presents a workshop-performance with other Byrd School members at Naropa in Boulder, Colorado. He spends part of the summer in Loos, British Columbia, where the Byrd Hoffman Foundation has acquired 300 acres for an educational center.

THE LIFE AND TIMES OF JOSEPH STALIN
An opera written and directed by Robert Wilson

Music: Alan Lloyd, Igor Demjen, with Julie Weber, Michael Galasso. Texts: R. Wilson, Cindy Lubar, Christopher Knowles, Ann Wilson. Choreography: Andrew de Groat. (Director, Act V: de Groat.) Scenery: Fred Kolouch, Lester Polakov. Lighting: Laura Lowrie. Costumes: Mary Brecht. Slides: Francie Brooks. Production manager: Melvin Andringa. CAST: R. Wilson, Sheryl Sutton, Lubar, Kenneth King, Stefan Brecht, George Ashley, de Groat, Demjen, Alma Hamilton, Hope Kondrat, Knowles, Lloyd, Carol Mullins, Jim Neu, Mary Peer, Sue Sheehy, Scotty Snyder, M. Sondak, A. Wilson, students from P.S. 47 School for the Deaf, et al. (Around 150 performers.) PREVIEW: Sept. 7-14. Det Ny Teater, Copenhagen. (A contingent of Byrd School members worked two weeks with 80 Danish per-

RICHARD NELSON

Richard Nelson, a prominent New York lighting designer, worked as a stage manager and designer on three Wilson productions, beginning with *The King of Spain* in 1969.

The first performance of *The King of Spain* was one of the most memorable days of my career. We had been working around the clock and the crew was literally sleeping out in the house. I was swept away by the performance and the impeccable clarity of Bob's vision. It really was an amazing evening. While I was drawn to Bob, his people really clinched it for me. Some were very sad and lonely figures but Bob seemed to have rehabilitated them with his presence and power. I was very impressed with his love for them and their love for him. They weren't professionals, they had no technique but they were believable and very touching. I especially remember Raymond Andrews, who began the piece by lighting all the candles on a shelf that ran around the the set. It was a very slow, deliberate, concentrated process and it was just extraordinary to watch this little kid light each candle—never rushing, never showing any sign of nervousness—with incredible precision and presence.

Later I went to Iowa to work on *Deafman Glance*. The company lived together in a farmhouse. I'd spend all day and night at the theatre and then come back and collapse into my sleeping bag on the floor. It was the dead of winter and the house was freezing. We'd have breakfast in the kitchen, which looked out over the snow-covered fields and a herd of cows. I sat there with Bob one morning drinking coffee and he was particularly quiet. Eventually he said, "I've been watching this cow all morning and in two hours he hasn't done more than move his head a little. That's what I'm going to do."

During the first performance in Iowa Bob got a lot of new ideas and started to change things. He'd get on the headsets and tell people to do something different. Chaos descended. At the end of the show Bob came running offstage screaming, "It can't end. It can't end." Total panic. The girl on the lightboard became hysterical because he was screaming at her and she didn't know what to do. We were working with a road board in those days and each cue was dependent on the previous one. I said, "Bob, I can't stop this, there's just thirty seconds left, we'll fix it later." But he screamed over the headsets to everyone on the crew, "This is *my* show, not yours. You'll do it my way." We were taking something away from him. The show ended but at that moment it seemed to me that Bob would never again leave anything to anyone else.

(New York City. April 1, 1985.)

formers developing the production, which was given with minimal scenery. Audience response was not favorable and two of the scheduled six performances were canceled.) PREMIERE: Dec. 14-5, 21-2. Brooklyn Academy of Music, Opera House. Presented by the Byrd Hoffman Foundation in association with the Brooklyn Academy of Music. SUBSEQUENT PERFORMANCES: Apr. 9-13, 1974. Teatro Municipal, São Paulo. (Under the title *The Life and Times of Dave Clark*.) NOTE: Acts I-III, *The Life and Times of Sigmund Freud* (1969); Act IV, *Deafman Glance* (1970); Act V, "some elements of music and movement" drawn from *Program Prologue Now: Overture for a Deafman* (1971); Act VI, "some elements of music, movement and libretto" drawn from *KA MOUNTAIN* (1972); Act VII, first version presented in Copenhagen. New material also included a series of entr'actes performed at the front of the stage and recurring appearances by and references to Joseph Stalin. Wilson received an Obie Special Citation for *Stalin* in June, 1974.

1974

DIA LOG/A MAD MAN A MAD GIANT A MAD DOG A MAD URGE A MAD FACE
(Performance by Robert Wilson and Christopher Knowles)

PERFORMANCES: Mar. 3. Contemporanea, Villa Borghese, Rome; May 30. Art Now 74, Kennedy Center, Washington, DC; Aug. 19-20. Delgocha Gardens, Shiraz Festival, Iran; Dec. 9. Galleria Ala, Milan. NOTE: Each version of *Dia Log* differed in its scenic elements, spatial configuration and participants. In Rome and Shiraz, Wilson and Knowles were joined by Ladan Chidani; in Washington by Robyn Brentano, Jessie Mullins and Ann Wilson; in Milan by Andrew de Groat and Michael Galasso. Various elements from *A Letter for Queen Victoria* and *BYRD woMAN* were incorporated into the performances.

THE LIFE AND TIMES OF DAVE CLARK [VIDA E ÉPOCA DE DAVE CLARK]

See *1973: The Life and Times of Joseph Stalin.* NOTE: Acts I, II, III were presented on Apr. 9, Acts II, IV on Apr. 10, Acts III, V on Apr. 11 and the entire work on Apr. 13. Portions of the upcoming *A Letter for Queen Victoria* were performed without scenery during Acts II, IV, VI on a platform covering the orchestra pit. (Political considerations necessitated the retitling of the work.)

PROLOGUE TO A LETTER FOR QUEEN VICTORIA
A Gallery Presentation

Director: Robert Wilson. Music: Kathryn Cation, Michael Galasso. Choreography: Andrew de Groat, Julia Busto. Artwork: George Ashley, Scotty Snyder, Kathryn Kean, Christopher Knowles, de Groat, Cindy Lubar, et al. Costumes: Fred Kolough, Carol Luiken. CAST: Sheryl Sutton, James Neu, Snyder, Knowles, Carol Mullins, Stefan Brecht, Lubar, de Groat, Busto, et al. PREMIERE: June 15-23. Six O'Clock Theater, Spoleto, Italy. (*Prologue* was presented in the basement of the Teatro Caio Melisso at 6:00 each evening before the main performance.) NOTE: "*Prologue* takes place inside and outside of ten rooms, each of which accommodates ten persons. The piece is in ten time sections. At the end of each of these sections, signaled by a bell, you may move from one room to another, or remain in the room you have chosen to be in. You may enter and exit during the interim between any two sections, or at the end, through either of the two doorways at opposite ends of the space. We ask that you please be quiet as *Prologue* depends on listening." Each room contained a burning taper and a suspended model airplane. De Groat and Busto spun at either end of the hall throughout the performance.

A LETTER FOR QUEEN VICTORIA
An opera in four acts, written and directed by Robert Wilson

Music: Alan Lloyd with Michael Galasso. Additional texts: Christopher Knowles, Cindy Lubar, Stefan Brecht, James Neu. Translations: Ann Metelli. Choreography: Andrew de Groat. Scenery, lighting, costumes: Fred Kolouch. Slides: Francie Brooks, Kathryn Kean. Musical direction: Galasso. (Scenery and costume supervision in New York were attributed to Peter Harvey and lighting supervision to Beverly Emmons, assisted by Carol Mullins.) CAST: Sheryl Sutton, Lubar,

Brecht, Kathryn Cation, Knowles, Mullins, Neu, Scotty Snyder, Wilson, de Groat, Julia Busto, et al. PREMIERE: June 15-22. Teatro Caio Melisso, Spoleto, Italy. Presented by the Diciassettesimo Festival Dei Due Mondi. SUBSEQUENT PERFORMANCES: July 3,5. Municipal Theater, La Rochelle, France; Sept. 19-22. BITEF Festival, Belgrade; Oct. 2-12, Dec. 5-31. Théâtre des Variétés, Paris; Oct. 16-8. Theater II, Zurich; Oct. 21. Maison des Arts et Loisirs, Thonon-les-Bains; Oct. 26. Maison des Arts et Loisirs, Sochaux-Doubs; Oct. 29. Théâtre Municipal, Mulhouse; Nov. 5-10. Théâtre Huitième, Lyon; Nov. 13-4. Palais de la Mediterranée, Nice; Mar. 19-Apr. 6, 1975. ANTA Theater, NY. NOTE: 1975 Maharam Award for best set design and Tony nomination for best score and lyrics (Alan Lloyd).

An exhibition of Wilson's sculpture and furniture is presented in September at the Musée Galliéra, Paris.

1975

A SOLO READING

Voice and drawings: Robert Wilson. Piano: Alan Lloyd. Lighting: Terry Chambers. Tape and records: Michael Galasso. PREMIERE: Feb. 2. Spring St. loft. Presented by the Byrd Hoffman Foundation.

THE $ VALUE OF MAN

Written and directed by Christopher Knowles and Robert Wilson. Music: Michael Galasso. Choreography: Andrew de Groat. Assistant director: Ralph Hilton. Scenery supervision: Gregory Payne, Terry Chambers, Charles Dennis. Lighting: Carol Mullins. Costumes: Richard Roth. Sound: Jan Kroeze. CAST: de Groat, Hilton, Knowles, Cindy Lubar, Mullins, James Neu, Scotty Snyder, et al. PREMIERE: May 8-11, 15-8. Brooklyn Academy of Music, Lepercq Space. NOTE: *The $ Value of Man* was divided into nine sections, "Free," "Casino" and "Vaudeville." The work was performed in a large rectangular hall with the audience seated on bleachers at either end and in two long rows running lengthwise at floor level. Black and red partitions suspended overhead could divide the stage into a

number of configurations. The audience was invited to move freely around the perimeter of the space.

DIA LOG [2]
(Performance by Christopher Knowles and Robert Wilson)

PERFORMANCES: July 29, 31. American Dance Festival, Connecticut College, New London; Aug. 7-9. Public Theater/Anspacher, NYC. NOTE: Two-performer version lasting 55 minutes.

TO STREET: ONE MAN SHOW

PERFORMANCE: Sept. 20. Kultur Forum, Bonn Center, West Germany. Presented by Bonn Center in association with the Byrd Hoffman Foundation. (An accompanying exhibition was presented at Galerie Wünsche.)

1976

THE SPACEMAN
Video Performance by Ralph Hilton-Robert Wilson

CAST: Hilton, Wilson, Christopher Knowles, Sue Sheehy, et al. PREMIERE: Jan. 2-4. The Kitchen, NYC. NOTE: "*Spaceman*, located within a $12' \times 3\frac{1}{2}' \times 65'$ tunnel of translucent plastic, represented Robert Wilson's first use of video as an integral part of the theatre experience. The images, portrait, still life and landscape, were conveyed by performers, props, lights and pre-recorded videotapes. Eight different sets of color videotapes were played on over twenty monitors placed among the sets and actors. The abstract theme of the work was that of an unidentified 'green thing' which had crawled up on the beach." (The Kitchen Center for Video and Music, 1975/76 Yearly Account)

DIA LOG [3]
(Performance by Christopher Knowles and Robert Wilson)

CAST: Knowles, Wilson, Lucinda Childs. PERFORMANCES: Feb. 19. Whitney Museum, NYC; Mar. 7. Douglass College, Rutgers University, New Brunswick, NJ; Apr. 14. Corcoran Gallery, Washington, DC.

RICHARD FOREMAN

The presiding genius of the Ontological-Hysteric Theater, Richard Foreman has been presenting his works—which he writes, directs and designs—in New York since 1968, the year after Robert Wilson moved into SoHo. Foreman's 1970 review of *The Life and Times of Sigmund Freud* was the first important piece of writing to appear on Wilson's work.

B ob had called Jonas Mekas, who used to write for the *Voice*, and said, "No one's reviewing my play, will you come and write about it?" Jonas, who had given me his theatre on Wooster Street to put on plays in and was my entrée into the whole SoHo art world, couldn't go for some reason and asked me if I would write something in his place. I think I'd talked to Jonas about Bob since I had liked *The King of Spain* so much. I had gone to see it a year before because of a strange ad in the *Voice* showing this big furry head. In those days I was hungry for anything and the strangeness of the ad attracted me. I was amazed to find there were only fifteen other people in the theatre, and they were obviously friends of the cast. It seemed incredible to me that such a strange ad didn't attract more people in New York City. I thought the piece was wonderful but what I found most interesting was something I later learned Bob was intending to correct: there were all these giant things happening with an awkwardness and silence and lugubriousness which made for something very real. Another thing I liked so much about Bob's early work was all the extraordinary different kinds of people in it. At that time I was also working with non-actors—something I've given up just as Bob has.

I think we were both influenced—as was everybody else—by Jack Smith. Jack was a seminal figure back in the middle sixties. He made a notorious and beautiful film called *Flaming Creatures,* which was seized by the police, and then he made performance pieces that were *very* slow. Jack taught that new material was best found in those things that would be rejected by a professional take—any kind of awkwardness or amateurishness, any slow or boring rhythm, framed the right way, was the real subject matter for one's art. Jack was in Bob's early pieces. I remember going to a rehearsal of *Deafman Glance* and waiting in the lobby to say "Hi" afterwards. Bob came out and lamented, Oh Jack, this is going so terribly, what should I do?" and Jack, who had a very funny voice, said, "Oh, just make it *s-l-o-w-e-r,* Bob, it should be *s—l—o—w—e—r.*"

(New York City. June 8, 1988.)

reconfirmation of reservations (Solo)

PERFORMANCES: June 7-10. Salone Pier Lombardo, Milan; June 25. Teatro Comunale, Brescia.

EINSTEIN ON THE BEACH
An opera in four acts by Robert Wilson — Philip Glass

Design/Direction: Wilson. Music/Lyrics: Glass. Texts: Christopher Knowles, Samuel M. Johnson, Lucinda Childs. Choreography: Andrew de Groat (choreography for Act I, sc. i by Childs). Scenery: Wilson and Christina Giannini. Lighting: Beverly Emmons. Costumes: D'Arcangelo-Mayer, Paris. Audio: Kurt Munkacsi. Stage manager: Julia Gillett. CAST: Childs, Sheryl Sutton, Johnson, de Groat, Wilson, et al. Music performed by the Philip Glass Ensemble. PREVIEWS: A runthrough of *Einstein* was presented at the Video Exchange Theater, Westbeth Center, NYC, Mar. 4-5. "The Knee Plays" (entr'actes) were presented at the Museum of Modern Art, Mar. 31. Musical selections were performed at The Kitchen Center for Video and Music, Mar. 19-20 (and the previous year at Town Hall as "Another Look at Harmony," May 6, 1975). PREMIERE: July 25-9. Festival d'Avignon, Avignon, France. Presented by the Byrd Hoffman Foundation, in association with the Festival d'Avignon, Festival d'Automne, Venice Biennale and the Region of Lombardy. SUBSEQUENT PERFORMANCES: Sept. 13-7. Venice Biennale, Teatro La Fenice; Sept. 22-3. BITEF, Théâtre des Nations, Belgrade; Sept. 28-30. La Monnaie, Brussels; Oct. 4-9, 11-3. Festival d'Automne, Opéra Comique, Paris; Oct. 17-8. Deutsches Schauspielhaus, Hamburg; Oct. 22-3. Rotterdamse Schouwburg; Oct. 26. Holland Festival, Theatre Carré, Amsterdam; Nov. 21, 28. Metropolitan Opera House, NYC. See separate entry for 1984 revival. NOTE: Awards included Prix de la Critique du Syndicat de la Critique à Paris, Grand Prize at the Belgrade Festival and the 1977 Lumen Award for lighting design.

BOB WILSON SOLO

PERFORMANCE: Oct. 28. Salle Vilar, Maison de la Culture de Rennes, France. NOTE: Wilson's solo included the murder scene from *Deafman Glance* (performed with two local children) and various fragments from past works. See 1977 entry for other performances.

1977

I WAS SITTING ON MY PATIO THIS GUY APPEARED I THOUGHT I WAS HALLUCINATING
A play in two acts by Robert Wilson

Codirection: Lucinda Childs, Wilson. Music: Alan Lloyd. Scenery: Wilson, Christina Giannini. Lighting: Beverly Emmons. Costumes: Scaasi. Film: Greta Wing Miller. Production coordinator: Robert LoBianco. PREMIERE: Apr. 2-3. Quirk Auditorium, Eastern Michigan University, Ypsilanti. Produced by Richard Barr. SUBSEQUENT PERFORMANCES: Apr. 8-9. Annenberg Center, Philadelphia; Apr. 12. Paramount Theater, Austin; Apr. 14. Bayou Building Auditorium, University of Houston at Clear Lake City; Apr. 16-7. Fort Worth Art Museum; Apr. 19. Wilshire Ebell Theater, Los Angeles; Apr. 21-2. Veteran's Auditorium, San Francisco; Apr. 26-7. Edith Bush Theater (Walker Art Center), St. Paul; May 10-29. Cherry Lane Theater, NYC; Jan. 16-29, 1978. Théâtre de la Renaissance, Paris. Jan. 31, Feb. 4, 1978. Schouwburg Theater, Rotterdam; Feb. 1, 1978. Royal Theater, Hague; Feb. 3, 1978. Staadsschouwburg Theater, Amsterdam; Feb. 6-8, 1978. Theater II, Zurich; Feb. 10-1, 1978. Théâtre de Carouge, Geneva; Feb. 14-9, 1978. Piccolo Teatro di Milano, Milan; May 26-30, 1978. Theatertreffen '78, Theater des Westens, Berlin; June 1, 1978. Württembergische Staatstheater, Stuttgart; June 5-10, 1978. Royal Court Theatre, London. NOTE: Television adaptation (unproduced), storyboards by Tom Woodruff, 1978.

BOB WILSON SOLO

PERFORMANCES: July 8-10. Malersaal, Deutsches Schauspielhaus, Hamburg; July 12-3. Kleine Zaal de Doelen, Rotterdam; July 23-4. Movie Star Club, Capri. NOTE: Wilson performed the *Deafman* murder scene and fragments from *A Letter for Queen Victoria* and *The King of Spain*.

[Reading • Performance]

Sept. 27. Franklin Furnace, NYC.

DIA LOG/NETWORK
(Performance by Christopher Knowles and Robert Wilson)

Text: Knowles. Scenery: Knowles, Wilson. PER-FORMANCES: Oct. 15-7. Spazio Teatro Sperimentale, Florence; Oct. 20, 22-3. Münchner Theater Festival, Munich; Oct. 27. Atelier Annick le Moine-Grand Palais; July 15-6, 1978. Institute of Contemporary Art, Boston; June 16-21, 1978. Mickery, Amsterdam; Aug. 4, 1978. Walker Art Center, Minneapolis. Aug. 5-6, 1978. Mo-Ming, Chicago.

1978

PROLOGUE TO DEAFMAN GLANCE *(SOLO)*

PERFORMANCES: July 12. Manhattanville College, Purchase, NY; Aug. 20. John Drew Theater of Guild Hall, East Hampton, NY.

VIDEO 50
(Television work by Robert Wilson)

Produced by Film/Video Collectif (Lausanne) in association with ZDF. (Taped at the Centre Georges Pompidou in Paris.) Director: Wilson. Music: Alan Lloyd. Lighting: Renato Berta. Production: Robert Boner, Caroline Arrighi. Storyboards: Tom Woodruff. CAST: Lucinda Childs, Philippe Chemin, Laura Condominas, Wilson, Bénédicte Pesle, Michel Guy, Louis Aragon, et al. NOTE: A 50-minute film made up of approximately 100 30-second episodes.

1979

DEATH DESTRUCTION AND DETROIT
A play with music in 2 acts/A love story in 16 scenes by Robert Wilson

Direction/Design: Wilson. Music: Alan Lloyd (additional material by Keith Jarrett and Randy Newman). German translation: Peter Krumme, Bernd Samland. Additional texts: Maita di Niscemi. Scenic collaborator: Manfred Dittrich. Lighting: Beverly Emmons, Renato Berta. Costumes: Moidele Bickel. Sound: Hans Peter Kuhn. CAST: Sabine Andreas, Philippe Chemin, Chris-tine Oesterlein, Otto Sander, Gerd Wameling, Günter Ehlert, et al. PREMIERE: Feb. 12. Schaubühne am halleschen Ufer, Berlin. (In May the production appeared at the Berlin Theatertreffen.) NOTE: German Press Prize for a new play. Television adaptation (unproduced), storyboards by Tom Woodruff.

DIALOG/CURIOUS GEORGE
A play in four sections and fourteen parts by Christopher Knowles and Robert Wilson (Reading Poems, Stories, Answers and Advertisements)

Direction/Design/Soundtape: Wilson, Knowles. Text: Knowles. Lighting: Beverly Emmons (NY). Stage manager: Philippe Chemin. PREMIERE: Apr. 29-30. Kaaitheater, Palais des Beaux Arts, Brussels. SUBSEQUENT PERFORMANCES: Mar. 10-3, 1980. Cabaret Voltaire, Teatro Nuovo, Turin; May 21-3, 1980. World Theater Festival, Warsaw; June 1-4, 1980. Holland Festival, Schouwburg Theater, Rotterdam; June 24-9, 1980. Mitzi E. Newhouse Theater, Lincoln Center, NYC (presented by Byrd Hoffman Foundation). NOTE: Television adaptation (unproduced), storyboards by Tom Woodruff, 1980.

EDISON
A play in four acts by Robert Wilson

Additional dialogue and research: Maita di Niscemi. Translation: Philippe Chemin. Music: Michael Riesman, with Gottschalk, Miles Davis, Puccini, Scarlatti, etc. Musical director: Tania León. Scenery: Wilson, Tom Woodruff. Lighting: André Diot, Robert LoBianco. Costumes: Jacques Schmidt. Sound: Jacob Burckhardt, André Serré. (Original film sequence by T.A. Edison.) CAST: Susan Berman, Randy Buck, Chemin, Ralph Douglas, Isabel Eberstadt, John Erdman, Saundra Johnson, Terrell Robinson, Joniruth White. PREVIEW: June 19-24. Lion Theater, NYC. Presented by Byrd Hoffman Foundation. PREMIERE: Oct. 9-13. Théâtre National Populaire, Villeurbanne (Lyon), France. A coproduction of Byrd Hoffman Foundation and T.N.P. SUBSEQUENT PERFORMANCES: Oct. 17-20. Teatro Nazionale, Milan (presented by Teatro alla Scala); Oct. 24-Nov. 11. Festival d'Automne, Théâtre de Paris, Paris. NOTE: Television adaptation (unproduced), storyboards by Tom Woodruff.

LUCINDA CHILDS

Lucinda Childs began her career as performer and choreographer in 1963 as an original member of the Judson Dance Theatre. In 1973 she formed her own company, which has toured throughout the United States and Europe. Her collaborations with Wilson include *Einstein on the Beach, Patio* and the full-length dance piece *Relative Calm.*

The first time I saw Bob's work was in 1975. I went to *A Letter for Queen Victoria* in New York and I think it was the first time I experienced something in theatre that excited me as much as the Cunningham movement had in dance. I was overwhelmed by the sense of performance and the composure of all the performers. You had the precision of a beautiful photograph that changed before you frame by frame. That summer I went to the American Dance Festival in New London where Bob was performing with Chris. We spoke briefly and out of the blue he asked if I would like to be in *Einstein on the Beach.* He said that he wanted me to play the role of Einstein but that he had no way of describing what it was until we actually started work.

Most of the working process was very intuitive and we didn't talk much about it. It combined some of the ideas I'd been working on in the sixties—the spoken text in the context of performance, moving with objects, moving with words—with things I was beginning to explore with my company at the time such as controlled accumulations of movement and very strict relationships of movement. So it touched on two different periods of my own work. But what was most interesting about *Einstein* was being involved in a full-scale production with singers and dancers for the first time. It was wonderful to perform in 2,000-seat theatres for all kinds of people, not just for the small avant-garde audiences who followed my work. Bob opened my eyes to the possibilities of the proscenium. He really transformed the traditional stage, playing into the nineteenth-century architecture and lines of perspective but also against them. What he did was very powerful and beautiful and it inspired me to deal with the architecture of the theatre. I had never thought of collaborating before and *Einstein* also inspired the works I later made with Phil Glass and Frank Gehry and John Adams.

Last year I did *Quartet* at ART in Cambridge and I found it interesting that Bob dedicated the production to Andy Warhol. Andy was the first personality I met in New York and I appeared in some of his very early films. As a director Andy seemed not to be paying attention, almost not to be there. It took me a while to catch on to the fact that this is how he engages you. That's one of the things I love most about working with Bob. There's this same kind of absent quality that's very present and gets you to do things that you just wouldn't do otherwise.

(New York City. February 1, 1989.)

THE BREAKFAST TABLE

Unproduced television work by Robert Wilson. Storyboards by Tom Woodruff. Feb. NOTE: An elaboration of an episode in *Video-50*.

1980

PROLOGUE TO THE FOURTH ACT OF DEAFMAN GLANCE *(SOLO)*

PERFORMANCES: Feb. 25. Raffinerie Plan K, Brussels; Feb. 26. Palais des Congrès, Liège, Belgium; Nov. 27. Performance Festival, Montreal.

Receives Guggenheim Fellowship, July 1. Major retrospective, organized by Robert Stearns, at the Contemporary Arts Center in Cincinnati, May 16-June 29, and the Neuberger Museum, State University of New York at Purchase, July 13-Sept. 21.

1981

SHIRLEY, KEEP OFF

A two-hour theatrical collage, the culmination of a week-long workshop with graduate students at Arts Magnet High School in Dallas. Sponsored by the Dallas Theater Center. Apr. 30.

For first *Medea* workshop (Feb. 26-Mar. 1) see 1984 entry.

THE MAN IN THE RAINCOAT *(SOLO)*

Text/Design: Robert Wilson. Tape-Collages: Hans Peter Kuhn. Associate designer: Tom Kamm. Lighting: Markus Bönzli. Slides: Gail Donnenfeld, Paul Bang. Assistant director: Garry Reigenborn. Stage manager: Joanne McEntire. PREMIERE: June 27-8. Theater der Welt '81, Köln Schauspielhaus, Cologne. NOTE: Twenty-four extras dressed like Wilson also appeared in the production. An adaptation by the Dutch director Rob Malasch was presented by the New Music Theater in Amsterdam on Apr. 20, 1987. The production, which was redesigned by Kamm and featured music by Laurie Anderson, marked the first time a Wilson piece was entrusted to another director.

the CIVIL warS
MUNICH: FIRST WORKSHOP

In August a group of performers, technicians and researchers met for nine days at the Bavarian State Opera in Munich to discuss the designs, shape the text and map out the action of Wilson's multinational epic. Participants included Hildegard Behrens, Donald McIntyre, Gavin Bryars, Hans Peter Kuhn, Cindy Lubar, Maita di Niscemi, Bénédicte Pesle, Garry Reigenborn and Gerd Wameling.

DEAFMAN GLANCE (also called THE MURDER) (Television work by Robert Wilson)

Direction/Design: Wilson. Associate designer: Tom Kamm. Lighting: Danny Franks. Storyboards: Tom Woodruff. CAST: Sheryl Sutton, Jerry Jackson, Rafael Carmona. 27 minutes. Produced by Lois Bianchi, Byrd Hoffman Foundation, for Corporation for Public Broadcasting. Taped at Matrix Studios, NYC. NOTE: Video adaptation of the *Deafman* prologue.

RELATIVE CALM *(DESIGN ONLY)*
A work in four sections for nine dancers by Lucinda Childs

Music: John Gibson. Lighting and decor: Robert Wilson. Lighting execution: Edward Effron. Projections: Kristine Haugan. PREMIERE: Nov. 16-7. Théâtre National de Strasbourg. SUBSEQUENT PERFORMANCES: Nov. 20. SYGMA de Bordeaux; Nov. 25-8. Théâtre Nouveau de Nice; Dec. 4-5. Maison de la Culture de Grenoble; Dec. 18-20. Brooklyn Academy of Music, New York.

Receives three-year Rockefeller Foundation grant. Visiting artist at Harvard University, 1981-2.

1982

For second *Medea* workshop (Mar. 4-5) see 1984 entry.

Designs landscape environment for Penn Treaty Park on the Delaware River, in collaboration with Carol Gangwere. The proposed design is exhibited at the Pennsylvania Academy of Fine Arts, Philadelphia, Feb. 19-Apr. 18.

THE GOLDEN WINDOWS [DIE GOLDENEN FENSTER]
A play in 3 parts by Robert Wilson

Direction/Design/Costumes/Lighting: Wilson. Music: Tania León, Gavin Bryars, J.C. Pepusch. Dramaturg/Translator: Michael Wachsmann. Lighting: Markus Bönzli. Dresses: Christophe de Menil. Sound: Hans Peter Kuhn. CAST: Peter Lühr, Maria Nicklisch, Edgar Selge, Irene Clarin. PREMIERE: May 29. Münchner Kammerspiele, Munich. SUBSEQUENT PERFORMANCES: June 5-6. Theater an der Wien, Wiener Festwochen. NOTE: Received Der Rosenstrauss, Tage Zeitung, Dec. 1982. For American production see 1985 entry.

the CIVIL warS
FREIBURG: SECOND WORKSHOP

Four-week workshop in Freiburg im Breisgau, West Germany, culminating in a five-hour "final review" on June 26. Participants, more than 60 in all, included Hildegard Behrens, Hans Peter Kuhn, Cindy Lubar, Robert Applegarth, Scotty Snyder, Ann Wilson, Maita di Niscemi and Nicolas Economou.

GREAT DAY IN THE MORNING
(A work by Jessye Norman and Robert Wilson)

Direction/Design: Wilson. Musical director: Willis Patterson. Musical arrangements: Norman, Charles Lloyd, Jr. Lighting: Beverly Emmons. Costumes: Françoise Tournafond. CAST: Norman, et al. PREMIERE: Oct. 12-4, 17, 19, 21, 23. Théâtre des Champs-Élysées, Paris. Produced by Kim D'Estainville. NOTE: Television adaptation (unproduced), storyboards by Tom Woodruff, May.

OVERTURE TO THE FOURTH ACT OF DEAFMAN GLANCE

CAST: Robert Wilson, Carol Miles (Freiburg), Chizuko Sugiura (Toga). PERFORMANCES: June 22. Audimax-Universität, Freiburg, West Germany; July 24-5. Toga Festival '82, Japan Performing Arts Center, Toga-mura. NOTE: The Freiburg performance was part of a benefit for the CIVIL warS which included appearances by Nicolas Economou, Cindy Lubar and Yoshi Oida.

STATIONS
Television work by Robert Wilson

Direction/Design: Wilson. Music: Jacob Stern, Nicolas Economou (second version). Choreography: Jim Self. Scenic Design: Tom Kamm. Lighting: Danny Franks. Storyboards: Tom Woodruff. CAST: Margaret Jane Linney, Robert Hock, Jamie Nodell, Larry Mataresse, Carole Davis, et al. 57 minutes. Produced by Byrd Hoffman Foundation in association with ZDF (Zweites Deutsches Fernsehen) and Institut National d'Audiovisuel. Producer: Lois Bianchi. Taped at Video Matrix, NYC. NOTE: Conceived in 1978 as a series of 13 half-hour episodes entitled *Robert Wilson Presents*. That same year Woodruff created storyboards for a single television work in 13 sections, *Video-13*, later retitled *Stations*.

1983

the CIVIL warS: a tree is best measured when it is down
ACT I, SCENE B (DUTCH SECTION)
An opera by Robert Wilson

Conception/Direction/Design: Wilson. Music: Nicolas Economou. Choreography: Jim Self. Research and additional texts: Maita di Niscemi. Scenery: Tom Kamm. Lighting: Wilson, Jérôme Visser. Costumes: Christophe de Menil. Sound: Hans Peter Kuhn. Film: Jeep Drupsteen. CAST: Thea Korterink, Cindy Lubar, Rinke Rooijens, Self, Scotty Snyder, Sheryl Sutton, Louis Vervoort, et al. PREMIERE: Sept. 6-11. Schouwburg Theater, Rotterdam. Presented by the Byrd Hoffman Foundation in association with Stichting Toneelraad, Rotterdam. SUBSEQUENT PERFORMANCES: Sept. 17-24. Festival d'Automne, Théâtre de la Ville, Paris; Sept. 28-Oct. 1. Théâtre Municipal/Opera, Nîmes; Oct. 5-8. Maison de la Culture, Grenoble; Oct. 12-5. Théâtre National Populaire, Villeurbanne (Lyon); Oct. 19-22. Nouveau Théâtre de Nice, Nice; Oct. 26-8. Salle du Conservatoire, Bordeaux; Nov. 4-5. Grand Théâtre, Lille; Nov. 9-10. Maison de la Culture, Le Havre.

[Lecture • Reading • Performance]

June 18. Space for Art, Produzentengalerie, Hamburg.

JESSYE NORMAN

Wilson's friendship with the celebrated American soprano dates from the mid-1970s. Together they conceived *Great Day in the Morning,* a work inspired by Negro spirituals which was produced in Paris in 1982.

About twelve years ago I was giving a recital in Paris and Bob Wilson came backstage after the performance. I'm sure Bob hadn't spent much time going to lieder recitals and I think he was taken by the fact that it was possible to stand absolutely still on an empty stage and create a tremendous sense of drama, which is what he attempted to do in his own work. He was terribly polite and shy, very conservatively dressed, and he spoke in calm, measured tones. I remember thinking he didn't seem like someone from the theatre at all. He might have been a banker. I was about to begin a concert tour of America and I gave Bob my schedule and he would just turn up in some of the cities where I was singing. It was very sweet. He would always have flowers backstage. I have a favorite photo of my mother with an orchid in her hair and very often he would send me white orchids. Our friendship grew very fast and hot and I must say it was lovely to have found a soulmate not only in art but in life.

A little later Bob invited me to see *D D & D* in Berlin, which was the first time I saw his work on stage. It was perfectly serene and beautiful and I was completely taken over by it. By then we both wanted to make a work together. I was interested in doing something with the Negro spiritual and that was the beginning of *Great Day in the Morning,* which evolved over a period of more than a year. During that time we would get together and I would tell Bob what a song was about and then sing it for him, and he would draw while I was singing or while we were listening to a recording of the music. It was wonderful working alone with Bob in a room, just practicing sitting in a chair or being still and quiet. He gave me more confidence to do what I already felt comfortable doing on stage and that made me very happy. What I didn't realize when I saw *D D & D* was the work needed to create such perfect serenity. There was a marvelous scene at the end of *Great Day* where I had to walk across the stage and slowly pour water from a pitcher into a glass and it had to take exactly six minutes. When the glass was about to overflow I began singing "Amazing Grace," which also had to be exactly timed so the water overflowed and spilled onto the floor at the right moment. I spent a lot of time with that glass and that pitcher, let me tell you.

(Croton-on-Hudson, New York. June 22, 1988.)

1984

the CIVIL warS: a tree is best measured when it
is down
ACT I, SCENE A, ACT III, SCENE E, ACT IV (GERMAN
SECTION)
An opera by Robert Wilson

Direction/Design/Lighting: Wilson. Collabora-
tor/Coauthor: Heiner Müller. Music: Philip
Glass, David Byrne, Hans Peter Kuhn, Frederick
the Great, Tallis, Schubert. Dramaturg: Wolfgang
Wiens. Scenic assistant: Regine Freise. Lighting:
Franz-Peter David, Heinrich Brunke. Costumes:
Yoshio Yabara. Sound: Kuhn. Film: Edgardo Co-
zarinsky, Hella Viezke. CAST: Ingrid Andree,
Anna Henkel, Fred Hospowsky, Hannelore Lü-
beck, Georg Peter-Pilz, Rainer Philippi, Ilse
Ritter, et al. PREMIERE: Jan. 19. Köln Schauspiel-
haus, Cologne. A coproduction with WDR. (Ap-
peared at the Berlin Theatertreffen, May 15-7.) For
American production see 1985 entry.

the CIVIL warS: a tree is best measured when it
is down
PROLOGUE AND ACT V (ITALIAN SECTION)
An opera by Philip Glass and Robert Wilson

Direction: Wilson. Music: Glass. Text: Maita di
Niscemi, Wilson. Choreography: Jim Self. Music
director: Marcello Panni. Choral director: Gianni
Lazzari. Scenery: Tom Kamm, Wilson. Lighting:
Beverly Emmons. Costumes: Christophe de
Menil. Sound: Hans Peter Kuhn. CAST: Seta del
Grande, Ruby Hinds, Luigi Petroni, Franco Sioli,
Luigi Roni, Franco Concilio, Gregor Leschig,
Self, et al. PREMIERE: Mar. 26. Teatro dell' Op-
era, Rome. SUBSEQUENT PERFORMANCES: Mar.
31, 1986. Scheveningen; Apr. 2, 1986. Utrecht;
Apr. 5, 1986. Eindhoven; Apr. 8-27, 1986. Am-
sterdam. Presented by the Netherlands Opera.
(New choreography by Ulysses Dove; Glass and di
Niscemi added a new duet for Hercules and Alc-
mena.) Dec. 14-30, 1986. Brooklyn Academy of
Music, Opera House. Produced as part of the
"Next Wave" festival.

the CIVIL warS: a tree is best measured when it
is down
the Knee Plays (AMERICAN SECTION)

Scenario/Direction: Robert Wilson. Music and
Words: David Byrne. Artistic assistance: Adelle
Lutz. Choreography: Suzushi Hanayagi. Design:
Wilson, Byrne, Jun Matsuno. Lighting: Wilson,
Julie Archer. CAST: Byrne (narration), Donald
Byrd, Maria Cheng, Frank Conversano, Gail
Donnenfeld, Denise Gustafson, Marilyn Haber-
mas-Scher, Hanayagi, Cho Kyoo-Hyun, Satoru
Shimazaki. PREMIERE: Apr. 26-8 (Preview Apr.
25). Walker Art Center, Minneapolis. Presented
by the Walker Art Center in association with the
Guthrie Theater. SUBSEQUENT PERFORMANCES:
Sept. 20-2, 1985. Schauspiel Frankfurt; Sept. 26-
Oct. 3, 1985. Maison de la Culture de la Seine-
Saint Denis, Bobigny; Oct. 7-11, 1985. Festival de
Otoño, Palacio de Exposiciones y Congresos,
Madrid; Oct. 16-9, 1985. La Biennale di Venezia
XXXIII, Festival Internazionale del Teatro, Tea-
tro Malibran, Venice; Oct. 25-7, 1985. Teatro Sala
Europa, Bologna; Oct. 30-Nov. 1, 1985. Schau-
spielhaus Köln, Cologne (Theater der Welt '85).
Sept. 19-Oct. 5, 1986. American Repertory The-
atre, Cambridge; Oct. 14-9, 1986. Doolittle The-
ater, Los Angeles; Oct. 24-5, 1986. Zellerbach
Auditorium, Berkeley; Oct. 28, 1986. Macky Auditorium, Boulder; Oct. 31-Nov. 2, 1986. Kemo
Theater, Albuquerque; Nov. 7-8, 1986. University
of Iowa, Iowa City; Nov. 13-6, 1986. Music Hall,
Detroit; Nov. 19-22, 1986. Warner Theater, Washington, DC; Dec. 2-3, 1986. Alice Tully Hall,
NYC; Dec. 6, 1986. University of Vermont Memorial Auditorium, Burlington. May 11-2, 1987. University of Texas, Austin; May 15-6, 1987. Cullen
Theater, Wortham Theater Center, Houston; May
17-29, 1988. Civic Theatre, Chicago; June 15-7,
1988. Aura Hall, Tokyo; July 7-9, 1988. Queens-
land Performing Arts Centre, Brisbane. NOTE:
Bessie Award (NY) for dance, Sept. 1987.

THE SPACEMAN
(Video installation by Robert Wilson)

Sept. 14-Oct. 28 (Preview Sept. 13). Stedelijk Museum, Amsterdam. Presented as part of "The
Luminous Image," an exhibition featuring the
work of 22 video artists. NOTE: A new version of
the 1976 video performance with one live per-

DAVID BYRNE

The lead singer and songwriter of the rock group Talking Heads and creator of the film *True Stories,* David Byrne provided the music, text and narration for *the CIVIL warS* "Knee Plays" and also contributed to its design. In 1988 Wilson and Byrne resumed their collaboration with *The Forest.*

Not long after I came to New York, a friend got a bunch of us tickets to *A Letter for Queen Victoria* and said, "You wanna go see this theatre piece?" I didn't know anything about Bob's work at that time. Nothing. So it was a pleasant surprise. I liked the music and the direction and the way it looked. I felt Bob's theatre was very alive and that he created a whole world that lasted the length of the performance.

We didn't meet until much later. I was on a Talking Heads tour in Japan during the time Bob was thinking about *the CIVIL warS.* He was in Tokyo with Christophe de Menil, who had given him a copy of the score I did for Twyla Tharp, and he liked it so there was an arranged meeting in a sushi bar. Bob came and saw a Talking Heads show and the next day we walked around and talked. I thought he was a fascinating man. Kind of enigmatic—you could never really get a handle on him or on what exactly a piece was about or how it would be done or what it would be.

Working with Bob on *the Knee Plays* was interesting because at the time I had limited stage experience and yet I felt our way of thinking had something in common, and that Bob's way of constructing a piece was very similar to the way I would put together a piece of music. The work doesn't start from a narrative or a text, it doesn't have one thing that everything else is based on or has to conform to. It's more like layering the melody on top of the rhythm and the text on top of that so it all fits together. It's a way of hodgepodging things together in an intuitive way and that seemed very comfortable to me. My work is like that a lot of the time. It's kind of externalizing a mental process, taking the process that you naturally go through in your mind when you're creating something and putting it physically in front of you. Anyway, that's how I saw it.

(New York City. January 11, 1988.)

former. (Wilson's original collaborator, the late Ralph Hilton, was not credited.)

MÉDÉE
An opera in five acts by Marc-Antoine Charpentier (1693), text by Thomas Corneille

Direction/Design: Robert Wilson. Prologue texts: Etel Adnan, Hebrew Kaddish. Musical edition: Edmond Lemaître. Musical director: Michel Corboz. Lighting: Heinrich Brunke. Costumes: Franca Squarciapino. CAST: Esther Hinds, Brigitte Lafon, Henri Ledroit, René Schirrer, Gilles Cachemaille, Danièle Borst, Evelyne Didi, Cindy Lubar, et al. PREMIERE: Oct. 22, 26, 29, Nov. 2, 5, 8. Opéra de Lyon, Lyon. NOTE: Wilson discarded Charpentier's original prologue and replaced it with Act II, a of the CIVIL warS, which absorbed some of the themes of Médée.

MEDEA
An opera in five acts by Gavin Bryars and Robert Wilson, after Euripides

Direction/Design: Wilson. Translation/Adaptation: Christine Friedel, Louis Méridier, Claire Nancy, Minos Volonakis. Additional texts: Prologue, Heiner Müller (Despoiled Shore/Medeamaterial/Landscape with Argonauts); Act III, sc. a, Wilson; Act III, sc. b, Vladimir Mayakovsky. Musical director: Richard Bernas. Lighting: Heinrich Brunke. Costumes: Franca Squarciapino. CAST: Yvonne Kenny, Steven Cole, Louis Otey, Evelyne Didi, Cindy Lubar, et al. FIRST WORKSHOP: Feb. 26-Mar. 1, 1981. Musical Theater Lab, Kennedy Center, Washington, DC. Presented by Musical Theater Lab and the Byrd Hoffman Foundation. (Music by Arthur Russell. Medea and Jason played by Sheryl Sutton and John Nesci. Adaptation credited to Volonakis.) SECOND WORKSHOP: Mar. 4-5, 1982. Aaron Davis Hall, New York City. Presented by the Byrd Hoffman Foundation and the Music Department, City College of New York. (Medea and Jason played by Wilhelmenia Fernandez and Stephen Dickson. Adaptation credited to Volonakis.) PREMIERE: Oct. 23, 27, 30, Nov. 3, 6, 9. Opéra de Lyon, Lyon. A coproduction of Opéra de Lyon, Théâtre National de l'Opéra de Paris, Théâtre des Champs-Elysées and Festival d'Automne. SUBSEQUENT PERFORMANCES: Nov. 21, 24, 27, 30, Dec. 2. Théatre des Champs-

Elysées, Paris. NOTE: Medea was first presented as a play with music in 1981, and afterwards reconceived as an opera with music by Gavin Bryars.

EINSTEIN ON THE BEACH [REVIVAL]

Supervised by Wilson and Glass, with new dances by Lucinda Childs replacing those of Andrew de Groat. Childs, Sheryl Sutton and Samuel M. Johnson returned in their original roles. Wilson danced in the final scene on a number of evenings. PERFORMANCES: Dec. 11-23. Brooklyn Academy of Music, Opera House. Produced as part of the "Next Wave" festival.

Workshops for the French and Japanese sections of the CIVIL warS are held in La Sainte Baume (Marseilles) and Tokyo in February. Neither section is ever completed.

1985

the CIVIL warS: a tree is best measured when it is down
ACT III, SCENE E, ACT IV (AMERICAN PRODUCTION OF GERMAN SECTION)

English translation of Act IV by Christopher Martin and Daniel Woker. Scenery credited to Robert Wilson and Tom Kamm, lighting to Jennifer Tipton and Wilson. CAST: Ben Halley, Jr., Priscilla Smith, Frances Shrand, Jeremy Geidt, Seth Goldstein, Thomas Derrah, Diane D'Aquila, Shirley Wilber, et al. PERFORMANCES: Feb. 27-Mar. 17 (Previews Feb. 22-6). Loeb Drama Center, Cambridge. Presented by the American Repertory Theatre, in association with Boston's Institute of Contemporary Art.

KING LEAR—A WORK IN PROGRESS

Direction/Design: Robert Wilson. Music/Sound: Daniel Birnbaum. Choreography: Paula Shelley. Dramaturg: David Rodes. Lighting: Jerry Enos. Costumes: Sylvia Moss. PERFORMANCES: May 17-9. Stage One, Metromedia Square, Los Angeles. Presented by UCLA Extension, "Distinguished Artist in Residency" program. NOTE: The cast included about 30 students who were enrolled in Wilson's two-week workshop/course.

LAURIE ANDERSON

A musician, performer and visual artist, Laurie Anderson has toured with her multimedia creations throughout Europe and the United States. In 1986 she created incidental music for Wilson's staging of *Alcestis* at the American Repertory Theatre in Cambridge.

B ob and I both lived in SoHo during the seventies but we moved in different circles. It was near the end of the minimalist period and art was supposed to be very pure and austere. The people I knew were mostly sculptors and musicians and they tended to think theatre was corrupt—it had too many connections to the world. But I did go to Bob's work. I'm not so sure what the first piece I saw was but I remember all these people walking across the stage with paper bags on their feet. Which one was that? They all fuse together in my mind. And that's the thing about Bob Wilson's work. It's so much like a dream. Of course, I saw *Einstein,* which was very important. It confirmed that there was an audience out there for this kind of work. In those days we called anything above 14th Street *De*-troit, so *Einstein* being at the Met opened up this other world. Everyone started writing operas. You'd walk down the street and your friends would ask, "How's your opera?" And you'd say, "Fine, how's yours?"

I probably met Bob eight times without really meeting him. We were in a number of benefit concerts together—everybody did benefits for everyone else back then— and I went to some of the open houses at his loft. The first time I talked to him at length was with Heiner Müller when he was getting ready to do *Alcestis.* We talked about animals for about six hours. I don't know why. We talked and looked at pictures of animals and at one point Bob and I got down on our hands and knees and crawled around the room, trumpeting like elephants. I have a collection of push toys from all over the world—like dinosaurs and a dragon that spits fire—and Bob came over to my loft and played with them one day. I have this memory of him down on his knees in the middle of all these little animals going in different directions. It was like a puppet show, which is what Bob Wilson's pieces are.

A couple of months later I went to a rehearsal in Cambridge. Bob had added an epilogue to the play based on a Noh comedy about a birdcatcher who is sent to hell. I have a large collection of bird sounds and I built a sound score by mixing pieces of that with human voices. It was pretty free. Bob wants people to do what they want to do within the context he creates. They just asked for a short piece of music but then Bob said, "Oh, I thought you were doing music for the whole thing." "Oh, you did?" I would have needed three months instead of the two weeks I had. It was all so slapdash. I didn't collaborate at all. I spent one day in Cambridge and never saw the show.

(New York City. May 27, 1988.)

KONRAD HENKEL FILM PORTRAIT
A Seventieth-Birthday Commemoration

Unproduced. Storyboards by Tom Woodruff. June.

READING/PERFORMANCE 1969-1984

Performed and directed by Robert Wilson. Texts: Wilson, Christopher Knowles, Ben Halley, Chris Moore, David Byrne. Design: Wilson. Sound: Hans Peter Kuhn. PERFORMANCES: Sept. 28. Dublin Theatre Festival; Oct. 30. Museum van Hedendaagse Kunst Gent, Belgium; Feb. 22, 1986. Brattle Theatre, Cambridge (Music: Byrne, Lighting: Jennifer Tipton).

THE GOLDEN WINDOWS [AMERICAN PRODUCTION]

CAST: David Warrilow, Jane Hoffman/Gaby Rodgers, Charles Whiteside/John Bowman, Cynthia Babak/Kimberly Farr. PERFORMANCES: Oct. 22-Nov. 3. Carey Playhouse, Brooklyn Academy of Music. Produced as part of the "Next Wave" festival.

Designs a multiroom installation (never realized) for the German National Gallery in Berlin.

1986

ALCESTIS

Adapted by Robert Wilson from the play by Euripides as translated by Dudley Fitts and Robert Fitzgerald. Additional texts: *Description of a Picture* (Prologue) by Heiner Müller, translated by Carl Weber, and the Japanese Kyogen *The Birdcatcher in Hell* (Epilogue), translated by Mark Oshima. (Excerpts from Rainer Maria Rilke's poem "Alkestis" were incorporated into the main text.) Conception/direction/ design: Wilson. Music: Laurie Anderson. Movement: Suzushi Hanayagi. Scenery: Tom Kamm, Wilson. Lighting: Jennifer Tipton, Wilson. Costumes: John Conklin. Audio Environment: Hans Peter Kuhn. CAST: Eric D. Menyuk, Rodney Hudson, Diane D'Aquila, Paul Rudd (Ken Howard in Bobigny), Harry S. Murphy, Jeremy Geidt, Thomas Derrah, John Bottoms. PREMIERE: Mar. 12-23 (Previews Mar. 7-11); June 27-July 13. Loeb Drama Center, Cambridge. Presented by the American Repertory

Theatre. SUBSEQUENT PERFORMANCES: Sept. 18-28. Maison de la Culture de la Seine-Saint Denis, Bobigny (Co-produced with the Festival d'Automne). See also German production, 1987. NOTE: Named best foreign work of 1986 by Association of French Drama Critics.

HAMLETMACHINE
A play by Heiner Müller

Direction/Design: Robert Wilson. Music: Jerry Leiber, Mike Stoller. Translation: Carl Weber (revised by the author, Anne Cattaneo and Wolfgang Wiens). Dramaturgs: Wiens, Cattaneo. Lighting: Jennifer Tipton, Wilson. Costumes: William Ivey Long. Sound: Scott Lehrer. PREMIERE: May 7-June 15. Mainstage Two, New York University. Presented by the Tisch School of the Arts, NYU and the Herrick Theatre Foundation (John Wulp, Producer). SUBSEQUENT PERFORMANCES: Oct. 1-4, 6-10, 1987. Théâtre des Amandiers, Nanterre; Oct. 14-7, 1987. Albéñiz Theater, Madrid; Oct. 21-4, 1987. Théâtre Comedie de Saint Etienne; Oct. 30-1, 1987. Théâtre de la Salamandre, Lille; Nov. 4-7, 10-4, 1987. Almeida Theatre, London; Nov. 18-21, 1987. Comedie de Nice; Nov. 26-7, 1987. Teatro Biondo, Palermo. NOTE: The play was performed by 15 NYU undergraduate acting students. Wilson received the 1985-86 Obie Award for his direction.

the CIVIL warS, *as produced by the American Repertory Theatre in Cambridge, is the sole nominee for the Pulitzer Prize; the board makes no award,* April.

OVERTURE TO THE FOURTH ACT OF DEAFMAN GLANCE *(SOLO)*

PERFORMANCES: July 16-9. Teatro Grec, Barcelona; July 21-2. Teatro Romano, Malaga (IV Festival Internacional de Teatro). NOTE: Wilson, who usually wears a coat and tie when performing the murder scene, appeared in a dark dress and blackface in this version.

HAMLETMASCHINE [GERMAN PRODUCTION]

Direction/Design: Robert Wilson. Music: Jerry Leiber, Mike Stoller. Dramaturg: Wolfgang Wiens. Lighting: Jennifer Tipton, Wilson. Sound: Peter J. Scholler. PREMIERE: Oct. 4-Nov.

30; Apr. 16-23, 1987. Theater in der Kunsthalle, Hamburg. Coproduction of the Thalia Theater and Hochschule für Musik und Darstellende Kunst. SUBSEQUENT PERFORMANCES: May 7-10, 1987. Theater Manufaktur, Berlin.

ALCESTE
An opera in three acts by Christoph Wilibald Gluck (1776), text after Euripides

Direction/Design: Robert Wilson. Choreography: Suzushi Hanayagi. Dramaturg: Klaus-Peter Kehr. Musical director: Christoph Eschenbach. Lighting: Hanns-Joachim Haas. Costumes: Joachim Herz. PREMIERE: Dec. 5, 9, 13, 17, 21; June 18, 20, 22, 1987. Würtemberg State Opera, Stuttgart. CAST: Dunja Vejzovic/Maria Russo, Sheryl Sutton, Jon Garrison/John Sandor, Michael Ebbecke, Carsten H. Stabell, Uwe Heilmann, Tomoko Nakamura, Mark Munkittrick.

EINSTEIN ON THE BEACH
(Film project by Robert Wilson)

Unproduced. Storyboards by Yoshi Yabara and Stephan Olson. Sept. Commissioned by Great Performances, PBS. Jac Venza, Producer.

1987

SALOME
An opera in one act by Richard Strauss (1905), from the play by Oscar Wilde

Direction/Design: Robert Wilson. Musical director: Kent Nagano. Scenery: Wilson, Giorgio Cristini. Lighting: Beverly Emmons, Wilson. Costumes: Gianni Versace. PREMIERE: Jan. 11-23. Teatro alla Scala, Milan. CAST: Hermann Winkler, Helga Dernesch, Montserrat Caballé/Carmen Reppel, Bernd Weikl/John Bröckeler, Neil Rosenshein. (The action was mimed by 16 NYU acting students, most of whom had appeared in *Hamletmachine* the previous spring.)

DEATH DESTRUCTION & DETROIT II
A play with music in 2 acts and 16 scenes by Robert Wilson

Direction/Design: Wilson. Texts: Franz Kafka, Heiner Müller, Wilson, Maita di Niscemi, Cindy

Lubar. Choreography: Suzushi Hanayagi. Dramaturg: Klaus Metzger. Lighting: Heinrich Brunke. Costumes: Moidele Bickel. Sound: Hans Peter Kuhn. CAST: Libgart Schwarz, Ernst Stötzner, Paul Burian, Gerd Wameling, Udo Samel, Gregor Hansen, Tina Engel, Peter Simonischek, Branko Samarouski, Elke Petri, Christine Oesterlein, Jezy Milton, Matthias Matuschka, Lucia Hartpeng, et al. PREMIERE: Feb. 27-July 4; performances continued through Dec. Schaubühne am Lehniner Platz, Berlin.

ALKESTIS [GERMAN PRODUCTION]

Translation: Friederike Roth, Ann-Christin Rommen. Dramaturg: Ellen Hammer. Lighting: Robert Wilson, Uwe Belzner, Jennifer Tipton. Costumes: Joachim Herzog, John Conklin. CAST: Thomas Goritzki, Sheryl Sutton, Anne Bennent, Stephan Bissmeier, Michael Mendl, Klaus Steiger, et al. PREMIERE: Apr. 19-July, Sept. 26-7; Feb. 1988. Würtemberg State Theater, Stuttgart.

QUARTETT
A play by Heiner Müller (suggested by Choderlos de Laclos' Les Liaisons Dangereuses)

Direction/Design: Robert Wilson. Music: Christoph Eschenbach. Dramaturg: Ellen Hammer. Co-designer: Klaus Baumeister. Lighting: Hal Binkley (Ludwigsburg), Uwe Belzner (Stuttgart), Wilson. Costumes: Frida Parmeggiani. CAST: Elisabeth Rath, Hans Peter Hallwachs, Klaus Steiger, Geno Lechner, Randy Diamond. PREMIERE: June 17-20. Stuttgart Schauspiel (presented at the court theatre of Ludwigsburg Castle outside of Stuttgart as part of the 1987 Theater der Welt Festival). In September additional performances were given at the Staatstheater in Stuttgart.

OVERTURE TO THE FOURTH ACT OF DEAFMAN GLANCE

CAST: Robert Wilson, Sheryl Sutton. PERFORMANCES: June 27. International Theatre Festival, Delphi; July 17-8. Alice Tully Hall, NYC (presented by Lincoln Center as the opening event of the "Serious Fun!" performance series).

ROLF LIEBERMANN

The Swiss-born composer and opera producer commissioned Wilson's 1988 *Cosmopolitan Greetings,* which was his final production as Intendant of the Hamburg Staatsoper. He also composed the music for the knee plays which punctuate its main scenes.

Always, I wanted to work with Bob Wilson. From the first time I saw his work, which is now years ago. What impressed me more than anything else was the way he combined fantasy with extreme precision. You would think one would exclude the other but with Wilson each is characteristic of the other.

The whole of *Cosmopolitan Greetings* was created in Bob's mind and it was fascinating to see it progress every day. Light is the way he makes his works. He would spend three hours lighting one hand with such concentration. We discovered — all of us — the piece when he lighted it. I also admired his personal kindness with the artists. He was very open and asked all the performers for their ideas but he is so sure of what he wants. He is absolutely 100 percent democratic but also 100 percent autocratic.

George Gruntz composed a jazz score and I did a completely different kind of music for the "knees" in a strict dodecaphonic style. John Rockwell wrote in the *New York Times* that it was like putting lemon ice between the warm courses of a dinner. You have hot jazz and in between this cool style of music. Nobody knew if it would work — I did not know — but it did. And we had a good time.

(Hamburg. June 20, 1988.)

ALLEN GINSBERG

A major figure of the Beat movement and one of America's most celebrated poets, Allen Ginsberg contributed the poems that make up the text of *Cosmopolitan Greetings.*

In 1973 I went to the Brooklyn Academy with Julian Beck and Judith Malina to see the night-long play *The Life and Times of Joseph Stalin.* We all stayed for the whole thing. I'd been to *Paradise Now* and was an old hand at this kind of thing. I had also spent three months at a meditation seminary doing sitting practice ten or twelve hours a day so I was equipped to sit through lots of time. The notion of being in one place at rest observing my mind and the phenomenon of the world around me fitted in very well with Robert Wilson's kind of theatre, which is in a sense a meditative theatre, and pleased me as such.

A few years later I saw his play *Einstein* in Paris and after the performance Robert and I had supper. I was intrigued by his method and asked how he arrived at his images and what his basic aesthetic was. He told me what he looks for is the lowest common denominator of universal images, just the most recognizable or communicative archetypes—like Mickey Mouse—and he uses these as building blocks, without regard to their content neccessarily. This interested me because it related to the work of people like Andy Warhol, Gertrude Stein and John Ashbery. In a way Robert Wilson was doing with theatre what others were doing in painting and poetry. This was also a time when an earlier generation of punks was displaying swastikas and hammer-and-sickles on their leather jackets, having absolutely no historical recollection of those symbols. So I was struck by Wilson's boldness in taking such deep and terrible names as Einstein and Stalin and using them as images, empty of their literal connotations.

A year or two ago Robert Wilson got in touch with me about a new work he was going to do in Hamburg. The possibility of some kind of collaboration intrigued me since his kind of theatre seemed to integrate ancient meditative practice with modern spontaneous inspiration like Kerouac or Burrows or my own work. He came over very late one night and gave me an outline of time sequences and scenes for what turned out to be *Cosmopolitan Greetings.* The work-in-progress title was "The Life and Times of Bessie Smith." I think Bessie Smith was another one of those archetypal names for him. I was very flattered that so Olympian an avant-garde figure as Robert Wilson was interested in working with me. My only problem was I have writer's block—I write fitfully and desultorily and only when I think of something and if I have a project I almost never can do it. So I explained that, gave him all my poetry books and some new poems I had done, and he said we would work something out. Later George Gruntz came over to the house and we went over my poems together. I gave him my most recent work, including the text of "Cosmopolitan Greetings," which became the title of the piece. That was Robert's idea and it was a good one, because that's what the production wound up being—a kind of international jamboree with pop, blues, Italian grand opera and serial music put together by American black singers, European mimes and dancers, a Swiss composer, an avant-garde artist from Texas. The whole thing was like a giant U.N. hodgepodge vaudeville circus. Some months after that meeting they said the thing was ready and did I want to come to the premiere? So I said great and flew to Hamburg a couple of days before the opening. Frankly, I had the best of the bargain. They did all the work and I had a free ride. I guess I'd done my work in writing the poems.

(New York City. January 5, 1989.)

PARZIVAL
"Auf der anderen Seite des Sees" ("From the Other Side of the Lake") by Tankred Dorst and Robert Wilson

Direction/Design/Lighting: Wilson. Co-worker: Ursula Ehler. Texts: Dorst, Christopher Knowles. Music: Tassilo Jelde. Dramaturg: Wolfgang Wiens. Costumes: David Hatchett, Sabine Birker. Sound: Gerd Bessler. CAST: Christopher Knowles, Elisabeth Schwarz, Klaus Pohl, Circe, Angela Schanelee, Hans Kremer, et al. PREMIERE: Sept. 12-5, 17, 22-4; performances continued through Apr. of 1988. Thalia Theater, Hamburg.

Designs environment "Erinnerung an eine Revolution" ("Memories of a Revolution") for Galerie der Stadt in Stuttgart. (An old man is seen sitting in a niche within the leg of an elephant. The vaguely Napoleonic figure is surrounded by rats and holds a model stage in his arms. The entire scene is glimpsed through a wall of prison bars.) July 3 to Aug. 16.

1988

QUARTET [AMERICAN PRODUCTION]

Direction/Design: Robert Wilson. Translation: Carl Weber. Music: Martin Pearlman. Lighting: Howell Binkley, Wilson. Costumes: Frida Parmeggiani. Sound: Stephen Santomenna. CAST: Lucinda Childs, Bill Moor, Jeremy Geidt, Jennifer Rohn, Scott Rabinowitz. PERFORMANCES: Feb. 10-Mar. 6 (Previews, Feb. 5-9). Loeb Drama Center, Cambridge. Presented by the American Repertory Theatre.

LE MARTYRE DE SAINT SÉBASTIEN
A mystery in five "mansions" with music by Claude Debussy and text by Gabriele D'Annunzio (1911)

Direction/Design: Robert Wilson. Choreography: Suzushi Hanayagi, Wilson. Dramaturg: Ellen Hammer. Scenery: Wilson, Xavier de Richemont. Lighting: Howell Binkley, Wilson. Costumes: Frida Parmeggiani. Sound: Hans Peter Kuhn. CAST: Sylvie Guillem, Michael Denard,

Patrick Dupond, Philippe Chemin, Sheryl Sutton, members of the Paris Opéra Ballet. PREMIERE: Mar. 23-6, 28-31, Apr. 7-9, 11-6. Maison de la Culture de la Seine-Saint Denis, Bobigny. Coproduction with Théâtre National de l'Opéra de Paris. SUBSEQUENT PERFORMANCES: July 7-9. Metropolitan Opera House, NYC; Nov. 4-10. Paris Opéra (Palais Garnier). NOTE: New prologue by Wilson. Prerecorded score conducted by Georg Schmoehe (live orchestra for performances at the Opéra).

COSMOPOLITAN GREETINGS

Design/Direction: Robert Wilson. Music: George Gruntz, Rolf Liebermann. Text: Allen Ginsberg. Scenery: Wilson, Xavier de Richemont. Lighting: Heinrich Brunke, Wilson. Costumes: Henning von Gierke. Sound: Hans Peter Kuhn. CAST: Dee Dee Bridgewater, Lutz Förster, Sheila Jordan, Mark Murphy, Carolyn Carlson, Sheryl Sutton. (Jazz instrumentalists Don Cherry, Howard Johnson, Larry Schneider, Mike Richmond, Adam Nussbaum and the Big Band of the North German Radio led by Gruntz; Liebermann conducted a string ensemble drawn from the orchestra of the Hamburg State Opera.) PREMIERE: June 11-July 1. Kampnagelfabrik, State Opera, Hamburg.

THE FOREST
A play by Robert Wilson and David Byrne based on the *Gilgamesh* epic (c.1200 B.C.)

Design/Direction: Wilson. Music: Byrne. Texts: Heiner Müller, Darryl Pinckney. Choreography: Suzushi Hanayagi. Scenery: Wilson, Tom Kamm. Lighting: Heinrich Brunke, Wilson. Costumes: Frida Parmeggiani. Sound: Hans Peter Kuhn. CAST: Martin Wuttke, Howie Seago, Geno Lechner, Eva-Maria Meineke, Günter Ehlert, et al. PREMIERE: Oct. 15-29. Theater der Freien Volksbühne, West Berlin. Produced in association with Werkstatt Berlin 1988 e.V. for Berlin—Kulturstadt Europas 1988. Subsequent performances: Nov. 5-12. Deutsches Theater, Munich; Dec. 2-10. Brooklyn Academy of Music, Opera House. Produced as part of the "Next Wave" festival. NOTE: Screen treatment (unproduced) by Byrne.

1989

LA FEMME À LA CAFETIÈRE
Television work by Robert Wilson based on Paul Cézanne's painting of the same name

Direction/Design: Wilson. Photography: Renato Berta. Sound: Hans Peter Kuhn. 6 minutes. Produced by Musée d'Orsay INA y la Sept. CAST: Suzushi Hanayagi, Consuelo de Haviland. NOTE: *La Femme à la Cafetière* is part of a series of short films based on paintings in the Musée d'Orsay collection.

DOKTOR FAUSTUS
An opera in three acts by Giacomo Manzoni (1989) based on the novella by Thomas Mann

Direction/Design: Robert Wilson. Musical director: Gary Bertini. Scenery: Giorgio Cristini, Wilson. Lighting: Uwe Belzner, Wilson. Costumes: Gianni Versace. CAST: Marcel Vanaud, Sylvia Greenberg, Fernanda Costa, Paolo Barbacini, Giovanni Lucini, Wilson, et al. PREMIERE: May 16-20. Teatro alla Scala, Milan.

DE MATERIE [MATTER]
An opera in four parts by Louis Andreissen and Robert Wilson

Design/Direction: Wilson. Musical director: Reinbert de Leeuw. Libretto: Wilson, Andreissen. Choreography: Suzushi Hanayagi. Scenery: Wilson, Vera Dobroschke. Lighting: Jennifer Tipton, Wilson. Costumes: Frida Parmeggiani. CAST: James Doing, Wendy Hill, Beppie Blankert, Marjon Brandsma, et al. PREMIERE: June 1-17. Netherlands Opera, Muziektheater, Amsterdam. SUBSEQUENT PERFORMANCES: June 20. Danstheater aan't Spui, Hague; June 24. Rotterdamse Schouwburg.

LA NUIT D'AVANT LE JOUR [PARIS OPÉRA GALA]

Design/Direction: Robert Wilson. Musical director: Georges Prêtre. Scenery: Wilson, Xavier de Richemont. Lighting: Uwe Belzner, Wilson. Costumes: Frida Parmeggiani. CAST: June Anderson, Teresa Berganza, Plácido Domingo, Barbara Hendricks, Alfredo Kraus, Shirley Verrett, et al. PERFORMANCE: July 13. Opéra Bastille, Paris. NOTE: Televised gala inaugurating the new Paris opera house on the eve of the bicentenary of the French revolution.

SELECTED BIBLIOGRAPHY

Alenikoff, Frances. "Scenario: A Talk with Robert Wilson," *Dance Scope*, Fall/Winter, 1975-6.

Aragon, Louis. "An Open Letter to André Breton from Louis Aragon," *Performing Arts Journal*, Spring, 1976 (trans. Linda Moses).

Baker, Rob. "The Mystery Is in the Surface," *Theatre Crafts*, October, 1985.

Baracks, Barbara. "Einstein on the Beach," *Artforum*, March, 1977.

Barnes, Clive. "Must There Be a Story?," *New York Times*, March 14, 1971.

Bird, Eugene K. *Prisoner #7: Rudolf Hess*. New York: Viking Press, 1974.

Brecht, Stefan. *The Theatre of Visions: Robert Wilson*. Frankfurt: Suhrkamp Verlag, 1979.

Brustein, Robert. "Advanced Machines," *New Republic*, June 16, 1986.

Cage, John. *Silence*. Cambridge: M.I.T. Press, 1966.

Chaillet, Ned. "Robert Wilson and the Language of Movement," London *Times*, June 10, 1978.

Cranston, Peter. "The Wilson Marathon," *Tehran Journal*, August 28, 1972.

Croyden, Margaret. *Lunatics, Lovers and Poets*. New York: McGraw-Hill, 1974.

de la Falaise, Maxime. "Einstein at the Met" (interviews with Wilson, Glass and Knowles), *Interview*, February, 1977.

Deák, Frantisek. "Robert Wilson," *The Drama Review*, June, 1974.

Denby, Edwin. *Two Conversations with Edwin Denby*. New York: Byrd Hoffman Foundation, 1973.

Donker, Janny. "Robert Wilson and Heiner Müller," *De Groene Amsterdammer*, February 8, 1984.

———. *The President of Paradise: a traveller's account of the CIVIL warS*. Amsterdam: International Theater Bookshop, 1986.

Faust, Wolfgang Max. "Tagtraum und Theater" (Daydreams and Theatre), *Sprache Im Technischen Zeitalter* 69, January-March, 1979.

Foreman, Richard. "The Life and Times of Sigmund Freud," *Village Voice*, January 1, 1970.

Frick, Thomas. "A Conversation with Robert Wilson," *Art New England*, June, 1985.

Fuchs, Elinor and James Leverett. "Back to the Wall: Heiner Müller in Berlin," *Village Voice*, December 18, 1984.

Fuchs, Elinor, ed. "The PAJ Casebook: *Alcestis*," *Performing Arts Journal* 28, 1986.

Funk, Phyllis. "Byrds of a Feather Act Together," *New York Times*, December 2, 1973.

Glass, Philip, "Notes on *Einstein on the Beach*," *Performing Arts Journal*, Winter, 1978.

Gold, Sylviane. "Light Show," *Wall Street Journal*, October 31, 1985.

Goldberg, Jeff. "Robert Wilson and *Einstein on the Beach*," *New York Arts Journal*, Spring, 1977.

Gruen, John. "Is It a Play? An Opera? No It's a Wilson," *New York Times*, March 16, 1975.

Hamilton, Alex. "Robert Wilson: The Browsing Playwright," London *Arts Guardian*, March 11, 1978.

Harris, Dale. "Robert Wilson's Epic Vision," *Connoisseur*, April, 1984.

Hart, Claudia. "Setting the Stage," *ID*, September-October, 1984.

Heimberg, Martha. "Sensored Theater," *Dallas Downtown News*, March 2, 1981.

Hoffman, William M., ed. *New American Plays*, Vol. III, New York: Hill & Wang, 1970.

Johnston, Jill. "Family Spectacles," *Art in America*, December, 1986.

Jones, Robert. "Listen to the Pictures," *New York News*, November 21, 1976.

———. "Robert Wilson's 'Einstein' Returns to the Stage," December 2, 1984.

Kidder, Gayle. "the CIVIL warS," *San Diego Union*, November 20, 1983.

Kostelanetz, Richard. "Writing Performance: A Symposium," *New York Arts Journal*, 1981.

Lang, Jack. *Éclats*. Paris: Jean-Claude Simoën, 1978.

Langston, Basil. "Journey to Ka Mountain," *The Drama Review* 17, June, 1973.

Leverett, James. "Democratic Vistas: Wholes, Parts, Sums," BAM program, December, 1986.

Lieberson, Jonathan. "Lovely to Look At," *New York Review of Books*, April 11, 1985.

Lotringer, Sylvère. "Phil Glass: Interview," *Semiotexte(e)* 3, 1978.

———. "Robert Wilson Interview," *Semiotexte(e)* 3, 1978.

McFerran, Ann. "I Was Sitting in This Theater . . . ," *Time Out*, May 26-June 1, 1978.

Manvell, Roger and Heinrich Fraenkel. *Hess*. New York: Drake Publishers, 1973.

Marks, Jonathan. "Frederick the Great: Foreign and Familial Strife," *the CIVIL warS* (ART program book), 1985.

Marranca, Bonnie, ed. *The Theatre of Images*. New York: Drama Book Specialists, 1977.

Müller, Heiner. *Hamletmachine and Other Texts for the Stage*. New York: PAJ Publications, 1984 (trans. and ed. Carl Weber).

Munk, Erika. "Enrapture the Eye, Detach the Brain," *Village Voice*, December 25, 1984.

Planchon, Roger. "Bob Wilson at Villeurbanne," *Le Monde*, October 11, 1979.

Quadri, Franco. "Robert Wilson: It's About Time," *Artforum*, October, 1984.

Rainer, Yvonne, Meredith Monk and Kenneth King. "R. E.: Croce" in *4 Live*, 1980.

Rockwell, John. "'Einstein' Returns Briefly," *New York Times*, December 17, 1984.

Rouse, John. "Robert Wilson: Texts and History," *Theater*, Fall/Winter, 1984.

Sargent, David. "Einstein on the Beach: The Met Will Dance to a Mysterious Tune," *Village Voice*, November 22, 1976.

Schoedel, Helmut. "Wilson, Wagner & Woody Allen," *Die Zeit*, June 4, 1982.

Searle, Judith. "How Long Does It Take to Peel a Red Onion," *New York Times*, November 12, 1972.

Shyer, Laurence. "Robert Wilson: Current Projects," *Theater*, Summer/Fall, 1983.

———. "Robert Wilson: *the CIVIL warS* and After," *Theater*, Summer, 1985.

———. "*The Forest*: A Preview of the Next Wilson-Byrne Collaboration," *Theater*, Summer, 1988.

Simmer, Bill. "Robert Wilson and Therapy," *The Drama Review* 20, 1976.

Smith, Ronn. "The Night Is for Dreaming," *On the Next Wave*, November, 1985.

Solomon, Alisa. "Theater of No Ideas: A Conversation with Robert Wilson and Heiner Müller," *Village Voice*, July 29, 1986.

Stayton, Richard. "What Happened in Los Angeles," *the CIVIL warS* catalogue. Los Angeles: Otis Art Institute-Parsons School of Design, 1984.

Strand, John. "Foreman and Wilson: New Glory for the Expatriate Avant-Garde," *Passion*, November, 1983.

Taylor, Sean. "*Einstein* on the Stage," BAM program, December, 1984.

Trilling, Ossia. "Ka Mountain and Guardenia Terrace," *The Drama Review* 17, June, 1973.

Tucker, Carll. "An Entirely Unfamiliar Human Way of Perceiving the World," *Village Voice*, March 24, 1975.

Wachsmann, Michael. "Brief Attempt Not to Interpret Robert Wilson," *The Golden Windows*, Munich Kammerspiele, 1982.

Wilson, Peter. "The Seven Story Mountain of Love," *Sixth Festival of the Arts*, September 8, 1972.

Wilson, Robert. *the CIVIL warS* (Dutch section). Paris: Editions Herscher, 1983.

——. *the CIVIL warS* (German section). Frankfurt: Suhrkamp Verlag, 1984.

——. *the CIVIL warS* (Italian section). Rome: Edizioni del Teatro dell'Opera, 1984.

——. *The Golden Windows*. Munich: Carl Hanser Verlag, 1982.

——. *Death Destruction and Detroit*. Berlin: Schaubühne am halleschen Ufer, 1979.

——. "Tale of Two Cities (D D & D)," *Performance Art* 1, 1979.

Wilson, Robert (and Cindy Lubar), "I Was Sitting on My . . . ," *The Drama Review* 21, December, 1977.

Wirth, Andrzej. "Death Destruction & Detroit," *Washington Review*, June/July 1979 (trans. Susan Winnett).

Robert Wilson: The Theater of Images, New York: Harper & Row, 1984.

the CIVIL warS. Act I, a. Cologne, 1984.

NOTES

INTRODUCTION

xiii   Ann Wilson. Phyllis Funk, "Byrds of a Feather Act Together," *New York Times,* December 2, 1973.

"one large structure." Claudia Hart, "Setting the Stage," *ID,* September-October, 1984.

xiv   Such borrowings and his failure. See "R. E.: Croce" in *Live* 4, 1980 for letters from Yvonne Rainer, Meredith Monk and Kenneth King refuting Arlene Croce's claim that Wilson "has been the biggest influence, after Cunningham, on choreographers working today."

xv   "I liked Balanchine." Interview with Sylvère Lotringer, *Semiotexte(e)* 3, 1978. Etel Adnan, a Lebanese writer who worked on several of Wilson's productions, has said, "A single picture is more important to him than an entire book." (Interview in *Robert Wilson,* a film by Howard Brookner.) Wilson once told a British interviewer that as a child he cared much more about how a book was placed on a shelf than what was inside it. (*Arts Guardian,* March 11, 1978.)

"Go like you would." Robert Jones, "Listen to the Pictures," *New York News,* November 21, 1976.

Clive Barnes. *New York Times,* March 14, 1971.

xvi   "Oh, you can speak." Calvin Tomkins, "Time to Think," *Robert Wilson: The Theater of Images,* p. 92.

time would provide the space. Wilson in a *Washington Star* interview, February 26, 1981: "I once saw a 15th century Japanese Noh play, on which an angel onstage barely moved for 45 minutes, or moved more than a tree in a breeze. It was very pleasant—all that space." Wilson in *Women's Wear Daily,* December 13, 1973: "If it's going to take me five minutes to pick up a spoon, first of all it's going to be painful just to control it. But what happens with my awareness of my body if I do it?" Wilson also believes that when movement is slowed both spectator and performer become more aware of internal bodily movement.

the viewer's own thoughts. Wilson in *Asahi Shinbun,* December 7, 1981 (trans. Alan Poul): "When watching a play that is seven hours or twelve hours long, the viewer falls into a half-sleeping, half-waking state in which his internal images are mixed with the external images on stage, and he ceases to make a distinction between the stage and reality. Some viewers see or feel things that never really appeared on stage. In this way the viewer himself participates in the creation of the drama. . . . By making the movement on stage extremely slow, one can open up spaces in time, so that while watching the play the viewer can also think about many other things. This too is a way of stimulating the viewer internally."

"People talk about slow motion." Robert T. Jones, "Robert Wilson's 'Einstein' Returns to the Stage," *New York Times*, December 2, 1984. Clive Barnes seems to have been the first to articulate this view: "Wilson drugs us with time. He rejects that speed-up, that Disneyesque concatenation of events all condensed like milk or *Reader's Digest*, which we accept as part of the theatre, and restores something of the pace of real time to his world. Some things are very s-l-o-w but this does not matter. At times it is like watching cloud formations, slowly evolving their figurative suggestions, and at times, naturally more rarely, it is like watching a street accident. . . .You wander rather comfortably through the landscape of Wilson's creation, pausing to ruminate, ponder or wonder about it. It is theatre that deliberately gives you time to daydream." (*New York Times*, March 14, 1971.)

xvii a greater collage. In a sense Wilson's commentary on his work—so often pieced together from other people's statements and views—constitutes another of his collages. (A number of Wilson's friends and associates have told me of hearing their own words and ideas issuing from his mouth.)

"It's just like when." Ronn Smith, "The Night Is for Dreaming," *On the Next Wave* (a BAM publication), November, 1985. A Byrd Hoffman Foundation prospectus for *The Man in the Raincoat* (1981) similarly tells us that "the visual and aural elements do not illustrate one another; indeed they may not even be related. If, on occasion, sound and image intersect and illuminate each other, that may be part of the author's designs—or simply a reflection of the spectator's own perceptions."

xviii Louis Aragon. "An Open Letter to André Breton from Louis Aragon," *Performing Arts Journal*, Spring, 1976 (trans. Linda Moses).

most radical innovations. Wilson in *Dancescape*, Fall/Winter, 1975-6: "My plays don't demand full attention." When Wilson began going to the theatre during his student years, he complained of the fatigue and mental strain of having to follow not only the action but every word of dialogue, a situation he would rectify in his own theatre.

Richard Foreman. "The Life and Times of Sigmund Freud," *Village Voice*, January 1, 1970. Wilson has said that he doesn't want a performer to do anything that would demand a particular emotional response from an audience: "I think there should be a freedom for people to feel however they want to feel and to respond authentically . . ." (Interview with Martha Heimberg in *Dallas Downtown News*, March 2, 1981.) He maintains that this allows the spectator to participate more fully in the theatrical experience (one of the things he never liked about the theatre, he says, was its lack of exchange; he felt everything traveled in one direction—from stage to audience).

the spectator is enlisted. Stefan Brecht in *The Theatre of Visions: Robert Wilson* (p. 212): "Wilsonian communication is not a transfer, but the making of something so that others can make something of it." Benjamin Henrichs in *Die Zeit*, March 2, 1979: "Wilson's theatre doesn't tell any stories, it causes stories." Stanley Kauffmann in the *New Republic*, January 5, 1974: "Perhaps [his imagery] will stimulate the viewer to invent his own play; perhaps not. No matter." Michael Wachsmann in "Brief Attempt Not to Interpret Robert Wilson," *The Golden Windows*, Munich, 1982: "It deals with—no, it does not 'deal with' at all. . . . [The spectator] will become an observer of an artfully live organism composed of tones, texts, sounds, pictures, movements, gestures, faces—no place for clear-cut thinking, for purposeful feeling, but for a multitrack-sensing . . . between the traces, cracks, passages for the imagination that can bind and unbind, make connections or stay with the riddles, as far as eye, ear, brain and wit will carry you. Therefore: if *The Golden Windows* is a play by four actors, too, then it is all the more a play by each reader, each spectator . . . and in this play that does not exist, he can find his own."

Wilson's works admit. Jacques Lemarchand in *Le Figaro*, June 25, 1971: "Truly there is no key to the peopled dreams of Robert Wilson. They are of free entry to all. I am convinced that if you would ask when the play was over those who had watched it to describe the events and the images they had seen, their reports would not coincide on a single point." John Perrault in the *Village Voice*, January 1, 1970: "*The Life and Times of Sigmund Freud* had so little obvious meaning that it contained all meanings." Byrd Hoffman Foundation prospectus for *The Man in the Raincoat*, 1981: "It is a work about many things—including some which the playwright himself may not yet have considered."

xix "The fact is." John Gruen, "Is It a Play?," *New York Times*, March 16, 1975. As Wilson told the journalist Peter Cranston in Shiraz, "I never know what I'm doing until it's over . . . I still don't know what *Deafman Glance* was about completely—maybe never will know." (*Tehran Journal*, August 28, 1972.)

It cannot be dispelled. The German critic Helmut A. Langh called Wilson's *Video-50* "an anti-puzzle" because unlike a puzzle the pieces do not produce a complete image. (*Die Zeit*, July 14, 1978.)

Imagery is rooted in biography. Jill Johnston has attempted to locate some of these biographical threads in her essay "Family Spectacles," *Art in America*, December, 1986.

"The theatre is a forum." "Bob Wilson Interview," Toga Festival, Japan, July, 1982 (NHK), BHF Archives.

xx Robert Kanters. From Kanters' review in *L'Express*, May 24-30, 1971, quoted in the *New York Times*, July 5, 1971.

antiquated art form. Meredith Monk was calling her multimedia works "operas" as early as 1971.

Edwin Denby. *Two Conversations with Edwin Denby*, November, 1973. Byrd Hoffman Foundation.

Stanley Kauffmann. *New Republic*, May 31, 1975.

Roger Planchon. Henry Popkin, "A French 'Titan' Comes to New York," *New York Times*, January 25, 1981.

PERFORMANCE AND PERFORMERS

SHERYL SUTTON

Unless otherwise specified, material in this section is taken from an interview with Sheryl Sutton (January 8, 1985). I have also drawn on performance documentation in Stefan Brecht's *The Theatre of Visions: Robert Wilson.*

6 *Deafman* prologue. This description of the murder scene is drawn from newspaper and magazine descriptions and the stage manager's book for the 1970 Iowa staging. In the original version of the scene, Sutton wore a single red glove which she later covered with a black glove. This effect seems to have been eliminated after 1974.

"It's hard to say." Wilson has said that at first glance the figure might appear to be a young boy: "You're not quite sure if she's a man or a woman." Wilson was evidently captivated by Sutton's androgynous appearance and insisted that the actress cut her hair very short. While the original performers of the Byrd School came in all shapes and sizes, Wilson eventually chose the body type of the ballet dancer—tall, thin, cool, finely chiseled features—as his ideal (an ideal personified by Sutton and Lucinda Childs). Ann Wilson: "He likes them long and skinny. When he's dealing with women he's really dealing with atttenuated fashion models. I also think those elongated women are men. They're him. His female persona. He's long and skinny too."

7 "the murders seem almost religious." Wilson has said the figure might be "an angel—an angel of death" and in the last frame of the television adaptation he made in 1981, a bare light bulb—a kind of incandescent halo—comes into view over Sutton's head.

the artist's late mother. Wilson may also have drawn some inspiration from Hitchcock's *Psycho.* Common elements include the tall, thin mother figure in the Victorian dress and the gleaming butcher knife that never penetrates the skin.

the seed of his stage adaptation. Sutton played Euripides' heroine in Wilson's 1981 workshop production at the Kennedy Center in Washington: "I think Bob always wanted to do *Medea* because of the murder scene. The Byrdwoman was Medea to him, a modern version of the mythological character."

8 "she seemed to represent." Wilson's notes on *Freud*, September, 1971. BHF Archives.

9 "strength, simplicity." *Waco Tribune Herald*, July 25, 1965. This interview with Waco's drama critic Gynter Quill reveals that Wilson was already attracted to theatre and dance forms making use of "complete naturalness, freedom and economy of means."

"I shall not teach." Quoted in the program to *Handbill*, 1970, BHF Archives. Wilson also seems to have taken up such Graham pronouncements as "the body doesn't lie" and "man danced before he spoke."

Richard Foreman. Quoted in *Dancemagazine*, April, 1974.

10 such ordinary acts. Wilson: "The trouble I had always was that . . . people had the idea that they would have to show a skill or that they'd have to perform . . . you're interesting just like you are, that's what really interests me—so just walk in and sit down, and that was very difficult for people to do because suddenly all their

crutches . . . they wanted to do always do something to show off . . . so then we tried to eliminate that—and try to get them to be confident and just be themselves and walk in and sit down . . ." (1970). Brecht, *The Theatre of Visions*, p. 392.

"extract from it." Peter Wilson, "The Seven Story Mountain of Love," *Sixth Festival of the Arts*, September 8, 1972.

liquid slow motion. Sutton describes her memorable slow cross as follows: "It's a step forward and a shift of weight to the foot, a relevé to demi-pointe and an exchange of the foot, relevé and descent on the other foot. It's an arch, like walking uphill. When both feet are planted in relevé you're either going up or down. You should never see the exchange of weight. It appears you're floating since the vertical movement is stronger than the horizontal."

11   "to move from the past." Frances Alenikoff, "Scenario: A Talk with Robert Wilson," *Dance Scope*, Fall/Winter, 1975-6.

"I peeled an onion." Wilson also took apart an onion in the performance, brutally tearing the bulb to pieces in a contrasting display of psychic energy.

smallest expenditure of energy. Wilson: ". . . to be able to use just the smallest amount of energy to express whatever they wanted to." Production notes to *The King of Spain* in William M. Hoffman, ed., *New American Plays*, Vol. III, p. 248.

"the audience is obliged." Edwin Denby similarly believed that one of Wilson's "great inventions . . . is that it's o.k. for actors if the audience doesn't pay attention to them." ("Two Conversations with Edwin Denby," November, 1973, BHF Archives.) Arthur Sainer in his review of *Deafman Glance* in the *Village Voice* (March 4, 1971): "P. Adams Sitney said of Richard Foreman's *Total Recall* that it could easily go on without us. So could Wilson's work."

"more than a physiological state." In his 1970 notes to *The King of Spain*, Wilson also suggested that audiences can see performers better when they're in a relaxed state. "It's difficult to see the persons if they're not relaxed—to look at them; have an exchange with them." Hoffman, *New American Plays*, p. 249.

12   "They're totally centered." Like Wilson, Sutton often speaks of centering, a Zen-derived term that denotes a state of calm, denial of the ego and wholeness of one's inner and outer parts.

"Actors can get very hostile." Sutton says that if an actor fails to achieve this state of centeredness, Wilson eventually "erases them, he puts them somewhere where their negativity and disjuncture works better."

14   "it's a denial of truth." At the same time she believes that because the performer has "very specific things to do, most of one's inner emotional response is masked."

highly trained professionals. On occasion Wilson will still take the lone performer off the street or from among his friends.

DAVID WARRILOW

The material in this section is drawn from an interview with David Warrilow (November 21, 1985) and my own observation of the New York rehearsals of *The Golden Windows*.

17   a company of American actors. Wilson also planned a French production with Jean-Louis Barrault and Madeleine Renaud which never materialized.

19 "almost forgotten the words." Stefan Brecht, *The Theatre of Visions: Robert Wilson*, p. 285.

20 "it's the same with Bob." Warrilow has worked with many of today's most innovative directors, among them Lee Breuer, JoAnne Akalaitis, Andrei Serban, Liviu Ciulei and Peter Sellars, and although he dislikes comparisons—"Wilson shares two things with these other people. He's a consummate artist and he had the good sense and taste to choose me"—he does acknowledge certain similarities to Richard Foreman: "Basically they're very similar. They do the drawings in their head. Foreman used to do it all too, he was like a man with a puppet theatre. Richard is far more clearly structured in his mind as to how it looks and how it sounds at every single moment. He's faster so there's less air."

"the actors were different." While the role in which Warrilow appeared was intended for a much older man ("I know I can speak for Bob when I say that I was not ideal casting for this part"), in true Wilsonian fashion he made no attempt to play age but rather "invested whatever maturity I have into it without any pretending."

"But he wouldn't say." While none of this posed any real problem for Warrilow, actors who are unaccustomed or ill-attuned to Wilson's methods are sometimes confused and frustrated by his seemingly contradictory directions—"don't project, more interior" while at the same time "your presence should reach the back row"—and his limited verbal means of expressing what he wants should they be unable to satisfy him.

"What I discovered." Martin Penrose, a New York painter who appeared with the Byrd School in São Paulo in 1974, pointed out to me the astonishing difference in time between backstage, where everyone was rushing wildly around and the piece seemed to go by in minutes, and the auditorium, where the action appeared slow and effortless—in Penrose's words, "one long stretch."

THE BYRD HOFFMAN SCHOOL OF BYRDS AND *KA MOUNTAIN*: THE SEVEN-DAY PLAY

28 Stefan Brecht. pp. 199-200.

31 *Dance Scope*. "Scenario: A Talk with Robert Wilson," by Frances Alenikoff, Fall/Winter, 1975-6.

37 a special performance. As it turned out, the Empress Farah did not attend *Overture*, though other Iranian notables were present.

44 The Seven-Day Play. Other attractions at the Shiraz Festival that year included Merce Cunningham, John Cage, Karlheinz Stockhausen, the Kathakali Dance Theatre of India and "Persepolis Event," a *son et lumière* spectacle with decor by Andy Warhol. Peter Brook's *Orghast* had been seen at Persepolis the previous year.

Allan Kaprow. *Happenings, Environments and Assemblages*, p. 188.

John Cage. *A Year From Monday*, p. 32.

Antonin Artaud. Margaret Croyden, *Lunatics, Lovers and Poets*, p. 95.

45 the journey of an old man. Wilson's interest in *King Lear* seems to have stemmed from this time; *KA MOUNTAIN* contained various references to Shakespeare's play.

53 Note in festival publication. *Sixth Festival of the Arts*, September 5, 1972.

66 Jerome Robbins. Calvin Tomkins, "Time to Think," *New Yorker*, January 13, 1975.

CHRISTOPHER KNOWLES

Unless otherwise specified, quotations are taken from an interview with Robert Wilson and Christopher Knowles (September 24, 1986), and from conversations with Kit Cation, Robyn Brentano and Lucinda Childs. I have also drawn extensively on Bill Simmer, "Robert Wilson and Therapy," *The Drama Review* 20, March, 1976.

74 "a bit autistic." Wilson's theatre is in some ways similar to the world of the autistic child, which Bruno Bettelheim describes in *The Empty Fortress* (1967) as a place where "neither time nor causality exist" (p. 84).

Dr. Lafave. Simmer, "Robert Wilson and Therapy," p. 106.

Ed Knowles. Ibid., pp. 104-5.

76 his movements and gestures. Chris provided performance material for a number of productions in a similar manner. Jim Neu remembers that during rehearsals for *The $ Value of Man*, "people would follow him and do what he did — and Bob would isolate a lot of those things and incorporate them into the choreography."

77 everyone is autistic. John Gruen, "Is It a Play? An Opera? No It's a Wilson," *New York Times*, March 16, 1975. Wilson: ". . . I believe in autistic behavior."

79 impressed and excited Wilson. Knowles perfectly fit Wilson's definition of the artist at the time; as he told an interviewer, "An artist is one who discerns patterns. If he is a painter, he sees visual patterns; if he is a musician, he finds patterns in sound." (Alex Volkoff, " 'Madness' by Robert Wilson," *Tehran Journal*, August 18, 1974.)

84 Erika Munk. "And Thereby Hangs a Tail," *Village Voice*, July 2, 1980. *Curious George*, the last of their "dialogs," received scathing reviews from the New York critics.

"If Christopher did." Francis Levy, "The Longest Show," *Penthouse*, September, 1975.

WRITERS, DRAMATURGS AND TEXTS

89 the isolated monologue. For example, Mary Peer's freefall monologue in *The King of Spain*, Wilson's opening speech in *Freud*, and the random remarks made by Liba Bayrak as the blindfolded woman in the *Deafman* banquet scene (Stefan Brecht says she was given a set of cards inscribed with various phrases and was allowed to choose "which [remark] to make, when to make it, how many of them to make." *The Theatre of Visions: Robert Wilson*, p. 64.)

"Keep that line!" Frantisek Deák, "Robert Wilson," *The Drama Review*, June, 1974.

90 DIEING DINA SORE. Wilson was fascinated by the various words and sound fragments within the word *dinosaur* and devoted considerable time to breaking apart its phonic components. (Ann Wilson says he was not amused when she told him he had overlooked Dinah Shore.)

Excerpts from Wilson's poetry. Wilson's *KA MOUNTAIN* journals, BHF Archives.

"Sometimes sounds." William A. Raidy, "The 'Silent' Opera," no date or source. BHF Archives.

John Gruen. *New York Times*, March 16, 1975.

"a dam bursting." Calvin Tomkins, "Time to Think," *Robert Wilson: The Theater of Images*, p. 92.

dialogue taken from television. In this Wilson was probably influenced by Christopher Knowles, who would incorporate commercials and songs he heard on the radio into his writings.

91 "a kind of huge graffiti." Frances Alenikoff, *Dance Scope*, Fall/Winter, 1975-6.

resembled his own plays. *Arts Guardian*, March 11, 1978. Stefan Brecht suggests that Wilson may have constructed sections of *Queen Victoria* in just this manner. "Wilson would come down . . . with sheets of lines he'd pick up stoned from late movies, etc. off a TV set he'd borrowed, assigned not to any characters but to '1' '2' '3' and '4' in regular alternation." *The Theatre of Visions*, pp. 272-3. Sheryl Sutton says that in the fourth act of *Queen Victoria* there were four concurrently running stories that were fragmented in this way. Mary Peer's taped monologue in *The King of Spain* seems to have been similarly organized. Wilson: "She sort of gets one thing going and then she starts another thing and then she'll start the third thing and then she goes back to the first thing and then she starts a fourth and a fifth and she's back to the second and the first and she keeps going back to all of them. . . ." Ibid., p. 394.

"The difference between." *Time Out*, May 26-June 1, 1978.

"tend to demand too much." Carll Tucker, "An Entirely Unfamiliar Human Way of Perceiving the World," *Village Voice*, March 24, 1975.

do not so much transmit. As Wilson told a writer for the London *Times* (June 10, 1978) during the European tour of *Patio*, "I get more involved in just listening to the sound of Lucinda's voice, than actually what she's saying."

Wilson likens his texts. Wilson: "Actually, I look at my speeches as singing. I'm interested in the natural sound of words." *New York Times*, March 16, 1975. "You'll have a theme that's introduced here in the text, then developed. I look at the text as being musical, it's used as much for the sound and rhythm as for what's being said. The text is structured like music, used like a score. . . ." *Performance Art*, vol. 1, no. 1, 1979. "When you listen to Mozart, you don't wonder what it means. You just listen. I consider what I am doing as a kind of music." *Semiotext(e)*, vol. 3, no. 2, 1978.

92 Richard Foreman. John Strand, "Foreman and Wilson: New Glory For the Expatriate Avant-Garde, *Passion*, November, 1983.

not until rehearsals. Wilson sometimes divides lines up among the still uncreated characters (who are designated as 1, 2, 3, etc.) in the first version of his texts.

Andrzej Wirth. *Washington Review*, vol. 5, no. 1, June/July, 1979, trans. Susan Winnett.

Colette Godard. *Le Monde*, February 22, 1979. (A review of *D D & D.*)

while others. *Le Figaro* on the Dutch *CIVIL warS*: "irritating words, insistent as a fly, constantly buzzing in our ears, with annoying ramblings, fragmented, snobbish stupidities. . . ." Quoted by Gayle Kidder in the *San Diego Union*, November 20, 1983.

the formula he has employed. Especially since Wilson's critics—particularly those in the United States—have grown increasingly impatient with this aspect of his work in recent years and the artist has always been sensitive to critical response. The New York production of *The Golden Windows* loosed just such a reaction. Frank Rich wrote in the *New York Times* (October 28, 1985): "*The Golden Windows* often sounds like a parody of *The Cocktail Party*. It is full of non sequiturs ('I don't need a screwdriver'), mock-Beckettisms ('Life is full of disappoint as they say'), self-consciously campy romantic bromides ('You cannot live without emotion') . . . Another line tells us that 'talk is cheap,' and, in this case, is it ever." Clive Barnes in the *New York Post* (October 30, 1985) pronounced Wilson "a charlatan of jargon. His language is at best cute and surprising. It has no poetic resonance, no provocative suggestiveness, no dramatic quality."

MAITA DI NISCEMI

Unless otherwise specified, material is drawn from interviews with Maita di Niscemi (January, 1985), her letters and published program notes, papers in the Byrd Hoffman Foundation archives and conversations with Philip Glass.

96   most of the critics. Di Niscemi says the Schaubühne considered Hess "politically dangerous" and discouraged Wilson from including his photo in the program. It may also be that Wilson chose to suppress the identity of his central character so critics wouldn't focus on historical and political issues to the exclusion of the work's other elements.

"about the fascination." Wolfgang Max Faust, "Tagtraum und Theater," *Sprache Im Technischen Zeitalter*, January-March, 1979.

97   a scene of Hess. A blurred enlargement of a section of this photograph was published in the program book, though few would have been able to identify the image.

98   "So much coal." The comment, which di Niscemi cited in her first letter, was taken from Speer's *Spandau*.

match text to image. Perhaps Wilson's most moving use of a displaced biographical text occurs in the epilogue when Frau Hess stands alone before the wall of Spandau. The end of her monologue is drawn from an incident di Niscemi found in *Prisoner # 7*: Bird had found some walnuts in the prisoner's coat, asked Hess about them and was told, "Oh yes . . . they're mine. I use them to play with like marbles as I walk around. They help me think" (p. 155). In the play, Frau Hess's last words are: "yes these are my walnuts/I'm playing with them/when I'm walking/it helps me thinking."

"How strange a thing." Roger Manvell and Heinrich Fraenkel, *Hess*, p. 188.

alighted on his shoulder. In *The Life and Times of Sigmund Freud* Wilson danced along the beach in striped pajamas with a stuffed bird on his shoulder.

99   "you're from Detroit." A postcard of the Ford automobile plant in Detroit from early in the century also appeared on the last page of the program book.

scenes are also duologues. *D D & D* was originally conceived as a chamber piece for four to six actors (with one young couple and one old couple), leading naturally to two-character scenes.

"Sometimes I cook." The speech, which appeared in Scene 9, is taken from di Niscemi's letter of November 21, 1978. The first part of the text, which was eventually deleted, contained several references to the play's themes: "I admit to finding refuge in sleep. And I am lucky in my sleep. I am able to control my dreams. I almost never dream of war or prison or death."

102   we see only the hand. This basic image would be seen again at the end of Act I, a of *the CIVIL warS,* this time with Frederick the Great clutching his cane in the darkness.

105   inserted these . . . fragments. Most of this historical material is concentrated in Act II, which is set in Edison's workshop.

characters, images and texts. As would also be the case with *the CIVIL warS,* Wilson paid tribute to the country sponsoring the presentation (*Edison* was performed in Lyon and Paris) by incorporating various references to its history and national heroes. These included the Marquis de Lafayette, the sudden appearance in the final act of the Statue of Liberty (a gift to America from the French people) and a scene set in the foyer of the Paris Opéra, one of the first buildings in France to be illuminated by electric light.

"The idea of the piece." Laurence Shyer, "Robert Wilson: Current Projects," *Theater,* Summer/Fall, 1983.

106   Lee and Traveller dialogue. The speech was eliminated when Wilson reconceived Act II, b as a prologue to his staging of *Médée* in Lyon.

109   "he wanted Hercules." The mythological hero also appeared in *KA MOUNTAIN.*

114   an offstage chorus sings. Di Niscemi was extremely uneasy about putting these concluding lines at the beginning of the scene. Her fears were quickly dismissed by the pragmatic Glass: "I told Phil they're going to boil us alive and he said, 'When was the last time that book was taken out of the library? Ahhh, 1962.'"

through a window. The image of the spaceship dates from Wilson's earliest sketches in 1979; at that time he did not know who would appear in the porthole, only that there would be "someone inside."

the incoherent outpourings. Wilson's texts are often most effective when placed within some kind of realistic context. In Act III, e of *the CIVIL warS,* for example, his assemblage of random comments and broken phrases suggested the unspoken thoughts and whispered exchanges of the soldiers as they woke at dawn and prepared for battle.

dressed as mythological figures. In subsequent productions the chorus was dressed in white triangular robes, identical except for color to those worn in the previous scene.

116   continue to influence. One of her ideas was to provide the foundation for the 1987 sequel to *Death Destruction and Detroit, D D & D II* : "I said why don't we do Hess and Kafka, the man who could not die and the man who could not live."

HEINER MÜLLER

Unless otherwise specified, material is drawn from an interview with Heiner Müller (March 7, 1985), my exchanges with him during rehearsals of *Hamletmachine* the following year, and conversations with Wilson, Wolfgang Wiens, Ann-Christin Rommen, Tom Kamm and Hans Peter Kuhn, all of whom were present at the Cologne workshop. I have also drawn on Carl Weber's introductory material in *Hamletmachine and Other Texts* (New York: PAJ Publications, 1984) and John Rouse's "Robert Wilson: Texts and History" in *Theater,* Fall/Winter, 1984, the best article that has appeared on the German section.

117   *Village Voice.* Elinor Fuchs and James Leverett, "Back to the Wall: Heiner Müller in Berlin," December 18, 1984.

"the genius of the aesthetic." Georg Hensel in *Frankfurter Allgemeine*, February 14, 1979.

119   "I tried to find." *New German Critique* 16, Winter, 1979. Translated by Jack Zipes with Nance Weber. Although the paper was delivered in New York, Müller was not able to attend the conference because his visa was delayed.

"no difference between actors." Although Wilson currently prefers to work with professionals, Müller believes that he will one day return to working with untrained actors but "on a new level."

"depicting the family." Quotation taken from Wilson's storyboard scenario created during the Freiburg workshop in 1982.

120   made up of disparate scenes. Müller says that, along with more conventional plays, he has been writing texts in this fragmentary mode since the early fifties, and that like Wilson's theatrical works, his body of writings is singularly lacking in "linear development."

121   "The words got in the way." Rommen says the actors' carefully timed countings were often disrupted because the texts proved longer than the action.

"putting something else." Although the fitting of texts to a preexisting staging was necessitated by Müller's late arrival, Wilson has always worked in this manner. With *A Letter for Queen Victoria,* he similarly began by creating the physical action and then layered on textual material.

122   an open-ended art. Michael Wachsmann, Wilson's dramaturg on *The Golden Windows,* could have been speaking for Müller when he stated back in 1982 that the task of the company was "to keep the whole thing open, to create space for the imagination to wander, not to clog the breathing pores by untimely pasting-over with interpretations." ("Brief Attempt Not to Interpret Robert Wilson," program essay, Munich Kammerspiele.)

"this year's concepts." Müller: "A danger always, especially in the German theatre, in European theatre, is that the director has a clear concept and then he breaks the text, you know, and kills the play with his concept. And so I always try to confuse them." ("The PAJ Casebook: *Alcestis*," *Performing Arts Journal* 28, 1986, p. 95.)

"There were no discussions." In a *Village Voice* interview ("Theatre of No Ideas," Alisa Solomon, July 29, 1986), Müller said that if you have to talk "you have to lie. The main energy of regular directors goes into lying to actors."

123   "maybe in the next four weeks." Wilson also remarked on the possibility of such a delayed reaction in his interview with Jonathan Marks in the Cambridge *CIVIL warS* program book: ". . . this piece doesn't tell one story; it tells many stories, some of them simultaneously; and *you* put them together, probably after you go home."

"It's very interpretive." Interpreters of all kinds have long been the bane of Müller's professional existence. In a 1983 interview in *Der Spiegel* (quoted in Weber, pp. 18-9) he explained, "My texts are frequently written so that every, or every second, sentence shows only the tip of the iceberg—and what's underneath is nobody's business. Then the theatre people put on their wetsuits and dive down, looking for the iceberg or building their own . . ."

Jonathan Marks. "Frederick the Great: Foreign and Familial Strife" in the ART program book for *the CIVIL warS*, 1985.

125   *Gundling's Life.* Frederick the Great also appears as a minor figure in Müller's *Germania: Death in Berlin* (begun in the 1950s, completed in 1971) in the guise of a vampire.

all wars are now civil wars. Müller says that this idea was originally reinforced by a scene, inspired by the painting *Washington Crossing the Delaware,* which contained a text about the execution of civilians in time of revolution. "It was one of the best scenes, I thought, but there wasn't enough time so we had to leave it out, which is a pity. What I tried to say was that until the eighteenth century, war was something between soldiers while now there is no difference between civil war and any other kind of war, it's one universal thing and this is the result of your revolution of democracy."

as well as selecting . . . texts. One of these texts was contributed by Maita di Niscemi. She had met Müller in Rotterdam during the Dutch workshop and after he returned to East Berlin he would call her late at night to talk about the project: "He asked me if I had any ideas for the German section and I said if you're going to have a Russian rocket in Act IV you should also have an American submarine. And he said, 'What would the submariners be doing?' And I said, 'They'd be singing.' And he said, 'What would they be singing?' And I said, 'They'd be singing about stocks. What do Americans care about? Money.' And, of course, what do Marxists care about? Money. They're fascinated by it. He's a Marxist and they love money with a passion because they don't understand it. As far as they're concerned money is magic. They don't understand interest, they don't understand credit, they don't understand any of it. So I told him I would write a 'Submariner's Cantata.'" Di Niscemi went out and bought a copy of the *Wall Street Journal,* creating a text based on the commodities listed on its back pages (". . . american motors/american capital/american control/american brands. . .monolit figgle federal screw/figgle national presto figgle. . .never/never/never/dream/of selling ibm"). "There's not a stock in there that's not quoted every day. Heiner loved it but Bob was incensed. He thought I was trying to muscle in on the fourth act and said, 'I forbid you to speak to Heiner Müller.'" (In Wilson's staging, a chorus of submariners, their faces grotesquely painted, rose from hatches in the orchestra pit to recite di Niscemi's text.)

fashioning the book. Müller also supplied texts for I, a and the epilogue.

126   selected a letter. The opening text in which Frederick I declared "I cannot stomach an effeminate fellow without manly inclination, blushing like a girl, who cannot ride nor shoot . . ." may have had personal associations for Wilson. As a young man he was similarly encouraged to be "a regular fellow" and take up "manly pursuits"; he had to accompany his father and the other men of the town on hunting parties and on one occasion climbed up a tree to escape the spectacle below (an image that brings to mind the little man in the first knee play of *the CIVIL warS*).

Dan Sullivan. March 10, 1985.

Racine's *Phaedre*. Both the *Phaedre* passage, which was intended "to show the homoerotic aspects of the personalities of Frederick and Katte," and the letter from Frederick I originally appeared in *Gundling's Life*.

127 "the resurrection of the dead." The phrase was to reappear in Müller's telegram to Wilson following the cancellation of *the CIVIL warS*: ". . . his theatre is a resurrection: the dead are set free in slow motion."

a procession of Black Scribes. The Black Scribes somewhat resemble the frock-coated, quill-carrying figures that haunt Robert Schumann in Balanchine's *Davidsbündler-tänze*, which Wilson may have seen.

"For me Hitler is the Erlkönig." In the workshop Hitler's face also appeared on the screen, an image that was later deleted.

128 The channels of response. There is a striking scene in Wilson's *Hamletmachine* that captures both the contradictory nature of Müller's dramaturgy and the director's manner of dealing with his text. Three young women sit at a long table laughing while another actor whose face is averted is heard weeping; neither party takes any notice of the other. (In a corresponding episode a short time later, broad smiles appear on the women's faces while a few feet away a female figure on a swivel chair turns slowly, revealing a grimace of horror.) There is no agreement, no consensus, no single view. The images literally contradict themselves, as in a sense the staging contradicts the text—this is Müller's world. (The playwright has said that the reason he prefers drama to other literary forms is that it enables him to "say one thing and say the contrary." Weber, *Hamletmachine*, p. 138.)

"I like destructive forces." Müller, who wrote in his PROJECTION 1975 that "in the century of Orestes and Electra that is upon us, Oedipus will be a comedy," believes the theatre's contribution to the prevention of "the apocalypse towards which mankind is working" should be its representation.

'Don't tell me what it is.' Rommen says that upon hearing the texts in English during rehearsals of the Cambridge production, Wilson was surprised by the content of some of the speeches and became "very interested in understanding what they meant."

129 staging contemporary works. In the late 1970s Wilson expressed interest in staging Beckett's *Happy Days*.

The play he chose. Wilson has never revealed why he chose *Hamletmachine* except to say he "liked it." While undoubtedly attracted to its powerful imagery and concentrated language, he may also have been drawn to the Shakespearean connection: he was already planning a *King Lear* with Müller for 1987 (later postponed), and the German section of *the CIVIL warS* featured a short scene from *Hamlet* (which happened to contain the tragedy's sole reference to "machine").

two independent tracks. Later Wilson added a layer of sound effects, again unrelated to either text or staging (wolf howls, bird cries, distant machine-gun fire, etc.) in much the same manner.

repeated the basic sequence. A silent prologue consisting of the same basic movements was later placed before the first scene.

130 Robert Brustein. "Advanced Machines," *The New Republic*, June 16, 1986.

than literal stage directions. According to Wiens, Müller never attempts to illustrate his texts when he directs his own works; in fact, he often intentionally sets out to confuse critics and spectators with his staging.

"texts have so many images." Solomon, "Theater of No Ideas."

131   He trusts the text. Wilson went even one step further by demanding that the performers give equal weight to each line of the text. "The first word is no more important than the last word," he would tell them.

"Just read it." At a rehearsal for the American production of *the CIVIL warS* in Cambridge the previous year, Müller asked one of the actors to read a passage without trying to understand or make understood what it meant. (Rommen recalls that Müller spoke frequently with the actors in Cologne, though rarely about interpretation or intonation: "It was usually 'Just say the lines. If you don't think too much about it, it will work,' and that's very similar to Bob's way.")

attuned to rhythms, intonation. Wilson and Müller also seem to share a similar distrust of language, though that is the medium in which Müller creates. When asked in a 1978 interview (*Semiotext(e)*) why he hadn't written a novel, Müller replied that he couldn't conceive of such a thing: "I don't believe in reading"—a response to gladden Wilson's heart.

132   but of affinities. Several years earlier Michael Wachsman called his theatre "the only true democratic art"; Müller has no problem with this designation, calling it simply "another word for the same thing."

"a very relaxed way of reception." This feature seems to have struck a nerve in Germany, where theatre is regarded as a forum for debate and an instrument of instruction. Wolfgang Wiens has similarly said that what most impressed him about *Einstein on the Beach*, his first encounter with Wilson's work, was that the audience was free to "leave the auditorium during the performance; you could go out and have a beer or a smoke and then come back in. It was a very relaxed way to see theatre."

than humankind. From Müller's telegram: "the history of mankind can no longer be separated from the history of animals (and plants, stones, machines)."

one must write for a majority. See Weber, *Hamletmachine*, p. 139; Fuchs and Leverett, "Back to the Wall," *Village Voice*.

133   "the colonization of fantasy." Müller has often spoken of his encounter with *Fantasia*, which he says he saw by mistake when he walked into the wrong theatre in an American cinema complex. He was horrified not only by the film's marriage of innocuous imagery and great music but by its reduction of "the symbolic force of images to one meaning, to make them immediately allegorical"—another face of the interpretation issue. Müller contrasts Disney's animated fantasies with the "torrent of metaphors" found in early Russian cinema and Elizabethan drama where a "world of images is created that does not *lend* itself to conceptual formulation and that cannot be reduced to a one-dimensional metaphor. That is what I try to do in my theatre." And that, of course, is what he also finds in Wilson's theatre. (Weber, *Hamletmachine*, p. 138.)

something almost inconceivable. Wilson in the *Daily Hampshire Gazette*, May 26, 1979: "I never could get involved in Shakespeare and Tennessee Williams and all that stuff. It requires too much thinking. I just like a pretty picture or arrangement."

a coming together of the American. The Dutch critic Janny Donker, writing in *Die*

Groener Amsterdammer (February 2, 1984), described Wilson's theatre as a still, elegant realm whose protective glass case had been shattered in this production, exposing it for the first time to the "wild vapors and harsh climate" of reality and history.

ANNETTE MICHELSON

Unless otherwise specified, material in this section is drawn from interviews with Annette Michelson (February 11, 1985) and Robert Wilson (July 10, 1985), as well as my article "Robert Wilson: Current Projects" in *Theater*, Summer/Fall, 1983.

136 exposure to Wagner. A few years later Wilson met his future scenic designer, Fred Kolo, at a performance of *Tristan und Isolde* at the Metropolitan Opera.

137 he saw for the first time. Wilson was later to see performances of *Parsifal* at the Bavarian State Opera in Munich, the Metropolitan Opera and the Salzburg Festival.
     they settled on *Parsifal*. In October Wolfgang Wagner informed Wilson that Rudolf Noelte had been chosen for the centennial *Parsifal* in Bayreuth (Götz Frederich eventually directed the production). Wilson believes that the conductor James Levine, who had already been contracted, refused to work with him.

138 an early version of *Tristan*. Wagner himself identified the wounded Tristan with Amfortas, who also yearns for death and the end of suffering.

139 his style of acting. In Wilson's 1987 production of *Salome* at La Scala, performers and singers were separated in just this manner.

140 had seized Wilson's imagination. A single sketch of a forest appears in the margins of a libretto Wilson studied while listening to his recording of the opera (it is unclear just when this drawing was made). He also sketched a group of cypress trees rising out of a lake at another point.

141 the expanse of water. To accomplish this transformation Wilson and his assistants devised a floor covered with polystyrene and silver-foil waves which could pivot upward to form a near-perpendicular wall. The surface was divided into three sections (with traps in between) and could be lighted from above and below.
     "Bob's idea was to have." This is an instance of Wilson subverting Wagner's control of theatrical time, or rather adapting it to his own uses. Although the swan is supposed to fall rapidly from the sky, Wilson intends to have the enormous down-covered creature descend slowly during the previous eight minutes of music: "I hope I haven't been disrespectful to Wagner," he told Jacqueline Brody in *The Print Collector's Newsletter* (September-October 1985), "but I want the eight minutes."

142 Wieland Wagner. Quoted by Geoffrey Skelton in *Wieland Wagner: The Positive Sceptic*.

144 He showed his designs. The previous four sketches date from March 1981.

146 A riveted metal tower. The surface of the tower is similar to the spaceship wall and the huge metal doors Wilson later created for *the CIVIL warS*.

147 "Here it's a rod." This effect was to be realized with the same mechanism Wagner used at Bayreuth in 1882—a spear (in this case a Plexiglas rod with fluorescent tubing) traveling diagonally down a wire.

150   The iceberg disappears and fire. Colette Godard, reviewing *D D & D* in *Le Monde*,
       February 22, 1979: "The alchemy of [Wilson's] art uncovers the hidden places
       where ice and fire melt into one another, the exclusive country of poetry."

152   has yet to be realized. In 1985 a projected stage and film version of *Tristan und Isolde*
       with Jessye Norman and Pierre Boulez also fell through (Michelson was again to be
       Wilson's dramaturg).

       The holy forest. Wilson's original design for Act IV, scene 1 of *The Forest* (1988), with
       its moving trees and hut, could be a traditional setting for the Good Friday scene in
       Parsifal.

       his 1979-80 collaboration. *Curious George* was presented in Europe and New York
       several months before Wilson went to Bayreuth in 1980. Perhaps he took the
       drawing from the souvenir festival program the Wagners had sent him prior to his
       visit and inserted it on impulse.

DESIGN

FRED KOLO

Unless otherwise specified, material is drawn from an interview with Fred Kolo (June 30,
1985). (The designer originally spelled his name "Kolough" and that is how it appears in
program credits of the period.)

155   "It was all gray." "Production Notes on *The King of Spain*" in William M. Hoffman's
       New American Plays, Vol. III, p. 246.

157   a cat so enormous. The image of the cat's legs stealthily making their way through tall
       grass—a row of which appeared near the curtain line—may have had its origins in
       the final scene of the previous year's *Theatre Activity*, where a photograph of a cat's
       face was slowly superimposed on a field of waving marsh grass. Wilson is a long-
       time cat lover. When asked as a child on a radio program what he thought "the
       nicest thing in the world" was, he replied: "a big, thick cat's paw." A live cat also
       appeared in *BYRD woMAN* (1968), where it was seen playing with a string that rose
       continuously out of the floor.

       lateral zones. The stage floor was often covered with real surfacing materials to create a
       greater sense of place and illusion: vermiculite for the beach in *Freud;* straw for the
       cave scene; dirt, leaves and grass for the forest in *Deafman Glance.*

158   discussion and exchange. Kolo says that in his experience Wilson's own storyboard
       sketches "usually came after the production."

       jointly designed. Because Kolo was in Pittsburgh and unavailable to work on the
       production, Wilson asked the designer's former teacher to do the show. Polakov
       created new scenes for Copenhagen but as it turned out there was no money to
       realize them. Wilson eventually secured a grant for the scenery from the Gulben-
       kian Foundation in Lisbon prior to the opera's scheduled presentation at the
       Brooklyn Academy of Music. Polakov was not able to go to Lisbon to oversee
       construction so once again Wilson approached Kolo, asking that several drops be
       reconceived as well. Kolo eventually repainted all the scenes, incorporating Polakov's
       ground plans and technical solutions.

a kind of "mirror." From the time he began compiling his existing productions, Wilson has been concerned with relating their divergent imagery and scenes. When *The King of Spain* became the second act of *The Life and Times of Sigmund Freud*, the Corot landscape that had been seen through the gap in the wall of the drawing room was replaced by the cloud-swept sky from the new first act ("The Beach"), which returned in the final act, this time glimpsed through the opening in a cave. Other visual elements were introduced to connect the three episodes; a small table with a green Egyptian statuette stood downstage in each scene and a wooden chair descended from the flies over the course of the performance (the first of Wilson's many scenic "timepieces"), reaching the floor in the final act, at which point Freud made his way onstage and sat down.

mature style. Wilson says that the spare and formal scenic design of the hastily conceived Paris *Overture* in 1972 already gave some indication of this. Mel Andringa feels that the scenic simplicity of the platform plays in *KA MOUNTAIN* and the empty skies of Shiraz made a deep impression on Wilson: "I think he realized that he didn't need all that painted scenery."

161 Andrew Porter. December 13, 1976.

Philip Glass. Conversation with Glass, 1985.

drops and sculptural elements. The design of *Einstein* brings to mind a number of scenic elements in Merce Cunningham's work: the floating glass cases in the spaceship scene recall Jasper Johns' 1968 decor for *Walkaround Time*, while the descending column of white light in the opening scene might be a positive image of the huge moving black column that Robert Morris created for *Canfield* the following year.

only its stylistic motifs. Marian Goodman, a New York art dealer who has exhibited Wilson's work, on his furniture and sculpture: "Bob is certainly part of the art history of our times and he knows a lot about art. I think you can see that in his work. He's really smart about picking things up and instantly aware of what other people are doing, so whatever's in the air he's going to use. Maybe Bob's a little like a magpie—certainly people have said that—but he's used references to others in a very original way and made them his own. Obviously, many of the pieces owe something to minimalism but Bob's work lacks the strict, cerebral quality that one associates with the minimalists. It's less mathematical, less theoretically engaged. There's a greater mystery and a real magical quality you don't find in the other people's work." (June 26, 1985.)

"the stage in *Einstein*." *The Theatre of Visions*, p. 360.

TOM KAMM

Unless otherwise specified, material is drawn from interviews with Tom Kamm (March 14, April 19, 1985; February 29, 1988).

164 "I work in a form." Laurence Shyer, "Robert Wilson: Current Projects," *Theater*, Summer/Fall, 1983.

165 "I was born." *Dallas Morning News*, May 20, 1984.

167   "The two things." Robert T. Jones, "Robert Wilson's *Einstein* Returns to the Stage," *New York Times*, December 2, 1984.

       rectangular platform. One of Wilson's earliest New York appearances took place on another white rectangle; the work was Meredith Monk's 1968 *Blueprint*.

       a theatre of transformation. The most basic kind of transformation occurs at the very beginning of the developmental process as Wilson reconstitutes a postcard view, a photograph or an image from a previous work. The opening scene of *the CIVIL warS*, for example, where the little man is chased up a tree by a lion and begins to read the history of the world, seems to have its origin in the New York version of *Overture*, in which Edwin Denby was roared up a ladder tree by a lion while reading aloud from the diaries of Nijinsky.

170   Wilson once claimed. Bill Simmer, "Touring Robert Wilson's *Einstein on the Beach*," *Theatre Design & Technology*, Spring, 1978.

172   "spaceship wall at the back." Wilson originally envisioned the spaceship in the final act of *Einstein* as passing so close to the earth that trees became visible through its window, an image realized nearly eight years later in this scene (though from a reverse angle).

       "The trees came to a stop." In the words of lighting designer Beverly Emmons, "It almost seemed as if the trees were standing still and the whole proscenium was moving." The panorama was subsequently scaled down and redesigned for performances in Holland and New York with unsatisfactory results.

176   "I like to work." Shyer, "Current Projects."

       Christina Giannini. Simmer, *"Einstein."* Beverly Emmons confirms this view: "He doesn't want to make something of cardboard that looks fine from the fifth row, he wants a real object that looks great as you stand there holding it in your hand. He has a different set of standards."

177   perfectionism. This almost fanatical demand for precision and order may have had childhood origins. Wilson once told an interviewer, "When I was six or seven, I'd wake up in the middle of the night and go to my parents' kitchen and rearrange all the glasses on the shelf, because it was driving me crazy that the tall one was in this spot, and the short one in that spot." *Daily Hampshire Gazette* (Northampton, MA), May 26, 1979.

       "He's a real perfectionist." Despite such care and effort, things do go wrong on occasion; as Emmons has said, "When Bob's shows get messy, they get really messy."

THOMAS WOODRUFF

Unless otherwise specified, material is drawn from an interview with Thomas Woodruff (May 30, 1985).

178   old postcard scenes. These included the grove of palm trees and the large rock by the sea as well as the racing cars, which were taken from a postcard view of the Salt Flats in Utah. Woodruff has a large collection of old postcards which he uses in his paintings. Like Wilson, he often appropriates his imagery from existing materials.

179 "Television . . is a very different." "Arts Interview with Robert Wilson," ABC Video Enterprises, 1983.

"Television's scale." Robert S. Ryan, "The Arts," *OMNI*, September, 1980.

180 "working at three o'clock." Woodruff says the storyboards for four projects, *Edison*, *DD&D*, *Curious George* and *The Breakfast Table*, were created in a single summer.

181 "another window." "Arts Interview."

"looking out the window." Nigel Gosling in *The Observer*, June 4, 1978: "He himself had been what he calls 'a spaced-out kid.' He used to spend hours locked in his room, looking out the window."

182 divided into thirteen sections. *Stations* was first conceived not as a single work but as a series of thirteen half-hour episodes.

Joseph Stalin. One segment, the Victorian hospital or "Bees," looks simultaneously back to *Stalin* and ahead to *the CIVIL warS* (Act III, c).

183 follow the storyboards closely. With both *Deafman Glance* and *Stations* Tom Kamm worked directly from Woodruff's storyboards. Kamm on *Deafman*: "The kitchen scene was based on a postcard of a Texas kitchen from the Depression era which Wilson had. My idea was that the kitchen would be stark black and white: white tiles with black lines, white cabinets with black hinges, white steel enamel stove. Then when the mother figure moved into the hallway, there would be a shift to very muted colors: beiges or browns. The two rooms in which she murdered the children were complementary and had an even higher degree of color—one was bluish green and the other a pinkish color. The color scheme was my idea and Bob liked it."

CHRISTOPHE DE MENIL

The material in this section is drawn from an interview with Christophe de Menil (May 28, 1985). I have also consulted Grace Glueck's article on the de Menil family, "The Medici of Modern Art," in the *New York Times Magazine*, May 18, 1986.

188 principal backers of *Einstein*. Although de Menil was not aware of it, her late father was one of a number of people Wilson wrote for financial support—playing on his loyalties as a fellow Texan—when he was trying to put together *The King of Spain*. In 1971, Dominique de Menil purchased a set of Warhol drawings that Wilson had been given and the proceeds helped to finance the European tour of *Deafman Glance* (Wilson did not know the de Menil family at that time).

189 "very often a triangle." These triangular robes had previously been seen in *A Letter for Queen Victoria* and *Great Day in the Morning*. The prototype was devised by Cindy Lubar while improvising with a white sheet at Royaumont in 1972.

John Conklin. *Performing Arts Journal*, Summer, 1986, p. 91.

monochromatic use of color. Brilliantly colored costumes have since been seen in *Alcestis* ("The Birdcatcher in Hell") and *Quartet*.

BEVERLY EMMONS

The material in this section is drawn from interviews with Beverly Emmons (January 4 and 23, 1985) and conversations with Richard Nelson and Fred Kolo.

191 John Rockwell. December 17, 1984.

196 approach to lighting. Wilson's highly refined lighting methods have their detractors, among them Fred Kolo: "When I go to the work now I see specials, everywhere specials. When you see a light on someone it's just a light." Kolo offers as a contrast the highly atmospheric lighting for the planet scene in *The Life and Times of Joseph Stalin*, which was bathed in "a pinkish glow like the light from some dying sun."

SOUND AND MUSIC

ALAN LLOYD/IGOR DEMJEN

Unless otherwise specified, material is drawn from interviews with Alan Lloyd (March, 1985) and Igor Demjen (November 6, 1985).

205 Gene Rickard. *Patio* program, Veterans Auditorium, San Francisco, April, 1977.

206 Jacques Lonchampt. January 18, 1978.
Together the two sections. *Patio* program.

207 their final collaboration. Lloyd also provided music for one of Wilson's solo pieces in 1975 and for *Video-50* (1978), which featured brief pieces from the composer's sketchbooks.

208 Demjen assembled and mixed. Julie Weber and Pierre Ruiz also provided taped music for some of these productions.

209 "based on the same principles." September, 1971, p. 20. BHF Archives.

PHILIP GLASS

Unless otherwise specified, material in this section is taken from interviews with Philip Glass (November 19 and 26, 1985). I have also drawn on Maxime de la Falaise's pieces on Wilson and Glass in *Interview* (February, 1977) and Barbara Baracks' excellent article on *Einstein* in *Artforum* (March, 1977).

215 *New York Times*. December 14, 1973.

217 Stefan Brecht. *The Theatre of Visions: Robert Wilson*, p. 245.
"I found it beautiful." *Die Zeit*, October 15, 1976. Interview with Renate Klett.

218 The trial in *Einstein*. The courtroom scenes seem to have had their origin in a short play depicting a murder trial that Wilson presented at Royaumont Abbey in 1972. The setting, which is described by Margaret Croyden in *Lunatics, Lovers and Poets*, also suggests the scenography of *Einstein*: "only tables, chairs, benches—[it] was like a stark drawing, all black, gray and white, all straight lines and no curves" (p. 217). Wilson's father, incidentally, was a city attorney and had hoped his son would follow him into his profession.
"we're all washed up." Erika Munk in the *Village Voice*, December 25, 1984.

220 "those drawings were before me." Wilson's final designs often differed considerably from those in Glass's workbook. At this point, for example, the knee plays were to be performed by a tall man in a cowboy hat (rather like Wilson in *Dialog/Curious*

George), while Act IV, sc. 2 featured a "bed with Japanese war monsters" (dark, wavy shapes looming at the back of the stage) rather than the glowing bar of light audiences would eventually see.

"felt the emotional content." Sean Taylor, "*Einstein* on the Stage," BAM program, December, 1984. (Glass is the speaker.)

"It didn't really matter." See Jeff Goldberg's interview with Glass in *New York Arts Journal*, Spring, 1977, for a contrasting view of the opera question.

and even incorporated material. Glass says he was writing "Another Look at Harmony" when Wilson first drew the image of a train for him. "I just said, 'Oh, this music will go with that image,' and I brought it in one day and asked Bob how he felt the two went together. That was the beginning of *Einstein*. It was fairly easy after that."

221   "developed a vocabulary." From Glass's 1976 program notes on *Einstein*.

222   "I thought of the dances." The first dance sequence (Act II, sc. 1) was also based on material from "Another Look at Harmony" (1975).

"ideas of the opera." For a detailed musical description of the opera see Glass's own "Notes on *Einstein on the Beach*" in *Performing Arts Journal*, Winter, 1978.

"a conventional theatre formula." Glass: "Once Bob heard the finale that I wrote he said, 'I think we better have something after that, I don't want the people to leave the theatre with that as the last thing they hear.' So then the fifth knee play was added as a way of coming out of it."

"I wrote a piece." Taylor, "*Einstein* on the Stage."

224   "What makes a piece new." From an interview with Sylvère Lotringer in *Semiotext(e)* III, 1978. The full quotation reads: "Even when using the language of Satie or Brahms we can still write pieces that are extremely radical; something that Rzewski knows. And John Cage knows. People that are working in this way found that what makes a piece new isn't a new harmony or a new kind of tonal organization; it's a new perception."

From *Queen Victoria*. In the final scene of *Queen Victoria* the window unit tilts to form a triangle in space and in the first scene of *Einstein* the tower on which the small boy is standing similarly slants to create that shape. (From *The $ Value of Man* comes the idea of independent dance sequences; in fact, the field dances were originally given the name "free sections" after those in the 1975 work.)

("Once you start looking.") Barbara Baracks, "*Einstein on the Beach*."

April Kingsley. December 2, 1976.

ordinary piping materials. Wilson also admired a table Willem de Kooning had made for Edwin Denby out of piping and plywood.

"The only person he carried." Dancers who had previously appeared with the Byrd School included Andrew de Groat, Charles Dennis and Ritty Burchfield.

226   Glass sees the two. Shortly after *Einstein*'s New York performances, Wilson did acknowledge the bond between music and staging: "The actions that I've done on stage have nearly always been tightly linked up with the music. For *Einstein*, when I was setting these actions Phil would tell me about the music and what the counts were and how many sections there were and I would map out something along those lines and they fit together with his music. Sometimes I worked against the music, sometimes with it." (*Interview*, February, 1977)

227   the trial/prison scene. Wilson found an engraving of a 1776 *lit de justice* (the royal
       parliamentary court) at Versailles and incorporated this image into the first trial
       scene as well. He must have been pleased to find that there really was such a thing as
       a "bed of justice."

       rewriting. Glass, however, did add the vocal solo accompanying the ascent of the bar of
       light in Act IV, sc. 2 in Avignon: "There was no aria in the piece and Joan
       LaBarbara (then a singer with his ensemble) said to me, 'If this is an opera there
       should be an aria.' So I said, 'Okay, I'll write you an aria.' "

228   "When people work with Bob." Lucinda Childs on the creation of her monologue
       about avoiding the beach ("I was in this prematurely air-conditioned super-
       market . . ."): "Bob asked me to speak spontaneously about the beach. I told him I
       didn't think I had anything to say about the beach and he said 'Well, that doesn't
       matter, just say whatever comes to your mind.' So I kept improvising, inventing
       things and he selected the part of the monologue where I discussed not going to the
       beach." The text, which Childs repeats over and over in the trial/prison scene, was
       actually created for Wilson's multimedia work *The Spaceman*: "*Einstein on the Beach*
       was in rehearsal at the time but Bob never mentioned he was looking for texts for
       Einstein. A typical Wilson maneuver."

230   a virtual catalogue of minimalism. When *Einstein* was revived at the Brooklyn
       Academy of Music, John Rockwell wrote that the "Wilson-Glass collaboration is the
       major achievement in the performing arts of the minimalist esthetic . . . [though]
       hardly minimal in any concrete sense. The end is minimal, in that the work aspires
       to a condition of meditative simplicity. Yet the accumulation of means is anything
       but minimal." (*New York Times*, December 17, 1984)

       "The piece was truly more radical." From *Einstein on the Beach: The Changing Image
       of Opera*, 1985, a film by Mark Obenhaus (edited transcript). Glass told me that the
       response of the art community had also changed by 1984: "They don't remember
       this but they were not so enthusiastic about the work in the beginning. Many of the
       artists among my friends didn't like the visual aspects of *Einstein* at all. Eight years
       later the same people came back and told me how much they liked it."

HANS PETER KUHN

Unless otherwise noted, material is drawn from interviews with Hans Peter Kuhn (March,
1985).

235   "you were completely covered." Philip Glass seems to have attempted something
       similar in *Einstein on the Beach*. As he told a reporter for *Libération* (August 3,
       1976), "When I look at a specific space area now, I see it as a volume of air which will
       be manipulated, move and produce sounds—what we try to achieve with the
       electronic device of quadraphony is to place all listeners in the middle of the sound.
       We take a certain space and try to fill it totally with sound."
       John Cage. *Silence*, pp. 9, 40.

236   "The voice accompanies." Jean-Pierre Thibaudat on *Edison* in *Libération*, November
       6, 1979.

Wolfgang Max Faust. "Tagtraum und Theater" (Daydreams and Theatre), *Sprache Im Technischen Zeitalter* 69, January-March, 1979, trans. Maria Hagadus.

Andrzej Wirth. *Washington Review*, June/July, 1979, trans. Susan Winnett. (Originally published in *Theater heute*.)

who now stands. Kuhn only miked a few of the performers in Wilson's production of *Alcestis* (1986-7), choosing to separate most of the actor's voices from the sonic environment for greater contrast. He felt that his work with Wilson was becoming "too easy and predictable" and the time had come to break the pattern they'd established.

Judith Gershman. *Performing Arts Journal* 7, 1983. (Review of *The Golden Windows*.)

"That was Bob's idea." Kuhn also procured a tape of the audio transmissions from a recent space-shuttle mission in which a German astronaut had participated and incorporated it into the scene: "It was like we really had contact with them up there."

layers of information. The earlier soundscapes of Igor Demjen and Christopher Knowles provided the model for Kuhn's work, though the designer is barely aware of their contributions. From the Byrd Hoffman Foundation's prospectus for *Dia log /Network* (1977-8): "A prerecorded audiotape of the two actors reading a written text by Knowles is played intermittently, at predetermined points, throughout the piece. Parts of the same text are also spoken aloud during the performance, in juxtaposition with the audiotape, a radio on low volume, and a cassette tape of Country and Western music." This audio environment is not unlike those Knowles created in Wilson's loft with simultaneously blaring radios and televisions when he was living there in the early 1970s. (Wilson seems to have discovered audial layering as a college student in the early 1960s. One of his dance pieces at Pratt was performed to music by the Renaissance composer Praetorius overlaid with the sound of a banging hammer.)

238   Eugène Ionesco. Letter from Ionesco to Bob Wilson, Paris, April 17, 1979: "Une scène significative est celle où un couple en maillot de bain continue une conversation mi-anglaise, mi-allemand, tandis qu'autour d'eux les mitrailleuses, les bombes, les obus, le fracas de notre mort les laissent insensibles. Comment peut-on encore vivre ici? Nous sommes au-delà de la menace, nous sommes déjà dans la réalisation de la menace."

John Cage. *Silence*, pp. 12, 83, 84.

239   audio score evolves. While the audio track is usually of Kuhn's devising, Wilson occasionally specifies the sound effects he wants in his text, as he did with *The Golden Windows*.

240   a theatrical form. Kuhn says his own audio pieces have been very much influenced by his work with Wilson. These include *Automusik*, in which he placed a microphone under a Berlin bridge and manipulated the sounds; *Das Audio Cafe*, an installation set in a cafe where the noises of everyday life issued from speakers on the tables; and his 1982 solo *Jenseits von Reden*, in which he started with a reel of blank tape and created an ever-thickening sound track by processing and layering his own voice. Kuhn has also composed scores for a number of German films.

BUSINESS AND ART: THE PRODUCERS

243   Stanley Kauffmann. May 31, 1975. (Review of *The $ Value of Man*.)
      Ross Wetzsteon. *Village Voice*, December 8, 1976.

HARVEY LICHTENSTEIN

Unless otherwise specified, material is drawn from an interview with Harvey Lichtenstein
(April 24, 1985).

246   "I would assume all." "Notes on *Freud*" (September, 1971), BHF Archives.
      "every cent I had." *New American Plays*, Vol. III, p. 262.
      Richard Foreman. *Village Voice*, January 1, 1970.

247   last-minute appeals for money. Richard Nelson: "Bob was an absolute genius at
      raising money. He always said there wasn't enough money and he always got it. The
      people closest to him felt he really did know exactly where to go and how to get hold
      of it."

248   *Stalin* finances. Calvin Tomkins in "Time to Think" (1975), *Robert Wilson: The
      Theater of Images*.

249   Wilson on Broadway. Bénédicte Pesle: "When Bob did *A Letter for Queen Victoria* he
      rented a Broadway theatre and couldn't understand why the American public didn't
      respond. He thought it was a natural place for his work to be seen. 'I show ordinary
      people on stage, everyone should be interested.' No one was interested. I think he
      was very naive at the time. Now he is more cynical. He has learned that it is not so
      easy."
      Victoria finances. Carll Tucker in the *Village Voice*, March 24, 1975: "Wilson is paying
      Broadway rents and falling into Broadway debt. He has borrowed on everything he
      and his school, the Byrd Hoffman Foundation, owns, to pay for this produc-
      tion. . . . It's an old story. Theatrical visions cost money." *Variety* estimated the loss
      at $100,000. Their calculations, based on commercial costs, may have been high;
      some of this would have been covered by grants and donations.
      Stefan Brecht. *The Theatre of Visions: Robert Wilson*, p. 268.
      New York Times. Stephen Holden, "The Avant-Garde Is Big Box Office," December
      16, 1984.
      Village Voice. Wilson's fundraising efforts are chronicled in Ross Wetzsteon's "Mount-
      ing *Einstein*: There's No Business Like the Avant-Garde Business," December 8,
      1976.

250   did not return to BAM. The Wilson-Bryars *Medea* and *Great Day in the Morning* had
      been scheduled in the intervening years but neither materialized. A run of *Einstein*
      performances had also been considered after Wilson's success at the Met.
      "wasn't even a new work." Most of the scenery used in the revival came from the
      original production.
      "fiendishly expensive." Beverly Emmons says that "the kind of time Harvey gave Bob
      was extraordinary. Ninety-one hours of cuing with the full cast standing around.
      Very few theatres in the world can afford that. Some in Europe, only some."

252   Meredith Monk. "Fuck the Curtain," *Village Voice*, May 21, 1985.

BOB WILSON IN FRANCE: PIERRE CARDIN/BÉNÉDICTE PESLE/MICHEL GUY

Material is also drawn from an interview with Robert Wilson (August 19, 1988).

254 Jack Lang. *Éclats* (1978), pp. 83-4.

256 "From the conservative *Figaro.*" Andreas Freund, "2 U.S. Plays in Paris Are Hailed at Close," *New York Times,* July 5, 1971.

257 *Belgrade Literary Gazette.* Interview with Vladimir Predic. Letter from Ionesco to Robert Wilson after seeing *D D & D,* April 17, 1979: "you are the greatest author of the century, and that says something for the people and the centuries." BHF Archives. A conversation between Wilson and Ionesco appeared in the magazine *Egoiste,* July-August, 1978.

 ". . . the miracle was produced." Louis Aragon, "An Open Letter to André Breton on Robert Wilson's *Deafman Glance,* art, science and liberty," *Performing Arts Journal* 1, Spring, 1976 (trans. Linda Moses). Alain Jouffroy: "It is a pity that Breton died in 1966. Aragon had a dream of reconciliation, he thought maybe the utopia of reconciliation was possible through this work." Aragon also went to Espace Cardin one afternoon and spoke with the group about how much he admired their work. Wilson and Aragon became friends and discovered they very nearly shared the same birthday (Aragon born on October 3, Wilson on October 4.) Many of Wilson's productions opened in Paris around that date and the elder writer was always invited.

258 ". . . you will see doors open." Roger Shattuck, *The Banquet Years,* p. 206.

260 something easy about Bob's work. Jean-Pierre Thibaudat in *Libération,* November 6, 1979: "Bob Wilson haunts the French theatre. He, and he alone. Because his performances are more immediately spectacular and seductive, he unknowingly smothers efforts often more radical than his own."

261 "we were just hoping." According to Mel Andringa, members of the company were nonplussed by their newfound celebrity. Upon being told that Samuel Beckett and Jean-Paul Sartre were in the audience, one Byrd replied, "Who are they?"

ROBERT APPLEGARTH

Unless otherwise specified, material in this section is drawn from an interview with Robert Applegarth (June 12, 1985).

274 "It was a huge risk." To offset the expense, Wilson eventually took the production to France, where Bénédicte Pesle organized an eight-city tour of cultural houses and state theatres, enabling Byrd Hoffman to break even.

278 economy measures. Act II, b, in which legendary figures of history and literature were seen floating in space, was the only scene to be actually deleted.

281 On March 9. Richard Stayton, "What Happened in Los Angeles," *the CIVIL warS* (catalogue for the Los Angeles gallery presentation), 1984.

282 "What people have contributed." Wilson says these figures do not really reflect the total cost of the project since many expenses (administration, technicians, scene painters, etc.) were paid out of the yearly operating budgets of the theatres.

283   Shrine Auditorium. According to Applegarth, Wilson toured the Shrine and said
      "'This is the place to do it.' Everyone said, 'No, not the Shrine, it's a big barn, it will
      cost twice as much there,' and Bob said, 'No negativity. This is right for it.' I flew to
      Los Angeles with Bob in December of 1982 and we went to see the Radio City
      Music Hall Christmas show there and it hit me like a bomb that he was right, this
      was the place to do *the CIVIL warS*. It had a sense of an event about it. Fitzpatrick
      said we will not allow the production to go into the Shrine and Bob then agreed to go
      into the Pasadena Civic Auditorium. The irony was that Fitzpatrick later bumped
      us out because he was keeping the Civic for all the dance events. Then there was no
      other theatre left in L.A. that could hold the project. The Dorothy Chandler Pavilion
      was off-limits."

285   *the CIVIL warS* had been lost. The cancellation also ended plans for performances of
      Act I, a, Act V and *the Knee Plays* at the Metropolitan Opera in New York later that
      summer.

      Dan Sullivan. Now a champion of Wilson's work, Sullivan admitted in his review
      (March 10, 1985) that he felt "quite foolish for not knowing what to make of [*the
      CIVIL warS*] last winter in Cologne. Clearly, this is a major work by a master theatre
      maker."

      pieces of a colossus. James Leverett, "You Have to Be There: Notes on Robert
      Wilson," *American Theatre*, November, 1984.

286   "I think he slept." Wilson told the *Dallas Downtown News* (March 2, 1981) that "one
      gets 50 percent of one's rest in the first two hours of sleep, and you can break sleep
      apart that way. Sleep two hours, work and sleep again. I can work for several days at a
      time, but I do it very restfully. I sleep sometimes while I'm thinking."

      "so overbooks himself." This frenzy of activity reached a peak in the fall of 1986 as
      Wilson jetted between rehearsals of *Hamletmachine* in Hamburg, *Alcestis* in Paris,
      the Rome *CIVIL warS* in Brooklyn, *Salome* in Milan and *Alceste* in Stuttgart, some
      of which were taking place simultaneously.

CHRONOLOGY AND WORKS

288   he presents plays. In an unpublished interview from the mid-1970s, Wilson said that
      one of these pieces consisted of the garage door going up and down, his grand-
      mother sitting in a chair sewing, himself sleeping and another figure dressed in a
      long fur coat walking quietly around the space (a motif that would appear in his later
      work). BHF Archives.

289   Wilson and a group of friends. Interview with Wilson, July 10, 1985.

      This half-hour piece. Interview with Wilson, July 10, 1985, and Stefan Brecht, *The
      Theatre of Visions: Robert Wilson*, pp. 27-9.

      The story of a young woman. Gynter Quill, "On the Aisle," *Waco Tribune Herald*, July
      25, 1965. Wilson never edited the footage, which he describes as "awful."

      Receives his BFA. For his thesis Wilson conceived a children's theatre with living
      units, what he calls "a kind of model city in miniature."

291   After attempting suicide. Brecht, *The Theatre of Visions*, p. 20, and Jill Johnston's
      "Family Spectacles," *Art in America*, December, 1986.

"Ten people sitting." Wilson's notes on *Theatre Activity* from the mid-1970s (edited), BHF Archives. According to notes compiled by Byrd School members, "most of the audience reacted negatively and left early."

During construction. Conversations with Robert Wilson (July 10, 1985), Cindy Lubar and Kikuo Saito. (It is possible that Wilson staged other performances when he revisited the Grail in 1971.)

293　The first part. James Neu's notes on *BYRD woMAN* (BHF archives), Cindy Lubar's typescript on Wilson's work and Jill Johnston's review in the *Village Voice*, November 7, 1968.

　　Watermill. Jerome Robbins, whose Long Island home was not far from where *Watermill* was filmed, appropriated a number of Wilson motifs (slow motion, horizontal movement, the figure of the runner, sowing grain) in his 1972 ballet which was also titled *Watermill.*

295　Wilson worked with. The Royaumont workshop is documented by John McEwan, Wieslaw Gorky and Lynn Thatcher in the 1973 winter and summer issues of *International Theater Information.*

300　*Spaceman.* Quoted in Brecht, *The Theatre of Visions,* p. 313.

ACKNOWLEDGMENTS

A book of this kind would hardly have been possible without the support and cooperation of a great many people, and I am hard pressed to acknowledge adequately my debt to them. First, I should like to thank Robert Wilson, who gave me permission to pursue the project and to contact friends and collaborators; granted me numerous interviews, access to his archives and entry to rehearsals; and finally allowed me to quote from his works and publish his drawings. Next, my thanks go to the primary contributors to this study, who gave generously of their time and memories: Laurie Anderson, Mel Andringa, Gilles Anquetil, Robert Applegarth, Dominique Boitel, Robyn Brentano, David Byrne, Pierre Cardin, Kit Cation, Lucinda Childs, Christophe de Menil, Igor Demjen, Maita di Niscemi, Beverly Emmons, Richard Foreman, Allen Ginsberg, Philip Glass, Michel Guy, Alain Jouffroy, Tom Kamm, Kathryn Kean, Christopher Knowles, Fred Kolo, Hans Peter Kuhn, Harvey Lichtenstein, Rolf Liebermann, Alan Lloyd, Cindy Lubar, Annette Michelson, Meredith Monk, Heiner Müller, Carol Mullins, Richard Nelson, James Neu, Alwin Nikolais, Pascal Ortega, Bénédicte Pesle (who also arranged my interviews in Paris), Kikuo Saito, Sue Sheehy, Scotty Snyder, Sheryl Sutton, Jean-Claude van Itallie, David Warrilow, Ann Wilson and Thomas Woodruff. I am also grateful to others whose names do not always appear in the text for advice, assistance or recollections: George Ashley, Gavin Bryars, Paula Cooper, Tankred Dorst, Joe Friedman, Richard Gallo, Julia Gillett, Marian Goodman, Elise Gorges, George Klauber, Elaine Luthy, George McNeil, Martin Penrose, Dennis Redmon, Jerome Robbins, David Rodes, Gordon Rogoff, Ann-Christin Rommen, Richard Shyer, Madame Takata, Pauline Tish, Gary Vodvarka, Ross Wetzsteon and Wolfgang Wiens. At TCG I should like to thank Terry Nemeth, Jim Leverett and my editor M. Elizabeth Osborn, who saw the manuscript through to publication. A special mention is due Bob Goldberg, until recently of Byrd Hoffman, for his helpfulness, infinite patience and enthusiasm for this project. I would also like to thank Robert Brustein for his kindness in writing a foreword; Annie Leibovitz for her splendid cover portrait; Ronald Vance, the director of Byrd Hoffman, for his many courtesies; and Joel Schechter at Yale, who encouraged this project from its inception.

The photographs and illustrations in this book are reproduced with the kind permission of the following photographers, individuals and organizations: p. xi, 124, 190, Richard Feldman; p. xii, Clärchen Baus-Mattar; p. 4, 154 (bottom), 159, 204, Martin Bough; p. 15, Ivan Farkas; p. 21, 168-9, Mara Eggert; p. 44, Basil Langton; p. 55, 59, Bahman Djalai; p. 75, André Morain; p. 85-6, Lincoln Center; p. 92, Carl Peller; p. 100-1, 195 (bottom), xxii, 240, Ruth Walz; p. 103, Enguerand; p. 115, Johan Elbers; p. 116, diBruno Bruni; p. 134, Bill Marshak; p. 139-51, Byrd Hoffman Foundation (drawings by Robert Wilson); p. 154 (top), 242, Jennifer Merin; p. 166, 320, Georges Méran; p. 171, Gerhard Kassner; p. 179-86, Byrd Hoffman Foundation (drawings by Thomas Woodruff); p. 195 (top), 225 (middle, bottom), 232, Babette Mangolte; p. 199 (top), Leo Van Velzen; p. 199 (bottom), Lelli and Masotti; p. 223 (top), 225 (top), Fulvio Roiter; p. 223 (bottom), Betty Freeman; p. 244, Dominique Ponzo.